VOYAGES

of the

PYRAMID
BUILDERS

Also by Robert M. Schoch, Ph.D.,
with Robert Aquinas McNally

VOICES OF THE ROCKS

ROBERT M. SCHOCH, PH.D.
with ROBERT AQUINAS McNALLY

Jeremy P. Tarcher/Penguin
a member of Penguin Group (USA) Inc.
New York

VOYAGES

of the

PYRAMID
BUILDERS

*The
True Origins
of the
Pyramids
from
Lost Egypt to
Ancient America*

Most Tarcher/Penguin Books are available at special quantity discounts for bulk purchase for sales promotions, premiums, fund-raising, and educational needs. Special books or book excerpts also can be created to fit specific needs. For details, write Penguin Group (USA) Inc. Special Markets, 375 Hudson Street, New York, NY 10014.

Jeremy P. Tarcher/Penguin
a member of
Penguin Group (USA) Inc.
375 Hudson Street
New York, NY 10014
www.penguin.com

First trade paperback edition 2004

The Library of Congress cataloged the hardcover edition as follows :

Schoch, Robert M.
Voyages of the pyramid builders : the true origins of the pyramids from lost Egypt
to ancient America / by Robert M. Schoch with Robert Aquinas McNally.
p. cm.
Includes bibliographical references and index.
ISBN 1-58542-203-7
1. Indians of North America—Transatlantic influences. 2. Indians—Transatlantic
influences. 3. Pyramids. 4. Indians—Transpacific influences. 5. Civilization, Ancient.
6. Egypt—History—To 332 B.C. I. McNally, Robert Aquinas. II. Title.
E98.T73.S36 2003 2002028988
970.01'1—dc21
ISBN-1-58542-320-3 (paperback edition)

Printed in the United States of America
1 3 5 7 9 10 8 6 4 2

Book design by Carol Malcolm Russo/Signet M Design, Inc.

Robert M. Schoch dedicates this book
to his parents,
Milton and Alicia Schoch,
and to his parents-in-law,
Robert and Anne Pettit.

Robert Aquinas McNally dedicates this book
to Gayle Eleanor:
"Doch immer mein Ewig-Weibliches."

Contents

Introduction   *1*

1. GIZA AND THE QUESTION OF TIME   7

2. THIS WORLD'S MANY PYRAMIDS   21

3. COINCIDENCE OR CONNECTION?
   THE MYTHIC FOUNDATION   54

4. THE PEOPLING OF THE AMERICAS   82

5. ACROSS THE ATLANTIC TO THE NEW WORLD   100

6. ACROSS THE PACIFIC TO THE NEW WORLD   136

7. HOW THE PYRAMID BUILDERS SAILED *166*

8. FLEEING THE ANGRY SKIES *191*

9. SEEKING THE SOURCE *237*

10. CIVILIZATION'S BEGINNING, ISOLATION'S END *270*

Appendix: Redating the Great Sphinx of Giza *278*

Acknowledgments *299*

Sources and Readings *305*

Index *331*

VOYAGES

of the

PYRAMID
BUILDERS

Introduction

B Y CONVENTIONAL THINKING, THE SO-CALLED ÜRÜMCHI mummies àre badly out of place. Discovered in the Takla Makan Desert of northwestern China, one of the driest, saltiest parts of Central Asia, and now housed farther north in the Provincial Museum of Ürümchi, these naturally preserved remains show what humans in that part of the world looked like between 2000 and 1000 B.C. The mummies are in an excellent state of preservation—the accidental result of winter burials in salty soil, which dried the bodies and protected them against the usual processes of decay—better in fact than Egyptian mummies embalmed at the same time. Curiously, the Ürümchi mummies wear brilliantly colored, well-made textiles that have no resemblance to Asian fabrics. Even more surprising are their facial features: round eyes, large noses, red or blond hair, and tall bodies. Both the fabrics and the remains suggest a tribe related to Europe's Celts.

But what are people connected with the ancestors of the modern Irish, Scots, and Welsh doing in this far corner of Asia?

Ürümchi's evidence is startling since it undercuts our ready division of cultures into European and Asian. Here is a people of European provenance buried in what is clearly an Asian cultural zone. Yet there is a way we can accept even this, simply because the link between Ürümchi and the Celtic heartland of the Caucasus lies overland. It is generally accepted that the Celts arose in the Caucasus Mountains, migrated westward into the Balkans and Central Europe, then into France, northern Spain, Ireland, and Britain. The Ürümchi mummies argue that some of them went eastward as well, settling in what is now China. Somehow we find it easy, if unconventional, to imagine these ancient sheepherders driving their flocks over deserts and mountains toward the rising sun in search of new, greener pastures.

But what if an ocean separated two ancient areas—one in the Old World of Europe, Asia, and Africa and another in the New World of North and South America—with human cultures that bear an uncanny resemblance to each other? By intellectual convention, we would assume that the similarity had to be coincidence. After all, aren't the two worlds just that—separate worlds? And besides, until Columbus navigated his three small ships across the Atlantic, Europeans and Native Americans supposedly knew nothing of each other's existence (with the exception of a brief contact between Norse and Native Americans circa A.D. 1000). According to the prevailing model of history, people on both sides of the Atlantic before Columbus lacked the drive to attempt a transoceanic journey and the competence to survive it.

This point of view, which has long dominated our way of thinking about the past, runs against a growing body of evidence that ancient peoples crossed the seas between the Old and New worlds many centuries prior to Columbus. They carried with them the ideas, tools, and elements that grew into what we call civilization. And this pattern of cross-cultural and intercontinental travel reaches far back, well into prehistory. In fact, it explains one of the most intriguing enigmas of the ancient world—the presence of pyramids in Africa, Asia, and both North and South America.

As much as they symbolize the mystery and magic of Egypt, pyramids are not uniquely Egyptian. Pyramids also appear in the ancient African kingdom of Kush, along the Nile between the third and fourth cataracts; as ziggurats in ancient Mesopotamia and Sumeria (the likely source of the biblical account of the Tower of Babel); in England and Ireland, taking such forms as Silbury Hill and Newgrange; in India and throughout Southeast Asia, in the distinct style of the Buddhist stupa; at Angkor Wat in medieval Cambodia; at Indonesia's Borobudur; in ancient China; at Teotihuacán, Tenayuca, Tenochtitlán, and other sites in the Valley of Mexico; in the ancient Olmec and Mayan realms of southern Mexico, Guatemala, Honduras, Belize, and El Salvador; in North America along the Mississippi at Cahokia and other ceremonial centers; and in Peru's coastal region, among the people who were the ancestors of the Inca empire, and in that country's northern Andes, the Inca heartland.

How can it be that a form as distinctive and powerful as the pyramid was built in such widely separated locales? It seems too much to believe that the world's many pyramids are the product of coincidence and convergence. Could it be that they share a common ancestor long lost to history, a primordial pyramid-building civilization that once navigated the seas and spread its way of life around the globe? Are they— like the modern Irish at one extreme and the startling mummies of Ürümchi at the other—evidence of migration from a single, ancient, and now-forgotten source?

Ever since I became involved in studying the Great Sphinx of Giza—a research project described in my earlier book *Voices of the Rocks* and updated in the appendix of this volume—I have pursued evidence suggesting that relatively sophisticated civilizations arose earlier than generally recognized. Some of these early civilizations apparently possessed high levels of astronomical knowledge and navigational expertise, giving them the ability to navigate across open sea. This evidence further suggests that the history of civilization is not a tale of slow, gradual, progressive change from primitive to sophisticated. Rather, history comprises a series of starts and stops, rises and falls. Periods of equilibrium, growth, and progress are interrupted, often suddenly, by natural catastrophes. Catastrophes can take many forms—volcanic eruptions, earthquakes, widespread floods, profound climate change, the spread of new diseases. The most devastating and far-reaching catastrophes of all, though, have come not from the earth itself but from the skies, in the form of cosmic run-ins with comets—experiences preserved in the religious mythology of skies turned vengeful and dangerous by angry gods who scorched the earth with the fire of heaven.

No structures that have survived from antiquity better embody the fascinating reality of civilization's rises, falls, and spread in response to celestial catastrophe than the pyramids. They are striking evidence of earth's long-lost protocivilization, the physical remains of the deepest taproot of the cultural, social, and technological inheritance from which our modern way of life draws its energy.

The evidence, as we shall see, leads us to site civilization's deepest and oldest root in Sundaland, the now-drowned continent of Southeast Asia, which once connected the mainland with what are now the many islands of Indonesia. Our planet's repeated collisions with the remains of comets affected the climate, raised sea level, flooded Sundaland completely by eight to six thousand years ago, and forced the migration of this protocivilization out from its point of origin. That movement, and its cultural legacies over the following millennia, provides the best explanation for the spread of pyramids across the globe.

Voyages of the Pyramid Builders tells this story, overturning some of our most cherished assumptions about prehistory and the rise of civilization in the process. Chapter 1, "Giza and the Question of Time," spells out the evidence that the Egyptian pyramids at Giza and certain associated structures, or at least portions of them, were built earlier than conventionally believed. Chapter 2, "This World's Many Pyramids," describes the various pyramid cultures in Africa, Asia, and the Americas and explores the significance of the striking similarities between them despite the long distances of land and sea separating them. Chapter 3, "Coincidence or Connection? The Mythic Foundation," investigates the rituals, beliefs, and stories that underlie the pyramids. We have to understand how ancient peoples migrated from the Old World into the New before we can explore the connections between pyramid cultures. This is the topic of chapter 4, "The Peopling of the Americas." The striking similarities between Old World and New World pyramids and the possibility of a connection spanning the Atlantic is the topic of chapter 5, "Across the Atlantic to the New World." Chapter 6, "Across the Pacific to the New World," details intriguing evidence that pyramid builders also entered the New World from the West and influenced the rising civilizations of Central and South America. Of course, the pyramid builders could have crossed the oceans only if they had sufficient maritime skill. Such is the focus of chapter 7, "How the Pyramid Builders Sailed." Next we look at why ancient peoples went to the trouble of moving vast distances, investigating the compelling theory that their migrations were responses to catastrophic encounters with comets—the topic of chapter 8, "Fleeing the Angry Skies." Chapter 9, "Seeking the Source," looks into the possibility of a lost pyramid-building civilization in the period before 3000 B.C., the generally accepted date for the earliest pyramids. The book concludes with chapter 10, "Civilization's Beginning, Isolation's End," which summarizes what we now know, points out what we still have to find out, and looks at what it means to know that the high civilizations of our planet have been interconnected for much longer than we previously imagined. Understanding that all civilization shares a common origin deep in the past reminds us what a precious gift civilization is and how assiduous we must be in tending this irreplaceable legacy.

Science is less a body of knowledge than an attitude, a willingness to lift the sacred veil and look behind it. That is what *Voyages of the Pyramid Builders* does. It offers the challenge of a fresh look and the thrill of exploring the new and unexpected.

One
Giza and the
Question of Time

AN ARABIC PROVERB SAYS OF THE THREE FAMOUS PYRAMIDS along the Egyptian Nile at Giza, "All the world fears Time, but Time fears the Pyramids." Indeed, these stoneworks contain many of the secrets of the origins of humankind, wrapped in a silence that seems eternal. The stones, though, have a voice. They speak, if only one knows what questions to ask and how to listen for the answers.

Ancient Egypt's Great Flowering

According to the conventional story, civilization is but the latest step in humankind's long and steady journey up the ladder of progress.

Hundreds if not thousands of millennia before the first word of history was written, humans stood up, fashioned stones into tools, and foraged for game, roots, seeds, and fruits. Of necessity, humans were nomadic. The depletion of food supplies in one area forced our ances-

tors to move to another, often on a rhythm that followed seasonal fluctuations in the abundance of animals and plants. Hunting, gathering,
and moving about characterized human existence until approximately
8000 B.C., when nomads in the Middle East's Fertile Crescent gave up
their wandering ways to settle in permanent villages. This transformation of lifestyle is called the Neolithic Revolution. The villagers had
taken control of their food supply by learning how to cultivate and harvest grain and by raising animals, particularly cattle, sheep, and goats,
for meat, milk, wool, and hides. This settled way of life allowed increasing cultural, economic, and political complexity to evolve, as villages expanded into towns and towns into cities.

The cities that arose among the people called the Sumerians, who
dwelled along the Euphrates River in what is now Iraq, gave humankind its first taste of civilization in about 3500 B.C. The Sumerians
recorded the legendary flood story later associated with Noah in Hebrew scripture, and they were said by subsequent Babylonian legend to
have arrived in their Mesopotamian realm after a sea journey from
some long-forgotten and distant homeland. The Sumerians were an accomplished people. They irrigated and farmed the desert, traded far
and wide, expressed themselves artistically in metalwork and stone
sculpture, and built extensive temples and palaces. Above all else, the
Sumerians could write—creating clay tablets in cuneiform by pressing
the characters into wet clay with a wedge-shaped wooden stylus.

Eventually Sumeria collapsed under the attack of outsiders even
more warlike than they were, but well before that end-time the nation's ideas, techniques, and methods traveled along the trade routes
into other lands. Thus it came to be that Sumeria planted the seed of
civilization that grew to full flower in Egypt.

In the fourth millennium B.C., the Egyptian population along the
Nile was organized into small communities called nomes, each of
which paid homage to its own gods and accepted the rule of a single
chief. Rivalry and warfare drove the nomes into alliances that eventually merged into two kingdoms. Lower Egypt, in the northern portion

of the Nile Valley toward the river's mouth in the Mediterranean, was composed mostly of peoples who had immigrated from the Middle East. The people of Upper Egypt, farther south along the Nile toward the river's source in the highlands of east-central Africa, came originally from Ethiopia, Sudan, and the eastern Sahara. It fell to the half-legendary king Menes—who is sometimes identified with the early ruler Narmer, or Scorpion—to beat the two kingdoms into submission, form a single political entity from them, and establish the first dynasty of pharaohs in about 3000 B.C.

Ancient Egypt became a land of civilized accomplishment that even today, thousands of years later, continues to stir awe and amazement. Some of that emotion arises in response to the stunning artistic accomplishments of the ancient Egyptians. Some of it arises too from the shock of recognition. Much of what we in the civilized world take for granted arose in Egypt and was passed on to the Western world, first through the Greeks and later the Romans, by the fortunes of trade and war. When we look at ancient Egypt, we are looking at ourselves in a distant, defining mirror.

Obsessed with religion and dedicated to achieving immortality as god-kings, the Egyptian pharaohs constructed immense religious complexes of temples, shrines, and tombs to preserve their mummified remains. As we shall examine in more detail in chapter 2, the earliest tombs were made of mud brick, and the first-generation stone pyramids were limited architectural successes. By the time of the Fourth Dynasty, which ruled the united kingdom of Egypt from 2575 to 2465 B.C.,* the stage was set for the building of the Giza pyramids.

Giza, which lies at the very edge of the Sahara overlooking the Nile just outside modern Cairo, is the site of the three monuments known far and wide as the very essence of what pyramids are supposed to look like. The largest of them, commonly referred to as the Great Pyramid

---

* Exact dates for ancient Egypt remain a source of scholarly controversy. We are following the chronology used in John Baines and Jaromír Málek's authoritative *Atlas of Ancient Egypt* (New York: Facts on File, 1980). Some Egyptologists date the Fourth Dynasty 2613–2498 B.C.

due to its size, is associated with the pharaoh Khufu (Cheops in Greek), who ruled from 2551 to 2528 B.C. Khafre (Chephren), a son of Khufu who followed an older brother as pharaoh and held the throne between 2520 and 2494 B.C., built the slightly smaller second pyramid. The third and by far smallest of the Giza pyramids was the work of Menkaure (Mycerinus), who ruled as pharaoh from 2490 until 2472 B.C.

It is a commonplace of both academic Egyptology and popular belief to assert that the pyramids are elaborate tombstones. Clearly there is no doubting the obsession with death that filled the ancient Egyptian soul. Only a people fixated on the afterlife could have been so devoted to the ghoulish dissection and embalming it took to produce a royal mummy. Yet it remains a curious, and no doubt important, fact that to date no Old Kingdom remains have been discovered within the Giza pyramids. A mummy was recovered from the Menkaure Pyramid, but radiocarbon dating of the bones showed it to be a Christian-era corpse in a Twenty-Sixth Dynasty sarcophagus. Obviously it was placed inside the pyramid more than two millennia after the pyramid was built. The Khufu Pyramid has yet to yield a mummy, and a sarcophagus in the Khafre Pyramid contained the bones of a bull—one of the many discoveries in the pyramids that led the well-known academic archaeologist Mark Lehner to write in *The Complete Pyramids* (p. 52), "These mysterious facts . . . hint that the history of the pyramids is not always as straightforward as Egyptologists may think." He has a point. As we shall see in chapter 8, the bull's bones point in a fascinating, distinctly nonstraightforward direction.

Despite all the attention focused on the pyramids of Giza, we should not forget that the site also contains a great many other structures, such as temples, causeways, and tombs. Then there is the Great Sphinx.

An Old, Old Sphinx

The Great Sphinx of Giza is immense: 66 feet high and 240 feet long with a headdressed human face 13 feet wide, all carved from solid limestone bedrock. It is also precious and irreplaceable. Standing in the shadow of the Great Pyramid of Khufu, which is the sole survivor of the Seven Wonders of the ancient world, the Great Sphinx serves as a living messenger from an age long past.

Egyptologists have long assumed that the principal monuments of Giza were built during the Fourth Dynasty, and they have ascribed various monuments to the legacies of specific pharaohs. The Great Sphinx, it has been agreed since about 1950, belongs to Khafre.

There is, however, a major problem with this idea: It fails to fit the evidence. The issue comes down to climate and the weathering of stone.

The monuments of Giza show two types of weathering. The first comes from sand blown by the strong desert winds, which scours the limestone like a sandblaster, leaving a horizontal, sometimes steplike pattern as the softer rock strata are worn away and the stronger strata survive. This kind of weathering is obvious on all the monuments of Giza. But there is another, very different kind of weathering found prominently on the Sphinx and its surrounding enclosure. This kind of weathering creates a rolling, undulating surface with deep vertical fissures, or runnels, which are often wider at the top than the bottom. Water, not wind, does this.

And there the problem begins. When the Sphinx is conventionally said to have been carved, Egypt's climate was pretty much as it is now: hot, dry, and windy. In fact, structures reliably dated to the period 2600–2300 B.C., supposedly roughly contemporaneous with the Sphinx, display weathering by wind, not water. The water-weathering pattern on the Sphinx makes sense only if the structure had been carved at a time when the Egyptian climate was much wetter than it is today. This indeed was the case at the end of the last Ice Age, circa 12,000 years ago, and extending (with alternating relatively wetter and drier periods) to sometime between 3000 and 2350 B.C. At that point, arid conditions more or less the same as the current climate set in, and water weathering yielded to wind.

Research by me and the seismologist Thomas L. Dobecki on the depth of weathered rock surrounding the Sphinx leads me to the conclusion that the Sphinx was originally carved sometime between 7000 and 5000 B.C., millennia before Khafre.* Certainly the head of the Sphinx was recarved, probably during early dynastic or Old Kingdom times, to give it a pharaonic look. But even at the time of this refurbishing, the Sphinx was already an old, old monument.

The Time of the Pyramids

If the Sphinx dates to a time before that which conventional Egyptology assigns it, what of the pyramids themselves? How sure can we be that they were actually built by Khufu, Khafre, and Menkaure?

The standard historical case for dating the Great Pyramid to the Fourth Dynasty rests on two pieces of evidence. The first is the testimony of the Greek historian Herodotus, who reported from his visit to Egypt circa 443 B.C. that Khufu had needed 20 years and 100,000 men to build the Great Pyramid. The second is a number of inscriptions found deep inside the Great Pyramid that bear Khufu's name. The inscriptions were discovered in 1837 by Richard Howard-Vyse (1784–1853), one of the early generation of pyramid explorers.

The historicity of Herodotus' accounts is always open to question. A dedicated traveler with a reporter's ear for a hot story or lusty legend, Herodotus sometimes got it right and sometimes got it wrong, at least by modern standards. He is but one source among many, and practically all of the others claim that the Great Pyramid existed before Khufu.

---

* The appendix on pages 278–298 details the scientific argument for redating the Sphinx and evaluates the unworkable countertheories that have been offered.

One of those sources is the Inventory Stela, which dates from the sixth or seventh century B.C. and which bears an inscription supporting an older date for the Sphinx (discussed in more detail in the Appendix). According to the stela, Khufu discovered and rebuilt an existing temple sacred to Isis, the great goddess of Egypt, which was located "beside the house of the Sphinx, northwest of the house of Osiris [the great god of Egypt and Isis' consort]." The inscription also suggests that a pyramid already stood on the site where Khufu built a pyramid for himself and another for Princess Henutsen, his wife. But which pyramid does the stela refer to—the Great Pyramid itself or one of the smaller pyramids close by, one of which was indeed intended for Princess Henutsen? If the inscription is correct, then the Sphinx is certainly older than Khufu, and the Great Pyramid may also be.

Most Egyptologists dismiss the Inventory Stela as an ancient forgery. The same charge has been leveled at the inscriptions discovered inside the Great Pyramid by Howard-Vyse.

Howard-Vyse was an Egyptologist of the old school, the kind who stormed ancient history like an enemy fortress and literally blasted his way into its monuments with gunpowder. His discovery of the Khufu inscriptions came at a convenient time in his archaeological career. In 1837 his money and his permit from the Egyptian authorities were both about to run out. He needed a big find to guarantee a new round of funds from his backers and an extension of the permit from the Egyptians. Howard-Vyse was also nursing a bruised ego. His Egyptological arch rival, Captain Giovanni Battista Caviglia of Italy, had created a stir among ancient-history buffs by uncovering quarry marks and inscriptions in tombs close to the Great Pyramid. These hieroglyphics, daubed in a red-ochre paint still used by the local people, told pyramid workers where to place each block. Howard-Vyse was hot for a discovery as earth-shaking as Caviglia's, and the Khufu inscriptions filled the bill.

A number of writers have argued that Howard-Vyse forged the inscriptions in order to further his career. The claim makes for a good story, a mystery tale worthy of an Agatha Christie tale, one built on fraud, skullduggery, and Howard-Vyse's unquestioned megalomania. However, the scholarship on which the claim is based qualifies as shoddy at best. It comes from the work of Zechariah Sitchin, who has a deep and abiding faith that ancient Egypt, and indeed the human race, was actually begun by space aliens. Sitchin twists and turns the Howard-Vyse story to his own purposes and makes an argument that is finally incredible. However unlikable and self-aggrandizing a character Howard-Vyse was, the inscriptions he found are almost certainly genuine.

Still, just what do genuine quarry marks and inscriptions on stones deep within the Great Pyramid actually tell us? The hieroglyphic cartouche for the name Khufu was a powerful charm that has been found on any number of tombs and monuments throughout Egypt, many of them accurately dated to well after the Fourth Dynasty. The cartouche was used as a holy symbol in the same way that the cross was inscribed here, there, and everywhere by Christians in later centuries. The inscriptions don't necessarily prove that Khufu built the Great Pyramid. They might mean only that Khufu was himself named for the Great Pyramid, which perhaps existed before he did.

The Inventory Stela suggests the possibility that Khufu added to, repaired, or augmented a structure that was already standing when he took the throne. Interesting physical evidence on this score comes from a carbon-14 study performed in the mid-1980s by the American Research Center in Egypt under the direction of Robert J. Wenke, a prehistorian at the University of Washington. Carbon-14 dating works only with organic materials and therefore cannot be used to date stone carving. The inner cores of the pyramids, which are out of sight and less precisely fitted than the outer courses of stone blocks, are held together with large amounts of mortar that often contains charcoal, wood, and reed. The mortar, like stone, cannot be dated, but the organic material embedded in it can be. Wenke's team took mortar samples from the exteriors of all three Giza pyramids and the Sphinx Temple for testing at

Southern Methodist University in Dallas, Texas, and the Eidgenössische Technische Hochschule (Federal Technical University) in Zurich, Switzerland.

The results were curious. Despite careful refinement and calibration, the samples averaged 374 years earlier than the accepted dates of the pharaohs with whom they were associated. Even more anomalous were the individual findings within single monuments. Two charcoal samples from an upper course in the Khufu pyramid were dated to 3809 B.C., with a margin of error either way of 160 years. This means that the samples could date to as early as 3969 B.C. A wood sample from the same site, however, tested to 3101 B.C. (± 414 years). Another thirteen samples, all but two of them charcoal, from lower in the Khufu pyramid spanned a range from 3090 to 2853 B.C., with the margin of error between one and four centuries. Seven samples from the Khafre pyramid were dated 3196–2723 B.C.; six from the Menkaure pyramid, 3076–2067 B.C.; and two from the Sphinx Temple, 2746–2085 B.C.

Some of these curious findings may be due to the technical difficulty of carbon-14 dating. The concentration of carbon-14 in the atmosphere is not constant, and samples can be contaminated with carbon from the environment that is younger or older than they are. It can also be the case that the organic materials do not in fact date from the same time period as the inorganic object being studied. For example, wooden beams used in the tracks over which stones were hauled to build the pyramids at Lisht, in Middle Egypt, were much older than the Twelfth Dynasty, to which those same pyramids are known to belong. Apparently the pyramid builders were using wood from trees felled long before, possibly taking advantage of the same timbers over and over again, a recycling strategy that makes eminent sense in a country with as little forest as Egypt. It is possible that the same pattern was followed at Giza, with charcoal being made from wood that was already a few hundred years old when the mortar surrounding it was mixed. However, the researchers involved in the project noted that at least some of the material used to arrive at dates included reeds and other "short-lived materials," which would be unlikely to yield the same results as presumably old wood.

A second radiocarbon survey of the Giza Plateau was undertaken in 1995, the detailed results of which have still not been fully released. Preliminary reports, however, suggest that although the discrepancies are not as great as in the 1980s study, radiocarbon dates from the Old Kingdom pyramids are generally a century or two older than the traditionally accepted dates. The researchers involved in this latest study concluded that the Old Kingdom Egyptians must have utilized massive quantities of wood, so they took whatever they could find, including wood that was already hundreds of years old. This, they suggested, gave the anomalously old dates.

But other explanations for the curious carbon-14 findings are possible. Many of the Giza samples from the 1980s study are much older than the pharaohs who supposedly commissioned the monuments. If we take the results of the radiocarbon dating at face value, the charcoal-tainted mortar at the top end of the margin of error in the upper course of the Great Pyramid was put into place over 1,400 years before Khufu became pharaoh. In the case of Khafre, the span is almost seven centuries. There is also the matter of the long span of dates within individual monuments, which reaches almost a millennium for the Menkaure and Khufu pyramids. And there is the curious finding that the samples from the area toward the top of the Great Pyramid are older than those at the bottom. If we assume that the Great Pyramid was built all at once, then this finding implies that the structure was constructed from the top down.

The older samples at the top do make sense, however, if we assume that the Great Pyramid was built, rebuilt, and rebuilt yet again in stages. No doubt the Giza Plateau was a holy site whose importance reached back into a time well before the Fourth Dynasty, possibly even to before the original sculpting of the Great Sphinx. Then the pharaohs of the Fourth Dynasty laid claim to it, built their tombs and temples there, and raised new pyramids atop old structures or repaired existing stoneworks, just as Khafre refurbished the Sphinx.

Even the language of the ancient Egyptians points to this possibility. According to the Egyptologists John Baines and Jaromír Málek, in ancient times the Khafre Pyramid was referred to as the Great Pyramid, while the Khufu Pyramid was known as "the Pyramid which is the place of sunrise and sunset." Could the ancient designation of "Great Pyramid" for the Khafre Pyramid indicate that the site, if not the pyramid itself, was of supreme importance and that it predates many other developments and structures on the Giza Plateau?

Indeed, my own research suggests that at least the base of the Second, or Khafre, Pyramid may predate the Old Kingdom. A close examination shows that the courses close to the pyramid's base differ distinctly in style from the upper tiers. Furthermore, the Second Pyramid's lowest course was faced with red granite, which appears to date to no later than the Fourth Dynasty. The rest of the pyramid, however, was faced with fine white limestone, with the result that in Khafre's time a horizontal red stripe ran around the base of the otherwise-white Second Pyramid. Why this difference in color and material? The answer may come from the fact that the ancient Egyptians favored granite for renewing or refurbishing older structures. Possibly the Fourth-Dynasty Egyptians were rebuilding and adding to a much older, preexisting structure, with the red granite demarcating the older, refurbished form that lies within the newer, white-limestone pyramid above. Likewise, the third, or Menkaure, Pyramid has a surviving outer casing of granite on its lower courses. Was it, too, refurbished, either by generations after the Fourth Dynasty (during the Twenty-Sixth Dynasty, circa 600 B.C., according to one suggestion) or possibly by Fourth-Dynasty Egyptians working on a site and structure that predated their own time? Furthermore, after studying the Tomb of Queen Khentkaus at Giza (late Fourth Dynasty), I have concluded that this tomb is built on and incorporates an older structure dating from very early dynastic or predynastic times. Finally, as detailed in the Appendix, not only the Great Sphinx, but also the Sphinx Temple, the Khafre "Valley Temple," "Khafre's Causeway," and a portion of Khafre's "Mortuary Temple" may all predate their conventional attributions.

The pharaohs Khufu, Khafre, and Menkaure played key roles in developing Giza as we now know it. But when they began their work, the place was already very, very old.

The Way Back

The tidy scenario of a civilization that began in Sumeria in 3500 B.C. and flowered in Old Kingdom Egypt of the Fourth Dynasty runs aground at Giza. The Great Sphinx was freed from the limestone bedrock well before Menes united the two Egypts into one pharaonic kingdom. And the pyramids themselves draw on this ancient, unknown time, at least for models and inspiration.

Scholars who argue vehemently against the hypothesis of an older Giza maintain that no group of people in the 7000–5000 B.C. period had the skill and organizational capacity to carve the Sphinx, much less build even an early version of one of the three pyramids. On the face of it, they have a point. Only two major Neolithic settlements, Fayum and Merimde, are known in Lower Egypt from the fifth millennium B.C., and they are rough places, the camps of people who lived on the brink of starvation and thought more about finding food than developing a high culture. But to suppose that these two sites are all there is to be discovered of predynastic Egypt is to make a dangerous assumption.

Giza is a convenient archaeological site to study because it lies above the Nile floodplain and has escaped the annual flooding that, before the damming of the Nile at Aswan, typically deposited one millimeter of soil each year. Over the 10,000 years between the beginning of the Neolithic Period and now, a little over 26 feet of soil has accumulated, burying any ancient sites to be found there. The Nile itself has changed course many times during that same period, and the Mediterranean coastline has also shifted. The heavy post–Ice Age rains that deluged Giza and weathered the Sphinx raised the sea level hundreds of feet, drowning any cities, villages, or holy sites on what used to be the shore. It is possible that the ruined settlements of the people who carved the Sphinx and held holy the site of Khafre's Pyramid lie hidden under silt or sea.

The recent excavation of the Nabta Playa archaeological site, located about 65 miles west of Abu Simbel in southernmost Egypt's Western Desert, shows that more was going on in predynastic Egypt than we previously suspected. The playa is a basin that fills with water when rainfall is sufficient. Beginning in about 9000 B.C., nomadic cattle herders brought their animals to the playa during the wet season and let them graze until water and grass dried up. By 7000 B.C. the nomads had settled in the area, digging deep wells to allow year-round habitation in the desert and building organized villages of small huts arranged in straight lines. Following a major drought, these people disappeared, to be replaced circa 5500 B.C. by a people with a social system more complex than any yet seen in Egypt. Their religion centered on sacrificing young cows and interring them in roofed chambers marked by burial mounds. By the fifth millennium B.C. they were erecting large stones in alignments, building a calendar circle to mark the summer solstice—the earliest astronomical measuring device known in Egypt—and constructing over 30 complex structures. Nabta grew into a ceremonial center that drew people from all over the Western Desert to participate in rituals that probably confirmed social and religious unity.

Building the alignments, circles, and structures of Nabta required a political or religious authority that could control large numbers of workers over extended times. It hints at the organization that was required to excavate the Great Sphinx and build the pyramids. And the centrality of cattle in the religion of Nabta, which also echoes the religious symbols of the Old Kingdom but not those of Mesopotamia, indicates that this area likely contributed important elements to the cultural mix that nourished ancient Egypt.

Nabta was not alone in its predynastic cultural sophistication, either. Recent research in the Eastern Desert of Upper Egypt—a now-forbidding region between the Nile and the Red Sea—has uncovered a series of elaborate rock paintings. Dated to circa 4000 B.C., the paintings have been called "the Sistine Chapel of predynastic Egypt" by Toby Wilkinson, the Cambridge University archaeologist who made the discovery. The paintings show a wetter, more abundant land, and they use a number of symbols, such as the boat for the voyage through the underworld and figures with plumes in their hair, later known from dynastic Egypt.

Nabta, the Great Sphinx, the Eastern Desert paintings, and the pyramids point toward a high level of social and religious complexity, technological ability, and overall sophistication much earlier than 3500 B.C. They hint at a mystery: the existence of civilization before civilization is supposed to have existed. When we consider that pyramids are found in many places around the world other than Egypt, that mystery grows even more fascinating.

Two
This World's
Many Pyramids

BY NO MEANS ARE THE PYRAMIDS OF GIZA THE ONLY SUCH structures to be found in Egypt itself, the Middle East, or even the Old World. In fact, pyramids exist in a wide variety of locations—some clearly connected by ancient cultural contact, some curiously distant from one another—on every continent except Australia and Antarctica. How they were constructed, by whom, and when are key questions whose answers point to a rethinking of the story of civilization and the capacities of our ancient ancestors.

What Exactly Is a Pyramid Anyway?

Say the word "pyramid" and most North Americans and Europeans think immediately of the great structures of Giza, southwest of Cairo, with their characteristic geometry and well-known reputation as the tombstones of pharaohs. The backside of the United States one-dollar bill even includes a pyramid surrounded by the cryptic Latin motto, *"Annuit coeptis, novus ordo seclorum"*—"he [God] smiles on what we have begun, a new order of the ages." This image, with its powerful spiritual overtones, colors our very use of the word "pyramid."

Yet, as we are about to see, the Giza pyramids are unique, local variations on a wider, global theme. Giza is a single example of an ancient architectural paradigm, not the type or source of that paradigm.

Spirituality is central to pyramids. Every pyramid is a metaphorical expression of a particular understanding of the relationship between humankind, the wider world of nature, and the yet wider world of the cosmos. Those understandings do differ. Aztecs at the time of Cortés or third-century B.C. Indian Buddhists under the king Açoka saw their world in very different religious colors than did Khufu, Khafre, and Menkaure in the Egyptian Old Kingdom. Still, a sacred cosmological understanding expressed in religious ritual is an indispensable aspect of each and every pyramid's meaning and reason for existence.

Of course, sacred cosmology underlies other religious architecture, such as France's cathedral of Chartres, India's Taj Mahal, Greece's Parthenon, or Tibet's Potala. As the great religious philosopher Mircea Eliade points out, holy buildings separate the space of the universe into the sacred and the profane. They create a point of sacred certainty, an axis from which the world begins. Pyramids achieve this purpose in a specific way. They stand apart from temples, cathedrals, and shrines by incorporating an architecture of mass. Chartres or the Taj Mahal are a religious experience inside as outside; both create immense, soaring interiors that tell as much of their builders' cosmologies as the buildings' exteriors. A pyramid, by contrast, has little or no internal space. The point of a pyramid is its mass, the piling up of stone, earth, or brick into an immense and weighty shape—a mountain built by human hands.

That shape takes a number of forms and may be based on the circle, square, or rectangle. The Giza pyramids, for example, are based on a square, with each course of stone block leaning inward from the next, a shape known as a battered profile. Some pyramids use vertical walls and achieve their height by placing successively smaller stages one atop another. In South Asia, circles, squares, and rectangles are super-imposed to achieve mixed shapes that contribute to an overall plan.

Giza, then, isn't the standard for the world's many pyramids. Nor is it the first fully developed example of the pyramid builders' art.

An Old Form in the "New" World

Curiously, what may be the oldest indubitable pyramids by classical dating are to be found on the coast of Peru, in a place called Aspero.* The Peruvian coast is a narrow band of beaches, valleys, and dunes that lies against the precipitous rise of the Andes. The area is ex-tremely dry, with rainfall infrequent and sparse, making its inhabi-tants dependent for fresh water on rivers arising in the Andes and running to the Pacific during the winter rainy season. In the fourth millennium B.C., the people of Aspero did not yet have fired pottery, considered one of the markers of the Neolithic agricultural revolution, but they were living in settled villages, raising crops of squash, gourds, and cotton, foraging for plant foods in the desert and river valleys, and fishing along the coast and possibly even out at sea in the rich coastal currents of the Pacific. Despite their supposedly primitive conditions, these people accumulated enough surplus labor and resources to build pyramids, possibly beginning as early as 3500 B.C. and ending some-time between 3100 and 2700 B.C. All told, the people of Aspero con-structed seven platform mounds and six pyramids.

The two largest structures are known today by their dramatic Span-

---

* The mounds at Aspero earn this distinction in part because they fit the conventional idea of a pyramid. A three-story stone platform that could be classified as a pyramid and was recently discovered in northern China may actually be older than Aspero, but archaeological work at this site remains preliminary and the site's chronology uncertain. Also, the precise dating of these and other very early pyramids around the world is open to much de-bate and will most surely be refined in the future, at which point a pyramid at Aspero may or may not prove to be the winner of the title "earliest pyramid." Indeed, as we explored in chapter 1, the dating of the classic Egyptian pyramids at Giza may need to be revised, an effort that could place their origins long before Aspero's.

ish names, Huaca de los Idolos (Holy Place of the Idols) and Huaca de los Sacrificios (Holy Place of the Sacrifices). Both structures are truncated pyramids, flat-topped monuments on which small multiroomed buildings were erected. The method of construction was unique. Workers wove strong, reedy grasses into nets that held about a half bushel of rubble. The filled net bags were then laid in place to construct the mass of the pyramids, much as the Egyptians used blocks of stone or the Mesopotamians mud brick. The net-bag fill method was employed only for the pyramids. Other structures at Aspero were constructed of adobe faced with stucco or plaster, a more typical way of building in desert climates.

Another, even larger ceremonial complex was built at El Paraíso between 3200 and 2500 B.C. Nine pyramids laid out in a U frame a plaza that covers over 17 acres and faces into the towering Andes. A strikingly large, rectangular mound—the base is over 400 feet by almost 500 feet and is about 40 feet high—was erected at Huaca Prieta sometime between circa 3000 and 2600 B.C.

Recent excavations of yet another site in a remote Peruvian valley have revealed an even more impressive set of pyramids surrounded by the oldest known city in the New World, dated to as early as 2627 B.C. Called Caral and located in the Supe Valley, about 14 miles from the coast, the 170-acre site centered around a huge, sunken circular plaza over one third of a mile across and surrounded by large stepped pyramids. The largest of the pyramids stands 65 feet tall and covers an area larger than a football field. The dwellings of Caral's elite, made of stone with large rooms and plaster walls, were built close to the pyramids, whereas lower-class dwellings, constructed from mud and cane, lay farther out, closer to the edges of the city. Like the pyramids at Aspero and El Paraíso, those at Caral were made of rubble and stone carried in woven reed bags and piled up behind retaining walls.

We know almost nothing beyond the fact that these ancient people constructed the earliest monumental pyramids. Exactly who these people were or why they built these curious and fascinating structures remains an unanswered and potentially very important question.

The Land Between the Rivers

If we shift from the New World to the Old just after the first mounds at Aspero, we find the next phase of pyramid building beginning among the Sumerians of Mesopotamia. At the site of the modern Iraqi city of Warka—known as Uruk in ancient times and as Erech in the Hebrew scriptures of the Old Testament—the Sumerians created their most impressive city. Swelling to 50,000 residents and encompassing over 1,100 acres within its fortified walls, Uruk became the world's first known urban center. It was a religious site as well as a political and ad-ministrative capital, dotted with temples and shrines. One of the sa-cred buildings of Uruk was constructed upon a truncated mound or pedestal of inward-sloping walls that reached approximately 40 feet in height. It has been named the White Temple, from its coating of lime. Because it was larger than the other temples of the same 3000 B.C. time period, archaeologists suggest that it was likely sacred to Anu, supreme god of the sky and the Sumerian equivalent of the Greek god Zeus.

Like all Mesopotamian buildings, the White Temple was con-structed from mud brick. The palm trees common in the Tigris and Euphrates valleys yield poor lumber, and the wide alluvial valleys offer little stone usable for building. The Sumerians mixed clay with straw, formed it into bricks, left them to dry in the sun or baked them in kilns, then mortared them into place with bitumen, which was im-ported from what is now western Iran.

Over the following centuries the platform temple grew into the zig-gurat, or staged tower. "Ziggurat" derives from a later Babylonian verb, *zagaru*, which means "to be tall or lofty." Essentially, a ziggurat was a stepped pyramid built by setting successively smaller platforms one upon another. This form flowered in the city of Ur under the king known as Urnammu, the first king of Ur's Dynasty 3 (2112–2016 B.C.). Rebuilding and extending an original structure that was probably contemporary with the White Temple, Urnammu created a massive ziggurat. According to the reconstruction completed by Sir Charles Leonard Woolley between 1929 and 1939, the ziggurat of Ur comprised three terraces linked by majestic staircases. The third and last terrace supported a temple or shrine dedicated to the moon god Nanna. Unfortunately, only the first two terraces, still impressive for their mass and architecture, remain. The lines of the ziggurat were built with slight curves that prevented the optical illusion of weakness had they been straight—a principle used by the Greeks of Periclean Athens in building the Parthenon over 1,600 years later and one that shows the artistic sophistication of these long-ago people.

A second flowering of the ziggurat came during the reign of the Babylonian king Nebuchadrezzar II, who ruled from 605 to 562 B.C. An earlier Babylonian kingdom had been destroyed by the Assyrians in 689 B.C., and Nebuchadrezzar's father, Nabopolassar, established a new dynasty and rebuilt the ruined city. According to the story told by Babylonian inscriptions, Nabopolassar himself carried clay and brick to build the great ziggurat in thanks to the god Marduk for restoring the city. It fell to Nebuchadrezzar to finish this monumental task. Named Etemenenanki (meaning "House of the Foundation of Heaven and Earth") and rising in seven steps to a height of 295 feet, this massive ziggurat in the city of Babylon is thought by many scholars to have been the inspiration for the Tower of Babel, whose story is told in the Old Testament book of Genesis. Nebuchadrezzar built another ziggurat at Birs Nimrud, one side of whose base measured 270 feet.

Today only the outline of Etemenenanki and the ruins of the ziggurat of Birs Nimrud still stand. Time has been hard on the ziggurats. A quarter century after Nebuchadrezzar's death, Persia conquered Babylon and made it an imperial province. As the old ways collapsed, people cannibalized the ziggurats for bricks. And, although it rains relatively little in the Mesopotamian desert, precipitation eventually wears away mud brick like salt on ice. No longer maintained in the way they required, the ziggurats melted into ruin.

The largest surviving ziggurat stands not in Mesopotamia but farther east, at Tchoga Zanbil in the ancient kingdom of Elam, located in what is now western Iran. Sited some 18 miles from Susa, the capital of Elam, the ziggurat was built around 1250 B.C. by Untash-Napirisha, whose royal name was stamped into the mud bricks used in the edifice. The ziggurat had five levels and reached more than 170 feet in height, supporting a shrine to the Elamite god Inshushinak. Elam was politically separate from Mesopotamia, but the two areas were joined by trade, which apparently involved ideas and religious practices as well as the usual goods and commodities.

The World Mountain in the Two Lands

Aesthetically, the Mesopotamian or Elamite ziggurat is very different from the Egyptian pyramid. Clearly, the Egyptians did not simply import Mesopotamian ideas and imitate them, nor did such copycat emulation apply the other way around. Still, pyramid building was a major fact of religious, social, and political life in both regions in about the same time period, at least according to the standard chronologies. Different as they appear, the pyramids of Egypt and those of Mesopotamia are roughly contemporary and were a focus of the energies of both societies in the second and third millennia B.C.

According to the standard explanation, the building of Egyptian pyramids can be traced to the graves of the predynastic period, when important personages were interred in pits marked by a simple mound of sand and gravel. Just before the time of Menes (circa 3000 B.C.), the founder of the dynasty that joined Upper and Lower Egypt into one kingdom, burial pits had developed into neat boxes of mud brick sunk into the earth and divided into rooms or chambers. During the first two pharaonic dynasties, this pattern became more complex. Built in the desert near the high cliffs of Abydos, the chambered burial pit was marked by large stelae, a mound, and an imitation royal palace, or mastaba, a flat-roofed, rectangular, mud-brick structure that served as a dwelling space for the departed spirit of the interred ruler. Although some of these complexes are large, they are not monumental. Rather, they have a homey feeling. In fact, the word "mastaba" comes from an Arabic root meaning "bench," referring to a sitting place attached to the walls of an ordinary house.

In the Third Dynasty (2649–2575 B.C.), friendly domesticity gave way to a monumental size that quickly exceeded the dimensions of day-to-day life. According to the ancient Egyptians, Imhotep, architect to Pharaoh Djoser (2630–2611 B.C.), turned an experimental take on the mastaba into the first Egyptian stepped pyramid, a feat that won him immortal status among the gods. Djoser's complex in Saqqara contains an original four-step pyramid encased within a six-step pyramid, and it is surrounded by a walled array of courtyards, palaces, and temples, many with false entrances that give the place the feeling of a labyrinth or maze. Built of gleaming white limestone, Djoser's pyramid is generally accepted as one of the oldest existing stone buildings.

This new tradition was followed by Djoser's successor, Sekhemkhet (2611–2603 B.C.), who added yet another stepped pyramid at Saqqara. Interestingly, the last two pharaohs of the Third Dynasty, Khaba (2603–2599 B.C.) and Huni (2599–2575 B.C.), built no pyramids as far as we know. With them the so-called Early Dynastic Period of ancient Egypt came to an end.

The Fourth Dynasty launched the Old Kingdom (2575–2134 B.C.), which turned pyramid building into a defining activity of political, social, and religious life along the Nile. Sneferu (2575–2551 B.C.), first pharaoh of the Fourth Dynasty, was a ruler with a penchant for grand gestures. In the 24 years of his reign, three major pyramids were erected, each representing a step along the way to the climax represented by the pyramids of Giza.

The first of Sneferu's pyramids (which some scholars suggest was actually begun by Huni), was located at Meidum, about 30 miles south of Saqqara, and it turned out to be an unequivocal disaster. The Meidum structure was the first attempt by the Egyptians to turn a stepped pyramid into the pure geometric form we now think of on hearing "pyramid." Eight steps were constructed, then stone blocks were added to fill in the steps and create a smooth exterior. That was when the trouble began, according to one theory. The angle of the pyramid was too steep to support the weight of the fill blocks, and the entire external structure collapsed—possibly all at once, a catastrophe of enormously fatal proportions. The stone may have yielded to gravity in an immense megalithic avalanche that would have crushed, sheared, and ground up many of the thousands of workers laboring on the structure.

The disaster at Meidum explains the peculiar shape of Sneferu's second effort, the so-called Bent Pyramid of Dahshur, which lies just south of Saqqara. Shaped like a trapezoid with a triangle on top, the lower portion of the Bent Pyramid rises at an angle of 54.5 degrees, then the slope shifts abruptly and gracelessly to 43.5 degrees. Apparently work was already in progress on this pyramid when the Meidum disaster occurred. Realizing that they were setting the stage for yet another megalithic avalanche, the builders changed the angle of elevation from the daring to the conservative and saved the structure. (Of course this tidy hypothesis to explain the shape of the Bent Pyramid fails to work if the Meidum pyramid was never finished or if it collapsed long after Sneferu's time, possibly as the result of an earthquake, as some researchers have suggested.)

The North, or Red, Pyramid, Sneferu's third effort, also located at Dahshur, followed the same conservative angle. The pyramid is 345 feet high and was at the time the tallest pyramid in Egypt, but its angle of elevation gives it a somewhat squat appearance.

By the time Sneferu's son, Khufu, took the throne of the Two Lands (he reigned from 2551 to 2528 B.C.), Egyptian builders had figured out that the greatest possible angle of elevation from the horizontal for a pyramid is approximately 52 degrees. They used this angle in erecting the Great Pyramid of Khufu at Giza, which was, as we have seen in chapter 1, a holy site that predated the Egyptian pharaohs by thousands of years. Perhaps the holy antiquity of the place inspired Khufu, for the structure attributed to him represents the triumph of monumentality in pyramid building along the Nile. Khufu's Pyramid is only a little longer on each side of the base than Sneferu's North Pyramid, 756 feet compared to 722. But the steeper angle of elevation makes it nearly half again as tall and massive. At a height of 481 feet and a volume of approximately 3 million cubic yards, it is far and away the largest pyramid built in the Old World. It remains a marvel that a structure of such ambitious immensity could have been built in the mere two dozen years Khufu held the throne.

When it was first complete, Khufu's Pyramid was a sight we can now only imagine. It was finished with a layer of fitted, polished white limestone that gleamed like a thousand full moons. Long after the Old Kingdom had passed, people who knew nothing of that lost glory pulled the limestone off and carried it away to build Cairo.

Khufu's successor, Djedefre (2528–2520 B.C.), built a much smaller pyramid at Abu Roash. Khafre (2520–2494 B.C.), who followed Djedefre, focused again on Giza. He built his pyramid—which may have been erected on the site of a much older structure—in a spot integral to a ground plan created by the Sphinx and Valley temples, the wide path now called Khafre's Causeway, the oldest portion of the structure known as Khafre's Mortuary Temple, and the Great Sphinx. His pyramid is slightly steeper than Khufu's, achieving an angle of a little over 53 degrees. It is about 50 feet smaller on the side (base) and 10 feet shorter.

Khafre's successor, Nabka, ruled for only four years (2494–2490 B.C.), too little time to finish the large pyramid he began south of Giza and north of Saqqara, at Zawyet el-Aryan. After him came Menkaure (2490–2472 B.C.), who returned to Giza and built the last and smallest of the three major pyramids on the plateau. It is only about half as long on the side as the Khufu and Khafre pyramids and reaches a height of just over 213 feet.

The next two pharaohs settled for funerary structures inspired more by the mastabas of early dynastic times than by Giza. Kings of the Fifth (2465–2323 B.C.), Sixth (2323–2150 B.C.), and Seventh/Eighth dynasties (2150–2134 B.C.) built pyramids, but only one exceeded Menkaure's in size. The workmanship is generally considered inferior to the grand designs realized at Saqqara, Dahshur, and Giza. Thereafter, Egypt collapsed into political upheaval, an event whose causes we shall examine more closely in chapter 8. Pyramid building resumed only with the Twelfth (1991–1783 B.C.) and Thirteenth (1783–1640 B.C.) dynasties. The 10 structures left from this period are all approximately the size of Menkaure's pyramid or smaller. The cores of these Middle Kingdom pyramids were rubble held in place by retaining walls, and later mud brick, rather than the solid stone blocks used in the Old Kingdom. The golden age had long passed.

Renaissance to the South

Egyptian pyramid building spanned a millennium. In that long reach of time more than 90 pyramids were constructed, counting the smaller satellite structures as well as the larger and better known monuments. Remarkably, about twice that number were built over another millennium, in Nubia, far up the Nile in what is now the northern Sudan, beginning about 800 years after the last royal pyramid was raised in Egypt.

The kings of Kush, as this land was known to the Egyptians, posed an apparent threat to the pharaohs of the Twelfth Dynasty, who built a frontier outpost to keep the Kushites out of their realm. Egypt's New Kingdom (1550–1070 B.C.) annexed Kush as part of Egypt's Nubian province, but this control ended with the breakup of the Egyptian kingdom into a series of unfriendly principalities that quarreled and made war on one another.

About 770 B.C. a powerful Nubian kingdom extended its control north, into the Egyptian heartland. Taking first the southern city of Thebes and then advancing north, the Nubians assumed control of the ancient Two Lands. The Nubian king Piye (750–712 B.C.) united Egypt once again and founded the Twenty-Fifth, or Nubian, Dynasty, which held power for almost a century.

Up until the time of Piye, the kings of Kush were buried unmummified beneath large, round mounds covering circular underground pits divided by walls. Piye returned to the ancient customs of his newly conquered domain. Choosing the site of el-Kurru, his father's burial place, for his own memorial, Piye was the first Egyptian king to be interred in a pyramid in over 800 years. It was a relatively small structure, with a base just 26 feet long and a steep, 68-degree slope of elevation. Although Piye's body was not found when the pyramid was excavated in 1918 and 1919, the presence of canopic jars in the burial vault indicated that it had been mummified.

Piye launched a renaissance, a return to the Egyptian customs of old, or at least those customs as they were imagined to be. Three of his successors were buried at el-Kurru, along with 14 queens, each in her own pyramid. The site also yielded two dozen buried horses and two dogs. Taharqa (690–664 B.C.), the next-to-last Nubian pharaoh, moved his pyramid site to a place called Nuri on the other side of the Nile.

The Assyrians forced the Nubian Dynasty out of Egypt and back to Nubia, taking the throne of the Two Lands for themselves. The Nubian kings, however, continued their pyramid burial practices, complete with mummification, creating a new Egypt outside Egypt. The mummy of the Nubian king Aspelta, who died in the middle of the sixth century B.C., was placed in a massive granite sarcophagus whose four-ton lid was decorated with excerpts from the Pyramid Texts (texts found inscribed on the walls of various burial chambers and antechambers in some pyramids, beginning in the late Fifth Dynasty), the Egyptian *Book of the Dead*, and images of various Egyptian deities. Until the end of the fourth century B.C., pyramids continued to be built at Nuri. Thereafter, Meroe, farther upriver, between the Fifth and Sixth cataracts of the Nile, became the royal cemetery. It remained in use until about A.D. 350.

A number of important characteristics distinguish the Nubian pyramids. For one thing, they are relatively small and remarkably standardized, varying little from one to the next. Nubian pyramids were
also used by more members of the royal family than just the king and
his queen. And many of these important personages took a great deal
with them into the other world—jewelry and other finery, weapons,
horses and dogs, and even companions and servants who were apparently sacrificed to accompany the dead on the journey to the other world.

Just as the Nubians copied the Egyptians, the Romans during late
Republican and Imperial times adopted many Egyptian styles and influences. A Kush-style pyramid was built in Rome circa 12 B.C. for the
praetor Gaius Cestius, during the reign of Augustus. Another, larger
pyramid stood in the necropolis on Vatican Hill, but it was largely destroyed by the sixteenth century A.D. It is very likely that more pyramids once took their place among the tombs that lined roads leading in
and out of Rome.

The Realm of the Lotus

East of the traditional center of pyramid culture in northeastern Africa
lies another, as yet little-known realm, of pyramid building that stretches
across southern Asia from modern Pakistan and India into Indochina.

Centering the Universe

Protopyramid structures first appeared in the Indian subcontinent during the Harappan civilization, named for the city Harappa, in the extensive and fertile Indus River Valley from circa 4000 to 1800 B.C. At its
high point in the middle of the third millennium B.C., the Harappan
civilization reached a grandeur to rival Egypt's Old Kingdom and traded
actively with Mesopotamia. Over 70 cities arose, some of them large
enough to accommodate about 40,000 residents, such as Mohenjo-daro
on the Indus River and Harappa itself on an Indus tributary, the Ravi.
Public structures in the cities sat atop mud-brick platform mounds.

Two of these mounds in Mohenjo-daro, called the Citadel and Lower Town, were massive, representing the same kind of major investment of time and effort evidenced by the similar structures raised in Mesopotamia and Egypt in about the same era.

The next appearance of a pyramid-type structure in India, the stupa, does not actually seem to be a pyramid, at least on first glance. Lacking the angularity of the pyramids of Egypt, the ziggurats of Mesopotamia, or the mud-brick platforms of Harappa, the stupas of ancient India seem only distant relations, like cousins so many times removed that the rest of the family has forgotten where they belong on the family tree. A careful look, however, shows that their relationship is much closer than we might at first imagine. The architects of the stupas use an architecture of mass, which vaults outside over inside. And stupas, like the ziggurats and Egyptian pyramids, are described as world mountains, peaks that divide the sacred from the profane and mark the place where time and space begin.

With the Egyptian and Babylonian monuments, we have to make educated guesses about meaning and significance. In the case of India's stupas we are fortunate to know a great deal more, owing to the living continuity of the Buddhist and Hindu religions. The meaning of a stupa does not have to be guessed; it need only be understood.

Ancient Indians buried their dead, as did predynastic Egyptians, under round burial mounds shaped like the huts in common use. The stupa's round, circular vault elevated this basic form into the image of Mount Meru, the mythological peak that serves as the center of the Indian cosmos. Meru (called Sumeru by Buddhists) is identified with Mount Kailas, a 19,000-foot snow-clad Tibetan peak that to this day is a destination for pilgrims from all over southern and central Asia.

This conception of the stupa as Mount Meru reaches far back into the prehistory of the Indian subcontinent. The first surviving expression of the idea dates to the middle of the third century B.C., when Buddhism became a state religion under the emperor Açoka (circa 274–237 B.C.). Around this time, perhaps under Açoka himself, Stupa 1 (also known as the Great Stupa) was erected at Sanchi to house the relics of the Buddha. Since then it has been rebuilt and enlarged repeatedly, but the original structure and plan remain. Basically a great dome mounded up on a circular base with a compacted-rubble core, the surface is faced with brick, slabs of stone, and stucco. A gallery that circles the base and opens through four gates allows pilgrims to walk around the dome in a counterclockwise direction, just as they would do at the base of Mount Kailas. Metaphorically, the mountain-like dome becomes the vault of the cosmos. The mast that rises from the dome represents the axis around which the universe turns and reaches across the great span from Earth to heaven.

A common feature of all stupas is a ground plan that follows the outlines of a mandala, a symmetrical nesting of squares and circles. The structure that best exemplifies this artistic reality is also the largest and best-preserved of all the ancient stupas: Borobudur, built on a plain in the center of the island of Java, about 30 miles from the modern Indonesian city of Yogyakarta. Borobudur began as a Hindu structure in the middle of the eighth century A.D. Construction was stopped, then was resumed later in the eighth century by a Buddhist dynasty that transformed the great stone mass into a memorial for its religion. Shifts in the political winds caused Borobudur to fall into decline and finally to be abandoned in the tenth and eleventh centuries. Volcanic dust and jungle growth obscured the site until it was first cleared by European colonizers in the early nineteenth century. The site was fully restored only in the 1970s, at a cost of more than $20 million.

The Borobudur stupa is massive and symmetrical; it extends over 220 yards on each side and peaks with a low sculpted hill, and is divided into nine rising terraces. Like Stupa 1 at Sanchi, it represents a model of the universe centered on Mount Meru. The lower terraces are decorated with panels that depict Buddhist doctrines and show scenes of everyday life in eighth- and ninth-century Java. The upper three terraces contain 72 small stupas, each of which houses a statue of the Buddha. Most of these images are headless, having been decapitated by antiquities hunters and museum collectors. A large central stupa crowns the whole structure. Representing nirvana, the Buddhist state of enlightenment, it is, appropriately, empty.

The Ceremonial Cities of the Khmers

At about the same time that construction was beginning on Borobudur, the Khmer people of what is now Cambodia began building temples echoing a Hindu architectural form known as the tower, or *sikhara*— testimony to how far into Asia the architectural forms and religious ideas of India reached. Melding the *sikhara* with the stupa created a form that showed Indian influence yet was distinctly and uniquely Khmer.

The early temples of Cambodia, such as Baksei Chamkrong, which was built in the tenth century A.D., comprise five terraces of declining size set one upon another that support a single temple on top. Four stairways, one on each side of the square structure, allow approach to the temple. The temple bears a clear resemblance to both the Mesopotamian ziggurat and the New World pyramids of the Maya, which we will soon examine.

The Khmer tower temple is the basic unit of the ceremonial cities the Khmers built in later centuries. The most striking and best-known example is Angkor Wat, which was constructed during the reign of Suryavarman II (A.D. 1112–1152). Built in what is now a thick rain forest, Angkor Wat is but one complex in an enormous center encompassing other, similar compounds connected by canals and artificial lakes. The core of Angkor Wat is a structure with five temple towers rising from a square, stepped platform—in essence, pyramids supported by a pyramid. The tallest of the towers stands in the center of the square and climbs to a height of more than 200 feet. The four remaining towers, which look like slightly smaller copies of the central pyramid, occupy the corners of the square. Galleries frame the complex, all of which is constructed with a mortarless drywall technique that evidences a high level of artistry and workmanship.

Temples in the other ceremonial cities surrounding Angkor Wat are oriented to the east, but Angkor Wat alone faces west. Many scholars argue that, since the gateway to the next world was thought to lie in the west, Angkor Wat served as a mausoleum for the temple's patron, Suryavarman II.

Mountains for the Kings

Starting in about the late third century B.C., about the same time as the original construction of Stupa 1 at Sanchi, the kings of China's Q'in (also known as Ch'in) Dynasty began marking their tombs with pyramidal mounds. The custom was followed during the succeeding Han through Tang dynasties, not only by kings but also by lords wealthy enough to afford such monuments to themselves.

But the Q'in pyramids did not rise from a vacuum; they had antecedents. One such predecessor is a contender for the title of oldest pyramid, a structure dating back to approximately 3000 B.C. or earlier that was discovered recently near Sijiazi, about 230 miles northeast of Beijing, in the Inner Mongolia Autonomous Region of northern China. Located on a mountain ridge and attributed to the Hongshan Culture (variously dated from before 4000 B.C. to 2000 B.C.), the structure is described as a three-story, pyramid-shaped, layered stone platform whose base measures nearly 100 feet long and 50 feet wide. The top of the structure contains seven tombs and the remains of an altar. Pottery fragments found around the altar that bear the ancient Chinese character for rice, stone statues of goddesses in some of the tombs, and a symbolic phallus (*lingam* or *linga*) carved on the wall of one tomb may all point to rituals associated with the site. The Chinese archaeologists involved with the excavations have suggested that there could be an astrological, and thus an astronomical, significance to the monument.

Additionally, there is evidence for numerous and substantial burial mounds during the Xia Dynasty of the late third and early second millennium B.C. During the Shang and Zhou dynasties, which ruled from circa 1600 B.C. to the late third century B.C. and preceded the Q'in, ruling elites were buried in underground pits constructed to preserve the body and the rich array of goods and artwork interred with it. As with the burial pits of Nubia, companions and retainers were sacrificed as part of the funeral ritual. During the last centuries of the Shang Dynasty, circa 1300 to 1100 B.C., kings were buried under large grave mounds, or earthen pyramids, at a site near the modern village of Hsiao-t'un in Honan (Henan) Province. Under one of these Shang pyramids the remains not only of the king but also of over 160 sacrificial victims were found. Some of the numerous—and still unexplored and undated—tamped-earth pyramids found in China may date to the Shang Dynasty. During the Later (or Eastern) Zhou Dynasty a mound supporting a temple or ceremonial hall was built over the grave. Zhongshan Mausoleum, built during this period in Hebei Province, is constructed according to an architectural plan that nests squares and circles within one another and shares many formal features with Angkor Wat, including the five stepped pyramids supported on a single raised platform. Apparently the central pyramid represented the burial of the king, and the smaller, corner pyramids represented the internment sites of his sacrificed consorts.

Chih-huang-ti (also known as Shihuangdi), the first emperor of Q'in, who is best known for building the Great Wall of China during his reign (220–210 B.C.), constructed an immense funerary center at Lishan, east of the modern city of Xi'an in Shensi (Shanxi) Province. Using a rectangular double-walled plan like that of the Zhongshan Mausoleum, the complex centered on a tumulus made of tamped earth, possibly with a natural hill as its center. The pyramid mound is immense, measuring over 1,000 feet on each side and rising to an approximate height of 130 feet. Erosion has been working on the tumulus over the more than 2,000 years since it was built, so it may well once have been higher. To date, the mound has not been excavated, so what lies within or under it remains unknown. According to uncertain historical records from the time, a tomb was built under the pyramid following the architectural plan of a royal palace, then was filled with treasure. Drawn and cocked crossbows connected to trip wires were set as booby traps to impale any robber foolish enough to enter.

The most extraordinary discovery thus far at Lishan came from three large pits outside the eastern wall of the funerary center. There archaeologists uncovered a complete army of life-sized ceramic figures—horsemen, infantry, and archers, equipped with horses and chariots. Unlike toy soldiers cast from the same mold, the fighters of Lishan are individuals, each with unique features that suggest distinct personalities. Apparently these figures served as stand-ins for the bloody ritual slayings that had accompanied Shang and Zhou burials.

There may be similar mountain-like pyramid structures on Japan, now long eroded and practically unrecognizable as pyramids. Writers on the topic have pointed to a number of curiously shaped hills in Japan and argue that they are in fact "lost" pyramids. Whether they are or not will remain unknown until a serious investigation is undertaken.

The Long Leap to Mesoamerica

Conditioned as we are by the continuing preeminence of the Giza pyramids to think of their form as distinctly Old World, it may come as a surprise to realize that the Americas contain more of these monumental structures than the rest of the planet combined. The brave scholar May Veber has suggested that 100,000 pyramids, some of them admittedly quite small, remain to be discovered in Mexico alone. Count in the other countries of Mesoamerica—the region that encompasses eastern and southern Mexico, Guatemala, Belize, northern El Salvador, and Honduras—and the total number becomes staggering. Mesoamerican cultures built pyramids from the beginning of the first millennium B.C. until the Spanish Conquest in the early sixteenth century A.D., a 2,500-year reach that equals the span of the pyramid-building activity of Egypt-Nubia and Mesopotamia.

The Olmec Beginning

Located on the Gulf of Mexico in what is now the Mexican state of Veracruz, La Venta seems an unlikely place for the beginning of Mesoamerica's pyramid cultures. An island set in a tangle of swamps, grasslands, and dense forests, this low-lying region is swept by heavy wind and rain for much of the year. Yet it was here that the people we know as the Olmecs first arrived in about 1100 B.C.

The new arrivals, whose origins are unknown, cleared the land and built a ceremonial center along a natural ridge in the island's middle. The focal point of the complex is a great pyramid of tamped clay, which today has a height of about 100 feet. Set upon a wide, low platform, the pyramid looks something like an upside-down cupcake: a truncated cone with a flattened top and fluted sides carved by 10 enormous gullies. Although deepened by erosion over the millennia, the flutes were part of the original construction and were created by the pyramid's builders. One hypothesis to explain La Venta's curious shape casts it as an imitation volcano. It does indeed resemble the volcanic cones common in the Tuxtla Mountains 60 miles up the coast. Since the Olmec homeland remains unknown, it is possible that the people migrated from the mountains and built a reminder of home in their new abode.

There is more to La Venta, however, than immigrant nostalgia for an abandoned past. The pyramid forms the center of two large complexes of buildings, plazas, monumental sculptures, offering pits, and tombs that were built in stages from 1000 B.C. until about 400 B.C., which is when the Olmecs abandoned the site. Much of the material was brought from far away—colored clays from distant regions, basalt from the Tuxtla Mountains, tons of jade and serpentine from a still-unknown source. Though we know little of the concerns that drove them, the Olmecs lavished every luxury on their religious center.

Teotihuacán: City of the Old Gods

Even the Aztecs who built the city of Tenochtitlán, the ancient site of modern Mexico City, had no idea who was responsible for Teotihuacán, an abandoned and ruined urban center northeast of Tenochtitlán, whose name means "Place of the Gods." Beginning in the last two centuries B.C., the Teotihuacános built a stunning city, which remained the preeminent city of Mexico until the eighth century A.D. At its height during the fourth to seventh centuries A.D., Teotihuacán covered more than seven and a half square miles and housed a population variously estimated at 100,000 to 200,000 people. Built in the highlands of central Mexico along a well-plotted north–south axis, the city followed an ornate, precise, and careful master plan that made Rome, then the center of the Western world, look haphazard and chaotic by comparison.

Beginning in the first century A.D., the Teotihuacános began what we now know as the Pyramid of the Moon, the name it was given hundreds of years later by the Aztecs. This pyramid was enlarged and rebuilt five times over the next two centuries—a common pattern with Mesoamerican pyramids—with a major leap in complexity occurring in the fourth phase.

At about the same time that the initial phase of the Pyramid of the Moon was completed, the Teotihuacános started the Pyramid of the Sun, completing their most stunning achievement by circa A.D. 250. Rising from a square base that is 730 feet on a side, the pyramid reaches up through five stepped terraces to a height of some 200 feet. The flat top may well have supported a temple that has since disappeared. A great staircase leads up the western side of the pyramid.

Like most of the Mesoamerican pyramids, the Pyramid of the Sun was built around a core of rubble fill held in place by retaining walls. These walls were then faced with adobe bricks, which were covered with mortared cobblestones. Originally another layer of stone and a coating of stucco finished the pyramid's exterior, but the dynamiting used to excavate the structure from 1905 to 1910 in readiness for the centennial celebration of Mexican independence destroyed much of the two outer skins. Sloppy blasting stripped away over 20 feet of material in some places.

A long, broad boulevard called the Avenue of the Dead joined the Pyramid of the Sun with the Pyramid of the Moon and was itself lined with important civic and religious buildings. Teotihuacán was a place of great economic power, functioning as the center of a trading network that supplied obsidian for utensils and weapons throughout Mesoamerica. The cosmopolitan city drew immigrants and pilgrims from as far away as the Yucatán and Guatemala. They came to trade and to worship not only at the two great pyramids but also among the many smaller pyramids and temples.

Excavation of one of the smaller sites, called the Feathered Serpent Pyramid, provided evidence that the Teotihuacános practiced human sacrifice. More than 130 skeletons, clearly soldiers and possibly prisoners of war, were found. Even more sacrifices, complete with military gear and including animals as well as humans, have been uncovered in the Pyramid of the Moon by recent excavations conducted by Arizona State University and Mexico's National Institute of Anthropology and History. Leopoldo Batres, who oversaw the first destructive excavations of the Pyramid of the Sun, found the bodies of sacrificed children buried at the corners of each of its five levels.

About A.D. 700, the population of Teotihuacán fell dramatically; then the remaining inhabitants deliberately burned the city and moved to the east. Consigned to the elements, Teotihuacán was soon covered by dust and vegetation. Ironically, this fate ultimately saved it from destruction by the Spaniards, who, fired by the Inquisition's fierce cruelty toward non-Christians, destroyed much of ancient Mexico's heritage. Clueless as to what lay beneath those tree-dotted, oddly shaped hills in the northeast of the Valley of Mexico (the area around modern Mexico City), the Spaniards let Teotihuacán be.

The Magnificent Maya

Some of the immigrants and pilgrims who made their way to Teotihuacán's pyramids and temples were Maya from southern Mesoamerica, particularly the Yucatán peninsula and bordering areas. Inspired
perhaps by what they saw in that great metropolis and possibly influenced by Teotihuacános, the Maya began building pyramids of their
own. Between the second and thirteenth centuries, and particularly
during the Classic Period, circa A.D. 550 to 950, the Maya erected a
series of religious complexes whose most prominent structures were
stepped pyramids. Many of these structures survive today in such
places as Palenque, Uxmal, and Xpuhil in Mexico; Tikal, Kaminaljuyú,
and Seibal in Guatemala; Copán in Honduras; Tazumal in El Salvador;
and Altun Ha and Caracol in Belize.

Like the Mesopotamians and the Buddhist builders of the Great
Stupa of Borobudur, the Maya constructed step pyramids whose topmost level supported a temple. And, like the Teotihuacános, they built
and rebuilt the same structures again and again. The name Uxmal actually means "thrice-built" in the Mayan language. In fact, the famous
Pyramid of the Magician or Sorcerer at that site actually underwent
five phases of construction (circa ninth and tenth centuries A.D.). Apparently this rebuilding renewed the relationship of succeeding Mayan
kings with the realm of the gods.

Mayan pyramids served various and unique purposes. According to
legend, the Pyramid of the Magician or Sorcerer was built by the god
of magic, Itzamná, as a site for training healers, astronomers, mathematicians, shamans, and priests. The Mayan-Toltec Temple of Kukulcan (also known as the Feathered Serpent, the same deity honored at
Teotihuacán), which was built between the eleventh and thirteenth
centuries at Chichén Itzá in the Yucatán, is a storehouse of information
about the sophisticated, accurate Mayan calendar. Each of the pyramid's four staircases contains 91 steps, which, together with the shared

step of the top platform, adds up to the 365 days of the year. The central staircase divides the pyramid's nine terraces into 18 segments, which equals the number of Mayan months. And the Temple of the Inscriptions at Palenque, a stepped pyramid of nine levels, which was begun about the middle of the seventh century A.D. and was finished in the early years of the eighth, encloses the hidden tomb of its royal patron, Pacal (A.D. 615–683). The tomb is reached through a hidden entryway that descends through 13 vaults to the actual burial chamber. The vaults were filled with rubble to deter invaders, a stratagem that worked against over a millennium's worth of potential grave robbers. The archaeologists who discovered and excavated the tomb in the early 1950s found the jade-covered body of Pacal resting in an ornately carved sarcophagus, just as it had been buried 1,300 years before. The tomb was no afterthought in the pyramid's construction. Located near ground level and just under the pyramid's center of mass, the burial chamber and the vaults leading to it had to have been designed into the pyramid from the time the first stone was laid. Similarly, Pyramid I at Tikal, one of six pyramids at this immense site, served as the funerary structure for the king known to archaeologists as Ruler A.

The Maya culture centered in Guatemala, Belize, and the southern Yucatán collapsed by about A.D. 1000, apparently owing to an ecological crisis brought on by too large a population on agriculturally marginal land. That vacuum invited invasion by the Toltecs, a fierce warrior people whose capital of Tula lay in the modern Mexican state of Hidalgo, about 50 miles north of Mexico City. Obsessed with warriors and war, whose images cover their pyramid temples, the Toltecs controlled an empire that spanned Mexico from Pacific to Atlantic and reached into the Yucatán. Much of the famed ruin of Chichén Itzá was built or remodeled by the Toltecs. And when the Toltec empire itself collapsed under the equally fierce Aztecs, who first appeared in the late twelfth century, some of the remaining Maya reoccupied then-abandoned Chichén Itzá, further rebuilding and refurbishing the great monuments of their heritage, including the Temple of Kukulcan.

The Aztec Ascendancy

Like the Maya, the Aztecs built their pyramids again and again. One of the largest Aztec pyramids, Tenayuca, went through at least eight rebuildings, of which six were major additions and enlargements. Originally raised by the Chichimecs in A.D. 1304, a tribe the Aztecs defeated and then ruled, the pyramid was transformed into an Aztec shrine. In its final form, Tenayuca has four stepped platforms with sloping profiles and a grand double staircase that end in two temples, surrounded by an immense sculpted serpent, on the top terrace. This same basic plan was followed in the massive Templo Mayor, which lay at the heart of the ritual complex in the Aztec capital of Tenochtitlán, now Mexico City. Remodeled eight times beginning early in the fourteenth century, Templo Mayor supported two temples. One was dedicated to the war god Huitzilopochtli, whom the Aztecs considered their ancestral deity, and the other to Tláloc, a divinity of fertility often associated with water. Offerings buried in Templo Mayor include the bones and skulls of children. This find indicates that, as at Teotihuacán, humans were sacrificed as part of the ritual of pyramid building.

Indeed, human sacrifice was central to the function of the Aztec pyramids. The Maya, particularly in the later centuries of their ascendancy, ritually slaughtered prisoners of war. The Aztecs developed this practice into a cultural obsession that claimed hundreds and even thousands at a time. Victims were led up the pyramid and stretched face-up over a stone altar, their arms and legs pinioned by priests. Another priest wielded a flint knife to slice open the victim's chest and pull out the beating heart, which was offered to the gods of the sky. It is thought that the body was then rolled down the long staircase to the ground level, where it was butchered and consumed.

Such displays of slaughter and cannibalism scandalized the invading Spaniards under Hernán Cortés, a man who himself murdered no small number of people, typically with immense treachery and boundless cruelty. Cortés made an example of the holy city of Cholula, where the Aztecs had appropriated an immense earthen pyramid originally built by the Toltecs and remodeled it—as usual, again and again—into a structure sacred to Quetzalcoatl (the Feathered Serpent, known to the Maya as Kukulcan). Suspecting an uprising in the making, Cortés ordered the massacre of 5,000 to 10,000 people. He then vowed to build a church for every Aztec shrine he destroyed in Cholula. One of these churches sits to this day atop the pyramid, the final rebuilding of this immense structure, one that aimed to stake a Christian claim on what had for centuries been an indigenous holy place.

The North American Echo

Even though the political influence of the Mesoamerican pyramid builders did not extend into what is now the United States, their cultural ideas apparently made themselves known far to the north. Between A.D. 600 and 1400, a culture called the Mississippian dominated the long fertile floodplain between what is now St. Louis and New Orleans and influenced much of central, eastern, and southern North America. The Mississippians were vastly more flamboyant and sophisticated than any previous culture in the area. In place of the simple burial mounds built by their ancestors, the Mississippians constructed large ceremonial centers comprising plazas and truncated pyramids with staircases rising to the temples on their summits. The central mound at Cahokia, Illinois, one of the major ceremonial centers, covered 16 acres, and the temple on its summit was over 100 feet high. Smaller mounds surrounding the central temple supported warehouses, administrative buildings, and the houses of the ruling elites. The religious symbolism of Cahokia, which reflects a fascination with human sacrifice and the sun, along with the architecture of pyramid and plaza, has an unmistakably Mexican air despite its great distance from the pyramid centers of Mesoamerica.

Peru: Closing the Circle

South of Mesoamerica, in Peru, where humans erected early pyramids at Aspero, the tradition of pyramid building continued, shifting and changing as it moved from culture to succeeding culture.

Beginning circa 1900 B.C., coastal peoples in Peru built a series of ceremonial centers that mirrored the more ancient site of El Paraíso— truncated pyramid mounds in a U shape facing the Andes. Between the Huaura and Santa rivers, about 100 such complexes were built, the largest at Sechin, in about 1400 B.C. There the mound measured almost 1,000 by over 800 feet and reached a height of more than 130 feet.

The same U-shaped, mountain-facing plan is found in the northern Andean highlands at Chavín de Huántar, which is the site of one of the earliest known South American civilizations. Built of monumental stone blocks over several hundred years of the first millennium B.C., the Temple Complex comprises two principal monuments, the Old Temple and the New Temple, connected by labyrinthine passageways and water channels. Within a cavelike space at the intersection of the structure's vertical and horizontal axes sits a stela over 13 feet tall called the Lanzon Slab. Sculpted in shallow relief, the slab depicts a divinity that is part human, part serpent, and part caiman.

At about the same time that initial construction was launched at the Temple Complex of Chavín de Huántar, pyramid building also started farther south, on the shores of Lake Titicaca. There a large platform mound was built at Chiripa by 1000 B.C. Around 400 B.C. the city of Tiwanaku (also known as Tiahuanaco, it is located in modern Bolivia) came into being, covering about two and a half square miles and housing as many as 40,000 people. Laid out in a north-south grid pattern, Tiwanaku was centered about a 50-acre plaza with pyramid temple mounds. The mound known as Akpana, built of stone quarried over 60 miles away and ferried across the lake, measures over 650 feet on each side and rises to about 50 feet in height. The Tiwanaku culture became the largest regional culture in the Andes before the advent of the Incas, and the city remained an important center for 1,400 years, a long reach of time on any continent.

Meanwhile, back along the northern Peruvian coast during the first millennium A.D., the rise of the Moche culture initiated another phase of pyramid building. The Moche people erected a ceremonial complex centered on two massive adobe structures. The larger of the two—in fact, the largest adobe building constructed in the New World—is known as the Huaca del Sol, or the Holy Place of the Sun. Although treasure hunters during Spanish colonial times diverted the Moche River, which washed away some two thirds of the monument, archaeologists have been able to reconstruct its original size. The platform measured approximately 785 feet by 520 feet and reached a height of almost 100 feet. According to scholarly estimates, over 140 million molded mud bricks, mostly arranged in columns, went into the structure.

Facing the Huaca del Sol is a smaller but still massive monument known as the Huaca de la Luna, or the Holy Place of the Moon. The Huaca de la Luna comprised three large platforms, each topped by a spacious plaza. Like the constantly reconstructed pyramids of Mesoamerica, the Huaca de la Luna went through at least six phases of remodeling over a 600-year period. And, again like Mesoamerica, human sacrifice, as depicted on Moche murals and ceramics, formed part of the pyramid rituals. The evidence, however, indicates that human sacrifice among the Moches occurred much less frequently than it did among the Aztecs. Since sacrificed victims were discovered under thick layers of sediment, modern archaeologists believe that ritual killing took place only during floods brought on by heavy El Niño rains. Those same rains over the centuries have turned other Moche sites, such as Túcume in the Lambayeque Valley, into badly eroded mounds that look like ice cream left to melt in the sun. These many ruins have yet to be fully surveyed, explored, and excavated.

Pyramid building was still going on under the last great indigenous Peruvian culture, the Inca, when Europeans came to South America.

About 80 years before Francisco Pizarro and his conquistadors descended on the Andes, the ambitious Inca ruler Pachacuti Yupanqui (A.D. 1438–1471) inaugurated construction on the Fortress of Sacsahuamán at the northeastern end of Cuzco, the Inca capital. According to the sixteenth-century Spanish chronicler Pedro de Cieza de León, the great structure took 20,000 workers and 50 years to complete. It was finished not by Pachacuti Yupanqui but by his son, Topac Yupanqui. Unfortunately, much of Sacsahuamán's massive stonework was carried away by the Spaniards to build colonial Cuzco, yet even the remains of the monument are awe-inspiring. Consisting of a series of stepped terraces built into the natural contours of a hill, Sacsahuamán was built from massive stones fitted together with exquisite precision—no mortar was used. Inca masons shaped the stones with a protrusion in the center, giving them the invitingly cushy look of pillows. Like the Temple Complex of Chavín de Huántar, Sacsahuamán contained many channels and pools and was the site of water rituals. The center of these rituals was very likely a prominent rounded structure still visible in the ruin. Garcilaso de la Vega, another sixteenth-century chronicler, reported that the round structure was a tower that went as far into the earth as it did into the sky. Although this remark is apocryphal rather than archaeological, it is strongly reminiscent of the world axis concept embodied in Buddhist stupas.

Perched high in the Andes, the well-known Inca city of Machu Picchu (middle second millennium A.D.)—the name means "Old Peak" in the Quechua language—is not, strictly speaking, a pyramid, but it draws from the vocabulary of pyramids. Built on a mountaintop that rises some 2,000 feet from the Urubamba River, Machu Picchu contains temples, palaces, baths, storage rooms, and about 150 houses built from the mountain's own gray granite. Building blocks of 50 tons and more are fitted with the same exquisite perfection as those at Sacsahuamán. In its way, Machu Picchu is analogous to the pyramids of Mesoamerica: the mountain serves as the pyramid, and the city at its top plays the role of the summit temple.

Pyramids or Not?

If Mexico alone contains 100,000 pyramids, many of them still undiscovered beneath centuries of geological change and jungle growth, then it may well be the case that pyramids are to be found in other places where no one has thought to look for them. In a manner of speaking, the existence of pyramids depends on the eye of the beholder.

Consider as an example the Irish burial mound known as Newgrange, one of four structures found in Brugh na Bóinne (Hostel on the Boyne), a site in northeastern Ireland dated to circa 3000 B.C. At over 260 feet in diameter and a height of nearly 40 feet, Newgrange has the massiveness of a pyramid. It also has the secret passage, a narrow entryway that begins in the mound and extends underneath it—something like Pacal's burial vault at Palenque. In fact, the chamber at the end of the passage contained basin stones filled, at the time the mound was opened, with cremated human remains. Newgrange was originally faced with tons of shining white stone brought from the Wicklow Mountains, many miles to the south, and most likely ferried up the coast. That whiteness is reminiscent of the gleaming limestone of Djoser's stepped pyramid and Khufu's Great Pyramid as well as the shining purity of the White Temple of Uruk.

Whiteness is a key characteristic of another pyramid candidate: Silbury Hill, which is located just south of the village of Avebury in England's Wiltshire. A massive artificial mound with a flat top, Silbury Hill stands approximately 130 feet high, with a base circumference of 1,640 feet that covers more than five acres. The hill contains over 12 million cubic feet of earth and chalk, the latter originally coloring it white. This monument was built in three stages, the first beginning in about 2660 B.C. Various legends and stories attach to Silbury Hill, but the monument's purpose remains unknown.

Another possibility, this one more traditionally pyramid-like, exists on Tenerife, one of the Canary Islands, off the coast of West Africa.

What have been explained as agricultural terraces may be the remains of a stepped pyramid built by Tenerife's first residents, a North African people called the Guanches, who may have first arrived about 200 B.C. At least that is the opinion of the noted adventurer and explorer Thor Heyerdahl, who rejects the notion that the terraces were built by the first Spanish invaders. Further research and careful exploration are needed to determine the archaeological truth of the situation.

A few writers have even suggested that New Zealand is the site of ancient, well-worn stone monuments similar to ones found in Ireland, Britain, and the Mediterranean. If true, the idea is most intriguing, but as yet the notion is only speculative.

Another site of interest, one I have explored and studied firsthand, lies at the end of Japan's Ryukyu Island chain in the East China Sea. In the mid-1980s, Kihachiro Aratake was exploring diving sites off the island of Yonaguni when he came across a submarine complex of geometric terraces separated by vertical stone risers. Dubbed the Yonaguni monument, the complex seemed anything but natural. Masaaki Kimura, a marine seismologist at the University of the Ryukyus on Okinawa, studied the Yonaguni monument intensively and became convinced that it had been fashioned by human hands. Since the monument would not have been built under water, its construction probably occurred when the level of the East China Sea was much lower, as in the 8000–6000 B.C. time period. (It is also hypothetically possible that the monument once stood higher and then sank during a catastrophic earthquake or subsidence, but as yet I have seen no evidence to support this idea.)

The possibility that Yonaguni represents a surviving structure from a lost protocivilization drew me there several times from 1997 through 2000. Numerous dives on the monument, however, convinced me that it is a natural form rather than a human-made complex. The apparently smooth terraces take their appearance not from the finished quality of the rock but from a thick coating of sponges, corals, algae, and similar organisms. Even when I scraped away this thick living cover

I could find no tool marks or quarrying scars. Also there was no evidence that the monument was constructed of separate pieces of stone. Rather, it is one large piece of bedrock whose angles are much less precise than they appear at first glance.

Further exploratory work on Yonaguni indicated to me that this peculiar form resulted from the unusual weathering pattern of the particular kind of very fine sandstone and mudstone that the formation is made from. Marked by numerous well-defined bedding planes crisscrossed at right angles by fractures and joints, the layers separate into square and rectangular chunks and fall away as the rock weathers. The effect creates the impression of steps, plazas, and platforms.

There remains the possibility that the Yonaguni monument is a natural form subtly altered by humans—in essence, a much earlier version of the brilliant synthesis of art and nature embodied in pyramid monuments like Borobudur, Sacsahuamán, and Machu Picchu. Ancient stone tombs of unknown age on Yonaguni look much like the monument, as if local people were imitating the forms that nature created on its own. In addition, ancient stone tools and carved stone vessels have been found on the island, and what may be a crude stone tablet with an X and a V inscribed on its surface has been found underwater near the monument. Professor Kimura has also identified what he believes to be quarrying scars at a couple of sites along the rocky shoreline and perhaps on the underwater monument itself. Thus it may be that the monument was altered by human hands or served as a quarry. Although Yonaguni does not currently qualify as another entry on the world's long list of pyramids, it does raise the fascinating possibility that ancient human builders were thinking in monumental terms much sooner and working toward that goal with greater skill than we currently comprehend.

Another underwater possibility has been suggested by scientists exploring the sea off the west coast of Cuba. Researchers using sonar equipment have found a large submarine plateau and have produced images that look much like pyramids, roads, and buildings viewed from above. The problem with explaining this as the work of humans is the depth of the water: 2,200 feet. At no time in the past 10,000 years has sea level been that much lower than it is today. The observed forms could be of human origin only if the land in this region subsided dramatically some time in the past. Further research is called for, but on the basis of what we now know, the Cuba discovery appears, like Yonaguni, to be an unusual natural phenomenon rather than the work of an undiscovered culture of pyramid builders.

Yet another possibility exists in India, under 15 to 21 feet of water offshore from the eastern seaport city of Mahabalipuram. The site consists of large submerged structures in which some observers see the work of human hands. Mahabalipuram may be a lost city of pyramid builders, but it may also be, like Yonaguni, a poorly understood geological formation. Only a rigorous scientific look will tell.

The Big Question

Even if the Yonaguni monument and Mahabalipuram are considered wholly natural, Newgrange is dismissed as only a pre-Celtic burial mound, and Tenerife's terraces prove to be hillside potato fields rather than pyramids, an impressive fact remains. From the end of the fourth millennium B.C. until the time of the Spanish conquest of Peru and Mexico in the sixteenth century A.D., humans were building pyramids. At almost every point in that 4,500-year span of time, a culture somewhere on the face of the globe dedicated itself with great energy and devotion to the construction of immense monuments bearing deep religious and ritual significance. Is it simple coincidence that this has happened in so many different times and so many different places? Or is there hidden within this pattern a story whose outlines we have only begun to imagine?

Three
Coincidence
or Connection?
The Mythic
Foundation

W HEN MOSES WANTED TO FACE HIS GOD, HE TOOK HIM-
self to Mount Sinai, and on its heights he received the stone tablets of
the Ten Commandments. In Homer's *Odyssey*, the summit of Mount
Olympus opens into a realm of blissful light as pure and perfect as the
sky itself. And at the end of the dream vision that informed the life of
the Sioux holy man Black Elk, he was transported to Harney Peak in
South Dakota's Black Hills. The deep-rooted religious and mythological traditions of both the Old and the New Worlds bathe mountains in
sacred light.

To understand the mythological significance of pyramids, we must
first do what Mohammed did. We must go to the mountain.

The Mountain Above All

Anyone who has climbed a high peak and taken in the panorama that opens all around knows how it feels to be at the center of the visible universe. The land falls away in every direction, fading into a final horizon that seems farther away than you could ever imagine. Yet the sky comes even closer, just beyond the hand's reach, as if you could seize the blue of the day in your fingers and snatch stars from the night.

This vision of the mountain as center is one of the many themes surrounding high places in world mythology. To the Sioux, who spent much of their nomadic year on the open flatness of the prairies, Harney Peak was the midpoint of the universe. The ancient Greeks placed the navel of the world, the holy stone they called the *omphalos,* in a shrine at Delphi, on the sacred slopes of Mount Parnassus. By far the most sumptuous vision of the mountain as center of the universe comes from the Buddhists. They saw Mount Sumeru—Mount Kailas in real-world Tibet—as a great cosmic axis rising 80,000 miles from hell to heaven, with continents spinning round it in an ocean enclosed by a ring of fire.

Even when mountains are depicted less extravagantly, they are seen to serve as the dwelling places of spirits, gods, devils, and immense powers. In the same way that the ancient Hebrews placed the abode of their own God, Yahweh, on Mount Sinai, the Greeks peopled the peak of Olympus with the multiple personages of their gods and goddesses. The Sherpas of Nepal's Khumbu Valley housed their gods on Khumbila, a peak—modest by the lofty standards of the Himalayas—that rises near the center of their homeland. The Sioux god Thunderbird nests on Harney Peak, then flaps its wings and blinks its eyes to make thunder roll and lightning flash.

Mountains, reaching up from the land like the very marrow of earth breaking into sky, offer access to the powers that dwell in the realm above. The Ruwenzoris of the Great Lakes region of Central

Africa are also known as the Mountains of the Moon, a name that betokens their heavenly association. The ancient Chinese named their sacred mountain range the T'ien Shan, which means the Mountains of Heaven. The Kikuyu people of Kenya referred to Mount Kenya as Kere-Nyaga, "Mountain of Brightness," referring to the solar brilliance of the sky god who claimed the snow-clad peak as his domicile. The Hindu god Shiva is said to sit in eternal meditation on the domed summit of Mount Kailas.

Sometimes the divine abode transforms the peak into a temple. According to Hindu mythology, the goddess Nanda Devi is to be found in a pagoda of gold on the Himalayan mountain named after her. The Hopis of the American Southwest see the San Francisco Peaks, a ring of mountains left from the explosive shattering of a volcano in northern Arizona, as an enormous holy dwelling, or *kiva*, that holds the spirits of the world and the souls of the ancestors.

Mountains can offer direct contact between divine powers and their human subjects, as happened to Moses when he received the Ten Commandments on Mount Sinai. The Transfiguration of Jesus told in the Gospels of the New Testament occurred on a mountain, and it was on Arabia's Mount Hira that Mohammed founded Islam upon hearing the first words of the Koran. For millennia, Hindu and Buddhist hermits have retreated into the Himalayas to meditate their way to holiness. And, in a desire to shed their sins and come closer to God, believers still walk barefoot up the stony path to the top of Croagh Patrick, the mountain on the west coast of Ireland where Saint Patrick is reputed to have banished the island's snakes.

Their easy access to the divinities dwelling in the sky makes mountains ideal places for sacrifices, which placate and please the gods and goddesses, and for sending prayers directly from the land below to the divine wills above. Wishing to thank the gods for the success of their dynasties, the emperors of China made offerings on the peaks of the T'ien Shan. When Yahweh ordered Abraham to sacrifice his only son, Isaac, he sent him to Mount Moriah. The Aztecs and the Incas likewise used peaks and hills as the sites of human sacrifice. The ark came to rest on Mount Ararat as the great flood subsided, and Noah immediately sacrificed to give thanks for God's rescue of himself, his family, and his boatload of animals.

This story of Noah from the Old Testament book of Genesis points to the role that mountains play in sustaining the right order of the world. A Sumerian cuneiform text dated to 2000 B.C. says that the earth began as a mountain rising from the primal sea. Much the same image informs the opening of the Old Testament book of Genesis, which recounts the creation of the world: "[T]here was darkness over the deep, and God's spirit hovered over the water. . . . God said, 'Let the waters under heaven come together into a single mass, and let dry land appear.'" This original separation of the dry from the wet dissolved when God chose to flood the earth to rinse away its abundant wickedness. Yahweh opened what the scripture calls "the springs of the deep and the sluices of heaven," so that all the earth, even the highest mountains, were submerged. When God allowed the water to drain back where it belonged, the peaks emerged first. There Noah found his first anchorage in the new, after-the-flood world, and he sacrificed to thank Yahweh for deliverance. Yahweh promised never again to upset the division of water and land on account of human transgressions.

Underlying Yahweh's promise is an ancient cosmological understanding of the break between earth and sky. In Sumerian mythology, the original world mountain rising from the sea was both male and female, and it was known as Heaven-and-Earth. The union of these two elements produced the god of the air, Enlil, who separated the female, earth portion of the mountain (Ki) from its upper, male, heavenly aspect (An). Almost exactly the same myth is found in Greece, where the god Kronos divided his mother, Gaia the earth goddess, from his heavenly father, Ouranos, eponym of the seventh planet from the sun. The Egyptians tell a similar tale, except for them the sky was female, the goddess Nut, and the earth was male, the god Geb. When a priest climbed a mountain to sacrifice, as Noah did on the slopes of Mount

Ararat, he healed this ancient division and restored the cosmos to its original oneness.

Building the World Mountain

The ancient Sumerians were explicit in their purpose of incorporating the world mountain into tower temples and ziggurats. Their astronomers saw the world as a peak rising in stages from the waters and straining toward heaven. The stages of this elevation from the sea were marked by the orbits of heaven's circling bodies: the moon, Mercury, Venus, the sun, Mars, Jupiter, and Saturn. The ziggurat replicated this sacred cosmology. Its towering monumentality represented the world mountain, and the successively smaller stages stood for the circling bodies that defined the peak's long reach from Earth to Heaven. Thus the ziggurat of Birs Nimrud, built at Borsippa by Nebuchadrezzar II in the seventh and sixth centuries B.C., bore the name E-ur-imim-an-ki, which means "House of the Seven Divisions of Heaven and Earth."

The Sumerians celebrated the power of the world mountain to heal the division of earth and sky with rites that rejoined the male and female in a sacred marriage. The temple at the top of the ziggurat housed a bed where priest and priestess made ritual love. Their physical union reconnected the elements separated at the creation of the world and restored the universe's right order, just as Noah did in his sacrifice upon Ararat. This connection between sex and right order survived for centuries after the Sumerians. A Chinese visitor to Cambodia in the thirteenth century A.D., about 100 years after the building of Angkor Wat, reported that the king made love to a princess in a tower temple, an act of ritual sexuality that guaranteed the continued welfare of the kingdom.

Like the Sumerians, all the world's pyramid traditions see these monumental structures as world mountains that represent the cosmos. The central vision informing a pyramid is always the same: This holy place stands for all that has been, is, and will be. It is a human-made microcosm that epitomizes the form and order of the universe.

Pyramid traditions do differ from one another in significant ways. Remarkably, these differences make the similarities among them even more striking.

The Egyptian and Nubian pyramids functioned primarily as monuments, objects to be admired from a distance. From the perspective of the general populace, they invited no human participation beyond the rites surrounding the death and internment of a pharaoh, king, or local ruler. The Egyptians and Nubians built their pyramids outside their cities, in places like Giza, Saqqara, and el-Kurru, creating sanctuaries dedicated to the purpose of memorializing the dead. It is also possible that the pyramids were used for various rites, rituals, and cults, particularly those associated, like the pyramids of Giza, with a particular dynasty.

This same notion of pyramid-as-distant-monument informs the Olmec fluted pyramid at La Venta. An island in a difficult-to-traverse swamp, La Venta was a long way from the villages that supplied the labor that raised its mountain of tamped earth. The Chinese pyramids of Lishan and the temple towers of Angkor Wat had similar mythological roles.

In Mesopotamia, India, Indonesia, Mesoamerica outside La Venta, and South America, pyramids are less monuments than settings for staged events. They elicit human participation. The staircase on the Pyramid of the Sun at Teotihuacán, the Pyramid of Uxmal, and Etemenenanki in Babylon provide ready access. To this day, tourists at Tikal in Guatemala or Altun Ha in Belize clamber up the steep stone steps to experience for themselves the fright and exhilaration felt by the participants in the rituals who made their way to the tiny temples located on the pyramids' summits. The Aztecs sacrificed on the peaks of their pyramids, making bloodletting a public rite. The stupas of Sanchi and Borobudur invite pilgrims to enter and retrace the holy passage that marks the journey from suffering to spiritual enlighten-ment. The pyramid mounds of Aspero and the Moche adobe pyramids supported temples used for regular rituals.

Pyramids that function as stages often stood in the very centers of cities and were a dominating element of urban life. This is true of the Mesopotamian ziggurats, Teotihuacán's Pyramid of the Sun, the Aztec pyramids, and the Mayan centers. A city resident did not have to jour-ney some distance to reach the holy site, as an Egyptian had to do in or-der to get to Giza or Saqqara. It was right there, practically around the corner, an inescapable fact of day-to-day existence.

Standing on Common Ground

The difference between pyramids-as-monuments and pyramids-as-stages is important. Equally significant are the many commonalities of form and function that unite pyramids located at opposite ends of the Earth from one another.

Architecture, Ground Plan, and Construction

From the outside, the battered profile of a classic Giza pyramid and the stepped shape of a Mesopotamian ziggurat seem to share little except the grandiose scale of the world mountain. Yet at the core they are the same.

In the late twelfth or early thirteenth century A.D., Caliph Malek Abd al-Aziz Othman ben Yusuf of Egypt, dreaming of long-buried Old Kingdom riches just waiting to be discovered, cut a deep hole into the Menkaure Pyramid at Giza. This excavation revealed that the inner structure of the building was a stepped pyramid. Some 1,700 years ear-lier, the Greek traveler and historian Herodotus, reporting on local Egyptian legend, had written, "The pyramids were built in tiers, bat-tlementwise, as it is called, or according to others, stepwise." Apparently he had it right. The buttress walls of the collapsed pyramid at Mei-dum, which have the same structure as Djoser's pyramids at Saqqara and reveal the original stepped structure, as well as similar walls in the badly preserved Fifth Dynasty pyramids at Abusir, show that these structures have a stepped pyramid at their core. Given the immense size and excellent preservation of the two pyramids at Dahshur and the Khufu and Khafre pyramids at Giza, their internal structure is uncertain. Likely they too began as stepped pyramids.

Putting a step pyramid at the core of a battered-profile pyramid solves a major construction problem. If a Giza-style pyramid is to be built from the ground up, its edges must remain absolutely straight as every new layer of rock is put into place. In a stepped pyramid small errors of alignment are hard to see and can be readily corrected as the next stage is built. But a battered-profile pyramid (which in profile looks like a triangle) allows no margin of error. As big as the Khufu and Khafre pyramids are, misaligning the edges by only two degrees at the bottom results in an error of almost 50 feet at the top—with no way to fix the problem except to go back and start over again.

The Egyptians solved this vexing problem by building a core stepped pyramid, then placing a central marker at its top. As outside layers were added to transform the structure into a battered profile, the construction crews sighted on the central marker—much as a modern builder uses survey marks to stay on track. This method of aligning the Egyptian pyramids was discovered accidentally in 1899 by the Egyptian Survey Department, which was working on the Meidum Pyramid. One member of the survey crew climbed to the top of the unfinished pyramid to place a flag on a mast and found a one-foot-deep hole cut into the summit's very center. Apparently this hole once held a flagpole-like mast that the builders used to align the edges. Very likely, similar summit center points lie buried under the topmost courses of stone in the Giza pyramids.

That center point served not only as a surveyor's convenience but also as an important element in the mythology surrounding the pyramid. Pyramids, like holy mountains, are the center of the universe. They become the axle around which the cosmos turns like a wheel, the point from which all that exists begins. Scholars of religion call this concept the *axis mundi,* a Latin phrase meaning "axis of the world" and a mythological theme found in many of the world's religions. It appears repeatedly in pyramids. The apex of an Egyptian pyramid serves as the axis of this world mountain, just as the peak of a Buddhist stupa bears a mast that makes the *axis mundi* explicit and obvious. So does the well that descends 120 feet beneath the central tower of Angkor Wat and the apocryphal story that the round structure at the center of Sacsahuamán is a tower that reaches as far into the earth as it does into the sky.

A pilgrim following the first rectangular gallery at Angkor Wat is told a story in relief sculpture that directly associates that monument with the center of the world. The sculpture's most extraordinary scene depicts the great serpent Vasuki wrapped, like a python on a pole, around the axis of the mountain of the world, atop which sits the dreaming god Vishnu. The gods wish to release the elixir of life from the cosmic seas and to do this they pull the immense snake one way, while demons tug it the other. The seesawing serpent stirs the ocean and releases the elixir, an action that gives the sculpture and the story its name: "The Churning of the Sea of Milk."

As the center of the earth in a cosmic or mythological sense, a pyramid defines direction. Many pyramids reveal careful attention paid to the cardinal directions of north, south, east, and west. Those at Giza are notable for being laid out with a nearly perfect orientation of their sides to the cardinal directions. Because the pyramid is based on a square, each of its sides carries equal weight, but the north side was preferred as the entryway to the burial vault. Sumerian ziggurats were oriented with equal precision, but with their sides directed to the intercardinal directions. Their *corners* pointed to the north, south, west, and east. The four gates leading into Stupa 1 at Sanchi mark the cardinal directions. Angkor Wat is oriented to the west, the direction of the setting sun, although the structures within the ceremonial center of which it is a part look to the east, where the sun rises. Thus death and life are set one against the other, and the tension between them is embodied in the ground plan. The complex surrounding the pyramid of La Venta was laid out on an axis that runs from north to south so precisely that it was clearly no accident. A number of important burials have been uncovered along this axis, further indicating its ceremonial importance. The city of Teotihuacán followed a north–south grid pattern that was as cosmologically significant as it was orderly.

Many pyramids share other similarities in building methods and material. Tamped-earth construction is found at Lishan, La Venta, and the temple mounds of the Mississippians. Stone, sometimes with megalithic blocks alone and sometimes used with a rubble-fill core, characterizes Egypt, Nubia, much of Mesoamerica, Sanchi, Borobudur, Sacsahuamán, and Chavín de Huántar. Mud brick occurs not only in Mesopotamia but also in the Moche pyramids of Peru. However, this similarity is not particularly striking, simply because humans have long been limited to a short list of building materials. More remarkable is the way that pyramids do not stand alone but are incorporated into large ceremonial complexes of which the pyramids are a part. Teotihuacán is notable not only for its two great pyramids but also for its immense plazas and the hauntingly wide Avenue of the Dead. The Aztecs, Mayas, Toltecs, and Mississippians likewise blended pyramids and plazas into sacred wholes. In much the same way, Giza, Saqqara, and other Egyptian pyramid sites included a variety of temples, causeways, and even canals, and the Mesopotamians built equivalently complex centers incorporating a variety of buildings besides ziggurats. Angkor Wat blends pyramids, galleries, and courtyards, and is itself but one ceremonial center in a region dotted with a number of temple complexes.

Where Gods Become Kings, and Kings Gods

Except possibly for Aspero and other early sites in Peru, about which we know very little, pyramids were built by cultures ruled by powerful kings, many of whom were considered to be gods walking the earth or mortals preparing to become gods. Pyramids are the property of males who governed with an absolute power said to be derived from the divinities of the sky. In many pyramid cultures, the kings depended upon a strong priestly class that was also exclusively male. Mythologically, pyramids represent something of an old boys' club of temporal and spiritual power.

The Mesopotamian kings, from Sumer to Babylon, were fierce despots who made war at will and considered their subjects vassals for their bidding. When Nebuchadrezzar II decided that Babylon needed more inhabitants, he uprooted the Hebrews from their Palestinian homeland and brought them forcibly to his capital. The Egyptian pharaohs walked the earth as incarnations of the falcon god Horus, then became one with the underworld god Osiris at death. Açoka, the reputed builder of Stupa 1 at Sanchi, was an enlightened monarch who made Buddhism a state religion. Borobudur was the work of a Buddhist dynasty that ruled central Java in the eighth century A.D. Angkor Wat owes its existence to the ambitions of its patron king, Suryavarman II. The pyramid-building Q'in Dynasty kings of ancient China were grandiose enough to build great walls to keep barbarians out, erect mountains to themselves, and suppress dissent in a manner both righteous and ruthless. The Mayas, Incas, Aztecs, and other American pyramid builders all were societies governed by powerful royal and priestly elites who drew their wealth from an underling class of peasants and laborers.

Like high mountains, pyramids provided a pathway for the gods of the sky to come to earth and for humans to make direct contact with the heavenly deities. When the Sumerians celebrated the sacred marriage rite that joined priest and priestess on the ziggurat, they understood the two humans not as actors or stand-ins but as actual personifications of the divinities of earth and sky. For the god-kings of the pyramid cultures, pyramids embodied the interchange between earth and sky that made them divine as well as royal.

Death divides human from god. All humans, no matter how ambitious or powerful, finally die. Gods, by contrast, go on and on, their dreams troubled by no thoughts of eventual death. The pyramid cultures used their monuments to memorialize dead kings, to give them an existence that extended beyond the grave, to make them gods. For example, since Angkor Wat is oriented to the west—which, as the direction of the setting sun, was believed to open into the underworld—while the other temples built in the same ceremonial center face the east, it is thought to have served as a mausoleum for its royal patron. Pyramids marked the tombs of Q'in, Han, and Tang monarchs in China; King Pacal at Palenque in Mexico; Ruler A at Tikal; and of course numerous dynasties of pharaohs and kings in Egypt and Nubia.

Several pyramid cultures attempted to arrest the destruction of death by preserving the body of the king. The Egyptians were not the ancient world's only practitioners of mummification. The art of preserving the dead can be dated to at least 3500 B.C., according to the work of the Italian archaeologist F. Mori, who found the body of a black African child carefully dried then buried beneath the family shelter in the Fezzan region of the Libyan Sahara. The Incas also preserved the bodies of high-ranking dead. The burial of Pacal inside the Temple of the Inscriptions at Palenque points to a similar practice among the Maya.

The preserved god-king concept receives a particularly clear expression in the mythology surrounding Buddhist stupas like Sanchi and Borobudur, a belief system that echoes aspects of ancient Egyptian belief. Though a human and therefore mortal, the Buddha achieved the godlike status of a *cakravartin*, or ruler of the world, through his accomplishments in life. After he died, his relics were preserved in the stupas, so that each stupa had some small portion of the Buddha's earthly remains. This dismembering and dispersing of the holy corpse is strongly reminiscent of the fate of Osiris in Egyptian mythology. The god of the underworld, Osiris was killed by his evil brother, Seth, and was hacked to pieces. Seth then scattered the severed hunks of

Osiris' body across the Egyptian landscape, and it took Isis, Osiris' wife, much time and trouble to reassemble the corpse for proper burial. Putting the body back together worked something of a miracle, for Osiris' phallus rose, Isis made love with him, and their union brought forth a son, the falcon god Horus. Later, Horus defeated Seth and united Egypt, much as the historical first pharaoh, Menes, joined the Two Lands of ancient Egypt. The Egyptian belief system incorporated the divine interchange between Osiris and Horus by making the pharaoh Horus while he lived, Osiris after he died. In the same way that Osiris was scattered across the land, so the remains of the Buddha were dispersed throughout the realm of believers who, in achieving their own enlightenment, reunited his divided body. This association of the pharaoh with Osiris could explain why no royal mummy has ever been found in the Giza pyramids—why, particularly, the great sarcophagus in the heart of the Khufu Pyramid was both undisturbed and empty. The pyramid memorialized the fact of the pharaoh's death and his transition into Osiris, but his body was physically elsewhere, as Osiris' was after his death. In the same way, the stupa replicates the Buddha's immortal status as *cakravartin* and reminds the believer that only the smallest portion of his body lies in this one place. The rest of it is everywhere and nowhere.

Praying in Blood

The deaths of the Buddha and the pharaoh were metaphorical sacrifices, transformations that lifted mortals into immortality. Pyramid-building cultures also practiced sacrifices that were bloodily literal.

When a Sumerian king of Ur's Dynasty 1 (circa 2500–2350 B.C.) died, he was buried not alone but in the company of his queen and her maidservants, his concubines, a troop of soldiers, a few musicians, a variety of sacrificed animals, even heavy chariots drawn by yoked oxen— all of whom were interred alive along with the corpse of the king. A great deal of treasure was also buried: richly ornamented reins on the silver-collared oxen, harps sporting bulls' heads adorned with lapis lazuli beards, beaded death shrouds, shapely stone vases, a golden bull paired with a silver cow. These royal burials took place in the precinct surrounding the holy site where the ziggurat of Ur was built, and they were not infrequent. The early-twentieth-century archaeologist Sir Charles Leonard Woolley excavated 16 such tombs dating to Dynasty 1, which lasted 100 to 150 years.

Similar rites were practiced in Nubia during the time period, between circa 2000 and 1700 B.C., when the area was a province of Middle Kingdom Egypt. Working from 1913 to 1916, George Reisner excavated an immense funerary city, or necropolis, that over a 300-year period served as the site of a multitude of small graves and a number of large burial mounds, one of which measured over 100 yards in diameter. In tomb after tomb Reisner found the same pattern: wife was buried with husband. The larger, richer tombs contained not only the wife but also what was apparently the wealthy man's harem—50 to 500 individuals. Most of the bodies were female; the few buried males were presumably harem guards or attendants. The principal males were all buried the same way: lying on the right side on the grave's south wall, usually on a wooden bed, with the face looking north, toward Egypt, knees bent and arms positioned as if in sleep. Weapons, personal adornments, ostrich-feather fans, and rawhide sandals were placed near the corpse. The women's bodies were found in a variety of positions: sometimes doubled up, sometimes with the hands over the face, around the throat, or clutching the hair. Apparently, the men were buried after death but the women were still alive when the earth was shoveled in, leaving them to suffocate in the dark.

Since mass burials did not occur in the urban centers of the Middle Kingdom, a question arises: Was this provincial practice a carryover from the Old Kingdom, or was it somehow unique to Nubia? The mythology scholar Joseph Campbell made the former argument, holding that Nubia was clinging to an ancient custom—that it was a cultural backwater staying faithful to that old-time religion. If Campbell was right—and there is as yet no physical evidence in support of his position—then the death of an Old Kingdom pharaoh spelled the imminent ritual demise of his queen, subordinate wives, and multitudinous concubines.

Whatever the truth of Old Kingdom practice, mass burial was indeed followed by the Nubian pharaohs of the Twenty-Fifth Dynasty and their royal descendants. When a Nubian king went to his place of pyramid internment at el-Kurru, Nuri, or Meroe, his queens and wives went with him, as well as horses and dogs from the household.

Ritual wife sacrifice lasted well into modern times within India's Hindu heritage. Though Buddhists opposed the letting of blood and abhorred sacrifice, Angkor Wat incorporates at least a hint of the practice, with its single central pyramid to memorialize the dead king Suryavarman II and the four subordinate towers thought to be memorials to his queens.

The ancient Chinese buried queens and royal retainers with the same thoroughness as the Sumerians, the Nubians, and the provincial Middle Kingdom Egyptians. Although little archaeological work has been carried out at Lishan and similar sites, it is clear that during the Shang and Zhou dynasties humans were sacrificed as companions to the departed king. The ceramic army interred within the complex centered on the Q'in Dynasty tamped-earth pyramid at Lishan was most likely an artistic stand-in for the ritual slaughter of past times. Or perhaps the sculptures just reduced the death toll. According to the ancient Chinese writer Ssu-ma Ch'ien, the dead emperor's wives as well as workmen who helped build the pyramid were buried with the king.

In the New World, sacrifice at the time of royal burial is known from Peru. According to one source, the death of Guayanacapa, the last Inca king, resulted in the sacrifice of over a thousand individuals. Pedro de Cieza de Leon, who traveled throughout Peru between A.D. 1532 and 1550, soon after the Spanish conquest, described how the local people buried dead chiefs:

[T]hey make a very deep sepulchre in the lofty parts of the mountains, and . . . they put the body in it, wrapped in many rich cloths, with arms on one side and plenty of food on the other, great jars of wine, plumes, and gold ornaments. At his feet they bury some of his most beloved and beautiful women alive; holding it for certain that he will come to life and make use of what they have placed round him.

But for being on a different and distant continent, Leon could have been describing royal internment in Sumeria, Nubia, or China.

A similar custom is found in Mesoamerica. When King Pacal was buried in the Temple of the Inscriptions pyramid at Palenque, six young men were sacrificed, presumably as bodyguards and companions. Palenque is not an isolated instance; the Mesoamerican pyramid builders were more than enthusiastic about sacrifice. The Zapotecs of Monte Albán buried companions, food, and water to provide for the dead on their long journey to the other world. The Teotihuacános killed captive enemy soldiers and children and buried their remains in pyramids under construction. Particularly in the later centuries of their ascendancy, the Maya butchered prisoners of war as offerings to their gods, and young women and men were thrown into a deep pool, or cenote, at Chichén Itzá to carry messages to the zone of the divine. Conveying their victims to the tops of their tall pyramids, the Aztecs offered still-beating hearts to the god of the sun by the hundreds, even thousands, and rolled the butchered bodies down the long, steep stairs to the crowd gathered below. According to the Spaniards who conquered Tenochtitlán, the temple plaza of the Aztec capital reeked with the rot of countless victims' heads displayed on racks and left to decay—but at least to some extent they were creating propaganda about their enemy's barbarity to justify their own murderousness. Similar, if less exuberant, sacrificial customs were followed among the pyramidal temple mounds of North America's Mississippian culture.

What Lies Beneath, What Flows

Because they reached from the earth into the sky and healed that ancient mythological division, pyramids were ideal sacrifice sites. Many
pyramid designers augmented this span between the below and the
above by erecting pyramids over or incorporating caves and subterranean spaces.

This association begins with the word *huaca*, used to name the very
ancient pyramids at Aspero. *Huaca* is a Spanish version of *guaca*, a
word from Quechua, the Inca tongue that remains the first language of
many of the people who live in the Andes. *Guaca* refers to an ancient
tomb, a hidden or buried treasure, or a holy place, whether a natural
feature like a cave or a human-made structure such as a cairn or temple. By blending all these meanings, *huaca* points to an ancient equa-
tion between caves, holy sites, and tombs.

The connection between caves and pyramids occurs again and again
in New World pyramids. At Chavín de Huántar, the Lanzon Slab,
which looks very much like a stalagmite, is positioned within a cavelike space formed by the crossing of the vertical and horizontal axes of
the Old Temple. The round structure that formed the center of Sacsahuamán was said to descend into earth as far as it reached into the
sky, an image that connects the cave to the *axis mundi*. In 1972, archaeologists exploring the Pyramid of the Sun at Teotihuacán discovered a
cave that opened near the front of the pyramid and ran to its center. A
natural feature, the cave had been remodeled to make it look like the
flower shape described in Mesoamerican mythology as the place where
the world began. The tomb of Pacal deep in the heart of the Temple of
the Inscriptions at Palenque was more than a simple cave created by
human hands. The 13 corbeled vaults leading to the burial chamber
replicated the 13 levels of heaven in the Mayan belief system, and the
nine stages of the pyramid repeated the nine levels of the underworld.
The Temple of the Inscriptions reversed the logic of normal reality

and turned the world on its head. One climbed up to get to the bottom of all things, then went down to reach the heights. Magnetometer readings at La Venta suggest that a hollow rectangular structure lies buried within 10 to 33 feet of the pyramid's top. Possibly a temple constructed under the surface, it suggests a cave in a mountain.

Below the central tower of Angkor Wat lies a well that is 120 feet deep. The Chinese pyramids of Lishan are built over elaborately constructed underground burial chambers.

As we saw in chapter 2, the Egyptian pyramids began as mounds heaped up over subterranean internment pits. This basic design continued through the golden age of pyramid building in the Third and Fourth dynasties and, even though pyramid-building skills declined, into the Fifth and Sixth dynasties as well. In almost all of the pyramids from this long period, the burial chamber was located under the pyramid proper. A striking exception is Khufu's Great Pyramid at Giza, where the chamber with its empty sarcophagus sits very close to the center of the structure's immense mass. Even here, though, a long shaft connected in a roundabout way to the burial chamber extends well under the pyramid to a subterranean chamber.

Burial in a vault beneath the structure was de rigueur in the standardized pyramids of the Nubian renaissance. A stairway in front of the pyramid proper led down into the chamber, where the body was placed in a recess cut into the floor. The chamber's vaulted ceiling added to the impression of a cave.

Water also played an elemental role in pyramid construction and ritual, even in a land as dry as Egypt. At Dahshur, a lake extending from the Nile reached to the base of the pyramids. In the days of the Fourth Dynasty, Khafre's Valley Temple at Giza, also known as the River Temple, could be approached by water. Archaeologists have uncovered a number of full-sized wooden boats first dismantled, then buried around the Khufu Pyramid. The largest of these is impressively huge—a little over 145 feet long and nearly 20 feet wide. Called solar barques by some authorities, the buried boats may have been equipment that the Osiris-becoming soul of the departed pharaoh needed to navigate the sky on his starry voyage to immortality.

Mesopotamian religious artwork of the late third millennium B.C. shows a similar association between water and ziggurats. In one scene, a god sailing the sea of heaven waits for the workmen below to finish the ziggurat so he can disembark and descend to Earth. Yet another shows a deity traveling the cosmic waters in a boat whose high stern and bow closely mirror the design of the vessels buried near the Khufu Pyramid.

Lakes and canals that look like watery boulevards lace the ceremonial center that contains Angkor Wat, which itself is surrounded by a vast moat. Angkor Wat is built as a series of expanding rectangles, with the moat the outermost. Over two and a half miles in total length, the moat represents the cosmic ocean that surrounds the world, the same body of water commemorated in "The Churning of the Sea of Milk."

Water appears again and again in the pyramid centers of the New World. The hauntingly mysterious cenotes of Chichén Itzá are both caves and deep wells, divine water sources that lie below the superficial world occupied by ordinary mortals. Chavín de Huántar contains a pattern of channels and pools through which water flowed, creating the sonorous rush of a stream or river. Similar structures at Sacsahuamán indicate that this ancient Peruvian site was also the site of water rituals.

Lining Up with the Heavens

In the same way that pyramids served to draw into themselves the chthonic power of the underworld and the life-giving force of water, they also incorporated connections with the dominions of the sky. Some pyramids are aligned with the sun, others with the stars and planets, yet others with solar, stellar, and planetary events.

Pyramid E-VII at Uaxactún in Guatemala near Tikal was built and rebuilt several times beginning in the first century B.C. The sides of the pyramid line up with the cardinal directions, and a stairway on the eastern face shows that that orientation was favored. East of the pyramid lies a lower platform, raised in the third century A.D., that supports three small temples. If one climbs the pyramid staircase on the day of the equinox and looks east, the sun rises directly over the central temple. At the winter solstice the sun rises over the left-hand, or northern, temple, and on the summer solstice it appears above the right-hand, or southern, temple.

Even though Teotihuacán lies along a precise north–south grid, the Pyramid of the Sun is set at an odd angle, 15 degrees north of west. There is a reason for this. If observers stand on the pyramid's west-facing staircase on the day of the zenith sun (when the sun reaches the highest point during the year above the horizon, on the summer solstice), they can watch it set directly in front of them. An ancient monument on the hill known as Cerro Colorado, which is located some four miles west of the city of Teotihuacán, marks the same line of sight.

Some of the pyramid temples of the Maya are oriented to the planet Venus, which in their mythology was identified with the great god Quetzalcoatl. In their complex way of reckoning time, the Maya began their calendar with the "birth" of Venus, an event they dated in modern terms to approximately August 12, 3114 B.C. The House of the Governor at Uxmal is one of a number of Mayan monuments that show an alignment to Venus. An observer standing in one of the doorways at dawn would have seen Venus rise as the morning star above the top of a solitary mound about three and a half miles away as the planet reached its southerly extreme in A.D. 750. Temple I at Tikal marks a point in the sky where Venus periodically aligns with Jupiter.

Venus, which in Mesopotamia was the heavenly form of the love goddess known as Ishtar, Aphrodite, and Inanna, may have played a central role in the retainer-burial rituals of Ur. When Sir Charles Leonard Woolley excavated the royal tombs, he wondered why they numbered 16 over the period of approximately 150 years represented by Dynasty 1 of Ur. The number 16 has a certain aesthetic precision to it, as the square of a square ($2^2 = 4$, $4^2 = 16$). Wives, concubines, and retainers were buried with the king at the time of his natural death, and one would expect that some kings ruled long, some short, making the number of burials appear odd or random. Rather, the burial number has that curious aesthetic quality, which leads one to wonder if a mythological pattern underlies it. Joseph Campbell, ever the insightful scholar who peers through the surface to the myth beneath, offers an explanation.

Over a 128-year period, the sun, the moon, and the planet Venus come into conjunction 16 times at regular intervals. Possibly, every time this happened the Sumerians changed kings. The king was sacrificed ritually, an example of sacred regicide known in many parts of the world, and his household was buried with him to complete the sacrifice and the transition to the new divine monarch, who ruled until the three brightest celestial lights once again lined up in the sky. One can imagine him, and his wives and servants, living out their royal days with anxious eyes ever turned toward the heavens.

The Mesoamericans were also intrigued with the constellation known to the modern world as the Pleiades. According to work done by the archaeoastronomer Anthony Aveni, the setting of the zenith sun in A.D. 150, which provided the orientation of the west-facing staircase on Teotihuacán's Pyramid of the Sun, was preceded by the heliacal rising (rising with the sun) of the Pleiades—that is, the day on which the constellation comes closest to the sun yet remains visible. The Aztec pyramid of Tenayuca also appears to be oriented to the Pleiades' heliacal rising, evidence that the Teotihuacános' interest in this star group extended beyond their culture.

Certainly no pyramids have been the subjects of more astronomical speculation than those in ancient Egypt. Unfortunately, many of these speculations are spurious, produced by sloppy thinkers and mystery lovers who have been unaffectionately dubbed "pyramidiots" and who read into ancient monuments more New Age freight than they can bear. Still, it is definitely the case that the Egyptian pyramids reveal meaningful astronomical alignments, more of which likely remain to be uncovered. One that scholars agree on is the curious 26-degree angle in the Khufu Pyramid's descending corridor, which leads down from the entry on the structure's north side to a subterranean chamber. An individual standing in the chamber and looking up the ramp on a clear night sees the northern polar node (celestial north pole). Today Polaris, the North Star, marks this point, but owing to the slow movement of the stars known as precession, this exact spot was empty some 5,000 years ago, around the time of Khufu. The stars then closest to the sky's northern polar node revolved around this point, never rising nor setting behind the horizon. The Egyptians called these stars the Indestructibles, a suitable place in the heavens to receive the soul of the immortal pharaoh. Many of the pyramids built after Djoser's stepped pyramid incorporate a north-facing ramp to ensure that the spirit of the departed king was sent off in the right heavenly direction.

A much grander hypothesis, that Giza's ground plan is actually a map replicating a heavenly paradise and pointing to an even more ancient time, has been advanced by Robert Bauval and Adrian Gilbert in *The Orion Mystery* and by Graham Hancock and Robert Bauval in *The Message of the Sphinx*. According to Bauval, Gilbert, and Hancock, Giza's curiously offset pyramids are a hologram for the three stars forming the belt of the constellation Orion, which was associated with Osiris. The Nile River itself stands in for the Milky Way, which, in a number of ancient mythologies, was the resting place for souls awaiting their next incarnation. In addition, Giza serves as a time marker memorializing the night sky of 10,500 B.C., the exact point when Sirius, the heavenly body we know as the Dog Star, near the constellation of Orion, but which the Egyptians connected to Isis, would rest precisely on the horizon. The causeways running from the pyramids mark the rising point of the sun on the cross-quarter days halfway between the solstice and the equinox in both summer and winter in the same year, 10,500 B.C. The Sphinx has a role in this scheme too. On those winter and spring cross-quarters long, long ago, the Sphinx's blank gaze fixed on the rising point of the constellation Leo, or the Lion, the prototype of the Sphinx's body shape.

Bauval, Gilbert, and Hancock can be criticized for being overly precise and exact in their correlations. It remains more difficult than they admit to get definitive measurements on ancient structures that have been battered by time and are no longer complete (for example, precisely where was the original corner of this pyramid located?). Furthermore, computer simulations of the night sky many millennia ago are not necessarily as accurate as they might seem; even experts disagree on minor nuances, such as the exact orientation of the Earth's axis in the past, which, of course, has an effect on relative solar and stellar positions at various times.

Still, these three authors make an important point: The astronomical associations of the Giza monuments are powerful, undeniable, and probably only partially understood. Like the Mesoamericans, the Egyptians marked the mythological terrain of the sky with their great monuments.

Invention Versus Diffusion

Comparing and contrasting the world's many pyramids lead to two inescapable observations. First, every culture that built pyramids gave the form its own twist. A Buddhist stupa in India has a distinctly different flavor from Djoser's six-step pyramid at Saqqara or La Venta's fluted volcano. Even in pyramid cultures as closely connected as those of Egypt and Nubia, one group did not slavishly imitate the monumental architecture of another. Nubian pyramids owe an obvious debt to Egypt, yet they remain an undeniably Nubian creation.

Yet—and second—the number of similarities among pyramids, even those at great geographical remove from one another, is equally striking. Pyramids re-create the world mountain that centers the cosmos; they serve as monuments to, or stages for, great religious events; they provide pathways for gods to walk among humans and for humans to enter the realm of the gods; they are the work of powerful male monarchies and priestly elites, some of whom embraced religions promising regal immortality; they are associated with sacrifices; and they incorporate in their structures mythological associations with water, underground spaces, and celestial bodies.

There are two ways to explain these obvious similarities. The first is called *independent inventionism*. Deriving their theories in part from evolutionary ideas developed in the wake of Charles Darwin's revolution in biological theory, independent inventionists argue that at similar points in their social development different human groups come up with, or invent, similar solutions to the same fundamental problems of material and spiritual life. This point of view was given a classic formulation by James G. Frazer, who wrote in his seminal *The Golden Bough* that such similarities are probably "the effect of similar causes acting alike on the similar constitution of the human mind in different countries and under different skies." Frazer, of course, has a point. All human groups face much the same challenges of securing food, shelter, and companionship and achieving a sense of meaning in their lives. It is hardly shocking to discover that at different times and in different places humans have come up with strikingly similar solutions and practices. Just like you or me, an ancient Egyptian needed to eat, sleep, connect with his or her family, and understand his or her place in the cosmos. These needs and urges, and the cultural artifacts they lead to, are part and parcel of the human condition.

The other way of explaining specific cultural similarities is to argue that they arose from a common point of origin. The original ideas later diverged in certain details, but their basic key aspects continue to point to a shared genesis, often in an obscure, long-ago time. This point of view is called *diffusionism*. The history of human languages, for example, is recognized as a history of diffusion. Almost all of the languages of Europe, including English, as well as many tongues of southwestern and central Asia and northern India share enough common points of vocabulary, usage, and syntax to betray their origin in a single long-lost proto-Indo-European language. A Polish farmer talking to his neighbors, a Buddhist monk chanting the Sanskrit sutras, and I myself typing the English words of this book into my computer are using words and sentence structures that all branched from the same linguistic source tens of thousands of years in the past.

Clearly, no competent scholar could be absolutely inventionist or diffusionist, because the extreme positions quickly become absurd and meaningless. Calling both English and Sanskrit Indo-European languages is a diffusionist idea pointing to their common origin, yet it is also the case that generations of Sanskrit and English speakers have contributed multitudes of invented words and sentence forms. If they hadn't, the two languages would still be the same, and English and Sanskrit would not be separate languages. By the same token, even the most ardent inventionist would never hold that every seemingly separate group came up with all of its own inventions. The native Indian nations of eastern and central North America spoke different languages, worshipped in distinct ways, and made war upon one another, yet practically all of them grew corn as a staple crop. Obviously corn growing was not invented independently by each nation. Rather, it was an agricultural practice that came from a common point of origin and spread, probably through the vagaries of war, trade, and intermarriage, from one group to another. The history of North America after the European influx includes a commonly retold account of one instance of this very diffusion. When the recently arrived Pilgrims were clueless as to how to grow crops in the strange, new land of what is now Massachusetts, the local Indians showed them the way, saving the whites from starvation. Thanksgiving celebrates this classic tale of cultural diffusion by a generous helping hand.

The Obvious, the Apparent, and the Unacceptable

The story of the Tower of Babel, recounted in both the eleventh chapter of the Old Testament Book of Genesis and apocryphal Hebrew scriptures, is an ancient diffusionist myth that explains the origin of language in the context of the building of a pyramid. The canonical authors of the Old Testament faced an important literary problem. The great flood that spared only Noah and his family meant that all humans came from this small original group—one man and three sons, with their wives—and must of course have spoken the same language. How then could one explain the multiplicity of different, mutually unintelligible tongues to be found in the Middle East? The story of the pyramid known as the Tower of Babel provided a solution to the problem.

When it came to pyramid building, the sixth-century B.C. priestly compilers of the Hebrew Scriptures knew what they were writing about. The Hebrew people had recently returned to Israel from Babylon, to which they had been forcibly relocated by Nebuchadrezzar II, the builder of great ziggurats in Babylon and Borsippa. No doubt Hebrew men had been impressed into the labor gangs that built the ziggurat. The priestly writers of Genesis used this firsthand knowledge to create the story of the pyramid they called Babel:

Throughout the earth men spoke the same language, with the same vocabulary. Now as they moved eastward they found a plain in the land of Shinar [Babylon] where they settled. They said to one another, "Come, let us make bricks and bake them in the fire." For stone they used bricks, and for mortar they used bitumen. "Come," they said, "let us build ourselves a town and a tower with its top reaching to heaven. Let us make a name for ourselves that we may not be scattered about the whole earth."

Now Yahweh came down to see the whole town and the tower that the sons of men had built. "So they are all a single people with a single language!" said Yahweh. "This is but the start of their undertakings! There will be nothing too hard for them to do. Come, let us go down and confuse their language on the spot so that they can no longer understand one another." Yahweh scattered them thence over the whole face of the earth, and they stopped building the town. It was named Babel therefore, because there Yahweh confused the language of the whole earth.

The name Babel itself results from the very linguistic confusion the story talks about. The mound under which the ruins of Babylon lay until their excavation in the early twentieth century was known as Babil by the local Arabs, a name that derived from the original name for the place, Bab-Ili, or "Gate of God." The Bible writers confounded Bab-Ili with the Hebrew verb *balal*, which means "to confuse."

Versions of the story of Babel from the Hebrew apocrypha embellish the original story's themes. In the apocrypha the tower is the work of Nimrod, a fierce hunter, ruthless king, and great-grandson of Noah. To solemnize his power, Nimrod built a pyramid upon a round rock, setting throne upon throne, first copper, then silver, then gold, and finally a great gem. There he sat to exact homage from all the people he ruled over. Nimrod built the tower as a way of assaulting heaven in revenge for the drowning of his ancestors. He wanted to throw Yahweh out and replace him with idols of stone and wood. Soon the tower rose 70 miles high, and Nimrod's archers launched arrows into the sky. Angels hurled them back dripping blood, deceiving Nimrod into thinking he had destroyed the inhabitants of heaven.

Actually Yahweh was laying a trap, allowing Nimrod's pride to go before his fall. Yahweh and his angels descended unseen upon the tower and turned the one language of the workmen into 70. Suddenly the well-coordinated construction project broke down, as the builders and laborers could no longer understand each other. Nimrod had to abandon his tower, which fell into disrepair.

The biblical and apocryphal accounts of Babel touch on much of the mythology of the pyramid, from the ego of the ambitious ruler to the structure as a pathway to the heaven-dwelling sky gods. They even detail the brick-and-bitumen materials used in building the great ziggurats. And they raise an interesting possibility: If language moved out across the earth from a single point, could it be that pyramid building did the same?

Scholars who have worked on this question have no trouble seeing the interconnections joining certain pyramid cultures within the Old

World or the similarities linking specific pyramid cultures within the New World. The stupas of Sanchi, Angkor Wat's temple towers, and Borobudur's cosmic mountain spring from a common tradition. In addition to the architectural and mythological similarities among the three ceremonial centers, we know that Buddhist and Hindu religious ideas moved out from India across Asia. Likewise, there is an interplay among the pyramid cultures of Mesoamerica. Again, in addition to the common ground of mythology and architecture joining Olmecs, Teotihuacános, Mayas, Toltecs, and Aztecs, we know that each succeeding culture drew on the prior group, adding its own unique contribution to a growing heritage.

Yet, when it comes to considering the possibility of links between the pyramid cultures of the Old World of Asia, Europe, and Africa and the New World of North and South America, the established academic stand has been clear and absolute. Until Columbus sailed three small ships across the Atlantic and made his first landfall in the Caribbean, the Old World had nothing to do with the New World. Before 1492 the pyramids of Egypt, Sanchi, and Lishan had no connection with those in Teotihuacán, Tikal, and Cuzco. Thus, while scholars are willing to accept diffusion within the two worlds, they are adamant that the similarities between the two realms must be the result of independent invention alone.

Is that actually the case, a credible hypothesis based on solid data? Or does this position qualify more as ideology than science—one that ignores good evidence that the pyramid builders of the Old and New worlds knew of each other long before Columbus set his sails westward?

Four
The Peopling
of the Americas

THERE IS AN UNFORTUNATE REASON FOR THE OFTEN BITTER and acrimonious debate between independent inventionists and diffusionists. The two camps are engaged less in the dispassionate discussion of data than in a battle of the paradigms. Inventionists, which include all but the smallest minority of professional archaeologists and anthropologists in universities and academic research institutions, hold to an evolutionary theory that under similar circumstances humans will, like biological species on paths of parallel or convergent evolution, develop similar cultural traits. There is, of course, an undeniable wisdom in this point of view. Even human cultures at opposite ends of the earth share common elements like marriage, a sense of religion and worship, founder myths, and the like. Clearly, nature as well as nurture has played a role in the development of human society since the time of our primate forebears.

At the same time, academic archaeologists and anthropologists are poorly equipped to detect common traits that might provide evidence of diffusion. Graduate school creates narrow specialists, men and women who devote their entire lives to knowing everything there is to know about a very small area and who refrain, for fear of being labeled amateurs by the experts, from commenting on other specialists' areas of competence. This professional reality has a way of dividing academics into affinity groups, with the Olmec specialists in this corner, the Egyptologists over there, and the Q'in Chinese archaeologists in another room altogether. In the unending battle for position within academic bureaucracies, no one group of scientists wants to admit that its area may have derived from another and thus lessen its claim to primacy and significance. If someone can prove that the Olmecs are actually transplanted Chinese, for example, then the political stock of the sinologists rises, while that of the Olmec specialists drops. In such a climate even the least suggestion of cultural diffusion draws fatal fire.

People who take a diffusionist stand, however, have often offered easy targets for academic sniping by rejecting even the most minimal standards of scholarship. There are, for example, the true-believer epigraphers—students of inscriptions, almost all of them amateurs—who can convert natural flaws on the walls of a North Dakota cave into a third-century B.C. Hebrew graffito and come up with a handy translation at the drop of a hat. Some who call themselves diffusionists, such as the writers Zechariah Sitchin and Erich von Däniken, argue that human cultures share cross-cultural similarities like pyramids because our race is the product of ancient, nonhuman astronauts venturing here from an unknown planet. And there are yet others who grab at any cultural similarity as further proof of the existence of Atlantis, Mu, Lemuria, or some other lost continent—complete with advanced technology, mental telepathy, and cordial relations between genders and races—holding to a dreamy-eyed, backward-looking utopianism. Mix in a horse dose of crystal power, reincarnation, and other fuzzy New Age ideas, and diffusionism takes on the odor more of religious enthusiasm than science.

The debate between independent inventionism and diffusionism deserves a deeper and more serious look, for it cuts to the heart of the source of the gift of civilization—what it is that makes us human. The reward of understanding the origin of the pyramids is more than an academic debate. It offers the prospect of better knowing who we are.

Babylon and Beringia

The connection between Old World pyramids and New World pyramids plays out against a larger backdrop, one that extends much further back in history than the first monumental thought in Imhotep's fertile mind. It has to do with how the people of the New World got here in the first place.

When Columbus returned from his voyage of discovery, the Indians he brought back with him posed a significant theological issue to a pre-Reformation Europe that was still uniformly Roman Catholic. According to the literal interpretation of the book of Genesis then generally accepted in the Christian world, all the peoples of the earth issued from the three sons of Noah. Each of the sons was responsible for the cultures and races of the three known continents: Shem for Asia (thus the word "Semite"), Japheth for Europe, and Ham for Africa (the origin of "Hamitic," a term applied to a family of North African peoples and languages). The gradual understanding that Columbus had run not into Asia's backside but an entirely separate continent posed a problem of biblical interpretation. If the Indians did not arise from one of Noah's sons, where then could they have come from?

Pope Julius II solved the problem at the Fifth Lateran Council in 1512 by declaring that American Indians were indeed children of Adam and Eve and therefore human. Their ancestors were Babylonians expelled from that city for sinfulness in the days before Noah's flood. These people wandered so far into the wilderness and away from the centers of evil, which God sought to destroy, that they survived the deluge—not spared by divine design, like Noah and his family and his multitudes of paired animals, but somehow overlooked. The Indians were sinners who slipped through the cracks in the godly mind, as it were. The papal declaration of 1512 placed the origin of the American Indian in Asia. That idea has largely survived to the present day, not just because it makes theological sense but also because available anthropological evidence long seemed to point in that direction. In the early nineteenth century, the naturalist and scientist Alexander von Humboldt recognized the similarities between some American Indian tribes and the peoples of northeastern Asia; he proposed that the earliest Americans were migrants from Mongolia and neighboring regions of Siberia, a theory first suggested by the Jesuit missionary José de Acosta in 1589. Modified and refined by archaeological research in the twentieth century, a model for the peopling of the Americas from Asia developed.

The most recent Ice Age, which reached its greatest extent circa 20,000 to 18,000 B.C., lowered sea level as much as 350 to 400 feet by capturing much of the earth's water in massive continental glaciers. What is now the Bering Strait, which connects the Chukchi Sea and Arctic Ocean with the Bering Sea and North Pacific, was a stretch of dry land that archaeologists have dubbed Beringia. Nomadic hunters could have crossed over from Asia during the Ice Age, but once they reached North America, they could have traveled no farther. Two massive ice sheets joined over what is now Canada and the northern United States to make travel south impossible.

Then, according to the conventional story, between 13,700 B.C. and 12,000 B.C. (equivalent to 11,000 and 10,000 B.C. in uncorrected radiocarbon years),* the slow warming as the Ice Age ended parted the two

---

* Radiocarbon dating is based on the decay of radioactive carbon-14 in organic material. Because the amount of carbon-14 has not been constant in the atmosphere through time, classic uncalibrated radiocarbon "dates" and "years" do not correspond to true calendar dates and years. This presents a continuing problem in studying prehistory and archaeology, particularly for the period circa 10,000 to 25,000 years ago, when the true calendar dates can vary from about 1,400 to 4,000 years older than the classic uncalibrated radiocarbon dates. Unfortunately, even in the technical literature, true calendar dates and uncalibrated radiocarbon dates are not always distinguished—thus two sites may be cited as belonging to the same time period but in fact may be separated in time by thousands of years if one date is based on calendar years and the other is an uncalibrated radiocarbon date. For more information, see *Scientific American*, September 2000, page 84.

glaciers and opened an ice-free corridor into the heart of the continent. Since the native languages of America fall into three distinct groups, it appeared that Asians crossed Beringia into North America in three waves. The first of these, who quickly fanned out over the continent and moved south into Central and South America, were the Amerindians. About 500 to 1,000 years later came a second wave, who settled in the central section of North America. Called the Na-Dene, these people include the Athabascans of the Alaskan interior and northwest Canada as well as the Navahos of the American Southwest. Last, perhaps another thousand years later, came the Eskimo and Aleut peoples who settled in the most northern extremes of North America and pushed across the sea ice to Greenland.

The first Americans, known these days as Paleo-Indians, came as hunters who specialized in killing and butchering the huge animals, like bison, mastodon, and woolly mammoth, that flourished in North America in Ice Age times. This impression was based on the 1927 discovery in Folsom, New Mexico, of flint spear points lodged in the skeleton of an extinct species of bison. Dated to circa 9500 B.C. (radiocarbon 8,000 B.C.), Folsom offered the first unambiguous evidence of human occupation of the New World, interpreted at the time as a result of southerly migration from Beringia. This date was pushed back further in the early 1950s, when older artifacts such as stone spear points and other tools were uncovered in Blackwater Draw, near Clovis, New Mexico. Radiocarbon dating indicated that the site belonged to circa 11,500–11,000 B.C. (circa radiocarbon 9500 B.C.).

For 40 years, Clovis artifacts and presumed cultural complex (named after the area where they were first found) became the benchmark that both defined and proved the model of human settlement of the Americas by migration from Siberia in the immediate post–Ice Age era (the so-called Clovis model). It showed evidence of large-animal hunting, which fit with the supposed motivation drawing hungry, nomadic spearmen from the Old World into the New. And the timing worked. The appearance of Clovis artifacts followed the opening of the ice-free corridor by enough years that small hunting bands traveling on foot had time, over generations, to spread from the northern point of entry in Beringia to the hunting grounds of what is now the southwestern United States.

Then, from both north and south, came evidence that the Clovis model fell short—or, more to the point, that the people of Clovis were latecomers, not founders. Far to the south lay Monte Verde, Chile; here an ancient campsite was subjected to 20 years of intensive research by a team of American and Chilean scientists led by Tom D. Dillehay of the University of Kentucky. Overcoming intense initial skepticism from professional archaeologists, Dillehay's team has proved that Monte Verde was occupied in 12,700 B.C. (radiocarbon 10,500 B.C.), over 1,000 years before Clovis. The evidence is so good that practically every professional Americanist archaeologist now accepts this date as reliable, even though it overturns the Clovis model. Monte Verde lies 9,000 miles south of Beringia, separated by vast reaches of tundra, mountain, and open plains, as well as forest and climatic zones ranging from frigid arctic to sweltering tropics. There is simply no way that Stone Age hunters crossing even in the first wave of Asian migrants could have covered such a distance in but one millennium, unless they were traveling at lightning speed—perhaps, as suggested by Knut Fladmark, following the coastline in small boats. Anthropologists generally agree that it would take 7,000 years for progressive waves of land-bound immigrants to travel that far (based on assumptions concerning human dispersal rates), a calculation that pushes their entry into the New World to 20,000 to 19,000 B.C. Trouble is, the massive glaciers of that time precluded land travel south. Monte Verde makes sense only if its inhabitants' ancestors crossed even earlier, before the expanding glaciers prevented their passage.

Nor is Monte Verde alone at this early date. Abundant well-supported evidence from South America shows that early peoples had already adapted effectively to many different environmental zones, from the coast to 13,000 feet high in the Andes to the grasslands of

Patagonia, by the time of Clovis or earlier. The oldest of the sites, Taima-Taima, lies in the Caribbean coastal zone of Venezuela and may be either contemporaneous with Monte Verde or circa 2,000 years later. No one Stone Age culture unites these sites, nor do they owe anything technologically to Clovis. Rather, these ancient peoples had had enough time to develop their tools and weapons and to use them effectively in the ecological zone they inhabited. They were long-time inhabitants, not recent arrivals in a strange, new land. In addition, the abundant cultural richness displayed by these peoples simply could not have developed in the few centuries since a first entry into the New World circa 13,500 to 11,500 B.C.

Then came evidence from the north. Geologists working in Canada demonstrated that an ice-free corridor had indeed opened between the two glacial masses and connected eastern Beringia with the areas south of the continental glaciers, but not until circa 11,000 B.C. (radiocarbon 9500 B.C.) or later—more or less simultaneous with the Clovis site and well after Monte Verde. Paleontological research supports this conclusion. Digs in the ice-free corridor zone have uncovered no animal bones in the period spanning 22,500 to 10,500 B.C. (radiocarbon 19,000 to 9000 B.C.). Ice still covered this northern land even as the Clovis hunters were setting off after mammoth far to the south.

This finding raises a number of possibilities, which are not mutually exclusive. One is that the first Americans came much sooner than 11,500 B.C., a possibility underscored by a new finding in North America. The archaeologist Joseph M. McAvoy and his wife, Lynn McAvoy, have excavated an ancient habitation at Cactus Hill, near Virginia's Nottoway River, about 45 miles south of Richmond; they have uncovered evidence of occupation of the site by 13,000 B.C. and possibly as early as 16,000 B.C. Clovis culture tools had been found at the dig earlier. The McAvoys went deeper and found evidence of previous occupation by a hunting culture that lived on white-tailed deer and mud turtles. Much earlier dates await confirmation in South America. At Monte Verde, Dillehay's team found charcoal radiocarbon-dated to 31,000 B.C. and associated with possible stone tools, a preliminary discovery that is even now being further researched. Another South American site, a large rock shelter at the foot of a sandstone cliff in northeastern Brazil known as Toca do Boqueirão da Pedra Furada, has also yielded controversial radiocarbon dates ranging from 50,000 to 30,000 B.C. Johanna Nichols, a linguist at the University of California at Berkeley, calculates that development of the more than 140 languages spoken by the native peoples of the Americas would take at least 20,000 to 30,000 years, a date curiously consistent with the Monte Verde and Pedra Furada charcoals. If further research supports the archaeological finds and Nichols's calculations, then humans have been in the New World about three times longer than we thought possible until only a few years ago.

Another interesting idea is that the Paleo-Indians traveled in ways other than hiking overland. As the glaciers pulled back and opened the sea, small boats staying close to the coast and hopscotching from island to island might have crossed from Siberia to Alaska and then worked their way south. The Northwest Coast, covering southeast Alaska, British Columbia, and Washington, was ice-free by about 12,000 B.C. and could have been colonized then. As yet, though, no archaeological site earlier than about 8500 B.C. has been found in that area—no doubt in part because archaeologists have not been looking for something that until recently they were convinced could not be there. Farther south, Santa Rosa Island, which lies some 30 miles off the coast of the southern California mainland at Santa Barbara, has yielded what may be the oldest human remains yet found in North America, though not the oldest habitation site. Dated to between 11,000 and 9000 B.C. by two different types of tests, the bones point to the possibility of Paleo-Indians coast-hopping their way down the continent.

Then there is the possibility that the Paleo-Indians came from places besides Northeast Asia. In a strange and wonderful irony, one of the strongest pieces of evidence for this idea is, as we shall see, the Clovis culture itself.

Paleo-America as Melting Pot

The biological corollary of the Beringian land bridge theory is that all indigenous Americans are descended from people who originated in the same small region of northeastern Asia. In the same way that Pope Julius II saw American Indians as forgotten survivors of the sinful city of Babylon, contemporary anthropology has depicted the native peoples of the Americas as well-adapted transplants from Siberia.

Unwittingly but sadly, this idea once contributed to the ideologies that led to fearsome repression and even extermination of Indian nations throughout North and South America. Since the Indians came from a single uncivilized region of Asia, they were themselves relicts of a bypassed culture—human dinosaurs, as it were, beings out of place in the onward rush of progress and social development. In 1912, with the last Indian wars fought and the tribes confined to reservations, the British anthropologist Sir John Lubbock wrote, "Savages may be likened to children," and he compared them to living fossils—pure, pristine, primitive. Children, of course, never replicate the accomplishments of adults, and, if they refuse to grow up, they require punishment. This ideology regarding indigenous Americans had lurked in the European mind for centuries and led to the torturous workings of the Spanish Inquisition in Mexico and points south and, later, to the wars of extermination in North America and to slavery.

Underlying this ideology was an even deeper belief: Indians and Europeans are distinct and different. Though descended from the same original ancestors, like the Adam and Eve of Judeo-Christian belief, they had so long ago diverged from each other that no family resemblance remained.

We now know that people from northeastern Asia did indeed migrate into the New World, but they were not the only ones. Recent research is showing that there is common genetic ground between Native

Americans and Europeans. In fact, there may even be an ancient connection to Africa.

In October 1999, Brazilian scientists announced the results of research on an ancient female skull discovered at Lapa Vermelha, in Brazil's Minas Gerais state, and given the name Luzia. Luzia's skull was found in 1975, but 20 years passed before scientists took a close look at the remains. This work dated Luzia to circa 11,500 B.C. (radiocarbon circa 9800 B.C.), a figure old enough to make news on its own. Even more intriguing, sophisticated reconstruction of Luzia's face at a laboratory in England showed features that looked African. Indeed, the shortest linear distance between the Old World and the New lies between the west coast of Africa and Brazil. Even if Luzia's African connection fails to hold up to further analysis, one fact is certain: She is no Asian.

Nor is the owner of a skull that was discovered accidentally in July 1996 by Will Thomas and Dave Deacy, two young boating enthusiasts who were wading in the Columbia River near Kennewick, Washington, to watch a hydroplane race. At least, Kennewick Man is not an Asian from an eastern Siberian background. Follow-up excavation yielded an almost-entire skeleton, missing only the sternum, a few ribs, and some of the small bones of the wrists and feet. Estimated to date back to 9,300 to 9,500 years ago, the skeleton came from a male about five feet nine inches tall and approximately 45 years old, presumably a ripe old age in the days before aspirin, Alka-Seltzer, and angioplasty. He was also one tough customer. Kennewick Man was heavily muscled, and he certainly suffered nasty chronic pain from badly worn teeth and a three-inch-long stone spear point that was embedded in his pelvis. New bone had grown around the wound, indicating that he lived for a substantial time after he was injured.

The most surprising thing about Kennewick Man is that he did not look like someone descended from Asians originating in eastern Siberia. He was taller than other ancient human remains found in the Pacific Northwest, and his skull and face were narrower and his jaw less prominent than the same features in modern Indians. This finding gave rise to a number of newspaper reports that Kennewick Man was a Caucasian, which were accompanied by photos of a facial reconstruction by the anthropologist James Chatters.

A scientific panel that studied Kennewick Man's remains concluded that, despite the early hoopla, he was no European after all. Comparing his skull measurements to averages for the other human groups showed Kennewick Man to be least similar to Africans and Europeans and most like Polynesians of the South Pacific and the Ainu, who are the indigenous people of northern Japan and Sakhalin Island. Both Polynesians and Ainu are thought to have come from groups that originated in South Asia. Significantly, both groups were prodigious seafarers. Kennewick Man does not look like a European, nor does he look like a modern-day Indian.

Racial characteristics vary so widely from individual to individual that basing a theory of migration on only one set of remains is an unreliable enterprise at best. A number of skeletons are needed to account for individual variation and make a supportable generalization. D. Gentry Stele of Texas A&M did just that: He analyzed research reports on all available skeletal remains from North America dating back to 6500 B.C. or earlier. The bones came from widely separated sites—three in Minnesota, two in Texas, one each in Colorado and Arizona. Artifacts found with the remains indicated that some came from groups of big-animal hunters, others from unspecialized hunter-gatherers. Despite the physical and cultural distances, all the skeletons had longer, narrower brain cases and smaller, slightly narrower faces than modern northern Asians or American Indians. If you were to arrange the peoples of the earth on a continuum of facial width, American Indians and northern Asians would be at the broadest end, with Europeans at the narrowest. The Paleo-Indians would fall somewhere in the middle.

So, interestingly, do most ancient remains from the same pre–6500 B.C. time period from all over the Pacific Basin, including sites in the Japanese home islands, Okinawa, and China. Some scientists are sug-

gesting that northern Asians and American Indians came from an original group of people who looked much like the Paleo-Indians and lived
in Mongolia on the order of 20,000 to 30,000 years ago. Various groups
migrated in different directions out of this homeland and developed
the characteristics we now think of as racial definitions only millennia later.

Luzia's skull points to the possibility that Africans may also have
contributed to the human brew that fermented in the Americas. Clovis
adds a European wrinkle.

Clovis hunters used distinctive spear points and other stone tools, all
flaked in a unique way. The Stone Age technology most like the Clovis
culture's is found not in northeastern Asia, where it would be expected
if the Beringian land bridge was the route for these particular immigrants into the Americas. Rather, it occurs in Europe, in a culture
known as the Solutrean, which inhabited northern Spain and France.
Solutrean and Clovis tools are not simply similar; they are so much the
same that even a specialist can hardly tell one from the other. The archaeologist Bruce Bradley, a leading expert on the technology of
flaked-stone tools, has said, "The artifacts don't just look identical; they
are made the same way. I call these deep technologies. These are not
mere resemblances; they are deep, complex, abstract concepts applied
to stone."

The Solutrean culture ended in Europe circa 14,000 B.C.; then Clovis
appeared later in North America, with no apparent predecessors, a
point Bradley finds most significant. "There is no evolution in Clovis
technology," he continued. "It just appears full-blown, all over the
New World, around 11,500 years ago."*

Bradley and his colleague Dennis Stanford, chairman of the Anthropology Department at the Smithsonian Institution's National Museum of Natural History, hypothesize that since much of the European

---

* Bradley was referring to radiocarbon years. By the calendar the date would be 13,000 years ago, or approximately 11,000 B.C.

landmass was covered by glaciers during the last ice age, the Solutreans made their way to the New World in boats, skirting the edge of the glaciers. However they got there, these European immigrants brought their genes as well as their stone tools. Evidence of their presence is found in evolutionary genetic studies as well as archaeological digs.

Researchers trying to unravel the evolutionary history of a group of people look primarily at two systems of inheritance. The first is mitochondrial DNA (abbreviated mtDNA), short pieces of genetic material found outside the nucleus of the cell. The other is the Y-chromosome. Both systems are inherited; mtDNA passes through generations from mother to daughter (it also passes on to the son, but he does not give it to his children), whereas Y-chromosomes are passed from father to son. Thus mtDNA and the Y-chromosome provide genetic histories for each gender within a given population.*

Both mtDNA and the Y-chromosome have characteristics that make them ideal for evolutionary research. They mutate at a predictable rate, so the number of changes is a measure of age, serving as a kind of genetic clock. Also, many of the mutations in both systems correlate with the geographic region where the line of inheritance began, providing markers that trace migrations even over a distance of a dozen millennia or longer. Finally, mtDNA and the Y-chromosome data are sensitive to random changes in gene frequency, meaning that differences in those frequencies between groups can show when they split off from a common ancestor.

Most mtDNAs of Native Americans fall into four lineages—geneticists call them *haplogroups*—known as A, B, C, and D. Statistical analysis of haplogroups A, C, and D indicates that they arose in both Siberia and America between 35,000 and 25,000 years ago. Haplogroup B is uncertain. Some analyses indicate that it is as old as the other three, but there is also research that suggests a more recent origin some 15,000

---

* Recent preliminary research by a University of Edinburgh group headed by Philip Awadalla questions this assumption, maintaining that paternal and maternal mtDNA combine after fertilization. If Awadalla is right—his results need to be confirmed—rates of change in human evolution will need to be recalculated.

years ago. In either case, these findings can be interpreted to support human migration out of Siberia into North America before the last round of glaciers reached their icy maximum—plenty of time for the Paleo-Indians to reach Taima-Taima and Monte Verde. Haplogroup B may mean that a later wave of Asian immigrants followed the earlier group's foot trails or coastal sailing routes and brought a new genetic mix with them.

The presence of yet another lineage, haplogroup X, in Native Americans shows that Asia was hardly the only place of origin for the most ancient Americans. Haplogroup X does not occur in East Asians or Siberians, but it is found at low frequencies among populations from Europe, the Middle East, and western Asia. Haplogroup X, found primarily in North rather than South America, particularly among the Sioux and the Ojibway nations, arrived here a long while ago, some 15,000 to 30,000 years in the past. Somehow, it appears, people from Europe, the Mediterranean Basin, or the western regions of Asia made their way to the Americas not long after the first North Asian arrivals and contributed to the mix from which the indigenous peoples of the New World arose. And later, millennia later, some of them built pyramids.

Rending the Curtain of Isolation

Even as the model of an isolated ancient New World is giving way to a pattern of various migrations from different parts of the world, the concept of a more recently isolated New World remains intact. According to this version of prehistory and history, once the indigenous peoples of the Americas evolved into their many nations and cultures, they supposedly lived in continental isolation for thousands upon thousands of years. Only when Columbus and his three little ships from Spain landed on a Caribbean island was the veil separating the New and Old worlds irreparably rent.

Even the most die-hard independent inventionist has to admit, however, that the curtain of isolation was less than perfect, at least in medieval and modern times. If historian and retired Royal Navy submarine commander Gavin Menzies is correct, a Chinese fleet under the admiral Zheng He circumnavigated the globe between 1421 and 1423, reaching Australia, rounding the Cape of Good Hope, and traveling to the Americas, where they explored the Caribbean, the South American coastline, and Baja California. According to Menzies, at least some of the information in the maps and charts resulting from the Chinese voyages made its way to the West and was put to use by late-fifteenth- and early-sixteenth-century European explorers.

There is evidence of even earlier instances of transoceanic travel. The Irish saga of the Irish abbot Saint Brendan, which recounts the westward voyage of the great abbot and his monk companions (circa sixth century A.D.), may well tell of an actual island-hopping journey around the curve of the Atlantic from the west of Ireland to northeastern Canada and back. The sailor and explorer Tim Severin, who later wrote an account of his journey in *The Brendan Voyage*, built a hide boat of the same kind that Saint Brendan would have used and repeated the journey, showing that it was possible for such a craft to make the passage from the Old World to the New. The Vikings followed the same course. Excavations by the Norwegian archaeologists Helge Ingstad and Anne Stine at L'Anse aux Meadows in Newfoundland prove that a group of as many as 160 Vikings, presumably led by the famous Leif Eiriksson (also spelled other ways, such as Erickson), lived in the settlement for three years or longer in circa A.D. 1000. According to the sagas that record the voyages of the Viking mariners, the settlers battled and bartered with the locals, whom they called *skraelings*. They also pushed far north into what is now the Canadian Arctic, where they were attacked and driven off by Eskimos who proved even more fearsome than they were. Modern scholarship, though, dismisses Vikings as interlopers, people who passed through without making an impression. That may not be the case, however. The oral traditions of the Micmac people, the indigenous tribal nation of Nova Scotia and coastal Newfoundland, have never been seriously investigated, nor is there a good explanation for the origin of the Beothuks (also spelled Beothucks), a reputedly fair-skinned people who lived in the area in historical times but died out in 1829.

L'Anse aux Meadows shows the difference between contact and influence. If the Vikings simply came and went, their sojourn in the New World displays maritime skill, but it carries little meaning for cultural history. It was contact without influence. But if the Newfoundland Vikings entered the mythology of the Micmacs, and if they number among the ancestors of the Beothuks, then contact grew into influence. Only with influence can culture, ideas, or technologies diffuse from one place to another.

An important theoretical issue arises in trying to distinguish the influences that lead to diffusion between peoples from the apparent coincidences of "similar causes acting alike on the similar constitution of the human mind in different countries and under different skies," as Frazer put it in *The Golden Bough*. For example, if the Maya built towns with square boundaries and the ancient Egyptians did the same, the similarity proves nothing. There are a limited number of choices for municipal boundaries, potentially a circle, perhaps a square or rectangle, maybe just a ragged sprawl. Likewise, if both the Maya and the Egyptians wore earrings, this again proves nothing. There are, after all, only a limited number of body parts from which to suspend ornaments. But if the Maya and the Egyptians built square towns with temples at their centers, and if the temples were the sites of sacrifices aimed to ensure the fertility of crops, and if the priests in both cultures wore large gold earrings formed in the shape of serpents with flicking tongues, then coincidence becomes almost statistically impossible.

This hypothetical example points up the criteria that come into play in judging whether an apparent similarity between two phenomena, such as the pyramids of the Old World and those of the New World, are connected by something other than the happenstance of independent invention. First of all, the more unique the element in question, the more likely it is that it was invented independently. That is, if only a single point of similarity is common to two groups, it is likely that this item arose independently in each group. The same holds true for geographical distance between the two groups. Neighbors are much more likely to trade ideas, tools, and marriage partners than are peoples separated by thousands of miles. A single similar element in peoples far distant from one another is almost certainly a case of independent invention.

Conversely, the more elements shared by two groups of people, the higher the likelihood that one group influenced the other in some way. Still one proviso remains: There must be sufficient time. Should an element arise in the two groups at about the same time, then independent invention usually provides the best explanation. But if the element arises in one group, then appears in the other after some years, decades, or even centuries, it is more likely that the group with the older element influenced the group with the younger. The trouble with this theoretical principle is that it can be hard to apply practically. Often the geological and archaeological records offer only approximate evidence, and distinguishing simultaneous events from ones that happened before or after each other is often impossible.

Sometimes, though, we get lucky, and the archaeological record allows us to tell when one event occurred relative to another and to decide whether invention or diffusion offers the best explanation. A concrete example is the nearly perfect resemblance between Solutrean and Clovis stone tools. The two cultures are widely separated, the one in Spain and the other in New Mexico, so we would look first at independent invention to explain the similarity. The number of shared elements argue against this, however. Characteristic after characteristic of the Clovis tools matches those of the Solutrean objects. And the timing is right. The Solutrean culture disappears from the Old World, then appears fully developed several thousand years later in the New. Diffusion from Old World to New is obvious. The only mystery is where the Solutreans were keeping themselves in the intervening dozens of centuries.

Time supports the diffusion of pyramids from Africa and Asia to the Americas. With the important possible exception of Aspero (as we have seen, the jury is still out as to whether Aspero really is older than the oldest Egyptian pyramids), the pyramids of the New World are younger than those in Egypt and Mesopotamia. The big hurdle is distance; it is many thousands of miles from Giza and Uruk to La Venta and Teotihuacán or from Lishan to Tikal. And pyramids alone, possessing as they do many architectural variations and uniqueness from pyramid culture to pyramid culture, do not of themselves prove diffusion.

We have already seen in chapter 3 the many mythological elements that tie the world's pyramids together and that led Joseph Campbell to believe that ancient cultures drew on the same deep well of myth. But there is a strong counterargument: Myths from different places are alike because the human psyche is the same no matter where it finds itself. Therefore, to evaluate whether pyramids traveled across the oceans we have to look at more evidence than shared myths. We will do that in the next two chapters; chapter 5 explores the possibility of diffusion across the Atlantic, and chapter 6, across the Pacific. And then we need to find out whether ancient peoples had the skills to cross the great oceans that separate the Old World from the New, the substance of chapter 7.

Five
Across the Atlantic
to the New World

WHEN THE SPANIARDS FELL UPON THE NEW WORLD and claimed much of it as their exclusive prize, they saw the indigenous civilizations of the Americas as so much heathen excess requiring conversion and conquest. Driven by the notion that only Christian people, ideas, and objects had any intrinsic value, they destroyed the accumulated wisdom of the New World with the systematic thoroughness of generals mopping up the last pockets of resistance or inquisitors seeking sinners for the fire. Kings and chiefs were slaughtered; wise men and women, hunted down and tortured hideously; ancient books called codices written in exquisite hieroglyphics, consigned to the flames. In the same way that the destruction of the great library of Alexandria cut us off from all but the smallest remnant of writings of classical antiquity, the Spanish conquest erased millennia of knowledge and wisdom in the Americas. Out of the entire heritage of Mayan Mesoamerica only three of the magnificent codices survived. They were carried off to Europe and kept there as museum displays, one in Madrid, another in Paris, the third in Dresden.

In the middle of the sixteenth century an unnamed, educated Quiché Mayan, from the Guatemalan highlands, updated and edited the central scripture known as the *Popol Vuh*, "Book of the Community," transliterating the original hieroglyphics into the Latin alphabet. One hundred fifty years later, Francisco Ximénez, the parish priest of Santo Tomás Chichicastenango, borrowed this now-lost manuscript from one of his parishioners and—as if to make up for the mindless destruction perpetrated by his predecessors—copied the text and translated it into Spanish.

According to the *Popol Vuh*, the Quiché were migrants from the east who lived there in darkness, came west in ships in search of the sun, disembarked on the shore, and made their way up to their highland home. The text says that the ancestors came "from the other side of the sea," the direction "where the sun rises." By their own testimony, the Maya were the descendants of a people from somewhere else.

The Old Shared Stories

The *Popol Vuh* is notable not only for what it says but also for the role it played in the spiritual, religious, and community life of the indigenous people of the Mesoamerican highlands. It was nothing less than a scripture. Like the Hebrews, the Egyptians, the Buddhists, the Muslims, the Christians, and the Hindus, the Maya had a canonical scripture, a collection of revered and preserved writings that recorded the history of the community and outlined its ethos.

Many of the ancient narratives recounted in the *Popol Vuh* reflect well-known mythological tales from the Middle East, many of which are found in their Hebrew form in the Old Testament. For example, when the Mayan tribes made their way to the New World, they "crossed the sea, the waters having parted when they passed," an event that echoes the Red Sea's miraculous division to allow the Hebrews to escape their Egyptian pursuers in the book of Exodus. The Mayan deity Vicub-Caquix tore the arm off another god, Hun-Hunahpú, an event that is reminiscent of the one-armed Egyptian god Min. Like the Babylonians, the Maya believed that toothache was caused by a worm invading teeth and gums. Again, like the Hebrew story in Genesis, creation began with preexistent darkness and water, and the power of the divine was connected to the light, not the dark. Hun-Hunahpú, his sons Hunbatz and Hunchouén, and his brother Vucub-Hunahpú raised such a din that the divine lords of Xibalba wanted to destroy them. In the Hebrew scriptures it is the noisiness of the people of Sodom and Gomorrah that alerts Yahweh to their wickedness and leads him to destroy them. The same story is echoed in the Babylonian creation epic: The god Apsu could not sleep because of the irreverent clamor of the young gods, and he resolved to destroy them for their constant noisemaking.

Eve's misadventure with the fast-talking serpent and the forbidden apple in the Garden of Eden is easily the best-known story from the Old Testament. Eve knew that death was the punishment for eating the fruit, even if it did appear pleasing to the eye and appetizing to the mouth. Convinced by the serpent that eating it would open her eyes and make her like a god in the knowledge of good and evil, she gave the forbidden fruit a try. The *Popol Vuh* tells a similar tale. A maiden had heard of a miraculous fruit on a special tree, and, although she feared that eating it could mean death, she was drawn to try it. She, too, needed convincing. The skull of the god Hun-Hunahpú was hanging from the tree like an apple, and it told her to try the forbidden fruit despite her fears. The result of this transgression is similar in both Hebrew and Quiché tellings. No sooner had Eve sampled the apple and shared it with Adam than the two of them became aware of their nakedness and rushed to cover their bodies. Sex had entered the world. Soon Eve gave birth to Cain and later to Abel. The Mayan maiden in the *Popol Vuh* lost her virginity as well. The divine skull spit in her hand, and she became pregnant with the god twins Hunahpú and Xbalanqué.

Numerology was practiced with great devotion in the Middle East.

The Hebrews, as but one example, made much of the number seven. The last day of seven is the Sabbath, and seven weeks is the span of time from Passover to Pentecost. Seven years make a sabbatical cycle, and seven sabbatical cycles make a jubilee, when slaves are freed and debts forgiven. The same fascination with seven is found throughout the Middle East and even into classical Greece—consider, for example, the mythological story "Seven Against Thebes," which was told by both Aeschylus and Euripides. The Maya had the same focus on seven. For instance, the *Popol Vuh* tells how Gucumatz, the Quiché Mayan serpent-god who brought humans civilization and agriculture, spent seven days in the sky, seven days in the underworld of Xibalba, seven days as a snake, seven as an eagle, seven as a jaguar, and a final seven as motionless, clotted blood.

As we saw in Pope Julius's theological embarrassment over the existence of American Indians, Genesis portrayed all the world's peoples as descendants of Noah's three sons. The Quiché also gave the essential number of their founding families as three. And, just as the Hebrews recounted the genealogies of their rulers in the books of Kings and Chronicles, the *Popol Vuh* detailed each royal generation from the first day of creation through the Spanish conquest.

This curious assembly of similarities between Mesoamerican scriptures and those from the Middle East is not confined to the Maya. The Aztecs, who drew much from the Maya and the earlier Olmecs, tell of a world-destroying flood much like the biblical deluge Noah survived. Of itself, a flood story is hardly noteworthy, because narratives of a massive inundation are found all over the world. The story itself among the Aztecs is not remarkable—but the details are. Only two people, the hero Coxcox and his wife, survived the flood, by floating in a boat that came to rest on a mountain, just as Noah's boxlike ark grounded on Mount Ararat. In the Hebrew scripture Noah knew that the flood was over when a freed dove returned with an olive branch in its beak. An Aztec depiction shows a dove offering the hieroglyphic emblem of language to the children of Coxcox, who had been born mute.

A neighboring Mexican tribe added additional pertinent details. In their version of the story, Coxcox is called Tezpi, and he escaped the waters in a boat filled with animals and birds. Noah sent out a raven, which is a scavenger and has the habit of eating the dead, but the raven never returned. Only the vegetarian dove came back. Tezpi released a vulture, which stayed away, gorging on cadavers. Then he let a hummingbird go, and it returned to him bearing a twig.

As we saw in chapter 3, according to Genesis the Tower of Babel was built only a few generations after the flood as a way of gaining access to the heavens. In Aztec mythology, the great pyramid of Cholula (like the Mesopotamian ziggurat that Babel must have been, it was encased in unburned adobe brick) was constructed by giants soon after the flood. These huge people wanted to reach the clouds, but that ambition angered the gods, who scattered them with fire sent from the heavens. The Aztec myth lacks the language aspect of the Hebrew story, but it has the same themes of human ambition, divine anger, and the gods' action directed toward thwarting the humans' design.

The Aztecs traced their origin to the goddess Cioacoatl, said to be the first goddess and the mother of all. She also bequeathed the sufferings of childbirth to women and brought sin into the world. Cioacoatl was called Serpent Woman and commonly was depicted with a snake near her. She sounds strikingly like Eve, who took her cue from the snake, became the theological entry point for sin in the newly created world, and was cursed by Yahweh: "I will multiply your pains in childbearing, you shall give birth to your children in pain."

These obvious parallels between Mesoamerican and Hebrew scriptures do not mean that the Aztecs had access to an early version of the Bible and could read Semitic languages. Rather, they point toward an earlier source of fundamental mythology on which the Hebrews, other Middle Easterners, and later the Mesoamericans drew. An example is the *Epic of Gilgamesh*, recorded in its present form in the seventh century B.C. but making use of sources dating to between 3000 and 2000 B.C. It tells a flood story much like the biblical account of Noah. The hero Gilgamesh encounters Utnapishtim, who escaped the waters of divine wrath with his wife and a boatload of living creatures. When the flood subsided, he sent out a succession of birds, ran aground, and sacrificed to his gods, as Noah did to Yahweh on Ararat and Coxcox on the highlands of Mesoamerica.

A central common ground between the Middle East, particularly Egypt, and the indigenous American civilizations is worship of the sun. Many, many cultures practice sun worship in some form. In Egypt, though, sun worship dominated all other forms of devotion, amounting to a state religion that supported the pharaoh's divine right to rule. Particularly from the Fifth Dynasty onward, the sun god, Ra, absorbed many of the other divinities, including Horus, who incarnated himself as the living pharaoh. Much the same pattern holds true for Mesoamerica and Peru. There the sun reigned supreme, and the king represented the sun god's incarnation.

The Egyptian *Book of the Dead* names three gods besides Ra as the so-called western souls. They are Sobek, the immortal crocodile god; Bakhu, lord of the mountain in the west; and Seth, who fights the serpent demon. Gods strikingly similar to Seth and Bakhu are depicted in characteristic poses in pre-Columbian Mexican art. As for Sobek, his name phonetically resembles the Aztec Cipact, who is, not accidentally, an alligator god.

Similarities arise too in the conception of the underworld in ancient Egypt and ancient Mesoamerica, as pointed out by the scholar Rafique Ali Jairazbhoy. In both cases the underworld is divided into stages—a physical conception that is expressed most famously in Dante's *Inferno*—through which the soul must progress after death. In both the Egyptian and Mesoamerican underworlds, a serpent stands guard over the second stage, the fourth consists of open desert flats, and the eighth offers a watery paradise where departed souls can swim, dive, splash, and frolic.

That both Mesoamerica and Egypt have an underworld is hardly surprising. The striking thing is that they share such precisely identical elements, mixed in with other elements of their own creation. Just by the law of averages, this must be more than coincidence or "the effect of similar causes acting alike on the similar constitution of the human mind in different countries and under different skies."

Mythology Made Real

To the modern mind, one of the most disturbing aspects of Mesoamerican civilization was the heart sacrifice. Practiced by the Maya and the Toltecs and taken to a level of bloody overindulgence by the Aztecs, the heart sacrifice ritually offered a still-beating human heart to the sun god as propitiation. The Egyptians did practice human sacrifice, as we have seen in the burial of retainers in the provincial Middle Kingdom and in the subsequent Nubian renaissance, but there is no record of heart sacrifice in northern Africa or neighboring regions. Still, a fascinating parallel arises in Egyptian mythology.

The Egyptian *Book of Caverns* shows the enemies of the sun with their arms pinioned behind them and their hearts at their feet, blood fountaining from opened chests. The Egyptian *Book of the Dead* tells how the goddess Amemit ate the hearts of condemned sinners after they confessed their sins to her. The Mexican goddess Tlazolteotl performed much the same task by consuming sins confessed during one's lifetime. In Egyptian belief, the heart of the dead one was weighed by the jackal god Anubis to determine the worthiness of that individual to enter paradise. The Mexican equivalent was Coyotlinauatl, the god whose name survives in English as "coyote." The notion of sin, the centrality of the sun, the devouring goddess, and the form of a divinity drawn from a canid animal run parallel in both Egypt and Mesoamerica.

The heart sacrifice is a case of mythology made real. It is not merely story or belief, but a concept of the world that informs and permeates ritual. The ancient Middle East and Mesoamerica offer many commonalities in ritual.

Across the Atlantic to the New World

The ancient Egyptians had their own proclivities to bloodthirstiness, commonly practicing extraordinary cruelties on defeated enemies and prisoners of war. When Ramesses III defeated the invasion of Libyans—the so-called sea peoples—in the twelfth century B.C., he ordered the penises of all the captured Libyan soldiers cut off. Scribes counted the number of the defeated by tallying the piles of severed organs, an occurrence recorded in the Medinet Habu reliefs. An inscription reports that one heap numbered 12,535, another 12,860. Ramesses III was not only torturing and, in some cases killing, his enemies with this butchery, but also ensuring that there would be no offspring to mount a further attack against him.

The event had a mythological parallel. When Horus battled Seth in revenge for the death of Osiris, Seth lost his testicles in the fight. He was mocked for his infertility; in the words of the ancient text, "his seed will be destroyed."

A relief sculpture dating from the earliest stages of Mexico's Monte Albán culture, in the Valley of Oaxaca, circa 500 B.C., shows a large number of figures conventionally referred to as Los Danzantes, "the Dancers." Three of the dancers, all males, display oddly twisted limbs— possibly the result of agonizing pain—and they grasp their crotches as if they were wounded. Near the three stands a figure holding some kind of instrument, possibly a surgical device for amputating the penis. Yet another similar *danzante* relief shows a miniature figure holding such a device, and red paint that has survived the long passage of time since 500 B.C. stains the thighs of the dancer. In earlier Olmec artwork, jaguar warriors are depicted brandishing the severed penises of vanquished foes, just as North American Indian fighters displayed scalps they took in battle.

To the Egyptians the severed phallus was not just a tally for counting prisoners of war. It was also revered as the source of virile fertility, the fountain of seed that grew crops. Herodotus reported that Egyptian women carried models of greatly oversized phalluses around their villages and pulled strings to make the models move like the real thing.

The same Medinet Habu reliefs from the reign of Ramesses III that depict the piles of severed penises also detail the Egyptian religious cult of the phallus. A priest carries a life-sized statue of the phallic god Min, whose awesome male endowment greatly exceeded human reality, in a company of standard-bearers. Another relief, in Luxor, depicts the phallic god lying on his back, much like the reassembled corpse of Osiris experiencing the magical erection that led to the birth of Horus.

Many of the same details are found in ancient Mexico's phallic cult. To this day, the descendants of the Maya perform a ritual dance with string-manipulated mock phalluses. A drawing in the *Codex Barbonicus*, one of the few surviving ancient Mexican writings, depicts similar artificial phalluses. An Olmec relief at Chalcatzingo shows a procession of standard-bearers approaching a phallic figure who lies on his back with his erection pointing up like Osiris'. A statue of Min shows this Egyptian god displaying his immense phallus while he holds his right arm up and bent at the elbow, a posture very like the physical attitude of an Olmec painting of a phallic figure at Oxtotitlan.

In the ancient Middle East, incense played a key role in worship. Two of the gifts the Magi brought to the newborn Jesus were frankincense and myrrh, particularly costly and highly prized types of incense. The ancient Egyptians formed incense into small balls that were burned in a sticklike censer with a bowl at one end and the head of an animal carved at the other. At Medinet Habu, Ramesses III is shown tossing incense balls into such a censer. The *Codex Selden* depicts a Mexican priest likewise tossing balls of incense into a censer, and Mexican censers commonly had a bowl at one end and a carved animal head at the other. There is even a distant similarity in the names for incense. Plutarch, a Greek historian of the first century A.D., said that the Egyptians called incense *kephi*. The ancient Mexicans named it *copal*, a phonetically similar word still used today to refer to certain aromatic tree resins.

Both Egyptian and Mesoamerican art show gods or kings being

blessed by libation. A figure stands on each side of the divine or royal figure and pours water over his head from a jug. The ritual is much like the custom of baptism as practiced by the Aztecs. In the ceremony of naming a newborn baby, water was touched to the infant's head and lips and an invocation was made to Cioacoatl, the serpent-woman mother of all, to cleanse the child of the sin that tarred humankind before the beginning of the world. Another Aztec ceremony was strikingly similar to Christian communion. Corn flour was mixed with human blood to form a cake in the shape of the Aztec guardian god, which was then consecrated by priests and distributed to the people to be eaten as divine flesh. And in yet one more parallel to biblical practice, the Aztecs stoned adulterers to death, just as ancient Hebrew law demanded.

These similarities between Aztec practice and the Bible do not mean that early Christian missionaries reached the New World centuries before the conquistadors. Hebrew and later Christian practice drew on Middle Eastern rituals that in some cases date back to very ancient times. The practice of baptism used as a source of spiritual renewal by John the Baptist in the Jordan River began in Mesopotamia in the late third or early second millennium B.C. When the Israelite prophet Jeremiah decried those who still worshipped the great goddess, these worshippers replied, "We offer incense to the Queen of Heaven and pour libations in her honor, . . . We make cakes for her with her features on them." The Aztecs were doing much the same.

The parallels between the ritual handling of the dead in the Middle East—particularly Egypt and Mesopotamia, where funerary customs lie close to the heart of the pyramid culture—and in Mesoamerica are particularly striking. Egyptian priests delivered sacred texts penned on papyrus sheets or strips to the dead. The Mexicans entrusted pieces of paper to the dead as a way of ensuring their ability to cross over into the next life. Egyptian mourners displayed their grief for at least 70 days by smearing mud on their faces. Singing dirges called "songs of dirt," the Aztecs mourned for an 80-day period during which women did not wash their heads, faces, or clothes. The sarcophagus with an inscribed lid is found both in ancient Egypt and in Mesoamerica from Olmec times on. And inside that sarcophagus was a mummy.

In Mesoamerica climate ultimately defeated mummification. The combination of heat and high humidity that characterizes the Olmec and Mayan heartland soon defeats even the most skilled attempts at embalming. Still, in an attempt to overcome climate and preserve the body, ancient Mexicans wrapped the cadaver in mats bound by rope and placed a mask over the face. This arrangement is highly similar to the burial practices of the Nineteenth Dynasty (1307–1196 B.C.), during the Egyptian New Kingdom (1550–1070 B.C.), according to which wrapped and bound mummies were interred at Saqqara.

The New World mummification practice most like the ancient Egyptian method is found in Peru, where the high, dry climate of the Andes favored the preservation of the dead better than the sweltering humidity of Mesoamerica. As in Egypt, the Peruvian cadaver was eviscerated by insertion of a hooked instrument through the anus with which the insides were pulled out, then was preserved by being rubbed with various oils and resins. The Peruvians, like the Egyptians, embalmed the internal organs in special containers known as canopic jars. And like the Egyptians, the Peruvians mummified dogs and buried them with the dead.

These preserved dogs bear further testimony to the origin of indigenous Americans in places besides eastern Siberia. The Beringian hunters brought with them heavy, muscular, thickly furred, wolflike working dogs, which are the ancestors of the modern Malamute, Samoyed, American Eskimo dog, and husky. The dogs mummified in Peru are of smaller, lighter-coated, less muscular breeds similar to the basenji, very much like the pets preserved in Egyptian tombs.

Olmec tombs contain no canine mummies, yet they do have ceramic dogs that run on wheels turning on wooden axles attached to their feet, again of the same basenji-like breeds. Some archaeologists have classified these objects as toys, because they are reminiscent of the pull toys that toddlers love to tug along behind them. Toys, however, are rare and unusual in tombs. The ceramic wheeled dogs are more likely ritual objects used in the cult of the dead. Indeed, wheeled animals, birds and bulls as well as dogs, are known from tombs in the Levant and China as well as Egypt and Mesoamerica.

The Egyptians, as we have seen, buried boats with the dead pharaoh to equip him with a solar barque to sail across the sky. In addition to the magnificent and full-sized vessel found near the Khufu Pyramid, cedar and sycamore boat models were discovered in the tomb of Amenhotep II (also known as Amenophis II, 1427–1401 B.C.) at Thebes; and a whole fleet of ships, all with their prows turned westward toward the portal to the underworld, accompanied Tutankhamun (1333–1323 B.C.) on his journey toward immortality. Burials from Peru during the ascendancy of Tiwanaku yield not boats but the next best thing— *guaras,* the long hardwood centerboards that served as both keel and rudder on the ocean-going balsa-wood rafts used by ancient Peruvians. As we shall see in chapter 7, they were key to their maritime prowess.

The mythology surrounding Egyptian burial also provides a possible but clearly speculative explanation for the large stone spheres found in southwestern Costa Rica. Discovered accidentally in the 1940s by United Fruit Company workers clearing land in the Diquis Delta, some of the spheres measure over nine feet in diameter and weigh up to 20 tons. Similar large balls of rock have been excavated at the Olmec site of San Lorenzo, and some of the stones mark the boundaries of cemeteries, which evidences a connection to the dead. Egyptian mythology, as we have seen, sent the departed pharaoh into the sky, where he was transformed into a star. Egyptian artistic convention sometimes depicted stars as spherical shapes. The stone spheres of Costa Rica and Mexico may mark the apotheosis of the dead into heaven's lustrous lights, showing yet another overlap with the mythology of the ancient Middle East.

Faces from Elsewhere

Like guardians from a time long gone, colossal stone heads stand watch at the ancient Olmec pyramid site of La Venta. The heads have unique, individual faces that seem to have been carved from life; they are not repeated versions of the same stylized face. Curiously, the stone faces of La Venta do not look like what we think of as indigenous Americans. Rather, with their broad noses and full lips, they more resemble West Africans.

If the La Venta heads were the only ancient Mesoamerican art with such an African flavor, they could be dismissed as stylized takeoffs by an artist with a different eye. They are not, however, singular or unique. Similar faces are found at the Olmec sites of Tres Zapotes and San Lorenzo. Later sites along the coast of Veracruz, on the Gulf of Mexico, have yielded sculpted heads with African features and scar tattoos, which are unusual in the Americas but widespread in Central and West Africa.

Africans are not the only seemingly nonindigenous people whose images can be found in the art of ancient Mesoamerica. A La Venta stela figure, who has been dubbed Uncle Sam for his out-of-place features, looks less like a modern Mexican than like a Syrian, Lebanese, or Greek, with a large, convex nose and a beard. Like the African heads, Uncle Sam is not unique. A number of other sculptures and paintings, such as an incense burner with a sculpted human head from the Guatemalan site of Iximché and a Oaxacan effigy of the rain god Tláloc, picture individuals who look more like Caucasians from the eastern Mediterranean than indigenous Mexicans.

The Chichén Itzá structure known as the Temple of the Warriors houses murals that depict three separate races of humans in the same setting. One of the paintings represents a seashore battle scene, in which white-skinned invaders with long blond hair are driven off by dark-skinned warriors, some of them black as Africans, some of them brown like Indians. The whites are shown either naked or wearing short tunics, while the dark-skinned warriors are dressed in the kilt, shield, hand weapons, and elaborately feathered helmet of Mesoamerican fighting men. In one of the panels a white captive is about to be sacrificed by the black warriors, who have stretched him across an altar with his chest upraised to receive the knife that will open his chest for heart plucking.

A major hurdle in analyzing any depiction of race is that distinguishing characteristics exist largely in the eye of the beholder. Individual variation is great, and the differences among even distinct ethnic groups are less pronounced and more overlapping than the theorists of race would have us believe. In the days when apartheid ruled South Africa, government authorities came up with such finely detailed, ultimately absurd definitions of race that siblings from the same family sometimes ended up with different racial identifications stamped on their papers. In deciding racial distinctions, it is wise not to make too much of small things. For example, some published descriptions of the Temple of the Warriors mural assert that the naked white warriors are circumcised, and this is interpreted as a sign that they came from the eastern Mediterranean, where circumcision was a common custom. An anatomical distinction so small on a painting that may be as much as a millennium old is not up to bearing such weight. But the presence of white, brown, and black skins in the same scene remains telling.

Mythological evidence also suggests the presence of more than one race in Mesoamerica before the Spanish conquest. The *Popol Vuh* describes the first ancestors as "black people, white people, many were the people's looks, many were the people's languages." The Quiché Maya may well have understood race very differently from how we moderns do, but clearly they recognized that the people of those early days came not from one background but several. They were a polyglot assemblage of different origins.

Some physical evidence points in the same direction as the mythology. In a study of skeletons at Tlatlico and other Olmec burial sites, the physical anthropologist Andrezj Wiercinksi concluded that some of the remains revealed African ancestry, a finding that has stirred considerable controversy among other experts in the field. Farther south, two necropolises dated to about 300 B.C. on the Paracas Peninsula along the south-central coast of Peru have yielded several hundred mummies, some of which have hair that is wavy, light brown, even reddish. Such hair is more typical of a European than an indigenous American.

A Long List of Similarities

A scholar who has carefully studied the question of contact between the Old and New worlds in the days before Columbus, John L. Sorenson, once put together a list of all the cultural similarities between the ancient Middle East and Mesoamerica. Although Sorenson excluded Peru, which offers many additional parallels of its own, his list still ran to over a dozen pages. Not only is this compilation extensive, but it also points to similarities in concepts and ideas so fundamental that explaining them by convergent evolution or coincidence is like grasping at straws whizzing past in a hurricane.

Middle Eastern astronomers and mathematicians had the concept of zero and a sign for it, an idea missing from classical Greek and Roman civilizations and undiscovered in Western Europe until the Crusades, whose warriors brought it back as part of the intellectual legacy gleaned from the Arabs. The Mesoamericans, however, knew the concept of zero. They also made paper, as did the Middle Easterners, and both coated the writing surface with lime. Astronomy was a passion in the Middle East and in Mesoamerica that led to observatories and meticulously maintained records of eclipses. As we have seen, sacrifices in both areas were associated with pyramids, and many of the details in ritual and meaning run parallel. Both areas divided the world beyond into a paradise and a hell—which are by no means universal human concepts. Pyramids and other major public works projects in Mesoamerica and the Middle East were constructed with corvée labor—unpaid labor due from a vassal to his lord or rendered to a lord as part of annual taxes. Important personages were borne on litters in both areas. And when either an Egyptian smith or a Mesoamerican smith wanted to create a metal sculpture, he used the same method of lost-wax casting, a complicated and highly skilled process taught by master to apprentice. It is not the sort of thing two groups come up with independently.

Add Peru to the mix, and the list grows longer still. Looking at the megalithic architecture of Sacsahuamán, with its precisely fitted stones, reminds one of the smoothly fitted, white limestone casing that enclosed the Khufu Pyramid or the limestone and granite walls of the Valley and Sphinx temples. Old stone walls at Tiwanaku in Bolivia were apparently repaired with copper or stone bolts shaped much like the metal, wood, and stone dovetails used at Medinet Habu in Egypt. The design of the Kalasasaya Temple at Tiwanaku, which dates from the Inca occupation of the ancient city, is comparable to that of the Egyptian Temple of Seti (circa 1300 B.C.) at Abydos: Both were built on a lake with reeds and lotus flowers and were graced with gilt doors.

To this day the people who live on the shores of Lake Titicaca preserve a singularly striking artifact that points to a connection with the ancient Middle East. Mesopotamian and Egyptian paintings and inscriptions from the second and third millennia B.C. show the gods sailing through the heavens in high-bowed, high-sterned boats made of reeds tied in tight bundles. Boats of that design are still in use in the marshes of the Euphrates delta in modern Iraq, on Lake Chad in the southern Sahara, and on the Mediterranean island of Sardinia. The same kind of vessel is likewise found on Lake Titicaca, along the northern coast of Peru, and on Easter Island, 2,350 miles off the coast of Chile. Reed boats were used in Mexico as well, until the middle of the twentieth century. Set any of these vessels against the ancient Mesopotamian inscriptions, and even a nautical expert would have trouble saying which is Old World, which New.

Both Peruvians and ancient Middle Easterners practiced trepanning, surgically opening the skull for medical or ritual reasons. Trepanning is known from various locations around the world, and alone its existence in different places is itself not remarkable. Prehistoric Mexicans performed the operation too, drilling a round hole in the skull to expose its contents. The curious similarity between the Middle East and Peru is that the procedure was done in the same way. Rather than drilling a hole, the surgeon or priest made four overlapping knife or saw cuts in the skull, the same pattern as the start of a game of tic-tac-toe, then removed the square of bone in the middle.

After reading a list like Sorenson's and examining the evidence from Peru, it would be easy to fall into the trap of thinking that Old World civilization was simply transplanted wholesale to the New World. That is not the case at all; Tiwanaku or La Venta is no photocopy of Giza or Uruk. Rather, bits and pieces seem to have been selected from the source culture, modified in highly individual ways, and made distinct and unique. Cultural contact is a process more complicated and complex than we currently understand.

A good example is language. The Egyptians, as is well known, wrote in hieroglyphics. So did the Mayas and Aztecs. Writing among the Olmecs is a point of scholarly controversy, as we shall see in chapter 6. Still, their art includes a figure of a kilted individual who looks very much like an Egyptian scribe, holding what could be a scroll. Mesoamerican and Egyptian hieroglyphics share a similar conception of the relationship of the image to the word and follow similar principles, which are quite different from the ideas and processes that underlie an alphabet. An occasional claim has been made that Egyptian glyphs appear in Mesoamerica, but so far the idea cannot be sustained. The forms of writing in Mesoamerica and the Middle East look similar, but the content differs.

There may, however, be a close connection between the spoken lan-

116

guages. Mary LeCron Foster has presented a telling body of technical linguistic evidence that underscores a possible relationship between the ancient Egyptian and the Mixe-Zoque languages of southern Mexico, which include the Mayan tongues and are thought to have derived from the still-unknown Olmec language. Quechua, an indigenous language spoken to this day by the Indians of the Andes, is similar to the Mixe-Zoque languages and, according to Foster, contains additional words with Semitic roots, most likely from Arabic.

The Bearded White Gods

Reputedly ancient remains of possible Europeans in the New World and ancient Egyptian words in the Mayan vocabulary have been used to create a model that has ancient visitors coming with the gifts of Old World civilization to a still-primitive New World. The mythology of the New World even appears to support this idea.

Mesoamerica and Peru share ancient stories of culture heroes who traveled from afar and bestowed great teachings and institutions. In Mexico this hero is Quetzalcoatl, the Feathered Serpent, known in the Mayan realm as Kukulcan. The son of the invading king Iztac Mixcoatl, Ce Acatl Topiltzin Quetzalcoatl was elected priest-king of Tula, the capital of the Toltecs, over whom he ruled with beneficence and wisdom. An austere man given to doing penance, Quetzalcoatl opposed human sacrifice and religious excess. Yet for all its beneficence, the rule of Quetzalcoatl came to an end. Different versions of the legend give different reasons—he seduced a virgin, he lost a battle, he drank so much *pulque* (corn liquor) that he disgraced himself in front of his followers. Quetzalcoatl moved to Cholula (the site of the Great Pyramid and the Mecca of the later Aztec empire) and ruled there for 20 years more, again spreading his humanitarian message. Finally the great man made his way to the Gulf of Mexico, where he sailed away toward the sunrise on a raft made, in different versions, of balsa logs, of writhing serpents, or of reeds, like the vessels of Mesopotamia and

Lake Titicaca. As Quetzalcoatl sailed into the sunrise, he promised to one day return to his people.

Centuries later when Hernán Cortés appeared in Mexico with his conquistadors, some of the Aztecs wondered whether he was Quetzalcoatl returning. The Incas of the northern Andes similarly turned myth into reality by thinking that Francisco Pizarro, who was to Peru what Cortés was to Mexico, was the returning version of one of their bearded white-skinned gods known as the Viracochas. Like Quetzalcoatl, the Viracochas, who were said to have come from some distant but undetermined place, declared themselves descendants of the sun itself and ruled with benevolence and humanity. They settled on the Island of the Sun in Lake Titicaca, the legend says, and the marvelous stoneworks of nearby Tiwanaku stood as monuments to their good works. Before the legendary arrival of the Viracochas, Indian life was primitive, nasty, brutish, and short. This was the account given by the Inca uncle of the mestizo historian Garcilaso de la Vega (1539–1617), who recorded what his elder relative had to say, soon after the Spanish conquest, about the pre-Viracochas past:

> [A]ll this region which you see was covered with forests and thickets
> and the people lived like wild beasts, without religion, or government,
> or town, or houses, without cultivating the land or clothing their bodies,
> for they knew not how to weave cotton nor wool to make clothes. They
> lived two or three together in caves, or clefts in the rocks, or in caverns
> underground. They ate the herbs of the field and roots or fruit like wild
> animals, and also human flesh.

The Viracochas, under the leadership of the individual known as Con-Tiki Viracocha, changed all that. They showed the locals how to cultivate crops, established regular government and laws, created settled communities, founded sun worship, taught a religion of love and charity to all, and built temples and stepped pyramids. The Viracochas fanned out across Peru to spread their teachings of civilized life, but the Indians proved so hard-hearted that Con-Tiki Viracocha decided he and his followers should move on. After founding the Inca capital of Cuzco on his way out of the country, Con-Tiki Viracocha gathered with his white-skinned followers near what is now Manta in Ecuador and sailed westward into the Pacific.

This mythic tale worked to the advantage of Francisco Pizarro, who was white-skinned and bearded as the Viracochas had been. With only a small band of men, he crossed the heavily fortified valleys of Peru, assassinated the Inca king, broke his army, and conquered what was then the world's largest empire. When the conquistadors took Cuzco, they found marble and gold images of Con-Tiki Viracocha, the god who had, in an ironic way, allowed their conquest. Ungrateful, the Spaniards smashed the marble sculptures and melted down the gold. An immense stone image of the god in the great temple at Cacha escaped destruction for years, but the Spaniards finally smashed it too when they realized it had become an icon around which to rally rebellion.

Similar stories of great culture givers like Quetzalcoatl and Con-Tiki Viracocha appear all over Mesoamerica and northern South America. In Venezuela he is known by such names as Tsuma or Zume, and is said to have taught the people agriculture and preached his faith and laws from a high rock. He finally gave up his mission when the locals proved hard-hearted in the same way that had dispirited the Viracochas of Peru. The coastal Indians of Brazil called their culture giver Sume and said that he came to them by walking across the ocean from the east. Panama's Cuna Indians told the story of a great personage who appeared after a massive flood and taught the people how to name things and what rules of behavior to follow. In addition to Kukulcan, the Maya venerated a wandering pilgrim hero named Itzamná, who was the leader, guide, and teacher who invented hieroglyphics and devised the calendar. The Tzendal people of the Mexican states of Chiapas and Tabasco had a similar figure, named Votan, who came from far away in the east in the remote past. He too invented the hieroglyphics and the calendar, and he gave each nation its own unique language as well as the laws of good behavior. Myth made him the builder of the pyramids of Palenque. The Mayan king Pacal, who was buried in Palenque's Temple of the Inscriptions, added the name of Votan to his own as a way of identifying himself with this great ancient personage.

Contemporary writers who have dealt with these stories have tended to fall into the trap of seeing them as literal transcriptions of events in which barbarous Indians were civilized by sophisticated Caucasian visitors. It does not help that many of the accounts of the bearded white gods of old were recorded by Spanish colonizers, who were more than a little eager to portray the people they had conquered as the worst sort of barbarians and themselves as gentle civilizers. Such a myth provided a convenient rationalization for explaining away their own brutality. In fact, the Spanish identified Quetzalcoatl with Saint Thomas and Con-Tiki Viracocha with Saint Bartholomew. Some of them were convinced that these saints had made unrecorded missionary trips to the New World and tried to convert the Indians centuries before the conquistadors arrived to complete the task. Here, for example, is how Juan José de Betanzos, among the first Spaniards into Peru, described the Viracocha leader, on the basis of what he was told:

> [H]e was a tall man with a white vestment that reached to his feet, and . . . his vestment had a girdle; and . . . he carried his hair short with a tonsure on the head in the manner of a priest; and . . . he walked solemnly, and . . . he carried in his hands a certain thing which today seems to remind them [the Incas] of the breviary that the priests carry in their hands.

It is hard to take seriously a description that sounds so precisely like a sixteenth-century Spanish Catholic priest, probably of the Dominican order. And the confounding trouble of a report like that of Betanzos as well as accounts written by some contemporary authors is that it fits a subtle racial stereotype of primitive Indians civilized by more sophisticated whites.

To begin with, civilizing heroes are figures common to many mythologies. In the founding stories of the Hebrews, as but one example, Moses plays this role. Raised as an Egyptian, he gave his enslaved people the gifts of that civilization. He turned them from the old, orgiastic, pagan ways represented by the worship of the golden calf to the austere, clear-eyed, monotheistic dictates of the Ten Commandments. Some scholars, most notably the psychoanalyst Sigmund Freud, have argued that Moses, which is not a Hebrew name, was actually born an Egyptian and later was claimed by the Hebrews as one of their own. Among the ancient peoples of Mesopotamia, the goddess Inanna brought the gifts of civilization from the gods to the people. And the Romans, like the Hebrews, relied on a foreigner as their founding father in one version of their early days. In the epic *Aeneid*, the poet Virgil's paean to the emperor Augustus, the hero Aeneas survived the destruction of Troy and made his way west—after a side trip to North Africa and an intensely distracting dalliance with the beautiful queen Dido—to arrive in Italy and wrest the land that would be Rome from the nasty local barbarians.

If we look beyond the slavishly literal in the stories of Mesoamerican and South American culture heroes, even more of the rich mix that gave rise to the magnificent indigenous civilizations of the New World becomes apparent. Quetzalcoatl, Votan, Kukulcan, Itzamná, and the Viracochas are rooted no doubt in real persons, but details from different individual lives have been conflated to create single mythological characters. For example, the name Con-Tiki Viracocha combines three related deities. Viracocha is the Inca name for their white-skinned bearded sun god. In pre-Inca times, a similar god was known as Con along the Peruvian coast and as Tiki in the Andean highlands. Putting the three names together as Con-Tiki Viracocha made political sense for the Inca rulers, who ran an empire comprising many peoples. It also had mythological import. Like the Greeks with their various forms of Zeus gathered under a single name, the Incas created a single deity who collected into one supreme being the power of several lesser gods.

The physical description of the Viracochas along with their theology of the sun god definitely suggests that the origin of these curious travelers was the Mediterranean. The centrality of the serpent in the stories of Quetzalcoatl and his Mayan equivalent, Kukulcan, also shares something with the Mediterranean. In both the ancient Middle East and ancient Mesoamerica, snakes were associated with wisdom—the serpent in Eden told Eve how to gain the knowledge of good and evil—and with healing and fertility. There is also a distinctly African element in the story and imagery of Quetzalcoatl.

Like all tropical regions, Mesoamerica has a large complement of snakes. Though there are dangerous vipers like the rattlesnake and bushmaster, none of the native species grows to anything near the size of the immense serpent who stands for Quetzalcoatl. The largest snake to be found in the neighboring regions is the anaconda, an Amazonian species that reaches 20 feet in length in the wild and in legend is even longer. Despite its impressive size, the anaconda is rarely dangerous and actually is rather boring to watch. It is a nondescript olive-drab serpent that spends most of its life lying still under the surface of muddy rivers hoping to ambush capybaras, deer, and other unsuspecting mammalian prey.

The pythons of Africa are much more interesting—and dramatic. They are huge, and their coloring is as dramatic as the plumage of brilliant tropical birds. Also like birds, pythons live both on the ground and in trees. They are at times dangerous, and have been known to ambush, crush, and swallow humans. Many of the native peoples of West and Central Africa invest the python with spiritual power because of its threat, rainbow coloring, and habit of climbing trees toward the sun. This belief reaches far back in time. A carved relief of a python decorates a temple at Naga, Sudan, that dates to the kingdom of Kush during the second millennium B.C. Ancient Egypt, which lacks pythons, transferred much of the mythology of the serpent to the cobra. The pharaoh's crown sported a cobra's head, signifying wisdom.

Depictions of Quetzalcoatl from Mesoamerica look something like the python relief of Naga. Some of them show a man in the mouth of the Feathered Serpent, an image reminiscent of that in an Egyptian story called "The Shipwrecked Sailor," which was written during the Twelfth Dynasty (1991–1783 B.C.).

The tale, recorded on papyrus, tells of a sailor who survived a shipwreck on a voyage to distant lands and found himself cast up on an island ruled by an immense bearded serpent plated with gold. This snake even had jeweled eyebrows made of lapis lazuli. The snake asked the sailor where he was from, then carried him harmlessly in its mouth back to its favorite lair. There the snake proved itself benevolent, predicting the arrival after some time of another Egyptian ship that would carry the sailor back to his native land. When that ship did arrive, the serpent bestowed on the sailor a valuable cargo of incense, spices, elephant tusks, monkeys, and apes. But once the sailor left, the serpent said, he would never be able to return. "It will happen that when you depart this place, this island will never be seen again, for it will become water," said the bearded serpent, a prediction much like Plato's later account of the fate of sunken Atlantis.

"The Shipwrecked Sailor" is not an account of the discovery of the New World. Rather, it exemplifies the ancient image of a wise, bearded serpent carrying a man in its mouth, an image found in both Old World and New.

Distant Corroboration

Recent scholarship focusing on a sculpted head of supposed Roman origin and discovered in Mesoamerica underscores the possibility of early pre-Columbian contact between the two worlds. It also shows that the Mesoamericans paid attention to visits from the outside and that they incorporated objects and ideas from other places into their own unique thought and ritual.

The terracotta head in question was found in a burial offering made near what is now Mexico City; the offering was reliably dated to between A.D. 1476 and 1510, before the arrival of Cortés and his conquistadors. The style of the head is obviously and apparently Hellenistic-Roman, a realization that raises the issue of how it got to Mexico. A thermoluminescent age test—less accurate than standard radiocarbon dating in a mass accelerator but requiring a smaller sample of material—performed on the head itself at the Forschungsstelle Archäometrie (Research Center for Archaeometry*) in Heidelberg, Germany, dated the head's manufacture to around the late second or early third century A.D. (1,780 ± 400 years ago), a date consistent with the Hellenistic-Roman artistic style.

Even if we accept that Romans were sailing around the Gulf of Mexico, how did this terracotta head travel all the way to the center of the country, and why did it take a millennium to get there? The most likely explanation is that the Mesoamericans commonly reused objects from earlier times. We have already seen how they built new pyramids surmounting and incorporating older pyramids. They did something similar with ritual objects. For instance, an Olmec greenstone mask uncovered in an A.D. 1500 Aztec burial in Tenochtitlán's Templo Mayor has itself been dated to 1000 B.C. The terracotta head was an offering of the same order—an ancient object preserved from earlier times and used ritually again and again at different sites and for different reasons.

If we widen our point of view to include the Americas beyond the pyramid-building regions of Mesoamerica and Peru, we discover a large amount of additional evidence pointing to contact between the two worlds. Unfortunately, the popularity of ancient history has made inscriptions, coins, and pottery shards grist for the mill of many a con artist eager to work fraud on the gullible. I want to look here at a few select pieces of suggestive evidence supported by careful scholarship.

---

* Archaeometry is the application of scientific techniques to the dating of archaeological remains.

One is the so-called Bat Creek Stone, discovered by a Smithsonian Institution archaeology team in an eastern Tennessee burial mound in 1889. The inscribed stone had been buried under the skull of one of nine skeletons in the mound. All of the objects found in the burial were located close to this one individual, and it is thought that this skeleton represented a chief, with his wife lying at his side, and that the other seven were retainers buried with him. Of course, retainer burial has a Middle Eastern flavor, as does the language inscribed on the stone: Hebrew from the time of the Roman occupation. The Semitic scholar Cyrus Gordon has translated the inscription to mean "Year 1: Comet (= Messiah) of the Jews" and dates it to the late first or early second century A.D., when the Romans crushed rebellions by the Hebrews. Radiocarbon tests performed in 1988 on wood found in the burial mound yielded a date from A.D. 32 to 769, consistent with Gordon's linguistic analysis. Survivors of the rebellion, Gordon suggests, could have fled westward and ended up in the New World. Hebrew coins from the same era have been reportedly unearthed at a number of sites in the American Southeast, but since they were found by amateurs who knew nothing of good archaeological technique, skeptics have always argued that the coins may have been plants. Bat Creek remains controversial, but the evidence as we now know it suggests a genuinely ancient origin outside the New World.

Another interesting piece of evidence is the Micmac hieroglyphic system, investigated by the Harvard biologist and epigrapher Barry Fell. The Micmac, an Algonquian tribe, inhabit the eastern provinces of Canada and are closely related to the Maine people known as the Wabanaki, "People of the East." North American Indians are said to have been illiterate before Europeans came in number in the seventeenth century, and the hieroglyphic system the Micmac used in historic times was attributed to Pierre Maillard, a French missionary who died in 1761. Curiously, a significant number of the Micmac hieroglyphics are similar to the Egyptian symbols for the same thing or idea. Maillard could not have invented the system from his own knowledge of ancient Egyptian writing. He had been in the grave for 61 years before a French scholar, Jean-François Champollion, published his first deciphering of hieroglyphics. Rather, it appears that Maillard adapted a system already in use among the Micmac to disseminate the Catholic catechism and took all the credit himself.

But how did the Micmac get a form of writing that resembles the ancient Egyptian one? And is there significance in the eastern orientation of the Wabanaki tribal name?

Writing and symbolic inscriptions are the key aspects of a third piece of evidence: five small caves in a sandstone bluff in western Oklahoma known as the Anubis Caves. The inscriptions on the cave walls are written in alphabets that may be a Libyan script or Celtic ogam,* and the symbols in the rock may have an equally wide provenance. There is a large bull identified with the constellation Taurus, a cartoonlike version of the Egyptian jackal god Anubis complete with the pharaoh's official flail, and an anatomically explicit female figure known in Ireland as *sheila na gig,* which can be traced to a frog goddess dating to 6000 B.C. in the eastern Mediterranean. Equally fascinating, one of the cave's carvings shows a clear alignment with the equinox. This connection parallels the solar rituals common in the Mediterranean and in the Celtic regions of Spain, Ireland, France, and Britain during the first millennium B.C. and the early centuries of the first millennium A.D.

There is other evidence as well. Roman amphorae found near Rio de Janeiro could point to an ancient shipwreck in the area. A Mount Holyoke College geologist named Mark McMenamin has found what he thinks are cryptic world maps on Carthaginian coins dating to 350–320 B.C. In McMenamin's interpretation, the coins offer a schematic view of the Mediterranean and a landmass to the west that can only be the Americas.

---

* Also "ogham," a fourth- to seventh-century A.D. writing system used in Ireland, generally consisting of about 20 letters.

A Word from the Plant World

When people travel, they do not go alone. Other organisms accompany them: bacteria in the intestines, lice and fleas, domesticated pets and livestock, even plants, both wild interlopers and cultivated species. We have already seen how the dog breeds of Peru were much more like those in Egypt than ones common to the American north or to eastern Siberia. Equally fascinating evidence comes from botanical footprints left as ancient humans moved around the globe.

It is a commonplace of botanical history that some plants are Old World and others New World, and that the two realms exchanged but a few species—and those solely by accident—before Europeans established colonies in the Americas. The colonists exported the New World's maize, potatoes, and tobacco and imported the Old World's rice, wheat, and date palms, for example. The trouble with this neat scenario is that a number of important cultivated plants are out of place.

One is the common garden green bean *(Phaseolus vulgaris)*, which has been grown in Europe since at least the times of classical Athens, in the fourth and fifth centuries B.C., when it was mentioned in the writings of Aristophanes and Hippocrates. After the same plant was discovered among the indigenous peoples of the New World, historians assumed that the Spaniards had brought the common garden bean over and taught the Indians its cultivation. Then the same bean was discovered in sites all along the Peruvian coast that predate both the Incas and the Spanish. Somehow the garden bean had made the journey from Old World to New before the Spanish could have brought it.

The same pattern is true of the bottle gourd (known as *Lagenaria vulgaris* or *L. siceraria*). Long before 1492, this useful plant was known in Africa and the Middle East, where it was dried in a fire and used as a watertight container. The same gourd has also been found in the highlands of Mexico and Peru at sites that precede the Spanish by centuries. For example, eight bottle gourds uncovered in the Chicama Valley in Peru that were used as floats for a fishing net have been dated to 1500 B.C., some 3,000 years before Pizarro brought his soldiers to South America. Some inventive botanists have proposed that the gourd traveled as flotsam in ocean currents from Old World to New. There, the hypothesis goes, it was discovered by indigenous people who said something like, "Why don't we put this over a fire and see if we can't make a canteen out of it"—an unlikely deduction, given the sorry state of plant material that washes up on a beach after crossing thousands of miles of ocean. In addition, it is unlikely that bottle gourds could have survived floating at sea. The ubiquitous and persistent shipworm would bore through their skins almost immediately and quickly send them to the bottom. The only sensible way of explaining the Old World bottle gourd in the New World is to assume that ancient mariners brought it with them.

Cotton *(Gossypium)* presents even more compelling evidence for the same kind of intentional transoceanic movement. Like all domestic plants, cotton was once a wild species brought under cultivation and bred for desirable characteristics. Wild cotton, of which there are 16 extant species, has short lint and cannot be spun. To produce the plant that yields the cloth so many of us depend on for T-shirts and blue jeans, cotton was bred over centuries to yield four species with long lint that can be spun into thread. In the Old World at least, the debt that cultivated cotton owes to its wild cousins appears in the plants' genetics: Both wild and cultivated cotton have large chromosomes.

By contrast, New World cottons show a marked difference between wild and cultivated species. Wild New World cotton plants have small chromosomes, but the New World species cultivated since ancient times from Mexico to Peru have twice as many chromosomes as either the wild New World species or the Old World species. Furthermore, the cultivated New World species have a combination of equal numbers of small and large chromosomes. The cultivated New World species were created by cross-breeding, or hybridizing. The reputed discovery in Yucatán, Ecuador, and the Galapagos of cotton species living in the wild that have a combination of large and small chromosomes does not invalidate this analysis. Most likely they are feral—formerly cultivated varieties that have escaped to the wild. The question is, How did New World cotton growers get access to Old World cottons to breed the hybrids they needed?

Accidental dispersal of Old World cottons to the New World is highly unlikely. Cotton seeds do not survive long when soaking in salt water, although transport in the guts of birds is possible. Still, even assuming that cotton seeds did make it from Old World to New in the intestines of a migratory bird blown far off course by a storm, how would the indigenous people know that the fibers of this unassuming plant could be spun into thread and woven into cloth? There are so many steps from seed to shirt that independent invention of the same processes on both sides of the ocean is an improbable explanation at best.

Cotton use in both Old and New worlds dates far back into the twilight zone between history and prehistory. Cotton fabric has been found at Mohenjo-Daro in modern Pakistan that dates to 3000 B.C. The material is known from Huaca Prieta in Peru circa 2500 B.C. and from Mexico's Teotihuacán in the 3000–2000 B.C. period and possibly earlier. The cultivation and use of cotton must certainly go back much further, because growing and using cotton is a complicated process that no civilization, no matter how advanced, would have figured out in a few years or even a few decades.

And not just cotton is found in both New World and Old. The method of weaving used in Peru is practically the same as Old World technology. The Peruvians use two types of looms. One is a vertical-frame loom with two warp beams, which is the same as one used in New Kingdom Egypt and probably imported originally from Mesopotamia. The other is a horizontal loom staked out on the ground, which was also used in ancient Egypt.

When we look not only at the type of cotton grown but also at the loom used to weave it, we are studying what anthropologists and archaeologists call a complex: a collection of traits, artifacts, technologies, and ideas associated with one another and found together. The odds that related cottons would be cultivated on both sides of the Atlantic before Columbus are small, and smaller still are the chances of finding the same kind of loom. But when the cotton and the loom are found together, then the odds are so infinitesimally small that the only reasonable explanation is diffusion from one part of the world to the other.

Another complex concerns purple dye extracted from shellfish. The royal purple that indicated high rank in classical Greece and Rome came from an extremely expensive dye produced by the Phoenicians, a trading people of the eastern Mediterranean, after 1700 B.C. The expense was due to the labor-intensive, difficult tasks of extracting and processing the dye. The color began with a number of species of marine snails that secrete a material that is at first yellowish-white but turns to purple when it oxidizes. Dyemakers crushed the snails, mixed them with salt and water to steep for three days, and simmered them for another ten days in lead cauldrons. They then soaked raw wool in the liquid for hours, carded it, and dipped it again. The wool turned purple only after it was exposed to sunlight. Making purple dye took days of work and huge numbers of snails. A tiny yield of a half-ounce required thousands of the largest snail species, many more of the smaller varieties. No wonder the dye cost such a fortune that it could be afforded only by the wealthiest. No wonder too that Phoenician dyemakers protected their craft with extreme secrecy.

Shellfish purple was also used in the pre-Columbian New World, from the Mexican state of Michoacán to Ecuador. The mollusks in this area produce the purple directly, which made the extraction process less difficult, but it still took many snails to dye one piece of cloth. As in the Mediterranean, the color purple was equated with wealth and status in Mesoamerica and northern South America. In both regions, purple bore an association with fertility as well as royalty.

Again, it is highly unlikely that people in such widely separated regions would have independently figured out how to extract purple from marine snails, particularly when the process is so difficult, and would then have associated the color with royalty and fertility. The real question concerns which way the shellfish dye complex traveled. Did it go from the Old World to the New, or was it one of those cultural traits that made a west-to-east journey?

A west-to-east journey could explain another finding, this one highly controversial and still uncertain. In the early 1990s Svetlana Balabanova, a pathologist at the University of Ulm in Germany, found cocaine and nicotine in tissue samples taken from nine ancient Egyptian mummies stored in the Egyptian Museum in Munich. Since nicotine comes from tobacco and cocaine from coca, and since both are New World plants, Balabanova was surprised to find them in obviously Old World material. She had the tests redone by an independent laboratory, which reported the same findings. Intrigued, Balabanova tested hundreds of mummies from different Old World sites, ranging between 800 and 3,000 years old. She found nicotine in about one third of them. The cocaine came only from the Munich museum's Egyptian mummies.

It is possible that the Munich mummies were contaminated with tobacco and cocaine after they were uncovered. Someone might have been doing drugs with no companionship but the long dead, and some of the cocaine powder might have gotten into the preserved bodies. The nicotine is harder to explain. Perhaps it came from the New World. Perhaps a form of tobacco once grew in the Old World and is now extinct. Or perhaps the nicotine came from another, still unidentified plant that was used as a preservative. Until further research clarifies the issue, the cocaine and nicotine mummies are something that could prove to be nothing.

Where Did They Come From?

About 80 years ago, A. L. Kroeber, one of the founding fathers of American anthropology and a committed independent inventionist, defined what he thought it took to prove a case for diffusion:

The first observation to be made, is that resemblance must not be too close if independent development is to be the explanation. . . . If the resemblance includes any inessential or arbitrary parts, such as an ornament, a proportion that so far as utility is concerned might be considerably varied but is not, a randomly chosen number, or a name, the possibility of independent development is wholly ruled out. Such intrinsic features would not recur together once in a million times.

As we have seen in this chapter, Kroeber's criterion is met again and again. Resemblance after resemblance after resemblance—never exact but always tantalizingly similar—is found among artifacts and rituals in the Old World and the New. As Kroeber points out, resemblance is particularly significant in similarities that are arbitrary and inessential like the shape of the loom for cotton weaving, the breed of mummified dog, or the association of purple with wealth and status. Indeed, the fact of diffusion is so obvious that the question becomes not so much whether ancient mariners crossed the Atlantic, but who those mariners were and which group might have brought the idea of the pyramid along on their journey across the ocean.

The Egyptians of the Old and Middle kingdoms, seemingly the most likely candidates because of their place in the modern mind as the quintessential pyramid builders, are in fact unlikely candidates. The Two Lands never added up to a maritime empire, and the Egyptians of old were notably lacking in nautical skills. Proof of the point comes, surprisingly, from the large funerary ship called the Cheops boat, which is buried near the Khufu (Cheops) Pyramid. Made of Lebanon cedar planks that were up to 75 feet long and 4.5 inches thick, the vessel has the lines of an ocean-going vessel, with high prow and stern and a hull that was shaped to pitch and roll with the waves. The boat is no ceremonial mockup either; some of the planks are chafed by hawsers, indicating that this was a working boat before it served its funerary purpose. Yet the ship's internal ribs are inadequate to fully stabilize the planks, which are laid end to end and held in place largely with glue-and-rope seams. The first time the Cheops boat hit a good swell, it would come apart. For all its ocean-going lines, the Cheops boat is a river vessel. As far as we know, no purely Egyptian crew ever sailed very far into the Mediterranean, much less the Atlantic.

Culturally, however, Egypt was not an island. Many of the ideas, concepts, institutions, and artifacts that we think of as Egyptian are also found in the wider context within which ancient Egypt existed. The Two Lands belonged to the larger Berber (or proto-Berber) culture, which extended westward across North Africa and the Sahara from the Nile. The people to the west, called Libyans during Egyptian and classical times, lived in a manner that was much the same as Egypt's except that urban life was lacking. The Libyans shared fiber-tempered pottery with predynastic Egypt, used the same arrowheads and spear-throwers, practiced ritual trepanning, and mummified venerated dogs.

Many of the antecedents of Egypt's culture developed in the Sahara in the millennia before 3000 B.C., when the climate was wetter and what is now desert was then rolling grassland. As we have seen in chapter 1, the ceremonial center of Nabta Playa practiced an astronomically oriented, cattle-centered religion that looks like an early predecessor of Egypt's fascination with the movements of the heavenly bodies and its devotion to the sky goddess Hathor. Also the goddess of women, Hathor was often depicted with cow's horns or a cow's head or simply as a cow. The Egyptians themselves placed the land of their gods to the south and west, in the desert, in places like Nabta Playa. As the Sahara dried up and became less and less habitable toward the end of the fourth millennium B.C., some of its residents moved north, entering Egypt, the Berber countries, and southern Europe, particularly Spain. Others turned west, making their way toward West Africa. By 3000 B.C. people related to the Tassili culture of the Sahara had reached Africa's west coast. The connection continued. By 1200 B.C. the West Africans were weaving cotton like their counterparts in Egypt and using the lost-wax method of metal casting found in both the Middle East and Meso-america. The Ashanti people of what is now Ghana used gold weights shaped to look like pyramids, both stepped and battered-profile.

The African connection with Egypt proper intensified during the Twenty-Fifth Dynasty, which put the Kushite kings of Nubia on Egypt's throne. Facing the immense power of the Assyrian empire to the north, the Egyptians made first allies, then subjects of the Phoeni-cians, with whom they had been trading for centuries. Originally desert nomads who settled on the eastern Mediterranean coast, the Phoenicians redirected their wanderlust to the sea. They were expert mariners who sailed to Iberia for silver, Cyprus for copper, and Corn-wall for tin. The Phoenicians spread their mercantile influence by founding the colonies of Carthage, near modern-day Tunis on the coast of North Africa, and Gadeira (Cadiz) on the Iberian Peninsula. Accord-ing to the testimony of Diodorus Siculus, a first-century B.C. Graeco-Roman historian, the Phoenicians had accidentally discovered a land to the west when a storm carried a ship far off course sometime after 1104 B.C. Settlers from Carthage went to the new land to found a colony. The Etruscans, a Semitic people who lived in what is now Italy's Tuscany, had the same idea, but the Carthaginians stopped them forcibly in the fourth century B.C. Worried that other nations might also try to establish a trading beachhead in the new land, the Cartha-ginians forbade further immigration and killed all the settlers who had already arrived there.

This history leads to an interesting speculation. Did Phoenicians, Carthaginians, and Nubians crew together on vessels traveling from the Mediterranean into the Atlantic? And did they follow wind and currents to Mesoamerica? If so, this would explain the apparently Mediterranean and African faces to be found on artworks in places like La Venta, Monte Albán, and Tres Zapotes. It would also provide an ex-planation for the python imagery that underlies the legend of Quetzal-coatl and could also prove to be the source of the sun-worshipping

Viracochas of Tiwanaku, the megalithic architecture of Sacsahuamán, and the reed boats of Lake Titicaca.

Other groups also made their way across the Atlantic. The Bat Creek Stone and the Hebrew coins from the first and second centuries A.D. are evidence of the presence of refugee bands from Judea in the American Southeast. The Hellenistic-Roman terracotta head from near Mexico City, the possible shipwreck off Rio de Janeiro, and yet another possible shipwreck off the coast of Beverly, Massachusetts (suggested by fourth-century A.D. Roman coins that washed up on the beach) point to at least some Roman contact in the early centuries of the Christian era. And, if the Anubis Caves have been properly interpreted, Ogam-writing Celts from Spain, where they had mingled with Libyans who taught them about the Egyptian jackal god, made their way at least as far from the sea as western Oklahoma.

Yet, for all the transatlantic richness of the pre-Columbian mix in the Americas, a pyramid bringer is lacking. For one thing, the dates do not work out. Much of the transatlantic contact that current evidence makes likely came after the erection of La Venta's fluted pyramid, which began circa 1000 B.C. For another, where the later megalithic Peruvian architecture at Tiwanaku, Sacsahuamán, and Chavín de Huántar has a distinctly Egyptian, Libyan, or Nubian flavor, the pyramids of Mesoamerica do not. Palenque's Temple of the Inscriptions, as but one example, is much more similar to the temple towers of India than the ziggurats of Babylon and Uruk. As for La Venta, its tamped-earth construction reminds one more of Lishan, the great Chinese burial mound, than Giza.

To get a complete picture of the connection between the pyramids of the Old and New Worlds, we have to look in a different direction. We need to turn to that great body of water that washes both Asia and the Americas, the Pacific Ocean.

Six

Across the Pacific to the New World

VASTLY LARGER AND WIDER THAN THE ATLANTIC, THE Pacific Ocean seems to have been thought to offer an insurmountable barrier to human contact in the times before the European explorations of the sixteenth, seventeenth, and eighteenth centuries proved it could be crossed for reasons of conquest and trade. Indeed, belief in the Pacific as unassailable barrier has controlled the popular and the scholarly mind without challenge for the past century. As we saw in chapter 4, the conventional paradigm says that the Pacific could be crossed only during a brief period of time, around 12,500 B.C. (uncorrected radiocarbon 10,500 B.C.), when humans walked over the Beringian land bridge from eastern Siberia into Alaska. There are, as we have seen, fatal problems in that model. The body of evidence that humans crossed the Pacific from Asia to America repeatedly and that they carried many things back and forth is too significant. One piece of evidence is the pyramid itself.

Roasting Ears, Fine Feathered Friends, and Uninvited Guests

No cultivated plant is more quintessentially New World than the grain Americans call corn and much of the rest of the world knows as maize. First cultivated in the Valley of Mexico before 3000 B.C., the grain spread north and south. It became a staple crop throughout Mesoamerica, down the spine of the Andes, and up into the woodland planter cultures of eastern North America, where it saved the lives of Plymouth's starving Pilgrims some 5,000 years later.

The story goes that after their arrival in the New World, European colonizers recognized the potential of this new grain and exported it back to their home countries in the early sixteenth century. From Western Europe corn then made its way east and south. Today, 500 years after its introduction to the Old World, corn is grown in agricultural areas of suitable climate throughout Europe, Asia, and Africa as well as in the Americas.

However, a body of evidence points to the likelihood that corn found its way into Asia well before the time of Columbus and the European colonizers. The data begin with the results of an investigation into Asian corn varieties conducted by the Russian botanist N. N. Kuleshov in the 1920s. The maizes of Asia impressed Kuleshov with their variety. In fact, many of the Asian variations, such as dwarf cultivars and ears with waxy kernels, were either very rare in American corn or simply not present at all. Of course, plant breeders are clever people who can work startling transformations—as long as they have enough time. Understanding as he did the genetic realities governing plant breeding, Kuleshov doubted that all the varieties of Asian maize could have been developed in the time since corn was supposedly brought from the New World. He wrote, "Likely there was an earlier cultivation of maize in Asia than the time of the first landing by the Portuguese on

the shores of Asia in 1516. . . . The facts . . . return us anew to this sup-
position and this time with a great deal of conviction."

When Magellan reached the Philippines in 1521, he found corn already under cultivation there as a staple crop. Apparently it had been
brought by Arab traders, who carried Islam with them as well. Records
from China in about the same period also indicate that corn was widely
cultivated in that country in the sixteenth century. Between 1525 and
1563, extensive crops of maize were being grown in six prefectures and
two department counties, a sizable portion of the country. In 1575, 20
million bushels of corn were paid as tribute, an indicator that the total
crop was much larger. Had maize been introduced into the country by
the Portuguese only in the 1520s, it is simply impossible that the amount
of land under cultivation and the crop itself could have grown so large
so fast.

Farmers, particularly those who grow their own food, are by nature
cautious, conservative people. They know that tried-and-true crops
work, and they are reluctant to attempt something new for a simple
reason: If the new crop fails, they starve. No matter how excellent the
advantages of new crops, subsistence farmers switch over only when
they are convinced of consistent success. Corn had to have been in
China for a long time to have achieved such prominence as a staple by
the middle of the sixteenth century.

Evidence for just how long that could have been comes from China's
neighbor India. Temples in Karnataka state dating to the Hoysala dynasty of the eleventh to thirteenth centuries A.D. are decorated with
hundreds of sculptures showing what can only be corn. Each carved
ear is distinctive, showing different numbers, arrangements, and shapes
of kernels. These are not one model repeated over and over; rather,
artists depicted individual ears, which in real corn can vary greatly.
Likewise, the details the sculptors portrayed—such as specific size and
shape of the ears, characteristics of kernels, and their rows and ranks—
all correspond accurately to those of real corn. Some critics of this research have said that the shapes are actually pomegranates, an unlikely

possibility given the smooth roundness of the pomegranate. Others have said that they are versions of the traditional Indian cornucopia, or horn of plenty. Traditionally, however, the small end of the Indian cornucopia points down, whereas these corn ears point up. And why would handwoven basketry display such curious plantlike variation in shape and form?

The only fitting explanation is that the sculptors of the Hoysala dynasty were depicting corn as a sacred grain in the hands of gods and goddesses. And they were not the first in India to do so. Statuary dating from the fifth to tenth centuries A.D. shows gods holding corn. An example is the form of Vishnu in a sixth-century temple carved into a sandstone cave at Badami. It is unlikely that even these carvings mark the introduction of maize to India. To become a grain of such divine proportions, which found its way into the carvings of deities, corn had to have been in the country for some time. Whatever the actual date of entry, the grain was under cultivation in eastern and southern Asia long before the first Portuguese colonizers could have brought it.

Even Europe may have gotten corn earlier than 1492—from the other direction. If the early Spanish and Portuguese explorers had introduced maize to Europeans, it would have moved eastward from Iberia after 1492. Ambiguous Italian sources, however, may indicate that a grain much like corn was being grown around Milan before or just about the time Columbus returned from his first voyage. One of the first German botanists to describe maize, Hieronymus Bock, who wrote about 40 years after Columbus's voyage, indicated that it came from Asia, not America. He called it "wheat of Asia, great wheat," and said that it had been brought from a region of Arabia to Germany. Other authorities writing at the same time called maize *frumentum turcicum asiaticum,* a Latin phrase meaning "grain of Asian Turkey" (the Turkish empire extended deep into Europe as well as Asia at the time, hence the distinction between Asian and European Turkey). Some European common names for corn point also toward Turkey as the grain's source: for example, *grano turco* and *grano saraceno* in Italian, *turkish hvede* in Swedish, and *blé de Turquie* in French. It is notably curious that an American grain is associated so closely with western Asia, and even more curious that it would have traveled from Iberia to Turkey—regions divided by religion and highly hostile toward each other—before making its way to Italy, Germany, and France. Something is wrong with this picture.

Something is wrong, too, with the picture of how the chicken purportedly arrived in the Americas. The standard account says that the Portuguese explorer Pedro Alvares Cabral brought chickens to the coast of Brazil in 1500. The locals must have taken quite a liking to the birds and passed them on to their friends. Only 31 years later, when Pizarro and his conquistadors invaded Peru, they found numerous chickens scratching the dust of Cuzco and other Inca cities. Chicken raising had diffused across most of the breadth of South America in slightly more than three decades.

If that is actually what happened, it qualifies as the fastest known rate of chicken diffusion by leaps, bounds, and several orders of historical magnitude. Current archaeological evidence indicates that the chicken was first domesticated in the Indus Valley in what is now Pakistan in 3000 B.C. One might think that so eminently useful and toothsome a bird would quickly be adopted by the neighbors. But, as is the case with agricultural shifts, this new avian livestock traveled through Asia very slowly. One thousand years passed before it appeared in Persia; 1,500, in Egypt and Mesopotamia; 1,600, in China; 2,200, in Greece; and 2,900, in England. Even for good birds, diffusion works slowly.

Except apparently in South America. It is approximately 2,400 air miles from Cabral's landing point at Bahia on the Brazilian coast to Cuzco in the Andes, more than half again farther than the distance from the Indus Valley to Mesopotamia. Yet the chicken traveled this New World expanse in but 31 years, whereas it took 1,500 years in the Old World. That is hardly likely.

Nor is it likely that Cabral brought with him the kinds of chickens found among indigenous Americans. As chicken fanciers have long demonstrated, these seemingly ordinary birds are capable of astounding variation in the hands of clever breeders. As a result, specialty Asian chicken breeds are different from European varieties. One of the most striking variations is the melanotic Asian breed, which has black feathers, dark flesh, and dark bones and which was not found in the Mediterranean in the early sixteenth century. And Asians used chickens differently from the way Europeans did. In Asia chickens were raised less for the table than for sacrifice and the manly ritual of cockfighting.

The chicken breeds common among indigenous Americans were much more like Asian varieties than European. They even had a chicken as dark-fleshed and as dark-boned as the darkest melanotic Asian breed. Furthermore, before Europeans introduced indigenous Americans to the practice of eating chicken, the birds were kept for feathers, rituals, and cockfighting. The particular uses to which melanotic chickens are still put among the Maya and their linguistic cousins the Huastec closely resemble the ritual purposes to which dark-fleshed chickens were put in China. Similar rituals are found in western Bolivia and among the Mapuche of Chile. It seems unlikely that the folk belief in good luck brought by a melanotic chicken in the yard, for example, could have traveled from China to Guatemala, Bolivia, and Chile via Cabral, his fellow travelers, or some unnamed Spanish chicken aficionado.

The indigenous names for chickens in the Americas also point to Asia rather than Europe. The Spaniards called the chicken *gallo, gallina,* or *pollo,* depending on type and context. One would suspect that, if the Spanish or Portuguese had brought the chicken as some newfangled barnyard critter, the native tongue would have borrowed a form of the original name. Indeed, the Spanish words for chicken derive from the Hindu *pil,* which became *gallus* in Latin, the predecessor of Spanish, and which points to the bird's distant origin along the Indus. Yet, curiously, the indigenous words for chicken in the Americas show no connection to the Hindu-Latin root and instead mirror the linguistic complexity and vocabulary of chicken names in Asia. In India, the melanotic chicken is called *kharcha*; in the language of the Arawak of northern South America it is *karaka*. The Chinese names for chicken are *ke, ki,* or *kai,* depending on dialect. The names in the various Mayan tongues are *ke, ki, ek,* and *ik.* To the Japanese a hen is *mendori* and a cock *ondori;* among the Tarahumara of northwestern Mexico they are *'otori* and *totori.*

The Beringian land bridge had been gone for 9,000 years by the time chickens were first domesticated along the Indus River in 3000 B.C. The only likely method of travel from Old World to New is by boat, the very way they came with Cabral.

The Asians who likely brought their chickens to the New World also apparently brought something less welcome: intestinal parasites. Mixed infestations of two kinds of hookworms (*Ancylostoma duodenale* and *Necator americanus*) are found both in areas of Chinese culture in tropical Asia and among indigenous peoples in tropical America. Of course, there have been human parasites as long as there have been humans, but hookworms could not have been brought to the New World over the Beringian land bridge. Hookworms must spend part of their life cycle in warm, moist soil, and under subarctic and arctic conditions these hot-climate parasites quickly die. More likely, some vessel traveling across the Pacific in the warm latitudes carried the parasites from Old World to New inside the small intestines of ancient mariners.

Stone Age Reminders

Once, as a child who was already fascinated by the question of human origins, I watched a television program that followed an Indian hunter through the rain forest near the Amazon as he slowly, carefully stalked his prey. He worked his way to the base of a tree where a monkey was feeding and slipped a poisoned dart into his blowgun. Then, his cheeks puffing big as a blacksmith's bellows, the hunter propelled the dart into the monkey and watched the animal fall to earth as the poison took effect.

Maybe a month or two later I was watching another program, this time about a native hunter in Malaysia. He too stalked his game in a tree and, when the right moment came, slipped a poisoned dart into his blowgun. When the monkey fell, the hunter scooped it up and carried it home for dinner, following a pattern that seemed hauntingly similar to the routine of the South American blowgunner on the other side of the Pacific and the world.

The blowgun used to be cited as the classic example of what simply had to be independent invention. The weapon was no candidate for transport over the Beringian land bridge after the last Ice Age. The light projectiles used by blowguns work best in forests, where there is little wind to divert them from their intended path. In the arctic, which is nothing if not windy, a blowgun is a worthless weapon compared to the spear or bow and arrow. Since the nomadic arctic hunters wandering into the New World from Asia brought no blowguns with them, the weapons must have developed independently on both sides of the Pacific. It was, the anthropologists argued, a perfect test case of like technologies developing in similar tropical environments.

A careful look, however, dispels this conventional notion of parallel development of the blowgun. True, the basic physical principle of the blowgun may well have arisen independently at different times and in different places. But it is the details that matter. And the details, the meticulous scholar Stephen C. Jett of the University of California at Davis maintains, are simply too similar to be independent.

One particular kind of blowgun, the split-and-grooved form, is found in Malaysia, northern Borneo, and western Luzon (in the Philippines). The same weapon was used by the Houma of Louisiana, natives in the upper Amazon, and among the indigenous people near Barranquilla, Colombia. The hemispherical mouthpiece, common in America, also appears in Malaysia. Indonesian and South American blowgun hunters use different trees as the source of their dart poisons, but they tap these trees in the same way and call them by similar names. Both Malaysian and Amazonian hunters cut away the meat surrounding the dart wound before eating the kill, even though the poison has been metabolized and poses no danger to humans. Both Malaysian and Amazonian blowgun users employ salt and lime juice as antidotes to poison despite the lack of evidence, other than superstitious folk belief, that either actually works.

Another cultural complex found in both Southeast Asia and South America is the making of bark cloth. The process, which produces a heavy paperlike material by means of pounding and treating the bark of certain species of trees, is extremely complex. Paul Tolstoy of the University of Montreal, a scholar as meticulous as Jett, identified 121 steps in bark-cloth making, of which 92 are alike in Old World and New World. Of those 92, 42 do not depend on the prior step and are carried out in an arbitrary sequence, yet they are done in both Old World and New World traditions in the same order. That such coincidence in point after point could arise from independent invention defies the laws of chance. No gambler in even the last remnant of his right mind would ever get near that bet.

A number of other similarities link parts of South America, particularly the Amazon Basin, with Southeast Asia. In both areas, tribal warriors hunt human enemies for their heads and preserve them as trophies. People live not in individual family huts but in large communal longhouses built on piles. And dugout canoes are used for river travel in both cultures.

If we assume, as the evidence suggests, that Southeast Asia and South America are linked culturally, it would add to our understanding of cultural history to know when this contact occurred. Bark-cloth making and blowgun hunting, though, are Stone Age customs that have probably lasted largely unchanged for millennia. Dating them accurately is impossible with current methods. There is, however, one well-researched connection between the Old and New Worlds that has been dated accurately and gives us an idea of how old the transpacific connection may be.

The Pottery Bringers

The story begins in 1960 when Emilio Estrada, an Ecuadorian who was fascinated by archaeology, invited two professional archaeologists, Betty J. Meggers and her husband, Clifford Evans, to a place called Valdivia on the coast of Ecuador north of Guayaquil to look at some ceramics. The trio thought they were studying some of the very oldest New World pottery in existence. Radiocarbon tests confirmed that this was true. The Valdivia pottery dated to around 3000 B.C.; some later tests resulted in times as early as 3620 B.C. (with an error margin of 256 years either way).

The three assumed that the Valdivia style of pottery was related to shards found on the northern coast of Peru at Ancón and Guañape, but close comparison revealed few characteristics in common. Then Estrada noticed something odd. The Valdivia pottery bore a striking similarity to an earlier pottery from the island of Kyushu in Japan. Called the Jomon, this culture decorated its ceramics much as did the long-gone people of Valdivia. At first, Meggers writes, she had never even thought of looking for an antecedent pottery outside the Americas. Graduate school had taught her most emphatically that the Old World and the New World were worlds altogether separate. Yet when she looked at Estrada's pictures of Jomon pottery, she simply had to wonder whether he wasn't on to something.

Meggers and Evans traveled to Japan to look at Jomon pottery firsthand and to compare it to enlarged photographs of Valdivia shards. Meggers saw what she described as "an astonishing degree of similarity" in surface finish, decorative techniques, vessel shape, motifs and combinations of motifs, and rim treatment. Meggers dug deeper and deeper into the problem.

As she wrote one controversial scholarly paper after another, Meggers showed not only that the two pottery styles were similar but also that the odds against independent invention had to be impossibly small. The similarity was distinct, obvious, and repeated in one stylistic trait after another. None of these traits had any functional role. They did not, for example, make a pot do better what the pot was intended to do, like holding water or being used to cook food. Rather, the similarities were arbitrary, matters of style and aesthetics rather than purpose. The Jomon pottery had developed from simple beginnings circa 7500 B.C. through clear stages of increasing complexity to reach the level it held when its like was found in South America. The Valdivia pottery arose like a whole invention, with little or no connection to any earlier American pottery style.

The Jomon and Valdivian cultures were ecologically similar. Both are cultures of coast-dwelling peoples who took their food from the sea, particularly mollusks, and the land, primarily in edible plants and game. They fished, they hunted, they got around in boats. But whereas the Jomon people had pottery for cooking, eating, and storing food, the ancient inhabitants of Valdivia had wood, gourds, and skins. When it arrived, pottery must have caused a revolution as profound as the arrival of electricity would five millennia later. And apparently it got there with a group of Jomon people who, accidentally or intentionally, made their way across the Pacific, following the ocean current that runs across the North Pacific from the east coast of Japan to the west coast of Ecuador—a key feature, we shall learn in chapter 7, of ocean travel in ancient times.

Because it runs so profoundly counter to the prevailing paradigm, Meggers's work has drawn heavy academic fire. Her critics argue that the Valdivia pottery in fact derives from a New World antecedent and that its similarities with Jomon are purely coincidental. To date, no earlier New World pottery culture has yet been established as the ancestor of the Valdivian style. And the argument of coincidence is a bit of an ironic joke. Archaeologists depend on pottery as a distinguishing mark of culture because of its nearly infinite variability. Whenever two pottery complexes are connected by land, similarities between them are said to be due to contact. But if water, particularly the Pacific Ocean, lies between them, then coincidence becomes the explanation—an inconsistency seized upon to keep the prevailing paradigm in place.

Possible corroboration of the Jomon-Valdivia connection comes from a weapon found in similar versions in Japan and Korea and in Ecuador, Peru, and Bolivia. Called the star-holed mace, this weapon of war features a star-shaped head hafted onto a handle by means of a round hole. Made in stone, Asiatic star-hole maces date to the Late Jomon Period, in about 1000 B.C. In the Andes similarly shaped maces were made first from stone and later from bronze, and they date to the A.D. 500–1500 period. Since the star-holed mace is not found anywhere in South America outside the cultural area influenced by the Jomon Japanese, it too probably came with them.

A bit of intriguing medical evidence also points to a connection. A virus associated with the disease known as T-cell leukemia is prevalent among mummies preserved in northern Chile about 500 A.D. and also in people from southwestern Japan.

Meggers's model of contact between Japan and Ecuador circa 3000 B.C. or possibly even earlier is persuasive. The early Japanese, however, built no true pyramids as far as we know, and they are unlikely candidates as the Old World source for the New World's take on this kind of symbolic architecture. Yet Ecuador does provide evidence of later contact with a pyramid-building culture.

By about 500 B.C., coastal Ecuador had developed what is known as the Bahia culture, characterized by larger villages with more highly organized societies that had moved from hunting and gathering to agriculture. At this time, ceramic neck rests, which were unknown previously in the Americas but were commonplace in South and Southeast Asia in that era, appear. Certain other Bahian items manifest an Asian flavor. Small models of houses found at archaeological sites have a new un-American look because of their saddle roofs, whereas model houses elsewhere have a distinctly local appearance. Panpipes, which in the rest of South America are graduated from one side to the other, changed to a form graduated from both sides to the center—a distinctly Asian style. Figurines are seated so that the right foot rests on the left knee, a posture common in depictions of the Buddha from South and Southeast Asia.

The South Asian Connection

There is an important difference between what happened at Valdivia and at Bahia. Before the Jomon sailors appeared in Ecuador, pottery was little known and crude. The Japanese brought a new, even revolutionary, technology with them that was soon adopted in toto by the Valdivian people. When Asians again appeared on the seaside doorstep of the Bahia culture 2,500 years later, they worked a more subtle effect. The objects and ideas they brought did not cause a revolution; rather, they influenced the style of artifacts already in use. Something of the same must have happened with regard to the pyramids of Mesoamerica, particularly those in the Mayan realm.

Pyramids had already been built in the New World when the Maya began erecting their monuments after their culture crystallized in about A.D. 200. The Maya incorporated into this architectural concept a number of techniques and styles that, like the seated Buddha-like figurines of Bahia, have a characteristically South or Southeast Asian flavor.

One is the general impression made by the Mayan pyramids. Take a classic example like Temple I at Tikal with its stepped profile, single narrow staircase, and small massive temple at the top. These features are found again and again in the stepped Cambodian temples in and around Angkor Wat. The resemblance is more than skin-deep. Any number of the architectural details that make a Mayan pyramid look Mayan can also be found in South and Southeast Asia. Mayan pyramids were built around a solid substructure, just as was done in the Buddhist stupas of India such as those at Sanchi and the stepped temples of Cambodia. The long, narrow corridors of Mayan pyramids, such as at the Temple of the Inscriptions at Palenque, and accompanying structures incorporate the corbeled arch. The same type of arch and the same type of corridor are found in Southeast Asian temples. And the temples that top the pyramids are similar in both areas: small but massive, offering just enough room inside to accommodate a sacred image and a few priests, with roof heights boosted for no functional reason but rather to create proportions that are more aesthetically pleasing to outside viewers.

Then there are the long-nosed gods of the Maya. The glyph that stands for the Mayan city of Copán contains the image of a divinity with a long, tubelike nose. In the mid-1920s, Sir Grafton Elliot Smith named this figure an elephant, an identification rejected by American anthropologists such as Alfred Tozzer and Herbert Spinden, who pronounced it a macaw, a native form of parrot. A macaw, though, is an unlikely candidate, because there is nothing tubular about its large, well-proportioned beak. If the glyph is indeed an elephant, it points to a South or Southeast Asian influence. No modern form of the animal has existed in the Americas since mastodons and mammoths became extinct following the last ice age.

Evidence of a link arises in the distinct and unique Mayan city known as Comalcalco, located in the modern Mexican state of Tabasco, on the southern curve of the Gulf of Mexico. The city is linked with Palenque, which was built primarily during the reign of King Pacal (A.D. 615–683) and his two sons. The earliest levels of Comalcalco appear to be older, possibly constructed as early as the first or second century A.D. The ruins excavated to date reveal a large ceremonial complex of open plazas and pyramid mounds supporting temples. In overall design Comalcalco is a typical Mayan ceremonial center, but a number of its architectural features are unusual. One is the use of small window-like openings, which are rare in Mayan buildings. In addition, narrow slots were cut into the walls next to some of the windows, again an unusual and rare feature. The dead were buried in a distinct way at Comalcalco as well. The body was placed under a large overturned pot placed on a bed of oyster shells, a method found nowhere else in Mesoamerica.

Most curious is the building material. Comalcalco is the only known site, not only in the Mayan region but also in the whole of pre-Columbian America, where kiln-fired brick was used. Sun-dried, or adobe, brick was used in other locations, but as far as we currently know, Comalcalco is the only place where kiln-fired brick was employed. Why, one wonders, did the Maya forgo their usual limestone and rely on fired brick in this one place—a material that, so far as we know, they had never used before and would never use again?

Even more curious are the motifs and designs incised into a small percentage of the Comalcalco bricks before they were fired. Many of the motifs are typical Mayan glyphs and icons, but a small number do not fit what is known of Mayan writing. The epigrapher Barry Fell studied these anomalous designs and decided that they were Roman mason's marks. The Romans did indeed make extensive use of fired brick, particularly after the first century B.C., and their masons commonly decorated their bricks with signs much like those found at Comalcalco.

Yet there are several big flies in the ointment of Fell's identification of Comalcalco as a Roman monument. For one thing, the Romans were less than prodigious pyramid builders. It is more than a little odd that a people whose few pyramids followed the sharply battered profile used by the Nubians would, in the new wild land of Mesoamerica, erect a stepped pyramid in the Mayan fashion. Comalcalco also lacks the flanged roof tiles that are a virtually ubiquitous feature of Roman buildings. And, though Roman masons did mark their fired bricks in much the same way as the ones found at Comalcalco, they also added something else: Latin graffiti. To date, no graffiti in Latin nor any other inscriptions in the Roman alphabet have been found at the site.

Obviously something unusual was happening at Comalcalco. If that something wasn't Roman, what was it?

Fell followed the right path in looking outside the New World for an explanation of Comalcalco's marked bricks, says David J. Eccott, a professional musician as well as a gifted student of the archaeology of Central America. Still, Eccott argues, Fell didn't go far enough. As Fell recognized, the marks are much more ancient than the dates of the Roman empire (circa first through fifth centuries A.D.). Eccott traced the markings to the Minoan empire on Crete in the first half of the second millennium B.C. In fact, they go back even further, into the shadowy realm of "Old Europe."

That is the term used by the late Marija Gimbutas, an archaeologist at the University of California in Los Angeles, for an ancient, peace-loving, goddess-centered culture that flourished in much of southeastern Europe and the eastern Mediterranean between 7000 and 3500 B.C. The later Minoan civilization of Crete arose from one of the last vestiges of this very old culture. According to Gimbutas, Old Europe was subjugated by highly aggressive, god-centered people who originated in the Volga Basin in what is now southern Russia. The Old European culture, however, did not simply disappear when it was conquered. Rather, it went underground, making itself known in small but significant resurrections. One of those resurrections had to do with writing.

Gimbutas broke with the archaeological belief that writing originated among the Sumerians in Mesopotamia in the fourth millennium B.C., largely as an accounting method for trade and other commercial purposes. Backed by museums full of evidence, Gimbutas argued persuasively that many of the "decorative" markings on Old European artifacts were actually symbols drawn from a more ancient form of writing based in religion rather than economics. Old European symbols survived the subjugation of Old Europe and reemerged in the Linear A script used by the Minoans on Crete in the first half of the second millennium B.C. and in the syllabary of ancient Cyprus.

Now Eccott picks up the story. He suggests that the Old European symbols traveled even farther than Crete and Cyprus and that they were the basis of the Indus Valley Script. Many of the symbols in that ancient writing system resemble closely not only Old European but also the mason's marks found on Roman fired brick. Similar signs have been found in the rongo-rongo script of Easter Island, which lies in the South Pacific off the coast of Chile, and on adobe, or sun-dried, bricks in the Huaca Las Ventanas Pyramid along the coast of northwestern Peru, which dates to the pre-Inca Moche period.

Adding to the case for a transpacific connection linking the Gulf of Mexico with the Indus Valley is the fired brick itself. The first great Indian civilization, the Harappan, used fired brick extensively, but the technique was practically lost until circa 500 B.C. Then, with the rise of India's classic civilizations, it reemerged in the northern part of that country and along the Ganges River.

It seems highly unlikely that marked, fired bricks made their way directly from the Indus Valley to Mexico. Chronology gets in the way. The Indus Valley societies declined during the 1900–1300 B.C. period, yet Comalcalco's earliest layers were built no earlier than the first century A.D. Where were the bricks and their marks in the meantime? Most likely, the technique and the marks passed through at least one intermediate civilization, perhaps in India, perhaps in Southeast Asia, which has long been heavily influenced by India. Indeed, some of the bricks bear marks with motifs that could be Indian, such as a human-shaped creature with bird feet, a skull with water buffalo horns, and a man emerging from a flower, much like the Buddha rising from a lotus.

Of course, none of this evidence is anything more than circumstantial. But when the architectural similarities linking the Mayan realm with South and Southeast Asia are added to the sculpted ears of corn in Indian temples built during the same period, a pattern emerges. It becomes altogether more likely that Asia's Hindu and Buddhist heartland was connected to Mesoamerica in a way that proved central to the building of the Mayan pyramids.

The China Clipper

Teotihuacán's pyramids predate many of the Mayan monuments, and they have a different look. Where a Mayan pyramid soars vertically, a Teotihuacáno monument delivers a powerful sense of the horizontal. It stretches out as well as rising up. Where, one wonders, does the idea for this different form come from?

An intriguing answer lies in the research and long career of Joseph Needham, a British scientist and academic who died in 1995 at the age of 95. A faculty member at Cambridge University, Needham first worked as a biochemist and wrote three classic texts on the chemistry underlying the development of the embryo. In 1966 he retired from biochemical research to focus his efforts full time on the scientific and technological history of China, a topic that had long interested him. In celebration of Needham's ninetieth birthday, *Nature* magazine declared him "probably the world's greatest living scholar . . . a genius almost without parallel in our time." No doubt fans of Stephen Hawking would beg to differ. Still, Needham was an extraordinarily insightful and meticulous academic, a scholar who understood the making of both science and history.

In November 1947 Needham was working in Mexico City with a United Nations organization. He took the opportunity to examine Mexico's museums of antiquity, visit such sites as Teotihuacán and Chichén Itzá, and talk with leading scholars of ancient America. In a way, Needham wrote, he felt as if he had been there before: "This adventure, indeed, had some of the quality of the *déjà vu*, and I was deeply impressed during my stay with the palpable similarities between many features of the high Central American civilizations and those of East and South-east Asia. Was it not striking, to begin with, that the former all arose on the western side of the continent, as if fertilised or induced or stimulated from across the Pacific?" Indeed, the first similarity that Needham noted was "the predominance of the horizontal line in the terraces and monumental stairways of Central Amerindian temple and town patterns, the pyramidal *teocalli* notwithstanding."

Drawn by this sense of seeing something in Mexico that he had already seen in Asia, Needham looked more deeply at the question. He tackled it with his characteristic scholarly thoroughness.

Needham was particularly struck by the similarity between the pyramids and enclosed courtyards of the Mesoamerican ceremonial centers and the sacred enclosures and stepped pyramidal platforms of Peking and other traditional Chinese capitals. Like the Mesoamerican pyramids, which were used for making sacrifices, the Chinese platforms provided a setting for offerings to the gods. An example is the altar platform of Chou built sometime between 700 and 500 B.C. in Szechwan. It consists of three stacked platforms that measure approximately 113, 73, and 34 yards on their longest sides. Since such platforms were only 15 to 35 feet high at their summits, they create a profoundly horizontal feeling. By the time of the Han Dynasty in the late first millennium B.C., stepped platforms were used for both sacrifice and the burial of princes. The same pattern is seen at the Temple of the Inscriptions at Palenque, where the Mayan king Pacal was interred in A.D. 683. Pacal's face was covered with a magnificent jade mask that recalls the jade body cases used to cover the corpses of Liu Sheng, also known as Prince Ching, and his consort, who were buried in Hopei in 113 B.C. Chinese platforms used only three stages, less than is typical of Mesoamerica and more like Southeast Asia or Mesopotamia, but the horizontal line and gentle slope of the Mexican pyramids, particularly at Teotihuacán, have a distinctly Chinese cast.

That similarity can be seen in other aspects of Mesoamerican culture. The Aztecs, like the Chinese, saw not a man in the moon but a rabbit. In China this lunar rabbit occupied the Palace of the Lady of the Moon, where it endlessly pounded ingredients for the elixir of immortality. The Aztec rabbit of the moon was associated with the gods of the intoxicant *pulque*.

The Aztecs, Maya, Pacific Northwest Indians, and Chinese all prized jade and held this green stone dear. They also placed jade beads in the mouths of their dead, sometimes after coloring the beads with red paint made from hematite or cinnabar, a color thought to give life.

The Maya and the Chinese saw time in similar ways. Europeans of the sixteenth century considered Earth to be approximately 5,500 years old, a calculation made on the basis of biblical evidence. Such a period was a mere drop in the cosmological bucket to Pacal, whose inscription at Palenque sets the beginning of his ancestral monarchy at a point 1 million years earlier. I-Hsing placed the first general conjunction of the planets at 97 million years before his own existence, in the early eighth century A.D. In both Mesoamerica and China time was far more spacious than in Europe.

To measure time, the Chinese used two cycles, of 10 and 12 characters, to name days, months, and years, each of which returned to its respective starting point every 60 days, every 60 months, and every 60 years. The Mesoamerican calendars also combined two cycles, and the Mayan version of the system was even more complicated than the Chinese. Two primary cogwheels of 13 numbers and 20 days formed the religious year, or *tzolkin,* which meshed with the 365-day calendar year to produce a recurring period of 52 years. The details differ, yet underneath both the Asian and Mesoamerican systems lies the notion of meshing two cycles, about as arbitrary and unusual a plan as can be imagined.

Mayan glyphs recall traditional Chinese ideographs in their squareness, the way they are read downward, and their pattern of indentations. And there is the *quipu,* a recording device of strings and knots used as an aid to memory before the spread of writing in ancient times in both South America and China. The Maya wrote numerals with a bar and dot system much like the rod method the Chinese used. And both areas computed with the zero in place-value arithmetic, a mathematical system that was still a relatively recent introduction to Western Europe when Columbus first showed up in the Caribbean. The Maya used the zero before the Chinese did, and it probably was an American contribution to the developing Asian civilization.

Ancient Mexicans fertilized their fields with human waste, a practice unknown in the Mediterranean but commonplace in China. And both areas were adept at irrigation and hydraulic engineering.

Any number of parallels also can be seen in metalworking. Mesoamerican and South American smiths were adept at techniques like various methods of gilding and the diffusion bonding of silver and copper, which were also known in eastern Asia. Two alloys characteristic of Japan, one of gold and copper oxide and the other of copper, silver, and gold, appeared in South America by the end of the first millennium B.C. As early as A.D. 1000, the people of Ecuador and northern Peru were circulating copper money shaped like small ax blades. The Chinese used copper money in the shapes of half-moons, circles, spades, and knives.

Drawing all this information together, Needham stated his conclusion baldly:

> A mountain of evidence is accumulating that between the −7th century [seventh century B.C.] and the +16th [sixteenth century A.D.], i.e. throughout the pre-Columbian ages, occasional visits of Asian people to the Americas took place, bringing with them a multitude of culture traits, art motifs, and material objects (especially plants), as well as ideas and knowledge of different kinds. . . . We have to visualize the arrival from time to time of small groups of men (and doubtless of women also) with a background of high culture, never any massive invasion like that of the Europeans in the +16th century.

Needham made the right deduction. However, new research is pointing to a date even earlier than the seventh century B.C., one connected directly to the first Mesoamerican pyramid at La Venta.

The Arrival of the Shang

The Olmecs have long vexed American archaeologists. This earliest known Mesoamerican civilization was discovered by accident in the 1850s when workers dug up one of the colossal heads of Tres Zapotes at a sugar plantation in the Mexican state of Veracruz. At first, the sculpture was regarded merely as an oversized ancient curio, interesting but not particularly important. The full extent of the civilization was revealed only with excavations in the 1940s, 1950s, and 1960s, which showed this early civilization's accomplished sophistication. A Mexican archaeologist, Miguel Covarrubias, championed the Olmecs as the mother culture of Mesoamerica, in the same way that ancient Egypt, through Greece, was the source of European civilization. The Teotihuacános, Mayas, Zapotecs, Mixtecs, Toltecs, and Aztecs all drew from the Olmecs in creating their own distinct cultures. The Olmecs were key to the rise and spread of civilization in Mesoamerica.

The problem that the Olmecs pose has less to do with their influence than with their origin. These sophisticated people arose in the unlikely swampy surroundings of coastal Veracruz with a curious suddenness, as if they had moved into the area from somewhere else. A number of hypotheses have arisen as possible explanations. Michael Coe, who headed the team that did much of the excavation work at La Venta, has argued that the "suddenness" of the Olmec ascendancy is an illusion and that the civilization developed from earlier, simpler cultures in Veracruz and northern Tabasco. Others have looked to the highlands of Morelos and the Pacific slopes of Oaxaca and Guerrero as the Olmecs' place of origin. In 1964, Gordon Ekholm, then curator of Mexican archaeology at the American Museum of Natural History, made the bold assertion that the Olmecs owed at least something to Bronze Age China.

Now H. Michael Xu of Central Oklahoma University has proposed a model that unites the other hypotheses and that points, as Ekholm suggested, to China as the source of the La Venta Pyramid. In Xu's model, mariners from the Shang Dynasty (also known as the Yin Shang), which flourished in China between circa 1600 and 1122 B.C.,* crossed the Pacific and made their landfall somewhere along the Oaxaca and Guerrero coast. From there they moved into the highlands of Morelos, then descended toward the Gulf of Mexico, where the civi-

---

* The dates of ancient Chinese dynasties, like those of ancient Egypt, are the subject of considerable scholarly controversy.

lization achieved its greatest flowering, an achievement marked by the fluted pyramid and ceremonial center of La Venta.

The Shang made excellent ceramics and pottery, and they were masters at carving jade. They practiced astrology, offered humans as sacrifices, built large palaces, erected public statues, and built tamped-earth pyramids as burial mounds. Of course, the Olmecs did much the same. There is a Shang tradition that when the last emperor of the dynasty fell at the hands of his rivals circa 1122 B.C., 250,000 people fled east, into the Pacific Ocean. The number appears inflated, but the tradition of migration at a time that fits with the later rise of the Olmecs on the far side of the same sea is intriguing.

Still, broad similarities and fetching stories are too general to support a theory that the Shang Dynasty brought its pyramid-building skills across the Pacific. Proof requires details. Xu says he has them, in what is known as La Venta offering no. 4.

Uncovered in 1955 by an archaeological team working under Philip Drucker and Robert F. Heizer, offering no. 4 comprises 16 male figurines, all of jade or serpentine except one, and six celts, stones shaped like flattened chisels, in the same materials. The offering was buried under a ceremonial court, apparently as part of a funerary ritual. Four of the celts are painted with the same red cinnabar paint that Needham cited as evidence of the Chinese presence in Mesoamerica. The figurines, all of which appear to portray males, are arrayed in a rough semicircle in front of the celts, which stand on end. Several of the celts are incised with marks that scholars have long argued over, some saying they are undecipherable writing, some saying they are just decoration.

Xu says they are writing—the ideographs of Shang China. The inscriptions, according to his translation, make offerings to ancestors of the Shang Dynasty and to the 12 kings of An Yang, the capital of the dynasty's second period. This interpretation fits with the arrangement of the figurines, which suggests a group of men engaged in an ancestor-worship ritual.

Shang pictographs appear on other Olmec carvings, too, according to Xu, so the celts are not simply once-off curiosities. For example, he says one of the colossal heads of La Venta, the one with an apparently African face, is carved with the Shang symbols for "sacrifice" and "rain," a combination found again and again in the Olmec realm.

The similarities carry over into other aspects of religion. The Shang worshipped the eagle. The bird was also a totem to the Olmecs, and it appears even today on the national flag of Mexico, carrying in its talons and beak a snake that could be related to the Chinese dragon. The Shang prized the tiger for its power and courage, placing its symbol on tombs to guard them. Among the Olmecs, the jaguar conferred superiority to warriors, and the big cat's image appears again and again, often blended with a human element to make a jaguar-man. It would make sense that an Asian people who venerated the tiger would transfer that sense of awe to their new home's fiercest wildcat.

The jaguar-man also appears in the Chavín culture of northern Peru, which flowered at about the same time as the Olmecs. A key difference between the two areas, though, is that the Chavín people worked in metal, whereas the Olmecs had only stone. Still, the similarity in images is too close to be coincidental. Perhaps the Olmecs and the Chavín people traded ideas, or the two cultures represent divided off-shoots of the same migration from China.

Both the Shang Chinese and the Olmecs oriented their ceremonial centers to the north. Measured with a compass, the central axis of An Yang lies at 5 degrees east of north, that of La Venta at 8 degrees west. These might seem like different orientations, but in fact they both point to true north. True north differs from the magnetic north of the compass by an amount known as the angle of declination, which varies with position on the Earth. When the angle of declination is figured in for An Yang and La Venta, both sites orient to true north. The Shang are known to have been adept at astronomy. Apparently the Olmecs, who could also find true north by sighting on the stars, were accomplished astronomers as well.

There may also be a connection, through the Olmecs, between the calendars of Mesoamerica and those of China. As yet, no hard archaeological evidence of an Olmec calendar has been found, but the common ground between the Aztec and Mayan systems indicates the Olmecs as a point of origin. The eight rays of the Mayan and Aztec calendars resonate with the eight-pointed sun calendar of ancient China.

And finally there is the pyramid of La Venta, so like the Chinese pyramids of Lishan in its mountain-like shape and tamped-earth construction. Coincidence is an unlikely explanation for such striking similarity.

Absence of Evidence, Evidence of Absence

But before we rush to judgment and name the Shang Chinese as the progenitors of Mesoamerica's pyramids, two key questions must be answered. The first has to do with physical anthropology. Whatever happened to these people who supposedly carried high culture to the Americas?

In addition to the colossal African-looking heads of La Venta and other Olmec sites, a few human portrayals from the same period show people with apparently Chinese features. One, a terracotta head housed today in Mexico's Museo Diego Rivera, shows a face that looks undeniably Chinese, complete with the epicanthic folds that give the eyes of East Asians their characteristically almond shape. Another, a stone sculpture with exquisitely equipoised arms thought to depict a wrestler, has a chin-bearded and mustached face that looks very much like a contemporary Chinese. Most likely these images were made soon after the migration from China, before intermarriage melded genetic traits and made ancestry more difficult to determine. Now, after the passage of 3,000 years, the presence of Chinese—or Africans or Mediterraneans, for that matter—in the physical lineage of Mesoamerica can be detected only with sophisticated genetic techniques.

But those genetic traces can be found, if the investigator has the scientific knowledge to know what to look for. A marvelous example comes from a quite different place: the southern end of Africa. The Lemba are a Bantu-speaking, African-looking group of about 50,000 people who live in the region where South Africa borders Zimbabwe. According to tribal tradition, the Lemba claim descent from Middle Eastern Jews. The story says that they were led by a man named Buba who took them from their lost home, called Senna, to Africa. The Lemba practice circumcision, keep the Sabbath, and avoid eating the meat of pigs or piglike animals, including the hippopotamus, which is a relative of the barnyard hog.

But religious practices can be learned, and they are not evidence of true biological descent. Since Jewish history records no Buba, the Lemba tradition has been discounted as nonsense created by twisting the Sunday school lessons of modern Christian missionaries.

Genetics, however, tells a different story. Recent research has revealed that Jewish priests known as *cohenim*, who have duties different from those of rabbis and are said to be directly descended from Moses' brother Aaron, carry a distinctive pattern of DNA on their Y-chromosomes. The Y-chromosome is passed virtually intact from father to son and undergoes rare mutations. These few mutations provide a genetic footprint for the male lines in a people or tribe. The particular pattern of mutations found among the *cohenim* is a case in point. Among non-Jews the *cohenim* pattern is extremely rare. Among Jewish men of both European (Ashkenazic) and North African or Middle Eastern (Sephardic) origin, the frequency of the *cohenim* DNA pattern among priests varies between 45 and 56 percent and among laymen from 3 to 5 percent.

Exactly the same distribution appears in the Lemba. The *cohenim* pattern is found in 53 percent of the men of the clan that claims direct descent from Buba and in 9 percent of men who come from other clans.

Furthermore, there really is a Senna, a now-unoccupied place in the Hadramawt region of Yemen, an area once home to many Jewish villages. Local tradition holds that the town was wiped out by a burst dam circa A.D. 1000. The Lemba use clan names like Sadiqui and Hamisi, which are Semitic rather than Bantu, and which persist to this day in the Hadramawt.

Apparently, the Jewish ancestors of the Lemba left Yemen after Senna's destruction and sailed to Africa, whose southern coast lies only nine days away by sail. There they established new homes, intermarried with the local people, and developed a tradition that mixed imported Jewish practices with indigenous customs. The result is a distinctly African people who owe a portion of their physical and cultural inheritance to the Middle East.

No doubt similar stories could be told again and again about pyramid builders coming from the Old World to the New. Theirs was not a massive invasion of the sort the Europeans mounted in the sixteenth and seventeenth centuries. Nor did they have the religious ideology of the colonizing Europeans, who considered the local people worthy only of conversion, conquest, and finally extermination, and who brought with them the ecclesiastical institutions and military power to back it up. Like the Jews who came to the land of the Lemba, these ancients intermarried, contributed to the existing cultures, and blended into a developing New World identity.

It is the subtlety of this arrival and admixture model that provides an answer for the second question. If Old World pyramid builders brought the high culture of their pyramids to the New World, why were only certain traits transferred while others failed to make the trip?

An example, one often cited by independent inventionists to support the absolute and total cultural isolation of the New World prior to 1492, is the absence of the wheel before Columbus and the Europeans. In the Old World the wheel prompted a revolution in transportation and in warfare. Carts and chariots meant that heavy loads could be moved from place to place and that ground troops could be attacked swiftly and murderously by smaller numbers of mobile archers. Given the obvious advantages offered by the wheel, why wouldn't Old World people have transferred this technological marvel to the Americas?

To begin with, cultural transfer is an erratic, often slow process, even across distances smaller than the breadth of the Pacific Ocean. The ancient Mesopotamians had the true arch and the wheel for a thousand years before the Egyptians picked up these new ideas from their neighbors and put them to work. The wheel, the arch, and other such innovations gain their obvious advantage only in hindsight.

In the case of the New World, the answer to the question of the wheel is that it crossed the sea but to different effect. The ritual wheeled dogs and birds buried in Mesoamerican tombs and the wheel-shaped calendars of the Aztecs and Maya are obvious evidence of the wheel in the New World. The makers of the tomb objects understood the physics and engineering of the wheel, and the idea of a wheel as a thing that goes round and round is implicit in the shape of the Mesoamerican calendars. The New World, however, lacked large draft animals. Even if some Thomas Edison of the Incas had figured out the wheel, he would have had a hard time harnessing a llama to a buckboard. In addition, the religious implications of the wheel may have prevented its use in contexts as mundane as hauling freight or killing enemies.

The distinction between religious and secular contexts also explains differences in the ancient use of metals. In the Old World, tools and weapons made of metal became the basis of civilization and conquest. The armaments of the ancient Egyptians were made of bronze, and when the Hittites turned iron into swords, they gained a significant military advantage in an old conflict between neighboring empires. As we have seen, Mesoamerican metallurgists were extremely adept with copper, gold, and silver, yet they did not use their materials primarily to make weapons or tools, reserving their skills largely for ornaments and religious objects. The sacred realm triumphed over the secular, and metal was the stuff of the gods.

At least one remnant of this kind of thinking, the belief that certain materials—typically those that are precious and difficult to obtain—should be reserved for religious purposes, remains current in the modern world. In traditional Roman Catholic ritual any vessel or object that comes into contact with the consecrated bread and wine must be made of gold. Only this metal is worthy of touching what Catholics believe is the flesh and blood of Christ.

The absence of evidence of oxcarts and metal daggers in the New World is not evidence of the absence of Old World migrants in the Americas. Rather, it shows the complexity of cultural exchange and the marvelous intricacy of civilization, in both concept and execution.

The Big Picture, and the Water at Its Edge

So who built the pyramids of the New World? The cultural evidence shows that it was New World peoples working with ideas and techniques they adapted from Old World immigrants. As far as we can tell, there was no massive immigration across either the Pacific or the Atlantic. Rather, smaller numbers of Old World outsiders made landfall in the New World, blended with the locals, and contributed their skills, energies, and ideas to the mix that created the civilizations of the Americas.

At least three lineages—sometimes separate, sometimes mingled—can be traced to the pyramids of the New World. One of these arises in Africa and the Mediterranean. It appears in the colossal heads of the Olmecs and the megalithic architecture of Tiwanaku and Sacsahuamán. Another comes from South and Southeast Asia, which heavily influenced the Mayan pyramids at such sites as Palenque, Tikal, and Comalcalco. And finally there is the Chinese element, which affected the strong horizontal lines of the Pyramid of the Sun at Teotihuacán and whose tamped-earth technique provided the construction method for the fluted pyramid of La Venta.

Sometimes these elements crossed and influenced one another. La Venta perked away as a Mesoamerican melting pot, with Africans, Mediterraneans, and Shang Chinese all adding their flavors. Something similar happened in the northern Andes. The jaguar motif in the art of the people of Chavín de Huántar points toward Shang China, and Tiwanaku has an Egyptian, Berber, and Nubian flavor. Even in ancient times the Americas were a cultural crossroads.

Still, pieces of the background are missing, leaving the picture incomplete. Although the cultural evidence surrounding the pyramids points to a connection between Old and New World monuments, that does not prove the Old World pyramid builders could actually cross the seas to the Americas. To establish the connection as workable hypothesis rather than fantastic speculation, we have to show that ancient peoples could traverse the oceans. That is the issue to be addressed in chapter 7.

Even if we accept that the pyramid builders could sail the oceans, a second questions arises: Why? What would propel these ancient people to leave their homes and cross the open sea toward an unknown horizon? Was it greed, the intrigue of the unexplored, or some terrible calamity such as the catastrophe that caused the Lemba to move from Yemen to southern Africa? This will be the subject of chapter 8.

And finally there is the question of what it all means. Is the presence of pyramids in the Old and New worlds evidence only of an ancient melting pot, one that takes much of the air out of Columbus' sails? Or are we looking at something more important—namely, the newer branches of a very old tree? Could it be that the pyramids and the people who built them originated deep in the distant past in a still-unknown place and then moved out across the world, carrying their ways to places as distant as India, the Nile, Mesoamerica, and the Andes? Do the pyramids signal a civilization whose name we have lost? This is the critical question we will look at in chapter 9.

Seven

How the Pyramid Builders Sailed

THE INDEPENDENT INVENTIONIST BELIEF THAT THE PYR-
amids of the Old World have nothing to do with those of the New World
rests on a number of fundamental assumptions. The most critical is that
Columbus was able to "discover" the Americas—and forge the first connection between the Old World and the New since Beringia slipped under the arctic waves—because, at the time, Spain enjoyed the most highly
developed maritime technology on the face of the earth. All the ships
and sailing methods that had come before were necessarily more primitive. Only when the explorers of the Age of Discovery perfected the
mariner's art was it even remotely possible for humans to venture upon
the bluewater deep and discover the new lands on its far shore. Since no
one before Columbus had the skill to cross the Atlantic, much less the
Pacific, the notion that pyramid builders plied the seas and carried their
religious ideas with them is a not a question worth asking seriously.

Or is it?

The Reality of Ancient Sea Travel

The independent inventionist point of view is an untested cultural assumption, and nothing more. It subtly reflects the deep-seated assumptions of scholars who spring from an academic tradition that began in ancient Rome. The Romans had no love for nor trust in the sea. Although their triremes rowed by banks of galley slaves controlled the Mediterranean, they rarely ventured into the open Atlantic, whose longer swells and higher seas swamped their ships. To the Romans, roads were the preferred avenues of commerce and conquest, and they built a network of excellent highways linking all the many corners of their empire. The sea daunted them. They abandoned Britain as an outpost because of the difficulty of keeping troops supplied across the English Channel, and Ireland escaped the terror of the legions because the narrow Irish Sea was to the Romans a salty moat they preferred to admire from shore rather than cross by ship.

The Romans' landlubber mentality has crept into much of the scholarly thinking about the movement of pyramids around the globe, leading to an assumption that transoceanic movement was impossible because it appeared unthinkable. For example, it is a standard of archaeological thought that two similar cultures joined by land must be somehow connected, while the same two cultures separated by sea or ocean must have arisen independently. The unstated assumption that the land joins while the sea divides deserves a hard look.

Consider first the reality of transoceanic distances. The latitude lines of Mercator-projection maps lead us to believe that the shortest distance between two points lies along one of those seductively straight lines. We forget that the line represents a circle, which gets larger as it approaches the equator. As a result, the shortest route between two points at approximately the same latitude lies not along a line of latitude but along a so-called "great circle." A great-circle route lies in a plane that intersects the sphere's center and was known by mathematicians before the time of Columbus. An airplane flying from San Francisco to Paris takes a great-circle route instead of following the latitude line across North America and the Atlantic to Europe. Rather, it heads north on a course that takes it through eastern Canada, across the tip of Greenland, over the North Atlantic south of Iceland, then past Scotland and on into continental Europe. This apparent loop is in fact the shortest route.

The reality of the great circle also holds true for ships. If a vessel wants to cross from China to Mexico, a flat map suggests a direct route along the Tropic of Cancer, which neatly connects Hong Kong to Mazatlán. In fact, it is shorter to sail northeast, then strike out across the North Pacific.

Navigators following this geometrical reality find something else in their favor: currents. The sea does not stand still; much of it moves in great rivers. Find the right current, and it will take you where you want to go.

Columbus himself profited from a current on his trip to the West Indies. He traveled south from Spain to the coast of North Africa, then, near the Canary Islands, he picked up a westbound current that heads directly for the neighborhood of Cuba and Hispaniola. The Spaniards discovered another transoceanic conveyor belt, called the Urdaneta Route, in the Pacific in 1565. The mariner Andrés de Urdaneta was looking for a way from East Asia to Mexico, and he found out something that Asian mariners had likely long known: The northeast-bound Kuroshio Current carries warm water and mild weather from the Philippine Sea across the North Pacific toward the northwestern coast of North America, where the California Current continues the journey south to Mexico. The Spaniards used this route to send their treasure-laden galleons from the Philippines to Mexico.

A current that takes mariners in the direction they want to go effectively cuts the distance between the two points. Suppose, for example, that an ancient navigator wants to cover 4,000 nautical miles from launch to landing. The craft averages one knot under sail, and the current it follows also averages one knot. Every hour the vessel travels two nautical miles, a rate that doubles the effective speed and essentially cuts the distance in half.

Mileage is only part of distance. The Mediterranean is approximately 2,400 miles long, from the seacoast of the Levant to Gibraltar. A straight route from Africa's Cape Verde to Cape São Roque in Brazil is approximately 1,900 miles. The difference between the two is less mileage than the perception that the open ocean is more difficult to cross than a landlocked sea, another carry-over from classical times. The ancient Greeks rarely sailed at night. They hugged the shoreline during the daytime, dragging their ships up on the shore to camp as darkness fell. This longshore sailing, however, can often be more dangerous than bluewater voyaging. Even the best sailors cannot overcome a strong storm wind pushing their vessel into a rocky shore, a fate that has smashed many a ship. The same storm is actually less dangerous on the open sea.

Nor do transoceanic vessels have to be particularly large; it doesn't take an aircraft carrier to cross the Atlantic or the Pacific. The longer the ship, the greater the stresses set up by the swells, a fact that makes some smaller vessels more seaworthy than larger ones. And the ship need not be particularly tough or rigid—in fact, better that a vessel can flex and bend with the waves, or the first good storm swells may soon break it up and send it to the bottom.

To people who understand the sea, the ocean is a waving road that connects one land to the next. And humans have been making use of this transportation route for much longer than we computer-bound landlubbers might imagine.

The Most Ancient Ancient Mariners

The long chain of islands known as the Indo-Malaysian Archipelago, which reaches from Sumatra to the Philippines, comprises two distinct biological zones. The islands of the western end of the archipelago, which sits on the Sunda Shelf and contains Java, Sumatra, Bali, and Borneo, were connected by land bridges during the low sea levels of the ice ages. This western zone supports a rich fauna of Asian placental mammals. The eastern islands—Sulawesi, Lombok, Flores, Timor, the Moluccas, and the Philippines—are separated by deep trenches and lacked land bridges in ice age times. This eastern zone has a more limited and different mammalian community, made up of Asian and Australian species that reached the islands mostly by accident. The divide between the western and eastern zones is the so-called Wallace Line, a chain of deep sea channels that separates the two areas like a watery wall. It is named after Alfred Russel Wallace (1823–1913), who arrived at a theory of evolution by natural selection independently of Charles Darwin and who studied the southwestern Pacific extensively.

These days humans live throughout the Indo-Malaysian Archipelago. An early hominid species known as *Homo erectus* entered the western islands possibly as early as 1.8 million years ago. Like the placental mammals of this area, they crossed over when the sea was low and land joined what are now islands. But when did humans cross the Wallace Line?

Anthropologists have long assumed that the crossing could have been made only in the past 30,000 to 40,000 years. By that time *Homo sapiens*—humans like you and me—had displaced the earlier, smaller-brained *Homo erectus*. Surely only thoroughly modern humans had the intellectual power to survive an accidental crossing of the Wallace Line's sea channels or the wits to build boats and get there intentionally.

In 1994, however, a Dutch-Indonesian research team working at a site on the island of Flores announced the discovery of stone tools about 750,000 years old. The tools could have been made only by *Homo erectus*, the sole known member of the *Homo* genus in Southeast Asia at the time. The find meant too that even when the sea was at its lowest ice age level, these early hominids had somehow crossed the 12-mile-wide channel from the nearest island of Sumbawa. The announcement was met with suspicion not only because it upended the conventional model but also because the method of dating used, called paleomagnetic (based on the fluctuating, and sometimes reversing, magnetic field of Earth as recorded in magnetic materials in rocks), was too uncertain.

A follow-up study by Paul Sullivan and Asaf Raza of La Trobe University in Victoria, Australia, using a technique called fission-track dating, found that the Dutch-Indonesian date was actually too recent. Pioneered at La Trobe University, this method measures the tracks left by the spontaneous fission of uranium-238 in volcanic crystals like zircon. The two scientists tested zircon grains in volcanic-ash layers just above and just below the stone tools and obtained dates of 800,000 to 850,000 years.

It is highly unlikely that *Homo erectus* reached Flores by swimming. Twelve miles is a long, long way, even for practiced swimmers, whose open-water competitions are usually but two or three miles long. The best explanation based on what we now know is some kind of watercraft.

Vessels of one sort or another were definitely required to bring Australia's first inhabitants to its shores. Those immigrants most likely came from Timor or New Guinea, a route along which they hopped from island to island and which involved a final sea crossing of about 55 miles, well out of the sight of land.

Since the 1960s, researchers have thought that Australia was settled about 30,000 years ago. More recent radiocarbon dating has pushed this figure back to the 35,000–40,000 year range, a time that, for methodological reasons, is at the limit of the technique. A different dating method, called optical luminescence, used on sites in northern Australia, points to 60,000 years ago. Yet another technique, called thermoluminescence, underpins a report by Richard Fullagar of the Australian Museum in Sydney and Lesley Head and David Price of the University of Wollongong that Jimmium, a sandstone rock shelter in the north of Australia, yields stone tools up to 116,000 years old. Since thermoluminescence is less accurate than optical luminescence, many archaeologists question Fullagar, Head, and Price's claim. If it stands up to verification, it means that humans reached Australia by sea far earlier than generally thought. It also means that those humans were possibly *Homo erectus.*

Other archaeological work in Southeast Asia shows that the ability to cross from island to island arose long ago and developed steadily. In about 31,000 B.C. humans were visiting islands between Sulawesi and New Guinea. In the 18,000–8000 B.C. period, contact intensified. Obsidian was carried from New Britain to New Ireland, and humans from New Guinea transported marsupial mammals to small neighboring islands to stock them for later hunting.

One controversial research study argues that long-distance trade was going on by 4000 B.C. Stephen Chia of the Universiti Sains Malaysia and Robert Tykot of the University of South Florida analyzed obsidian discovered at an archaeological site in northern Borneo and found that the stone came from New Britain, some 2,400 miles away, in about 4000 B.C. If the data stand up to subsequent analysis, they point not only to open-water trading much earlier than expected but also to an ongoing cultural connection over the sea between these two areas.

There is no doubt that by 1000 B.C. New Britain obsidian was being hauled over the long sea journey to northern Borneo. At the same time, the Lapita people—thought by some scholars to be the ancestors of the modern Micronesians and Polynesians—traded it as far away as Fiji, 2,100 miles to the southeast.

Approximately 2,000 years ago, Asian vessels learned how to use the monsoon winds that blow across the Bay of Bengal to travel from India to the many islands of Southeast Asia. They transported trade pottery from the Indo-Roman site of Arikamedu in Tamil Nadu, on the eastern side of India's tip, to Sembiran on the Indonesian island of Bali, a distance of 2,700 crow-fly miles. This contact began a trade that brought the Romans spices from the Indies and that over the next thousand years carried into Southeast Asia the Indian cultural influence apparent in Angkor Wat and Borobudur. This trade also suggests a tantalizing connection between the Indo-Roman trade pottery of South-east Asia of the first century A.D. and the mixed Indian and Mayan marks found on the fired bricks of Mexico's Comalcalco, which was built in the first and second centuries A.D.

Widening the World

When Columbus set sail for Cathay (China) but instead discovered the Americas, he was breaking out from the limited vision of the world that had survived from the end of Roman times. As the Roman Empire collapsed into the Dark Ages, Europe pulled in upon itself. Knowledge of distant places vanished with the classics, and a world that had once been large and round became small and flat. In a way, Columbus was less discovering a New World than recovering a body of knowledge about navigation and sea travel that Europe had forgotten centuries and even millennia earlier.

A short inscription from the Fourth Dynasty (2575–2465 B.C.) about the import of cedar logs by ship, most likely from Lebanon, shows that Egypt's Old Kingdom made use of maritime trade. Since the Egyptians of that time were less than sterling seafarers, it is likely that the ships plying the lumber route hailed from Lebanon, probably the Phoenician port of Byblos. In about 1460 B.C. the Egyptian queen Hatshepsut dispatched vessels to the unknown port of Punt to fetch rare trees and woods, monkeys and apes, gold, and the incense myrrh. Scholars place Punt somewhere at the southern end of the Red Sea in modern Eritrea or Somalia, meaning a total round-trip journey of some 3,000 miles.

At some later date, the Egyptians may have made it as far as Australia—albeit almost certainly by accident. An inscription in Hunter Valley, about 65 miles north of Sydney, commonly known as the Gosford Glyphs, is thought by some writers to represent Egyptian hieroglyphics dating to anywhere from the Old Kingdom (2575–2134 B.C.) to Ptolemaic times (323–30 B.C.). If the inscription is authentic—and there is no proof as yet that it is—it tells of an Egyptian crew that was blown far off course, landed in a strange place thousands of miles from home, and wanted very badly to return.

To the west, the Egyptians apparently went no farther than Crete, perhaps because they didn't have to. The Minoans, who flourished in the first half of the second millennium B.C., were accomplished maritime traders whose great cities, like Knossos on Crete and Akrotiri on Thera, displayed both great wealth and a surprising sense of security. The Minoans had no apparent fear of attack. Their archaeological sites yield few weapons, their cities lacked walls, and only one of their exquisite frescoes shows a battle scene—and that one is at sea. From 2000 B.C. until their subjugation by the Mycenaean Greeks approximately 600 years later, the Minoans traded actively with Cyprus, Greece, Egypt, and Syria. They also ventured into the western Mediterranean, as indicated by ship graffiti on a temple on Malta. According to legend, King Minos, who gave the Minoans his name, led an expedition to Sicily.

The Mycenaeans traded their jewelry, weapons, and possibly wine for the amber, tin, copper, and gold of northwestern Europe. The shape of a twelfth-century B.C. Mycenaean dagger carved into one of the rocks of the later stages of Stonehenge underscores the connection between the Mediterranean and England. It remains uncertain, however, whether this commerce traveled over land and by river or through Gibraltar and into the Atlantic. The evidence of Greek culture indicates it went by sea. Greek epic mythology rests on great voyages: Odysseus' 10-year circuitously adventurous return from Troy to Ithaka, Jason and the Argonauts fetching the Golden Fleece from the farthest end of what we know as the Black Sea. Except for local coasting journeys, however, seafaring collapsed among the Greeks in their Dark Age, which began circa 1100 B.C.

The Phoenicians took over as the next great sailing nation of the Mediterranean. A Semitic people like the Hebrews, called Canaanites in the Old Testament, they had lived on the coastal plain below the mountains of Lebanon since at least the third millennium B.C., building ships and a maritime trading network. By 1000 B.C. the Phoenicians had constructed harbor towns, most famously Tyre and Sidon, and had filled the maritime trade void left by the Greeks.

The Phoenicians were not above working for hire. In the tenth century B.C. Hiram of Tyre organized a fleet for King Solomon of Israel to bring back a cargo of gold, precious stones, and other valuables from the realm of Ophir, which was probably located in southwestern Arabia. And, as we saw in chapter 5, the Phoenicians provided their sailing skill to the Nubian Dynasty of Egypt; possibly they traveled all the way to the New World. Unlike the Greeks, who trumpeted their exploits at sea in their epics, the Phoenicians were tight-lipped and close-mouthed about where they traded and how they got there. Secrecy propped up their trading network. Ignorance kept the competition at bay and leaves us wondering about the extent of their explorations.

It is certain that the Phoenicians ventured far enough west to set up a colony in Spain called Tarshish, which lay beyond the Strait of Gibraltar, on the Atlantic coast of Spain at the mouth of the Guadalquivir River. Jonah was on his way to that city when he ended up in the sea and then in the belly of the whale. Called by Yahweh to warn the people of Nineveh, a Mesopotamian city, about their sins, Jonah tried to head the other way as fast as he could go and boarded a ship bound for Tarshish. To the Hebrews, who were a land-loving people rather than seagoers, Tarshish was the edge of the earth. To the Phoenicians, it was just a stepping stone to what lay even farther beyond.

In circa 600 B.C. Pharaoh Necho II commissioned a Phoenician fleet to sail around Africa. The voyage, recounted in one terse paragraph by Herodotus, began in the Red Sea and took three years. The Phoenicians sailed all summer, then put in as the weather turned, sowed a crop, and resumed traveling after the harvest. In this seasonal way they traveled down the east coast of Africa, rounded the Cape of Good Hope, and came up the long western reach of the continent, heading back into the Mediterranean through the Pillars of Hercules, or the Strait of Gibraltar.

The sailors of Carthage, a colony established in the ninth century B.C. by the Phoenicians near modern Tunis, made the first known systematic explorations of the coasts of Europe and Africa. The Carthaginians wanted gold, and they traded cloth, pottery, and trinkets for it. As secretive as their Phoenician forefathers and as possessive—they blockaded the Strait of Gibraltar in about 500 B.C. and refused to let the ships of other nations through—the Carthaginians almost certainly reached the Canary Islands, the Azores, and the Madeiras. They certainly had the skill to cross the Atlantic and return, but whether they actually tried to do so is another matter.

Not until after the Romans made war on the Carthaginians and finally destroyed them in the Second Punic War (218–201 B.C.) did the Greeks make a habit of venturing into the Atlantic again. At least a few Greek sailors had been there before. About 630 B.C. a storm carried Colaeus of Samos beyond Gibraltar, where he made landfall at Tarshish and traded for silver. Pytheas of Massilia entered the Atlantic in about 300 B.C., when the Carthaginians were worried more about the Romans than about maintaining the blockade of Gibraltar. He and his crew rounded Spain, crossed the Bay of Biscay, sailed up through the Irish Sea and north of the Shetlands, followed the coast of Norway south, then headed east into the Baltic. On the way back, the Greeks retraced their course as far as Scotland, then came down the east coast of England through the North Sea and along the Channel and into the Bay of Biscay again. Pytheas covered some 8,000 miles and brought the Atlantic back within the Greek view of the world.

There is little to indicate that the Greeks knew of the New World. They did, however, have an understanding of the shape and size of the earth that was far more accurate than Columbus'. By the fifth century B.C., around the time of Plato, the idea of a spherical earth appeared in Greek thought. Aristotle (384–322 B.C.) argued for this model with the same reasoning found today in elementary school geography texts. For example, when ships sail over the horizon, the tops of their masts are the last part to disappear, an observation that shows the curvature of the earth. Eratosthenes (circa 275–194 B.C.), the director of the great library of Alexandria, calculated the circumference of the earth and came up with a figure that differs by only about 200 miles from our measurement. He understood the implications of a spherical world, saying that it would be possible to reach India by sailing west "if the width of the Atlantic sea did not prevent it." He also drew a map of the inhabited globe. His world included all of Europe (including Ireland and Britain), the Mediterranean shoreline, Asia as far as a line extending from the north shore of the Caspian Sea to the Bay of Bengal, Arabia and the Persian Gulf, the Red Sea and the Horn of Africa, and the Atlantic coast of Morocco. He figured, too, that this area took up only a corner of the earth's full extent and speculated about the existence of unknown worlds beyond the edge of the oceans.

Rome inherited and copied much of the Greek legacy. Still, landbound as the Romans largely were and hampered later by the experience of their empire's own collapse under the ceaseless hammering of the barbarians, the Roman world-view shrank. By the time of the Dark Ages the world was smaller and flatter in the human imagination. Europe was only just emerging from this backward slide when Columbus provisioned his three ships and set off from Spain toward the setting sun. He apparently knew less about what lay out there than had his Greek, Carthaginian, and Phoenician forebears. He was about to "discover" something they had already suspected—and some of them no doubt knew of.

Paper Boats

The written records that have come down to us from the time of the Mediterranean world's pyramid-building period contain little if any evidence of a New World beyond the far western sea we call the Atlantic. Commercial secrecy of the sort practiced by the Phoenicians and the Carthaginians may have been one reason. Or it could be that the people who made the trip never returned to tell about it. For there is evidence, both striking and perishable, that the trip was made.

One of the issues facing archaeologists investigating ancient maritime cultures is the fact that, before the advent of metal vessels in the nineteenth century, ships and their gear didn't last. Made of wood, cotton, oxhides, and similar materials, their physical remains soon decay under most climatic conditions. Boat-building techniques, however, remain. In traditional preindustrial cultures, boat builders construct their vessels in the same way generation after generation. A common type of boat-building technique, and the demonstration that such a vessel can actually cross the Atlantic from east to west, is the best evidence for the arrival in the New World of pyramid builders from the eastern Mediterranean region.

As we saw in chapter 5, both the Old World and the New have boats made of reeds tied in tight bundles. These vessels appear in carvings from the second and third millennium B.C. in Mesopotamia and Egypt, although they were probably used much earlier. Boats of the same design are used to this day by the so-called marsh Arabs of the Euphrates Delta. Similar boats ply Lake Chad in Central Africa and the coastal waters along the Mediterranean island of Sardinia. They are found too in Lake Titicaca, between Peru and Bolivia, along the northern Peruvian coast, on Easter Island, and, until the 1960s, at a number of locations in Mexico, including the eastern shore of the Sea of Cortez.

What makes this common artifact of the Old and New worlds even more fascinating is the association of the reed boat with the pyramids of Giza. In chapter 5 we discussed the Cheops boat, the large vessel excavated from a burial pit near the pyramid of Khufu. Although the Cheops boat is built from cedar wood, its lines are those of a reed vessel. Also, the Cheops boat lacks substantial ribbing, necessary for stability in a wooden vessel traveling in the open sea but quite unnecessary in a reed boat. The builder of the Cheops boat was attempting to imitate a reed ship in a longer-lasting material—wood. Presumably only this type of vessel was thought to have the ritual qualities necessary to ferry the departed pharaoh on his sky journey to immortality.

The experience of the Norwegian explorer and archaeologist Thor Heyerdahl shows just how deeply interwoven the Old World and New World reed-boat traditions are. It was one of those accidents that brings home something easily overlooked.

Heyerdahl made his name by sailing a balsa raft named *Kon-Tiki* from the coast of Peru westward into Polynesia as living proof of his theory that the South Pacific was settled not from Asia but from South America. In the late 1960s another transoceanic possibility caught Heyerdahl's fancy. Intrigued by the notion that the bearded Viracochas of the northern Andes were of European origin, he wanted to check the feasibility of the idea that sailors from the Mediterranean could have crossed the Atlantic in a reed boat and brought their culture with them. Heyerdahl isn't the kind to remain hanging around libraries, blowing dust off old books and drafting hypotheses. He goes out and does it. So he set about building himself a reed boat and demonstrating that it was capable of sailing across the Atlantic.

Ever conscious of context and publicity, Heyerdahl set about building a reed vessel at Giza, in the shadow of the Khufu Pyramid. Papyrus, the reed that the ancient Egyptians used for paper as well as boats, is now virtually extinct in Egypt, so Heyerdahl imported tons of the material from Lake Tana in Ethiopia. He also brought in two experienced traditional Buduma boat builders from Lake Chad. Their knowledge, combined with funerary drawings of papyrus vessels from the Old Kingdom, provided the design of a vessel constructed from tightly bound bundles of reeds. It was named the *Ra*, in honor of the sun god of the Egyptians.

Old Kingdom papyrus vessels have strikingly high, curved bows and sterns. The fishermen of Lake Chad cut their sterns off square, and they wanted to do the same to the *Ra*. Heyerdahl insisted that they follow the Egyptian design. There was nautical understanding in Heyerdahl's insistence. In a ship lacking a keel, as *Ra* did, highly placed buoyant material can prevent the vessel from capsizing in a strong gale or beneath a wave. But both Heyerdahl and his Buduma boat builders saw no purpose to the tight rope that, in the funerary drawings, ran from the end of the curving stern to the afterdeck. The stern looked so durable in its curve that the rope appeared to be an unnecessary add-on. So they left it off.

Not until the *Ra* was well out to sea did Heyerdahl and his six-man international crew understand the significance of the rope. They had set sail from Safi, Morocco, and quickly hit the same westward current that carried Columbus and his three little ships to the New World. The crew broke the heavy steering oars almost immediately in rough seas and continued to have trouble with them; nevertheless, the *Ra* performed admirably at first. Any seas the vessel shipped simply washed through the reed bundles, and its flexible design allowed it to undulate over the waves.

Then trouble came. Although the stern remained curved, the absence of the rope securing the afterdeck allowed the vessel to flex like a hinge. The ship buckled at the rear of the afterdeck, and the stern's elegant curve drooped into the water, allowing every following wave to break across the vessel. The dragging stern slowed *Ra* and made it impossible to steer in a straight line. The constant washing of the waves caused *Ra*'s wicker cabin to rub against the papyrus deck, severing the ropes that held the reed bundles together. The vessel lost so much papyrus that after a battering by a storm it was listing hard to starboard. At a distance of 2,662 nautical miles from Safi, about four fifths of the way along the planned course, Heyerdahl and his men abandoned *Ra*.

That first journey taught a couple of important lessons. For one, papyrus made for an excellent ocean-going boat. For another, drifting alone would carry the boat from Africa to the West Indies. All the trouble the *Ra* had with steering oars meant that the vessel more drifted than sailed—but that proved a sufficient method of travel from one continent to another.

Heyerdahl tried again, building *Ra II* and setting sail again from Safi 10 months after the *Ra* had been abandoned. To build the new vessel, he brought in Aymara Indians from Lake Titicaca. Curiously, the Aymara had closely preserved the Old World method of boat building for the sea. Since the waves on Lake Chad never approach the size of ocean swells, the Buduma saved themselves the trouble of building something unnecessarily overdesigned and squared off the sterns of their boats. The Aymara, though, had preserved the curved stern and bow of the old Egyptian and Mesopotamian design. Their boat consisted of three cigar-shaped bundles of reeds squeezed together by a spiral of ropes so tight that the smallest, center bundle disappeared from view. The bow and stern were turned upward, and two smaller bundles were added to widen the deck.

Ra II was smaller than *Ra*—not quite 40 feet long, compared to the *Ra*'s almost 50—and it had a rounder cross-section, with less cargo-carrying volume. Still, it proved eminently robust and seaworthy, even when laden with tons of supplies. *Ra II* stood up to bad storms, even to a merciless broadside pounding when yet another steering oar broke. It crossed the 3,270 nautical miles from Morocco to Barbados in the West Indies in 57 days.

Ra II again made the point that a reed vessel could cross the Atlantic. And it showed that the Aymara Indians of the New World had preserved a tradition of Old World boat building that exceeded their own lake-bound needs. They were constructing vessels designed not for Lake Titicaca but for the open sea. And whoever first brought them the prototype of that design and had taught them how to build it must certainly have crossed the Atlantic's blue water.

The Great Tradition of the Raft

Even as the reed boat is strong evidence for the arrival of pyramid builders from across the Atlantic, yet another style of ocean-going vessel provides evidence of the arrival of pyramid builders from East, Southeast, and South Asia.

The invading Spaniards of the early sixteenth century first met the people of Peru at sea, not on land. While scouting the Peruvian coast in A.D. 1527, Bartolomeo Ruiz, Pizarro's pilot, encountered a native raft tacking northward against the southbound current. This vessel was no insignificant affair. Carrying a crew of 20, the raft was ferrying a cargo of gold and silver ornaments, fancy clothing, jars, mirrors, and seashells that Ruiz estimated at some 40 tons. The vessel was built of balsa logs as thick as telephone poles that were lashed together and decked over with thinner canes. The superstructure, with hutlike cabins for the crew and cargo, remained dry even in a strong sea. Cotton sails every bit as good as the Spaniards' own propelled the raft.

The coastal mariners of Peru and Ecuador were not Incas but local peoples subjugated and ruled by the Andean highlanders. And they were highly skilled seamen, sailing their rafts up and down the coast and trading as they went. The rafts were so superior to European keeled vessels at approaching and landing on shallow beaches that until modern wharves were built, rafts remained the principal mode of transport along the Pacific coast of South America long after the conquest. Some of them were still sailing in the early twentieth century.

The word "raft" conjures up visions of those rickety, eminently sinkable contraptions boys build after they read *Huckleberry Finn* and decide to go off on a river adventure of their own. The sailing rafts of Peru and Ecuador were of another order altogether. Remarkably strong and light, the largest could carry 50 armed men and their horses, according to reports from the Spaniards. Because of their buoyancy and flow-through design, balsa rafts withstood storm seas readily and rarely broke up, even in the heaviest weather. The large square sail was hoisted up the bipod mast on a boom, and some of the rafts also ran up an extra foresail when the wind was favorable. And, though they lacked keel or rudder, South American balsa rafts could literally sail rings around Spanish ships.

Under full sail and traveling downwind, a Spanish vessel could over-take a balsa, but it was hampered badly when it came to sailing up-wind. The balsa raft was much more effective at moving against the wind, because of an ingenious mode of steering Europeans had not en-countered before.

When a vessel is trying to travel across the wind, the moving air pushing against it drives it downwind. This drift is called leeway. In modern sailing vessels, a deep heavy keel holds the vessel against the tendency to drift; also the helmsman maintains a position to counteract the drift. At the time of the conquest of Peru, the Spaniards had not completely figured this technology out. Their vessels could do little against leeway and moved poorly in a contrary wind.

The balsas of Ecuador and Peru lacked a keel, but they could move against the wind. They did it by compensating for leeway with long, thin, flat boards, called *guaras*, thrust down between the logs. By push-ing down and pulling up different boards in different locations, South American raft sailors steered their vessels with or against the wind as their course demanded. It was this combination of leeway boards and sails that gave the South American balsa raft its exceptional and char-acteristic maneuverability.

Rafts of log or bamboo that venture onto saltwater are found in many locations around the Pacific and along the Indian Ocean coasts of India and East Africa. Ocean-going rafts shaped like the South Ameri-can balsa rafts, in which the longest logs are placed in the center, were used in the Red Sea, the southeast of India, various islands in and around New Guinea and Australia, and in Vietnam, China, and Japan. Most distinctive is the combination of sails with leeway boards on a shaped raft. These are found in only a few locations, some of them sep-arated by great spans of open water: the Coromandel coast of India, the island of Java, northern Vietnam and southern China, and Taiwan in the Old World; and northwestern South America and the coast of Brazil in the New.

The similarity between the ocean-going raft vessels of East, Southeast, and South Asia and those of South America is so strong in detail after detail that it convinced the ever-scholarly and always-meticulous Joseph Needham that the connection could not be coincidental. He wrote, "[W]e would not hesitate to say that we believe the American sailing-rafts to be direct descendants of the Southeast Asian types through an influence mediated by trans-Pacific voyages over many centuries, voluntary or involuntary."

Needham makes an important point. It hardly seems likely that a chance visit by one wayward raft could have created a tradition of raft sailing as extensive and accomplished as the one the Spaniards discovered in Ecuador and Peru. Asian vessels probably appeared again and again, either because subsequent generations of mariners made a mistake at sea and found themselves transported unwillingly across the Pacific or because they chose to undertake the long voyage. And when they arrived on the American side of the Pacific, they imparted their knowledge of raft building to the people who were already there.

How far back into time the raft connection between Southeast Asia and northwestern South America reaches is unknown. Given the wide distribution of ocean-going rafts in the Old World, it may be the case that this boat-building tradition is older than either European planked boats or Chinese junks. According to documentary sources from China, ocean-going sailing rafts were in use there by no later than the fifth century B.C. and possibly as early as 2500 B.C. Thus the sailing raft with leeway boards may be contemporaneous with the reed vessels used in Egypt and Mesopotamia in the third millennium B.C.

Like the reed vessel, the sailing raft provides another connection between the pyramid builders of the Old World and those of the New. On the Asian side of the Pacific lies the immense cultural sphere of South, Southeast, and East Asia, with its sailing rafts and pyramids. And on the American side of the Pacific stands northern South America with its pyramids and sailing rafts. The evidence begs us to draw the link.

The Question of Intention

Did sailors from the Old World pyramid-building cultures come to the New World because they wished to or because some accident sent them in an unintended direction?

Accidental drift voyages have happened in historical times, and they no doubt occurred in prehistory as well. When the first Europeans reached the northwestern coast of North America, the area that runs from Oregon north through southeastern Alaska, they encountered a few misplaced Japanese fishermen kept as slaves by the Indians. Apparently the fishermen were caught in bad weather and carried far out to sea, where the Kuroshio Current drove their vessel across the North Pacific to North America. Similar mishaps have brought Asian sailors to North America any number of times in the past couple of centuries. No doubt many died before they completed this accidental crossing. But fishermen know how to catch fish, collect freshwater during squalls, and stay alive on the surface of the sea. History shows that some of them made it.

One such accidental voyage played a role in the birth of Japan as a modern nation. In the early 1850s a storm drove Nagahama Manjuro almost all the way to Hawaii, where he was picked up by an American vessel. Ashore, Manjuro was befriended by a clergyman who sent him to San Francisco, where he learned English. Making his way back to Japan soon after Admiral Perry arrived there, Manjuro found employment in the government of the shogun. Drawing on his knowledge of English and of American customs, Manjuro traded on his New World experience to become an adviser on foreign affairs.

Yet it does not seem overly likely that lost fishermen in times long gone would carry a culture of pyramid building with them. Pyramids are associated with royal and priestly elites. Common people provided labor, not expertise, to their building. Wayward fishermen might, once they cracked the language barrier, tell their new neighbors of the pyramidal wonders of home, but they would be unlikely to give them an idea of how to build such a monument. That knowledge would have to come from people who belonged to the elite, who were privy to its ways and customs.

A story from the history of ancient China tells of a voyage by just such elites that could have reached the New World. And it happened during the reign of a prodigious pyramid builder.

That was Chih-huang-ti, the first emperor of Q'in (220–210 B.C.), who built the tamped-earth pyramid and immense funerary center of Lishan described in chapter 2. Like the other Chinese emperors of his time, Chih-huang-ti didn't want to die. His royal ancestors looked endlessly for the holy sea islands known as Phêng-Lai, Fang-Chang, and Ying-Chou, where all the birds and beasts were white and the drugs to prevent death could be found. Obviously, Chih-huang-ti's ancestors had not yet discovered these mythical locations, because death claimed them and he had inherited the job of emperor. Chih-huang-ti continued the search where his predecessors left off. He put together a fleet, most likely of sailing rafts, captained by Hsü Fu. The vessels returned, Hsü Fu claimed, after coming close to three islands but being unable to reach them owing to contrary winds. Hsü Fu told the emperor that a divine guardian with the color of brass and the form of a dragon told him that if he wanted the drugs of immortality he must return with tradesmen of all kinds and virgins. Sensing a golden opportunity to keep death at bay, Chih-huang-ti organized an even larger fleet, one so immense that he complained of the expense. According to the account given by Ssuma Chhien, the emperor "set three thousand young men and girls at Hsü Fu's disposal, gave him (ample supplies of) the seeds of five grains, and artisans of every sort, after which (his fleet again) set sail. Hsü Fu (must have) found some calm and fertile plain, with broad forests and rich marshes, where he made himself king—at any rate, he never came back to China."

As for Chih-huang-ti, he died at Sha-chhiu on his way back to the capital near Xi'an.

This story may in fact be the account of an ancient voyage from China to the Americas in the third century B.C. Hsü Fu would have arrived with the people, agricultural resources, and elite knowledge needed to found a colony that could have passed on the idea of pyramid building to his new neighbors.

At first glance, though, there is something wrong with this picture. The tamped-earth pyramid of Lishan most closely resembles the fluted cone of La Venta. However, Hsü Fu would have arrived in the New World too late to have had any influence on that structure.

The significance of the Hsü Fu story is less the exact date than the matter-of-factness of the telling. The Chinese had clearly done this kind of major ocean expedition before. Tamped-earth pyramids were built by the Shang over a millennium earlier, and that same dynasty probably had access to sailing rafts. Yet, if they ventured upon the open sea, could they have known where they were going?

At least two centuries before Chih-huang-ti and Hsü Fu, the Chinese were familiar with the strong Kuroshio Current heading northeast. They called it Wei-Lü, a name that means "great drain" or "cosmic cloaca," or Wu-Chiao, which means "coming together and pouring away."

In addition, the sophisticated calendar systems and astronomy of China indicate a knowledge of celestial navigation. Chinese emperors and kings supported the development of these sciences, and sages in their employ kept meticulously accurate records of the heavens' many events. Texts dating to the second century B.C., not long after the legendary voyage of Hsü Fu, discuss the use of the stars for navigation, and the Chinese were the first to use a compass in the form of the lodestone spoon, a device that dates to at least 200 B.C. and possibly earlier than 300 B.C. By the first century A.D. the Chinese understood the earth to be a globe, and they were using a system of latitudinal and longitudinal coordinates—something the Europeans didn't get around to fully figuring out for another millennium and a half.

Still, if we use La Venta as the earliest marker for an East Asian influence on the pyramids of the New World, these dates all appear to be too late. Two considerations need to be kept in mind.

First of all, it takes little in the way of navigational smarts to hit a destination the size of a continent. As Pedro de Quiros, a late-sixteenth-century writer, said of the Spanish explorers, "[T]he most stupid can go in their embarcations . . . to seek a large country—since if they do not hit one part they will hit another." The issue in crossing either the Atlantic or the Pacific is less whether one will run into land than whether one will survive the several months the passage can require.

Second, the highly developed calendric and astronomical knowledge of the Chinese in the late centuries of the first millennium B.C. is very likely only the icing on the cake. Beneath it lay a richness of geographical knowledge passed down by oral tradition from master to master, raft captain to raft captain. Hsü Fu probably had more of an idea of where he was heading than he let on to Chih-huang-ti.

A contemporary example of the detailed geographic and navigational knowledge available in the ancient world comes from the Micronesians and Polynesians of the South Pacific. Although technologically less developed than the Chinese, these people piloted their large outrigger canoes across long reaches of ocean with stunning accuracy and without compass, clock, sextant, global positioning system receiver, or any map other than generations of knowledge memorized by master sailors. In the course of a millennium the Micronesians and Polynesians explored and settled islands scattered over 10 million square miles of ocean, journeying back and forth from place to place.

How they did it was demonstrated in 1976 by the voyage of the *Hokule'a,* an outrigger built in the manner of the ancient Hawaiian canoes. The purpose of the trip was to show that the round-trip voyages from Hawaii to Tahiti, a distance of 2,400 miles each way, celebrated in Hawaiian oral traditions were indeed based on historical reality. The builders of *Hokule'a* wanted to demonstrate that a canoe built and navigated in the old way could complete the journey. Since no Hawaiian sailor knew the ancient method of navigation without instruments,

Mau Piailug, a wayfinder from the Micronesian island of Satawal in the Caroline Islands, was recruited to pilot the vessel.

Piailug used his extensive knowledge of the rising and setting positions of the stars to guide the vessel east from its departure point on the island of Maui. When the wind shifted toward the southeast, he headed more to the south. In addition to watching the stars, Piailug paid attention to the moon and sun. Even when the sky was overcast, he kept the vessel on the correct heading by checking the direction, shape, and even taste of ocean swells and by watching for seamarks— water-places where, for example, sharks gathered or teeming birds announced the proximity of land. Fairy terns skimming over the sea told Piailug that the island of Mata'iva in the Tuamotus was near long before the low island appeared over the horizon on the thirty-second day of the trip. After a short layover, *Hokule'a* completed the journey to Tahiti, arriving 34 days after leaving Maui. The strong trade winds carried the canoe back to Hawaii even faster; only 22 days were required for the return voyage.

Compared to a continent, the island of Tahiti is very small indeed, yet *Hokule'a*'s navigator found it with striking accuracy, an accomplishment based on Piailug's mastery of the accumulated navigational knowledge of generations of Micronesian wayfinders. Surely, if Piailug could find his tiny bull's eye, so might a Chinese master of the Shang Period locate the vastly larger target of the Americas.

Setting a Course for the New World

For pyramid builders to cross the Atlantic or the Pacific to the New World and bring their religious culture of monumental architecture with them, they needed the same two necessities that Columbus did. One was a vessel sturdy enough to make the trip. The other was sufficient knowledge of navigation to keep them from sailing in circles or heading off in a wrong direction.

Clearly both of these requirements were met. In fact, many of the ancient mariners were Columbus' superior in both technology and know-how. Heyerdahl has demonstrated that a reed boat can cross the Atlantic safely and could thus have become part of the boat-building tradition of both South America and Mesoamerica. And the presence of the same type of ocean-going raft in both Asia and northern South America indicates that this vessel certainly crossed the Pacific, probably more than once, and more likely by intention than accident.

Clearly, too, ancient mariners reached the New World across both oceans. Those who came over the Atlantic had their greatest influence in the Andes. The Pacific travelers most affected Mesoamerica, contributing a number of the architectural features that give the pyramids of Teotihuacán and the Mayan realm their distinct flavor. Everywhere we look in ancient America, we see the tracks of these ancient voyagers.

But why did they come? For what reason did they leave hearth and home to venture upon the sea to so distant a place? What prospect—or what fear—drew them out to test the deep?

Eight

Fleeing the Angry Skies

CURIOSITY KILLED THE CAT, THE SAYING GOES, BUT IT HAS drawn many an explorer on, mountain climber up, and diver down. The desire to see what lies beyond is a powerful motivation, one that has figured into our natures since we first became human. Still, curiosity is a largely individual matter. It is not the kind of emotion that induces groups of people to cross an ocean to a new life in an unknown place. The people who brought their cultures and their pyramids to the New World were doing more than responding to the lure of curiosity over what lies on the far shore. Something drew them on—or pushed them out.

Bright, Shiny, and Missing

The search for precious metals drove many of the trading relationships of the ancient world. The Carthaginians, for example, had reasons other than the presence of a good harbor to establish a colony at

Tarshish in Spain. Up the Guadalquivir River lay some of the richest silver mines in Europe, and controlling the port gave the Carthaginians effective control of the mines' output. Tin, needed to alloy with copper to produce the much harder and more valuable bronze, drew ancient mariners to Cornwall, and gold's luster pushed seamen toward Africa, the Orient, and eventually the New World. More than any other resource, Columbus wanted to extract gold from his discovered land, and he was willing to kill and despoil in order to get it.

The most interesting body of archaeological evidence for possible Old World mining in the New World, however, pertains not to gold but to copper. Copper was one of the first metals used by humans. Later, when the method of alloying it with tin to make bronze was perfected, copper became an even more critical strategic material in the ancient world.

Except for a small amount of bronze made in Peru before Columbus, the New World never entered the Bronze Age. Copper was in use, though, for tools and ornaments, and North America offered a rich source of the metal, particularly in the area around the Great Lakes. There is no doubt that considerable mining occurred in the region. Sites like Isle Royale in Lake Superior and the Keweenaw Peninsula on Michigan's Upper Peninsula are dotted with shallow pits, typically 15 to 20 feet in diameter and 6 to 7 feet deep, that once served as copper mines. About 5,000 such mines have been identified to date. This mining may have begun as early as the seventh to fifth millennium B.C., with the major period of exploitation occurring through most of the third and second millennia, between 3000 and 1200 B.C.

For years archaeologists have assumed that the copper extracted from the Lake Superior mines went to make artifacts from the so-called Old Copper culture. In addition, popular writers of the Atlantis-was-here variety have proclaimed that up to 1 billion pounds of copper was mined in the New World, then carried off to the Old World during the second millennium B.C. James L. Guthrie recently gave the issue a meticulous analysis and came up with a reality that is less grandiose but still leaves one wondering what exactly was going on.

For all the obvious evidence of copper being taken from the Great Lakes, artifacts from the period are curiously uncommon. In fact, Old Copper tools and ornaments draw such a high price from collectors that unscrupulous dealers have been known to palm off as North American more abundant ancient Mexican, Peruvian, and Persian copper. All in all, only about 20,000 Old Copper culture objects are known to exist in museums and private collections. Put them all together and they probably weigh on the order of 10,000 pounds, obviously a number considerably smaller than the billion pounds of mined Great Lakes copper that some writers have claimed.

In addition, relatively few Old Copper artifacts have been found in the American Midwest, the area that surrounds the Great Lakes, nor were all the Old Copper artifacts found in other parts of North America made with Great Lakes metal. Other sources of copper exist on the continent—317 of them by one scholarly count—and Indians appear to have used the closest local source. An electron-probe microscopy study of 16 artifacts from Mexico, Wisconsin, Georgia, Missouri, Oklahoma, and Illinois identified only two spear points from Wisconsin and a pendant from Alabama as unequivocally fabricated with Great Lakes copper. The others looked more like Mexican metal, and a single piece from Oklahoma had a uniquely high aluminum content whose source could not be specified. Some of that 10,000 pounds of artifacts came from sources besides the Great Lakes.

And even by the most conservative estimate possible, much more than 10,000 pounds of copper was dug from the region. Given the volume of ore removed and the likely concentration of metal in the ore, somewhere between 3 million and 84 million pounds of copper were removed, with 20 million the most likely amount. That is considerably less than the 1 billion pounds that some nonscientific writers have claimed, but it also exceeds by a great deal the 10,000 pounds of known Old Copper artifacts.

So what happened to the missing copper? Might millions of pounds of Old Copper artifacts been melted down and reused—some of the recycled copper now being found in our pennies, for example? There is no evidence that this ever occurred, and for over a century Old Copper artifacts have been valuable collectors' items, a marketplace reality that makes recycling unlikely. Another possibility is that the missing copper simply has not been found. That is, the metal was made into tools and ornaments that were buried as part of funerary rituals and still lie underground. Curiously, though, less than 10 percent of known Old Copper artifacts have been uncovered in burials. Apparently these objects were not commonly buried, so it seems unlikely that some huge amount of it remains to be uncovered. And if large amounts of Old Copper artifacts had been buried, it also seems unlikely that, with all the digging into ancient Indian burial grounds archaeologists have done over the past century and a half, they would have found only .05 to .33 percent of the total. As imprecise a science as archaeology is, it is hardly so totally blind.

Another possibility is that the Indians were very poor miners who took copper off the surface, then kept digging bigger and bigger holes in the hope of finding more—which they never found. The hypothesis here is that the Indians did a gargantuan amount of digging to get a minuscule amount of copper. The trouble with this model is that it makes Indians not only the worst but also the stupidest miners ever to have stuck a spade in the earth. Who keeps digging a bigger and bigger hole when this hard work produces nothing more of value?

Finally, there is the possibility the popular writers have pointed to: The copper was hauled off for use in the Old World. The trade continued throughout the Bronze Age, then collapsed when iron replaced bronze and copper's strategic value dropped.

Certain similarities in the use of copper in the Old and New Worlds indicate that this idea is plausible. In the Mediterranean area, copper was often melted into an ingot shaped like a cured ox hide, called "reels" by archaeologists because they look like the home-made handles boys use to reel in kite string. Ingots of much the same shape have been found in North American burial mounds. It does seem curious that people separated by thousands of miles of water would have developed the same shape for transporting and storing metal, a shape that has no particular functional value. The reel-shaped ingot is one of those arbitrary similarities that suggests contact.

In addition, Old Copper socketed ax heads and gouges are similar to tools found in western Asia, and they strongly resemble implements from along the Volga River, in Russia. So-called half-socket hafting, which is common in Europe, is found among indigenous Americans only in the western Great Lakes region, near the major Lake Superior deposits.

Here and there, the Old World people who came to the New World for copper left small signs of themselves. One bit of evidence is the so-called Newberry inscription, found in 1896 under an uprooted tree in Michigan's Upper Peninsula along with three large clay statues. Although written in what is thought to be an American Indian language, the inscription uses a version of a syllabary that originated on Cyprus and was in wide use as a trading language from the sixth to third centuries B.C.

Even more telling from a scholarly point of view is the Peterborough stone, a major petroglyph site located about 100 miles northeast of Toronto, near the town of Peterborough in Ontario. The petroglyphs show a large ship drawn in a style common in Scandinavia, as well as a series of signs that the epigrapher Barry Fell identified as a Norse inscription written in an alphabet from North Africa. Fell, who joined brilliance with a tendency to leap to conclusions, dated the inscription to 1700 B.C.

David H. Kelley, a careful scholar and archaeologist who was involved in unraveling the complex code of Mayan hieroglyphics, disagrees with the date, suggesting 1000 to 700 B.C. instead, yet he agrees with Fell's basic linguistic analysis. The form of the petroglyphs argues for a Scandinavian origin and indicates that the words—which still defy transliteration, much less translation—are probably an early form of a Norse tongue. Even more fascinating, the characters used in the inscription come from an alphabet that Kelley names Proto-Tifinagh, one that is ancestral to the Libyan and Tifinagh alphabets, both of which are found in North Africa. In fact, Tifinagh remains in use to this day among the Tuareg, a fierce warrior people who have long lived in isolation deep in the Sahara.

But why, one wonders, were these early Norsemen writing their own tongue in a North African alphabet? The likely answer has to do with the remarkable ways cultures spread, change, and borrow. North Africa is part of the extensive Middle Eastern–Berber culture that spans land and sea from Mesopotamia to Morocco. Many of these peoples were accomplished navigators and traders, as were the Norse. Trade no doubt brought Berbers and Norse together, and in the course of that contact they learned something of each other's languages. But the Norsemen didn't have a written language. Proto-Tifinagh gave the unlettered Norse the ability not only to record their own language but to produce records intelligible to their Mediterranean trading partners. The Norse took the alphabet home to their fjords and then over the Atlantic to the New World, where some unknown artist carved the petroglyphs of Peterborough. In its time and way, Old Norse in Proto-Tifinagh is no stranger than modern Yiddish, a German dialect written in the Hebrew alphabet, or Maltese, the only Arabic tongue written in the Latin alphabet.

The missing copper and the Peterborough inscription support the concept of New World–Old World contact at least as early as the first or second millennium B.C. and possibly earlier. But the Norse were not pyramid builders, nor is the Great Lakes region known for its monumental architecture. To understand better why the pyramid builders came to the Americas, we have to make a journey that at first looks like an unlikely digression, one that links the pyramids of the Old and New worlds to the demise of China's Shang Dynasty, the growth rings of Irish bog oaks, and a zone of outer space just beyond our solar system.

Good Times, Bad Times, and Trees

As we saw in chapter 6, there is a tantalizing connection between the collapse of the Shang Dynasty in China and the rise of the Olmec civilization, its zenith represented by the building of the La Venta Pyramid on Mexico's Gulf coast. According to Chinese tradition, 250,000 people—presumably families still loyal to the collapsing dynasty and possibly at risk for their lives—fled eastward from China into the Pacific after the last Shang emperor, Chòu (also known as Zhou), was killed by his enemies in 1122 B.C. The anti-Shang forces were led by Wu Wang, founder of the Zhou Dynasty. Zhou kings ruled until circa 220 B.C., when they were overthrown by the first man to rule all of China: Chih-huang-ti, the first emperor of Q'in (220–210 B.C.). It was Chih-huang-ti who dispatched Hsü Fu to find the elixir of immortality on the holy islands in the sea to the east. Like the 250,000 Shang refugees before him, Hsü Fu and his 3,000 men and women never returned to China. In both cases the collapse of a Chinese dynasty is connected with the movement of a large number of people from China in the direction of the Americas, people who came from a culture that built pyramids and would have taken their pyramid-building ideas with them.

Among the ancient Chinese, an emperor ruled under a divine right known as the Mandate of Heaven. As long as he looked after his subjects, his power remained intact. But if he failed to place their well-being uppermost, then heaven removed his power and the emperor's overthrow was guaranteed. Such an event brought T'ang, the first Shang emperor, to the throne in about 1600 B.C. Chieh (also known as Jie), the last king of the preceding Xia Dynasty, was seen as corrupt, a charge later leveled against Chòu, the last of the Shang. Having lost the Mandate of Heaven, both Chieh and Chòu had to be overthrown and replaced.

In the Chinese world-view, human corruption manifested itself in the phenomena of the physical world. When the Mandate of Heaven was withdrawn, there was no mistaking what had happened. As Chieh lost his royal grip, the ancient records say that "the earth emitted yellow fog . . . the sun was dimmed . . . three suns appeared . . . frosts in July . . . the five cereals withered . . . therefore famine occurred." Misfortunes on earth mirrored calamities in heaven.

Since historians focus their scholarly energies on understanding the ins and outs, ups and downs, of human enterprise, the first conventional explanation for the collapse of one dynasty and its replacement by another is political. As a result it is easy to see heavenly events like the appearance of three suns as literary devices only. That is, the Chinese chronicler was indulging in a creative flight of fancy, inventing a cosmic event to veil happenings in the political realm; he relied on metaphorical invention rather than fact to explain political history.

Yet there is a growing body of evidence that the Chinese chronicler was recording actual events that brought an ancient pyramid-building society to its knees and may have resulted in large-scale emigrations across the Pacific to the New World. The chain of this evidence begins in Northern Ireland and leads in a loopily fascinating way back to those two waves of Chinese pyramid builders who crossed the Pacific to the Americas. Indeed, if we follow this evidence far enough, it even points to a surprisingly cosmic understanding of the creation of the pyramid in the first place.

As practically everyone learns in elementary school, trees add a single ring of wood for each year that they grow. Every annual ring of wood isn't the same, however. In good years, when sunshine and rainfall come in the right amounts, the tree puts on a wider ring than in tough years, when the rain is scant or the climate too cold or too hot. Leonardo da Vinci (A.D. 1452–1519) recognized this relationship, and he suggested that the pattern of ring widths could be used to reconstruct past weather patterns—a notion that, like many of Leonardo's proposals, was about 400 years ahead of its time.

Andrew Douglass, an astronomer based in Flagstaff, Arizona, picked up on the idea in the early twentieth century. Douglass was interested in changes in the sun's output of energy, and he began working with tree rings to determine whether solar energy peaked and fell in cycles. Douglass worked not only with living trees but also with ancient timbers retrieved from archaeological sites in the American Southwest. Meticulous work with these two sources allowed Douglass to create an accurate chronology going back to A.D. 701 and permitted the dating of ancient ruins in Arizona with a precision that archaeologists rarely enjoy. It also showed in what years rainfall was abundant and temperature was moderate and what years were dry and challenging.

Douglass had laid the foundation of what is now known as "dendrochronology," a deliciously academic word constructed from the Greek roots for "tree" and "time." By finding overlapping matching patterns in tree rings from different eras, dendrochronologists can develop time lines spanning thousands of years that not only accurately date events but also give a snapshot of what was happening climatically by year, decade, and century.

About 40 years after Douglass's original research, Martin Ross and his colleagues at the University of Arizona used the dendrochronological data to construct a chronology of the pueblo site known as Arroyo Hondo in New Mexico. The data showed that rainfall was abundant in the early part of the fourteenth century A.D., allowing the pueblo to grow to a hundred times its original size. Then the climate shifted, with long droughts broken only by brief wet spells. Crops must have failed again and again, for the pueblo's population dropped so precipitously that by 1345 the site was practically abandoned. Not until the 1370s did the Indians occupy the site again and begin a new phase of development.

The fascinating fact about this pattern was its curious synchronicity with events in other parts of the world. In 1347, the Black Death appeared, rapidly killing one third of Europe's population. Dendrochronological information from Tasmania, an island province of Australia, indicated that 1345 was one of the coldest years in the past three millennia. The same pattern was uncovered later in other tree-ring chronologies from areas as far apart as New Zealand and Scandinavia. Clearly some kind of major climatic upset had affected the earth in the mid-1340s, setting the stage for crop failures, hunger, and the spread of disease among weakened populations.

When Mike Baillie, a dendrochronologist at Queen's University in Belfast, Northern Ireland, began his work, scientists in the field held to the theory that volcanoes were responsible for such sudden, worldwide cold snaps when the sunlight was blotted out by dust. There were good, verifiable, historical examples of such events. When Tambora erupted in what is now Indonesia in 1815, the following summer was a miserable season to be a farmer. Unseasonable frosts in midsummer killed the crops in New England, and weather records from Ireland in the same season report an excessively wet and cloudy summer and autumn, with the average temperature markedly cooler than normal. The next summer wasn't much better.

The role of powerful volcanic eruptions in worldwide climate change was underscored by the research of the late Val LaMarche and Tom Harlan into bristlecone pines, high-altitude trees that grow in the White Mountains along the California-Nevada border and are, not incidentally, among the oldest living things on the planet. LaMarche and Harlan, both of the University of Arizona, found severe frost damage in the summer growth rings for A.D. 1884, 1912, and 1965, dates that correlated with the major eruptions of Krakatoa (1883), Katmai (1912), and Agung (1963).

A large volcanic blast causes a smaller version of the nuclear winter scenario, in which great clouds of dust vaulted into the atmosphere by bomb blasts cool the surface of the planet disastrously and take a terrible toll on plant and animal life. Volcanic explosions also send massive columns of ash into the air. When Tambora erupted, the ash reached 50 miles up and was spread around the globe by high-altitude winds. Within a year it had reached into the Northern Hemisphere and had begun to affect the worldwide climate. The high-altitude ash layer reflected sunlight back into space, so areas beneath it cooled. This not only dropped the temperatures on the surface but also disrupted the patterns of heating and cooling that drive weather cycles. Thus Ireland was both cold and wet, and summer frost killed the corn in New England.

This strong correlation between volcanoes and tree rings gave Mediterranean archaeologists and prehistorians an important handle on a critical event: the eruption of Thera, an island also known as Santorini that lies 75 miles from Crete. Today Thera is just a rocky shadow of its former self. During the second millennium B.C. the volcano erupted, collapsing most of the island into the sea, ending Minoan occupation of the city of Akrotiri, and dramatically affecting life throughout the eastern Mediterranean. That much the archaeologists knew. What they were unsure of was exactly when Thera blew its top.

Two dates were in contention. The later, and more popular, number came from Greenland, of all places. The ice that forms each year on Greenland's thick glaciers provides a climate record, something like tree rings. The ice also contains evidence of major volcanic eruptions. Chemicals in the ash and dust launched into the atmosphere react to form acid, mostly sulfuric acid, which later precipitates in ice or snow. Cores of ice taken from the Greenland glaciers covering the past six millennia of earth history showed nine major acid layers. One volcanic eruption happened in 1390 B.C., with an error range of 50 years either way. Most archaeologists asserted that this must be the date for the Thera eruption. The choice was comforting. It fit well with chronologies then in vogue for the second millennium B.C., particularly the ever-fluctuating history of Egypt.

There was, however, a dissenter: Val LaMarche. Working with his University of Arizona colleague Kathy Hirschboeck on the bristlecone dendrochronology, LaMarche documented a striking frost in 1627 B.C. The two authors suggested "the intriguing possibility of dating precisely the cataclysmic eruption on Santorini." In other words, Hirsch-boeck and LaMarche suggested pushing the Thera date back two and a half centuries, a date that worked major havoc on the finely constructed chronologies of Middle and New Kingdom Egypt.

By this time Baillie had constructed an Irish bog oak dendro-chronology spanning the period from 5000 B.C. to A.D. 1000. Intrigued by the Thera question, he went to his tree rings for a close look. The Irish data did indeed show a pattern of narrow rings around 1627 B.C. This meant that LaMarche and Hirschboeck's data applied to more than the White Mountains. But he noticed a couple of other things. First, the rings were so narrow in some of the trees that Baillie could barely mea-sure them. Conditions had obviously been not just bad but catastrophic. Second, the narrowest rings covered most of the 1620s. Instead of the distinct change lasting from one to three years that could be correlated with the Tambora eruption, for example, this period of pronouncedly poor growth spanned most of the decade. Either this was one amazing volcano that kept blowing its top with unimaginable violence for years or something else entirely was going on.

Then Baillie laid his dendrochronological data, which revealed sev-eral bands of powerful climatic disturbance indicated by very narrow rings, against the Greenland ice cores. A number of dates lined up, with the tree data falling well within the error ranges of the ice-core acid layers. Both the ice cores and the Irish bog oak rings pointed to major climatic disturbance in 210 B.C. ($\pm$ 30 years), 1120 B.C. ($\pm$ 50), 3150 B.C. ($\pm$ 90), and 4400 B.C. ($\pm$ 100). The correspondence grew even more fascinating when new data published in 1987 showed the exis-tence of yet another acid layer, this one in 1645 B.C. ($\pm$ 20). Use the margin of error for the ice-core data, and the overlap with the Irish bog oak dendrochronology's 1628–27 B.C. is obvious. Subsequent data from English and German trees also pointed to a major event centering on 1628 B.C., linking events on continental Europe, Ireland, western North America, and Greenland. Something very big affected no less than a major slice of the Northern Hemisphere at that long-ago time.

If you have been keeping track of all the archaeological dates dotting these pages, you realize that history has served up another major correlation: The narrowest tree rings of 1628 B.C. correspond to the end of the Xia Dynasty and the beginning of the Shang circa 1600 B.C. And, at the other end of the spectrum, the killing of the last Shang emperor in 1122 B.C. falls well within the Greenland acid layer dated to 1120 B.C. (± 50), the time when pyramid-building Shang refugees were fleeing into the Pacific. And the rise of Chih-huang-ti to be ruler of all China and the dispatching of Hsü Fu with his retinue of 3,000—followed soon thereafter by the rapid collapse of the short-lived Q'in Dynasty and its replacement by the Han Dynasty circa 206 B.C.—fall equally close to yet another band of extremely narrow tree rings Baillie found at 207 B.C.

There was no reason to doubt that a thick dust veil, with its attendant cooling, lay behind each of these events. The question was where the dust veil came from. Volcanoes were increasingly unlikely candidates; rarely do they erupt so violently for such long periods that the dust could cool the planet for a decade. The answer had to lie elsewhere. With their Mandate of Heaven, the Chinese pointed Baillie and the dendrochronologists to the sky. So did the dinosaurs, who had a sobering lesson to teach about the heavenly objects called comets.

T. rex and the Coherent Comets of Doom

The story has often been told of how the father-son scientist team of Luis and Walter Alvarez, both of the University of California at Berkeley, solved the problem of the sudden disappearance of the dinosaurs, including *Tyrannosaurus rex*, from the geological record. The rocks of the Cretaceous layer contain dinosaur fossils; the overlying, subsequent Tertiary strata contain no such remains. Between the two periods, a short span of time marked by a narrow band of clay called the K-T (for Cretaceous-Tertiary) boundary, the dinosaurs appear to have vanished into thin air some 65 million years ago. The Alvarezes discovered that the K-T clay contained an extraordinary amount of iridium, a rare element found in abundance only deep within the earth—from which it reaches the surface in volcanic flows—or within space rocks like comets and asteroids that date from the same extremely distant time as the earth's interior. Since no volcano of a size big enough to deposit so much iridium could be identified at the time corresponding to the K-T boundary, the Alvarezes argued that the element could be explained only by the impact of a very large comet or asteroid.

In 1990 the Alvarezes' scenario moved from bold proposal to sound idea with the discovery of an impact crater of the correct age at a place in the Mexican Yucatán called Chicxulub. The asteroid was several miles across, about the size and mass of Mount Everest, and it hit in an area of shallow water just off what was then the coastline. The explosion was immense. It equaled 10,000 times the combined current nuclear arsenal of all the earth's nations, and the blast carved out a crater 20 miles deep and more than 110 miles wide. The explosion itself and the earthquakes and tidal waves it set off killed everything for thousands of miles in every direction. Equally important, it raised an immense column of dust, one that was thousands of times larger than Tambora's. The dust spread across the upper layers of the atmosphere and blocked the sun for months if not years. The resulting cooling led to the sudden doom of most of the extant species of land animals. Nothing larger than a medium-sized dog survived the sudden calamitous chill of this cosmic winter.

A cometary impact could account for a dust-veil cooling that could last for years, such as the event that Baillie's data showed for the 1620s B.C. But another element was needed as well: periodicity. Chicxulub and the K-T extinction looked like a major-league, once-off catastrophe that happened long, long ago. It was an apparently singular, even unique event. The Greenland ice cores and dendrochronological data, however, agreed on five dates: 207 B.C., 1159 B.C., 1628 B.C., 3150 B.C., and 4400 B.C. (± 100). In addition, the Irish bog oak data pointed to dust veils at two further historical points, A.D. 536 and 2345 B.C. Whatever was happening to produce this pattern was obviously of a smaller order than Chicxulub—perhaps a less impressive comet, one big enough for its impact to affect a continent or a hemisphere but not sufficient to lead to mass extinctions. But even these smaller incidents kept happening, spaced at intervals from several hundred to more than a thousand years. The cause had to be something that repeated itself. Comet and asteroid impacts, it was thought, were unusual phenomena that occurred maybe once in every 100 million years, rogue elephants that swept their wild, destructive way through the solar system very rarely.

The periodicity needed to explain Baillie's repeated dates comes from the work of two astronomers based, like Baillie, in Northern Ireland. Victor Clube and Bill Napier overturned the random, rogue-elephant model of dangerous comets with a theory they call coherent catastrophism: The apparent chaos of destruction by comet has an underlying order that comes from the facts of astronomical life in our galactic neighborhood.

The farthest reach of the solar system, a frozen zone beyond the planet Pluto, contains perhaps as many comets as there are stars in the Milky Way galaxy. Called the Oort Cloud, this area includes objects of a great range of sizes, from about two thirds of a mile to over 185 miles across.

Astronomers thought the Oort Cloud was stable and fundamentally harmless to us until about 30 years ago. Then they discovered molecular clouds—cold, dark, massive nebulae that the solar system encounters in its movement through the Milky Way. Clube and Napier realized that whenever the solar system collides with a molecular cloud, the new gravitational force makes the Oort Cloud unstable. At the same time, the solar system and the Oort Cloud are subject to periodic tidal forces as they pass close to the spiral arms of the galaxy and the central galactic disk itself. The two forces—predictable tidal surges and unpredictable encounters with molecular clouds—pull comets out of their current orbits and send them in new directions. Some shoot away into the deeper reaches of outer space. But others plunge into our solar system, where they run the chance of hitting something, like the planet we live on.

Clube and Napier's model also builds on the newly understood behavior of comets once they enter the inner solar system. A comet isn't simply an immense chunk of ice, tar, and rock that comes down in one piece. Rather, comets, particularly large ones, break apart and create a trail of space-traveling objects like a cosmic stream of big and little bangs waiting to happen.

Astronomers had a chance to observe this phenomenon in close detail when the comet known technically as P/Shoemaker-Levy 9 collided with Jupiter less than 10 years ago. First pulled into an orbit around the giant planet, the comet broke apart because of gravitational forces. Six of the pieces were large, as much as a mile and a quarter across, and a dozen were of moderate size. Trailing them was a cloud of bits and pieces ranging from pickup-sized boulders to mere motes of dust. Then, over a seven-day period in July 1994, this stream of material dove into the Jovian atmosphere at speeds in excess of 130,000 miles per hour. The large fragments exploded into fireballs of hot gas that blew out into space like great plumes. For weeks afterward, dark scars left over from the explosions pocked Jupiter's usual salmon- and sand-colored atmosphere.

The fragmentation of P/Shoemaker-Levy 9 was not a unique event. Ancient astronomers in both Asia and Europe recorded the breakup of comets, with each piece taking on the characteristic head (or coma) and luminous tail. Nineteenth-century skywatchers observed Biela's comet split in late 1845 and early 1846 as its seven-year orbit passed close to Earth. A faintly visible piece divided off from the main part of the comet and quickly brightened, then the two comets that had been one disappeared into space. The two comet fragments were observed in September 1852. In 1865 the two fragments did not appear as they should have. On November 27, 1872, the day when Earth's orbit passed closest to Biela's, an immense meteor shower lit up the skies as an estimated 160,000 shooting stars passed through the sky in only six hours.

Called the Andromedid shower because it appeared in the portion of the sky where the constellation Andromeda is found, the fragments left by the continuing breakup of Biela and its companion lit up the sky spectacularly once again on November 27, 1885. There is still an Andromedid shower, though now it is much diminished. Only a fraction of the original number of fragments remains, and they are spread across the whole orbit Biela's comet once followed.

P/Shoemaker-Levy 9 also showed that comet fragments can detonate in the atmosphere. Such an explosion occurred over Tunguska, a remote region of forests and swamps in Russian Siberia, on the morning of June 30, 1908, when an immense fireball crossed the sky, then exploded with a force estimated at between 500 and 2,000 Hiroshima bombs. The blast left no major crater and not a single piece of meteoritic iron, yet it stripped and flattened trees over an area half the size of the state of Rhode Island. According to the best mathematical analysis to date, the explosion occurred three to five miles above the surface of the planet and sent out intensely destructive waves of fire and burning wind blasts.

The object that exploded very likely came from a comet. Regularly, Earth passes a stream of meteors called the Taurid shower—it appears in the region of the sky marked by Taurus, the constellation of the bull—that resulted from the fragmentation of a spent comet. This happens twice annually: once from April to June, and again from October to December. The June 30 explosion date underscores the likelihood that the Tunguska object was a fragment from the Taurid stream.

Tunguska and P/Shoemaker-Levy 9 exemplify the process that Clube and Napier place at the core of their hypothesis of coherent catastrophism. When a comet from the Oort Cloud tumbles into the inner solar system, it takes up a new path around the sun and fragments repeatedly, leaving a long, wide trail of orbiting debris as it speeds through space. Since the fragments keep breaking up, eventually the stream becomes nothing more than a stream of cosmic dust. Early on, though, when the fragments are large and the stream narrow, the comet poses its greatest threat to Earth. If Earth passes through such a young stream, the fragments can shower down onto the planet, causing explosions large, widespread, or both. At the same time, small particles fill the upper atmosphere like dust and add to the cooling effect of large amounts of debris injected into the atmosphere by explosions on or near the surface.

Meteor streams from disintegrating comets are something like cosmic Russian roulette. Earth passes through them year after year. Some years we dodge the bullet. In June 2002 an asteroid with a diameter between 50 and 120 yards, roughly the dimensions of a soccer field, missed Earth by just 75,000 miles and was detected only three days *after* that cosmic near miss. Now and again, though, all that speeding space rock, ice, and tar finds the target.

Clube and Napier figure it takes a comet 3 to 5 million years to travel from the Oort Cloud into the inner solar system. About every 100,000 years a giant, fragmenting comet enters a path that crosses Earth's orbit. After that, approximately once every millennium or so our planet's orbit directly crosses the debris stream trailing behind the comet. Depending on a number of variables, the danger would be greatest at one or two times of the year for a period of several hundred years. Some years would be quiet; in others the bombardment could last for hours, even days. Several years in succession might be singularly disastrous, with space debris actively bombarding the earth. Such periods can manifest themselves as well-marked events in the ice core and dendrochronological data. Periods of calm, about 500 to 1,000 years long, would intervene, then the cycle of catastrophe would begin again.

Right now, Clube and Napier suggest, we are in one such period of calm. It will end, though, and one day we will find ourselves looking up at the sky with fear in our eyes—as the people of 1628 B.C. must have done.

The Clube and Napier model adds two central points of fact to explain Baillie's dendrochronological data. One is the periodicity of the catastrophes. Space objects come in pulses or waves separated by long periods of time, just as the narrowest Irish bog oak rings and the acid layers in the Greenland ice cores do. And the meteor streams left by a disintegrating comet also explain why Baillie found not just one bad year of extremely narrow growth rings but clusters of them. Each year over a span of a decade or more, Earth encountered the same stream of flying objects and the planet went into cosmic chill. Then, when the orbital mechanics of our planet and the meteor stream carried Earth out of harm's way, the bombardment slowed or stopped, the dust settled, and the climate warmed again.

Ancient Encounters of the Cometary Kind

The next step in this investigation is to lay the pattern of tree-ring and acid-layer dates against the historical record and look for evidence of one of Clube and Napier's catastrophic swarms marking each event. The pattern that emerges is stunning. It tells us, too, what terrible times descended upon the world at those critical junctures when pyramid builders apparently emigrated from one area to another, even across the great oceans, and brought their cultural ideas with them.

A.D. 1178

On the evening of June 25, 1178, a group of monks at Canterbury, England, watched in horror as the crescent moon split in two and a torch of flame rose from it. Gervase, the monk who recorded the event, wrote that the body of the moon wavered and writhed "like a wounded snake." The flame and the writhing were repeated a dozen times, then the whole moon turned black.

Many years ago, the meteorite expert J. B. Hartung decided that Gervase had described not a vision rising from a monk's mind but the crash of an astronomical body into the moon. The torch of flame came either from a cloud of incandescent gas at the blast site or from sunlight reflected in dust rising from the crater. Dust spreading out over the surface of the satellite was also responsible for blackening the moon's face.

Research work completed since Hartung's original suggestion points to the crater known as Giordano Bruno as the likely scar left by the A.D. 1178 impact. The explosion that excavated the crater was so big—on the order of 100,000 megatons*—that it started the moon on a slow 50-foot wobble around its axis every three years.

The anniversary of the June 25 date of the lunar event lies close to the June 30 date of the Tunguska explosion, suggesting that what hit the moon was a large fragment from the Taurid meteor stream. In fact, A.D. 1178 was a year when the Taurid stream peaked.

Meanwhile back on Earth—the planet that had dodged the large bullet that hit the moon before the eyes of the Canterbury monks—various ominous occurrences were recorded. Large comets appeared throughout the late eleventh and into the twelfth century. Stars falling from the sky—that is, comets—were interpreted by European prelates as warning signs from God. They used these dramatic celestial visitors to justify mounting crusades to retake the Holy Land from the ungodly as a way of winning back the divine pleasure they feared was being withdrawn. On the other side of the world, Chinese astronomers noted a striking increase in the number of comets around A.D. 1150. According to their records, the number of these celestial objects was 10 times greater than normal.

At about the same time, according to the legends of New Zealand's Maoris, fire fell from the heavens and burned up the forests, killing off many of the large, flightless moa birds. A series of shallow impact structures, called the Tapanui Craters, date to circa A.D. 1200, and soot in geological samples from the same time period indicates the kinds of extensive fires the indigenous legends describe. At this same time, waves of immigration moved across Polynesia. For reasons unknown,

---

* A megaton equals 1 million tons of the explosive TNT. Currently the explosive potential of the world arsenal of nuclear weapons is estimated to equal 20,000 megatons.

whole peoples abandoned their old homes and moved to new abodes. Wars erupted, royal lines ended and new ones began, foreign customs and religious practices were introduced. On the western edge of South America the coastal civilizations that had built the Lambayeque and Túcume pyramids collapsed and were never rebuilt. Rather, a new civilization, the one we know as the Inca, arose high in the Andes sometime later. In Mexico the Aztecs migrated from the place they called Aztlán, which was probably located near modern Mazatlán on the Pacific coast, to the high-altitude Valley of Mexico. These uphill movements in both Mesoamerica and South America may have been attempts to escape tsunamis brought on by comet-fragment impacts. The Aztec obsession with human sacrifice could have arisen as a way of warding off the divine ill will that had brought down such tragedy.

On the other side of the Pacific in China, the weather was unusually severe in the second half of the twelfth century. In A.D. 1194 the Yellow River flooded so catastrophically that Kaifeng, the northern capital of the Song (Sung) Dynasty, was destroyed, and the mouth of the river moved nearly 200 miles south. The emperor having obviously lost the Mandate of Heaven in a big way, the Song Dynasty collapsed.

In the 1170s or 1180s the young Genghis Khan saw a sign in the sky—probably a comet—that he took as a portent of his mission to lead the Mongol hordes out of their homeland and across Asia. According to historical writings by the Persian chronicler Al Juvaini, the weather in Mongolia was so cold at the time that for a period of two generations apples would not grow.

From a purely human point of view, something major was happening in the second half of the twelfth century, yet on a cosmic scale these events hardly registered in the Greenland ice cores and the dendrochronological data. There appears to have been no major single impact, like the one Gervase and his monastic colleagues saw on the moon. Instead, the evidence fits a pattern of a swarm of smaller, Tunguska-sized objects exploding over land and in the sea, setting off widespread fires, leveling villages and forests, and setting up towering tsunamis.

A.D. 536

In the sixth century A.D. something much bigger happened. Even by the dismal standards of the European Dark Ages, the late 530s and early 540s were dark indeed. In Ireland, which had just become a Christian country, the grain crop failed twice, once in 536 and again in 538. Starvation depleted Ireland and England. In 542 disaster visited the eastern Mediterranean in the form of a plague that began in Egypt and made its killing way across Europe.

More than Europe and the Mediterranean were affected. Chinese chronicles from the same period tell of a widespread famine. Apparently whatever was affecting European farming was also wreaking havoc in East Asia. A combination of disease and famine weakened Teotihuacán and contributed to the city's decline. Although the Maya flourished in their Classical Period, which began circa 550, the decades just prior are curiously devoid of dated artworks or buildings.

Two accounts from the time describe a depopulated, ruined wasteland in the west of Great Britain. One of these accounts, a report by the Byzantine historian Procopius, tells of an island divided in half by a wall. One side was habitable, the other dangerous.

> For to the east of the wall there is salubrious air, changing with the seasons, being moderately warm in summer and cool in winter . . . but on the west side everything is the reverse of this, so that it is actually impossible for a man to survive there even a half-hour. . . . [T]he inhabitants say that if any man crosses the wall and goes to the other side, he dies straightaway, being quite unable to support the pestilential air of that region, and wild animals likewise which go there are instantly met and taken by death.

The other account comes from the *Confession* of Saint Patrick, an autobiographical document written in bad Latin by the missionary to Ireland toward the end of his life. A Briton by birth, Patrick had been enslaved by Irish raiders at the age of 16 and had been hauled off to Eire to tend animals. After six years Patrick escaped to the coast and found passage back to Britain on a ship. The sea journey took only 3 days, but for 28 days after the ship landed Patrick and his fellow travelers wandered through what he described as a desert, where there was no food to be had.

Between Patrick and Procopius, it appears that something untoward was going on in western Britain. What could have caused it?

One possibility is the release of gases trapped in deep-sea deposits several hundred yards under the ocean floor. The deposits contain three kinds of gas: methane, also known as natural gas; hydrogen sulfide, which smells like rotten eggs at low concentrations and is poisonous at high concentrations; and ammonia, which can also be poisonous. In ordinary times the gases remain trapped down below the water and the sediments, but they can be disturbed and allowed to break out by a movement of sufficient size in the earth's crust. Then they erupt as a cloud that can blow onshore and cause significant harm. The methane may catch fire, and the hydrogen sulfide and ammonia can asphyxiate and kill.

Such events are known to have happened at lakes. In 1986 hydrogen sulfide outgassing at Lake Nyos, in the African country of Cameroon, killed thousands of people and animals. The same outgassing may have happened from the sea at the time of the sixth-century wasteland. Describing a terrible earthquake that befell the ancient Syrian city of Antioch (now part of Turkey) in A.D. 526, John of Ephesus wrote that "moist dust bubbled up from the depths of the earth, and the sea gave off a great stench; and the dust could be seen bubbling up in the water as it threw up sea shells." The smell he describes certainly fits with the hydrogen sulfide of ocean outgassing.

Other writers describing the 526 earthquake in Antioch call attention to fire coming out of the sky like rain and fire shooting up from the earth. Some of that fire may have been the ignition of outgassed methane. And the rest of it may have come from meteors exploding in the sky and striking the earth. Those impacts could have set up the severe tectonic forces releasing buried sea gases, which then swept over the land, causing fires or—as happened in western Britain—poisoning all who breathed them in.

David Keys's recent *Catastrophe: An Investigation into the Origins of the Modern World* ascribes all the events surrounding 536 to a major volcanic eruption in Southeast Asia. Volcanoes, though, do not erupt long enough to account for the ongoing devastation of the 530s and 540s, all of which was apparently due to a dust veil. It is possible that there was unusual volcanic activity in the early sixth century, but such activity may have been triggered by impacts from outer space. The *Anglo-Saxon Chronicle,* one of the few documentary sources for England from this time, is noticeably silent about the decade from 534 to 544, except for two total eclipses of the sun, one in 538 and the other in 540. Curiously, even though there were eclipses of the sun in these years, they would not have appeared total in England. On both dates, according to the chronicle, the stars appeared after what should have been dawn and shone until nine in the morning. A partial eclipse could appear to be total and could draw out the stars usually hidden by daylight if the sky was already darkened by a high-atmosphere dust veil caused by a comet. In the same decade, chroniclers from the eastern Mediterranean told of what they described as a "dry fog," which lasted throughout 536 and 537 and sounds much like a dust veil. Tree-ring data also point to a deep chill. The years 535, 536, and 541 are extremely cold in the Sierra Nevada record; there was no summer in 536 in Fennoscandia (the region of Norway, Sweden, and Finland); and from 540 to 542 the Irish bog oaks show a profound decrease in growth. Ice-core data from the Andes indicate severe fluctuations in the South American climate as well. Everything points to a series of cometary impacts, large enough in scale and long enough in duration to raise a considerable dust veil into the high atmosphere and to set off earthquakes that allowed marine outgassing.

There is even one eyewitness account of a comet from this period, set down by Roger of Wendover: "In the year of grace 541, there appeared a comet in Gaul [France], so vast the whole sky seemed on fire. The same year there dropped real blood from the clouds . . . and a dreadful mortality ensued."

Recently I came across another fascinating piece of evidence from the eastern Mediterranean, one that corroborates Roger of Wendover's comet. Old coins fascinate me. When I was a child, a Roman coin discovered at a flea market led me into a longtime enthusiasm for ancient history and eventually to this book. Old coins also give us a look into history, for they may record, in imperishable metal, important events of the time.

The coin that caught my attention was minted at Antioch in ancient Syria during the sixteenth regal year (542–543) of the Byzantine emperor Justinian I, who reigned from 527 to 565. Two aspects of the coin are notable. One is the star appearing under the date. According to Edward Waddell, an expert on medieval Byzantine coins, the star device is unusual. The other is the date. The mint at Antioch produced coins through 539–540, the thirteenth year of Justinian's reign. No coins were minted in the fourteenth and fifteenth years, and only a few in the sixteenth. Then the mint was quiet again until the twentieth year (546–547), when it returned to business.

Antioch was no frontier outpost, and the cessation of the mint's activities for most of a decade points to a major crisis that led to suspension of business as usual. As we have seen, the so-called Justinian plague struck in 542, a catastrophe that followed closely on the heels of an invasion by the Persians. Byzantine coin makers associated these events with the star on the 542–543 coin. But is that a star, or is it rather a comet? Very likely it is the one that Roger of Wendover named as the source of bloody rain and mass death in Gaul.

207 B.C.

The Chinese were starving in this year, as they continued to do for three more years. Calamitous starvation meant that the Mandate of

Heaven had been withdrawn from the Q'in Dynasty, and the new Han emperors overthrew the old king and took over the throne. The ancient *Irish Annals* note a great die-off among cattle, the principal source of food and wealth among the Celts, at this very time. In 206 B.C., according to the Roman historian Livy, two suns appeared—probably both the real sun and a comet so bright it was visible in daytime—and a strange light illuminated the night skies during 204 B.C. Other historians record showers of stones falling frequently from the sky during 205 B.C. A plague of some sort beset Rome at this time, even as hostilities with the Carthaginians continued. State priests consulted the Sibylline books about this long string of misfortunes and took from them the lesson that they must bring to Rome the statue of Cybele, the *Magna Mater* or Great Mother, from its home in Asia Minor lest the city face destruction. Moving Cybele is significant not only because the event tells us how dire the Romans perceived their straits to be. Equally important is the form of the goddess: a large black meteorite* that had fallen from the sky into Mount Ida in Phrygia, a region of what is now Turkey, close to the site of Troy. The Romans received the meteorite with great pomp and circumstance and built a temple for it on the Palatine Hill that remained in active use until the fifth century A.D.

All these events correlate with climatological data from tree rings and Greenland ice cores. An acid layer in the Greenland ice dated to 210 B.C. ($\pm$ 30 years) indicates a dust veil. German oaks show reduced growth from 208 to 204 B.C. The year 206 B.C. was extremely cold, according to the bristlecone pines of the White Mountains. And in 202 B.C. the Irish oaks slowed their rate of growth to almost nothing. Shortly after the turn of the century it truly was nothing, as conditions became so severe that the oaks stopped growing at all.

---

* Technically, a *meteoroid* is any particle of matter in space, ranging from bits of dust to asteroids. A meteoroid that strikes Earth's atmosphere, becoming incandescent in the process, produces the phenomenon known as a *meteor,* or shooting star. In common parlance, however, the term "meteor" is generally used to refer to both the observed phenomena of shooting stars and to the solid meteoroid objects. A *meteorite* is the portion of a meteor or meteoroid that reaches Earth and collides with the surface.

1159 B.C.

In the twelfth century B.C. the tree-ring and ice-core data again match up. Greenland ice shows an extremely high level of acidity, and the trees display abnormal growth. Irish bog oaks offer the narrowest of narrow rings, evidence of a time of unspeakable cold. Curiously, oaks in Turkey grew very fast during this same period. Apparently the normally dry climate of that country became unusually wet, a kind of climatological flip side to what was happening in Ireland. In both places, the usual pattern was upset.

Upset characterizes cultural and political history at this time too. As we have already seen, the Mandate of Heaven was withdrawn from the Shang Dynasty as famine and chaos ruled, and a reputed quarter million people took refuge in the Pacific—possibly ending up in the New World, where they may have helped implant the pyramid as a cultural and religious icon. At the same time, the civilizations of the eastern Mediterranean came to a fiery end, beginning a dark age for the previously ascendant Greeks. Troy, whose defeat at Greek hands was told in exquisite hexameters by Homer, was destroyed, rebuilt, and destroyed again. The same fate befell almost every urban community of size in Greece and the Middle East outside Egypt and Mesopotamia between approximately 1200 and 1150 B.C., bringing the Bronze Age to an end throughout the region. No city in Anatolia in modern Turkey escaped destruction, and Cyprus's three principal cities, as well as Ugarit in what is now western Syria, were burned. The coast of the Levant, from Lebanon through what is now Israel, was hit heavily. All of the palaces of Late Helladic Greece, such as Mycenae, were destroyed. Although Egypt escaped the same kind of immolation that fell upon many of its neighbors, waves of armed refugees attempted to invade the country, so weakening its defenses that the New Kingdom soon came to an end. In terms of its effects on civilization, the end of the Mediterranean Bronze Age was a catastrophe greater than the combined wars of the twentieth century. In our own time the civilized nations picked themselves up and went on. Recovery after the Bronze Age required centuries.

Some of the oldest psalms in the Hebrew scriptures date to this period, and they tell in poetic form events that sound altogether like showers of meteors descending upon the earth. Consider, as an example, these lines from Psalm 18:

> *Then the earth quivered and quaked,*
> *the foundations of the mountains trembled . . .*
> *from his nostrils a smoke ascended,*
> *and from his mouth a fire that consumed*
> *(live embers were kindled at it). . . .*
> *Darkness he made a veil to surround him,*
> *his tent a watery darkness, dense cloud;*
> *before him a flash enkindled*
> *hail and fiery embers.*
> *Yahweh thundered from heaven,*
> *the Most High made his voice heard;*
> *he let his arrows fly and scattered them,*
> *launched the lightnings and routed them.*
> *The bed of the seas was revealed,*
> *the foundations of the world were laid bare.*

1628 B.C.

This was the date when tree-ring and ice-core data overlap with the Xia Dynasty's loss of the Mandate of Heaven; it first sent Baillie looking to the heavens for an explanation. Another event consistent with a dust veil from cometary impacts is evidenced in the Venus Tablets, a set of astronomical records kept by Babylonian astronomers during the reign of King Ammizaduga in the middle of the second millennium B.C. According to the tablets, the planet Venus disappeared from view for nine months and four days during the ninth year of Ammizaduga's tenure. This is a remarkable observation, for Venus is one of the brightest celestial objects, and the skies over Mesopotamia, with its desert climate, are more likely to be clear than cloudy. A thick dust veil, though, could indeed obscure the planet for a period of months. The problem is determining the exact date of the ninth year of Ammizaduga's reign, since corruptions in the Venus Tablets make exact dating difficult. The archaeoastronomer P. J. Huber studied the issue carefully and decided that the data in the tablets indicate four possible candidates for the beginning of Ammizaduga's time on the throne: 1701, 1645, 1637, or 1581 B.C. If the first year of his reign was indeed 1637 B.C., then Venus was obscured in 1628 B.C., the same year that the ice-core and tree-ring data reveal a major climatic event. In that case, the Babylonian astronomers were witnessing the very event recorded in the Greenland ice and Irish bog oaks farther north.

In Egypt the 1628 B.C. date falls within a time of turmoil, strife, and invasion commonly known as the Second Intermediate Period (1640–1532 B.C.), which separates the Middle Kingdom from the New Kingdom. A once-united Egypt was split up into a number of smaller fiefdoms. The Hyksos, foreign invaders who may have come from Asia, ruled the land in the north. Rulers based in and around Thebes controlled the middle of Egypt. In the southern part of Egypt, Nubian contenders were able to assert themselves against the people who had been their masters.

The catastrophe of 1628 B.C. may also explain the historical background of another major event in ancient history, one that had much to do with giving the modern world its form and content: the escape of the Hebrews from enslavement in Egypt.

For decades, biblical scholars have hotly debated the date of the Exodus. The Old Testament gives no name to the oppressing pharaoh. Working backward from known dates, some scholars have set the Hebrews' escape in the reign of Merneptah (1224–1214 B.C.); others, in that of his predecessor, Ramesses II (circa 1290–1224 B.C.); still others, approximately two centuries earlier, under the rule of Thutmose III (1479–1425 B.C.). All of these dates are essentially speculations made in

the face of a striking lack of hard evidence. It can just as easily be speculated that the Exodus occurred almost 200 years earlier than Thutmose III's reign, in 1628 B.C., at the very time Venus was obscured in
nearby Mesopotamia.

This suggestion, made by Mike Baillie, explains the plagues visited
by Yahweh upon Egypt and its pharaoh to convince them to let his
people go. Moses first demonstrated his god's power by turning the waters of the Nile into blood:

> He [Moses] raised his staff and in the sight of Pharaoh and his court he
> struck the waters of the river, and all the water of the river changed to
> blood. The fish in the river died, and the river smelled so foul that the
> Egyptians found it impossible to drink its water. Throughout the land of
> Egypt there was blood. . . . Meanwhile, all the Egyptians dug holes
> along the banks of the river in search of drinking water. . . . After Yah-
> weh had struck the river, seven days passed.

This excerpt from the unnamed biblical compiler of the book of Exodus is uncannily similar to the description by Roger of Wendover of apparently cometary events in A.D. 541: "The same year there dropped real
blood from the clouds . . . and a dreadful mortality ensued." A similar
image appears in the great Hindu epic the Mahabharata, which describes fireballs from the sky as the work of a horrific bird with one eye,
one wing, and one leg that hovered overhead and vomited blood. The
blood in the rain and the Nile could have arisen from iron-rich dust
thrown up in an impact blast or atmospheric explosion, then mixed
with water vapor and precipitating as thick, red rain. In the case of the
Nile, the bloody rain would have fallen in the East African highlands
where the river's two branches begin, then traveled downstream. That
would explain why groundwater in Egypt, which the people reached
by digging shallow wells along the riverbank, was not discolored and
polluted. And it would explain why the effect lasted for only seven

days. Once the flood of red water passed, the river would have returned to its normal color.

Then there was a plague that killed all the Egyptian livestock, an epidemic of boils on men and women—possibly caused by chemically reactive particulate fallout that "spread like fine dust over the whole land of Egypt"—and a rain of hailstones, possibly the result of unseasonable cold: "The hail fell, and lightning flashing in the midst of it, a greater storm of hail than had ever been known in Egypt. . . . The hail struck down everything in the fields, and it shattered every tree in the fields, man and beast." The plague of darkness sounds too like dust raised by a nearby impact: "Then Yahweh said to Moses, 'Stretch out your hand toward heaven, and let darkness, darkness so thick that it can be felt, cover the land of Egypt.' . . . [F]or three days there was deep darkness over the whole land of Egypt. No one could see anyone else or move about for three days." Moses called the darkness down from the sky. And the fact that it could be felt sounds like a long-remembered detail about air so thick with dust that it brushed the skin less like a wind than a thick, blinding blanket.

Taken as a metaphor for the extent of the calamity, the death of Egypt's first-born, the plague that finally convinced the pharaoh to release the people who claimed responsibility for all these events, underscores the terrible toll the catastrophe took on humans and animals. And the parting of the Red Sea, coupled with the drowning of the pharaoh's army when the waters rushed back in, depicts what happens when tsunamis are set off by a cometary impact. First the water pulls back—a phenomenon well described in Psalm 18's line "The bed of the seas was revealed"—then returns in a terrible rush that sweeps everything living before it.

2345 B.C.

In a period spanning five centuries, from 2500 to 2000 B.C., several major civilizations underwent sudden, unexplained declines: Early Bronze

Age societies in the Levant, Anatolia, and Greece; the Old Kingdom in Egypt; the Akkadian Empire in Mesopotamia; the Helmand civilization in Afghanistan; and the Harappan civilization in the Indus Valley of modern-day Pakistan. Much like the collapse marking the end of the Bronze Age, a dark age followed. Take Egypt as an example. The few pyramids built during the Middle Kingdom, which rose from the remains of the Old Kingdom, are but pale shadows of the monuments at Giza. Their engineering is sloppy, the workmanship poor, the art hackneyed. Egyptian culture had suffered a mighty setback, almost as if it had been the victim of a frontal lobotomy. Whatever events caused Egypt such damage, they were mighty indeed.

The Irish bog oak chronologies show a period of narrow rings beginning in 2354 B.C. and becoming narrowest in 2345 B.C. A similar change in growth pattern also appears in tree rings from England's Lancashire. There is suggestive evidence that Ireland's Lough Neagh, one of Europe's largest freshwater lakes, flooded suddenly at this time, while the water level in other lakes in Europe and Africa went down. Floods are a key feature of the reign of King Yao, the earliest historical figure in China, who is reputed to have taken the throne in 2357 B.C. Once-fertile areas like the edge of the Sahara, the plain around the Dead Sea, and northern India dried into deserts. Africa below the Sahara became wetter, absorbing migrants who moved south out of the new deserts. North America likewise became both wetter and cooler, while Mexico became distinctly more arid, as did the southern reaches of Europe. There is evidence too that currents in all the major oceans changed, probably in response to shifts in the atmosphere. The surface of the earth itself was moving around a great deal at this time. Every continent was affected by various patterns of uplift, subsidence, tilt, downwarping, earthquakes, and shifting riverbeds.

All these events match up in time to a sudden, significant cooling of the planet on the order of 4 to almost 6 degrees Fahrenheit. Before this change, sea level had been rising, as glaciers and polar ice caps melted and added their melt waters to rivers and oceans. Then the sea stopped rising, apparently as the arctic chilled and more and more water turned back into ice. The increasing glacial burden added to the cooling effect by reflecting sunlight into space. And, because it brought extra weight to bear on the crust of the planet, the sudden glaciation may have been the cause of the earthquakes, lake level changes, uplifts, and other geological events of the time. The cooling also explains the climatic changes. The band where air from the tropics flows toward the pole, called the intertropical discontinuity, shifted farther south, altering the patterns of winds that carry rainstorms. As a result of the cooling and the change in wind directions, dry areas became wet and wet areas became dry.

The only explanation for a sudden cooling is some equally sudden causal event, one that worked its effects across the whole globe. The Hekla 4 volcano on Iceland did erupt at this time, but one wonders: Could this single volcano have had such global effect? Or was it but one more geological result of the impact of meteors and comet fragments?

The latter possibility is supported by the recent discovery of a two-mile-wide meteoritic crater in the Al 'Amarah region of southern Iraq, north of the confluence of the Tigris and Euphrates rivers. First identified on satellite images by Dr. Sharad Master, a geologist at the University of Witwatersrand in Johannesburg, South Africa, the crater occurs in geologically young sediments and may date to the circa 2400–2300 B.C. period. More research will be required to substantiate this date. According to Dr. Benny Peiser of John Moores University, Liverpool, craters dating to the same time period have been found in Argentina. All of this evidence fits with a bombardment of meteors and comet fragments during the second half of the third millennium B.C.

3150 B.C.

At the long remove of more than five millennia, it becomes more difficult to correlate the overlap between the Irish bog oak tree rings and the Greenland ice cores with archaeological evidence, simply because that evidence is scanty. Depending on the method used, this particular event is variously dated to somewhere between 3195 and 3150 B.C. Yet there are bits of evidence that make one wonder.

One is the recent discovery of a meteorite associated with the death of Huangdi, also called the Yellow Emperor and reputed to be China's earliest ancestor. Huangdi—the word means "dread lord," and it became the standard Chinese public name for the emperor—is a founding hero along the mythological lines of Israel's Moses or Egypt's Scorpion King. His accomplishments are so many and munificent that he is almost certainly a composite built from several historical figures. Chinese legend credits Huangdi with inventing the cart and the boat, and his recorded conversations with the physician Qi Bo formed the basis of the first Chinese medical text. Huangdi's wife, Lei Zu, taught the Chinese how to weave silk from the cocoons of silkworms, and his minister Can Jie invented the original Chinese characters. Huangdi ruled until he was 110, the story continues. Then a dragon fetched him to heaven at a time when cataclysmic events, such as the destruction of Huangling town by nine other dragons, shattered the land and put an end to the beneficence of the first emperor's reign.

Dragons, as we shall see soon in more detail, are associated with sky events, particularly comets. Excavating near the mausoleum where Huangdi reputedly was buried, archaeologists uncovered a meteorite dating to approximately 3000 B.C., tantalizingly close to the 3150 B.C. dendrochronological date. Apparently the meteorite crashed to earth on top of the very mountain where Huangdi was buried. It is tempting to link the legendary death of Huangdi, the 3150 B.C. event, and the meteorite associated with Huangdi's burial place and create a scenario of an early civilization brought to a cataclysmic close by celestial events. The fly in this ointment is the traditional dating of Huangdi's reign, which is said to have run from 2697 to 2597 B.C., approximately 550 years too late. However, Huangdi's dates are based on calendrical extrapolations and are as much the product of legend as he is. Chinese archaeologists are far less precise about Huangdi's dates, placing the civilization over which he ruled within a span of time reaching from the second half of the fourth millennium into the first half of the third millennium B.C. It may well be that the story of his rise, rule, and demise chronicles the development and unexpected death of the first flowering of Chinese civilization, around 3150 B.C.

The dating is more certain in another line of evidence: the 1991 discovery of the Iceman, affectionately known as Ötzi (after the site of his discovery in the Ötztal Alps), a frozen male human discovered in a mountain pass at over 10,000 feet on the border between Italy and Austria. Remarkably well preserved in a frozen state, the body has been dated to circa 3300–3200 B.C. At the time of his death, the Iceman was carrying a copper-bladed ax, bow and arrows, and a flint dagger and was wearing shoes and clothes fabricated from leather, fur, and grass. About eight hours before he died, the Iceman had eaten his last meal, which consisted of unleavened bread made of einkorn wheat, some as yet undetermined plant, and a bit of meat. Based on the presence of pollen from the European hop hornbeam tree in the Iceman's stomach, he apparently died when the tree was in bloom between March and June—curiously, during the very season when the Taurid meteor shower lights the skies. But what is most fascinating is how the Iceman died—from an arrow wound. The missile entered his left chest from below, tore through various nerves and blood vessels and paralyzed the left arm, then shattered the left shoulder blade before lodging under the shoulder joint. The wound caused massive internal bleeding and led to a painful, protracted death within a few hours. So how did the Iceman get so high up in the mountains? Surely he could not have scrambled uphill after receiving such a severe wound. Unless someone else carried him, he must have been shot near where he died. Was he crossing the mountains with friends when things turned ugly and a fight ended in death? Could he have gone into the mountains for other reasons, perhaps to be held down, shot through the chest, and left to die as a sacrificial victim, whether willing or unwilling? Perhaps, in a grisly ritual similar to one attributed to the Celts millennia later, the wounded Iceman's agonizing death was observed by his comrades as a way of divining the future during a time of crisis. The Iceman may have uttered prophecies as he expired, and his body was then left in the mountains as an offering. Or perhaps the Iceman was shot during a skirmish between neighboring tribes. Was his a time of social unrest brought on by disturbing and dangerous events in the skies, when one tribe or people tried to take advantage of the situation and attack another?

The possibility of armed conflict high in the mountains at a time of great cultural distress instigated by dramatic celestial events is underscored by a fascinating coincidence: The end of the fourth millennium marks the first known phase of pyramid building. Very early pyramids rose at Aspero in Peru at this time, with construction activity peaking right around 3150 B.C. Curiously, too, the original White Temple of Uruk was built in Mesopotamia at just about the same period. A pyramid-like structure in the Inner Mongolia Autonomous Region in northern China dates from approximately this time, and may have astrological and astronomical associations. The pre-Celtic inhabitants of Ireland constructed Brugh na Bóinne during these years, and the first phase of Stonehenge rose as well. The Egyptians, who would soon be united under the ambitious Menes, began erecting burial mounds over the mastabas in which they buried their dead, laying the cultural foundation for what would become the great Giza pyramids of the Fourth Dynasty a few centuries later. The Maya, who were not yet building pyramids but would be in later centuries, began the dating of their calendar to a time between August 11 and 13, 3114 B.C., a point they called the Birth of Venus.

There is more to this apparent coincidence than coincidence. For one thing, the building of the Aspero pyramids occurred at a time of pronounced climatic change in Peru. A warm, wet, tropical climate along the coast became colder, drier, and less tropical. During this very period, from 3500 to 3000 B.C., the asteroid now known as Olijato had repeated close encounters with Earth. Clube and Napier think that Olijato resulted from the breakup of a larger comet about 4,000 years earlier. If that is the case, then other fragments traveling on roughly the same orbit as Olijato's may have actually hit Earth rather than passing harmlessly close by. Those frighteningly cataclysmic collisions may well have been the spur that led the ancient Peruvians to build their temple mounds, the Sumerians to erect the White Temple, the ancient Chinese to reach to the skies on stone platforms, the Irish to construct Brugh na Bóinne, the Britons to raise Stonehenge, and the Egyptians to heap tumuli up over their dead.

Were pyramids an independent invention hit upon by many different cultures aimed at addressing the same celestial phenomena? This might seem to be the case. However, as we will explore further in the next chapter, all of the pyramid-building cultures appear to share traditions and roots in a very ancient, long-lost, and common culture that itself may have associated pyramids with the natural catastrophes caused by falling space objects. As a result of cultural exchange between the continents that occurred well before such contact has been thought possible, pyramids had become a traditional way of addressing and appeasing the skies.

4400 B.C.

Pushing well into conventional prehistory, we are hard-pressed to correlate cultural, physical, and biological evidence over 6,000 years ago. However, I would like to point out three aspects of the circa 4400 B.C. event, give or take a century or two, recorded in the tree-ring and ice-core data.

First, the 4400 B.C. date is just slightly later than my upper, or most recent, estimate for the age of the original portions of the Great Sphinx in Egypt, as discussed in chapter 1. Is this significant? Is it possible that the circa 4400 B.C. event brought to a close the "Sphinx Age" civilization of the early builders of the Great Sphinx and related structures? We don't currently have sufficient data to judge, but the correlation is tantalizing.

Second, as discussed by John Anthony West in his book *Serpent in the Sky*, there is evidence to suggest that the ancient Egyptian calendar was established circa 4240 B.C. Perhaps the Egyptians began their chronology from the time of a traumatic event, the same one recorded at this period in the dendrochronological and ice-core data.

Third, what may be additional evidence comes from a hypothesis made by Stephen Blaha, a particle physicist and computer scientist with an interest in ancient Egypt. Blaha argues that the famous ankh hieroglyph was taken from the appearance of a comet in the heavens over predynastic Egypt during the period between 8000 and 4000 B.C. If Blaha is right, the comet memorialized in the ankh may have been the cause of the big chill of 4400 B.C.

Colors, Dragons, and the Bull in the Stars

Colliding comets and pyramids have something to do with one another. If we dig more deeply into the mythological associations surrounding pyramids, it becomes even more apparent that these great monuments, in Old World and New World alike, owe their genesis to those times when the sky reached down to touch the earth with its fire. Somewhere, a long time ago, in a now-lost culture, pyramids were built as a response to the dangerous skies. From that single point, the conceptual association of pyramid and comet spread out across the earth in culture after culture.

The mythological associations of comets and pyramids that suggest this common origin begin with the color white. White runs like a theme through a number of the earliest pyramids. There is, of course, the White Temple of Uruk. Newgrange at Ireland's Brugh na Bóinne was originally faced with white glowing quartz. Silbury Hill in England was as white as the chalk it was built from. In addition, the monument is thought to be sacred to the god the Celts knew as Lugh, the god of light whose name springs from the same Indo-European root as Latin *lux* and German *Licht*, both of which mean "light." The Great

Pyramid of Khufu, encased in its original white limestone, had the gleam and shine of a heavenly body.

Duncan Steel, an astronomer who has looked hard at the cultural influence of comets on Earth, is of the opinion that the color white is intended to be a heavenly association and that it explains the uniquely battered profile of the Giza pyramids. The key is a phenomenon called the zodiacal light, a diffuse sky glow caused by dust grains in space. The zodiacal light stretches above the horizon more than halfway to the zenith in a triangular shape and is best seen in tropical latitudes after sunset and before dawn. If a large comet is breaking up close to Earth's orbit, the cloud of space dust becomes thicker and heavier, and the zodiacal light grows into a luminous path across the sky. In fact, it would look something like the river along which the sun god Ra navigated his solar barque. At the end of the river of light would appear the pyramid-shaped body of the main zodiacal light, which the dead pharaoh would have had to climb to begin his own journey across the sky. Thus the pyramids of Giza, in both color and form, re-created on Earth the eternal realm of the sky—a sky shaped, in both color and form, by the close passage and breakup of a comet.

The Serpent of Many Colors

Knowing nothing of orbital mechanics or the Oort Cloud, the ancient and medieval Chinese described passing comets as dragons wrestling in pools of water. Here is a description of a comet recorded in the late thirteenth century A.D.: "[A]ll of a sudden there were two dragons which twisted around each other and, fighting, both fell into the lake. . . . In a short space of time a heavy wind came riding on the water which reached a height of more than ten feet. Then there fell from the sky more than ten fire balls, having the size of houses of ten divisions." Dragons fly, as do comets. And they kill with their fiery breath, as do comets.

The identification of comets with dragons and water extended far beyond China. The Hebrew prophet Isaiah (circa 750 B.C.) described his god as triumphant over this terrible power:

> *That day, Yahweh will punish,*
> *with his hard sword, massive and strong*
> *Leviathan the fleeing serpent,*
> *Leviathan the twisting serpent:*
> *he will kill the sea dragon.*

In the Christian pantheon of saints, Saint Michael fought Satan in the form of a dragon. One of the names for Satan is Lucifer, which in Latin means "bringer of light." The light in his name could well be the zodiacal light that brightens during a cometary interlude. Curiously, the cult of Saint Michael flourished in the middle of the sixth century A.D., when the tree-ring data point to a run-in with space rock and ice.

Moses played a role similar to Saint Michael's, but with an interesting twist. When Moses first encountered Yahweh, he needed convincing that the Egyptians would listen to him. His god granted him the power of miracles: "Yahweh asked him, 'What is that in your hand?' 'A staff,' Moses said. 'Throw it on the ground,' said Yahweh. So Moses threw his staff on the ground—it turned into a serpent and he drew back from it. 'Put your hand out and catch it by the tail,' Yahweh said to him. And he put his hand out and caught it, and in his hand the serpent turned into a staff."

Convinced now that his powers of persuasion were up to the task, Moses approached the pharaoh and displayed his abilities by turning his staff back into a snake. He and his brother Aaron threw their staffs upon the ground, and the staffs became serpents. According to the book of Exodus, the Egyptian court magicians pulled off exactly the same transformation, but Moses' and Aaron's serpents swallowed the Egyptian snakes, demonstrating the superior power of their god.

In Hebrew a comet is known as *kokbade-shabbit*, or "rod star," because of its tail. This suggests that there is more to the story of Moses' prowess than a simple magic trick or a god capable of shape shifting. The rod connects the snake to the comet-dragon of Chinese lore. Moses demonstrates that his god is the cause of the catastrophe falling on Egypt from the skies and that Yahweh is using this great power as a tool to rescue his chosen people. Saint Michael defeats the power of the comet; Moses harnesses it to Yahweh's purpose.

This connection apparently lasted for centuries. The Bat Creek stone, discussed in chapter 5, referred to the Jewish revolutionaries who fought against Rome in the first and second centuries A.D. as "Comet (= Messiah) of the Jews." One comet had freed the Hebrews from the Egyptians; now another would release them from the Romans.

The connection between a great serpent and a comet appears too in the Egyptian story "The Shipwrecked Sailor," which was written during the Twelfth Dynasty (1991–1783 B.C.). As we discussed in chapter 5, this narrative tells of a bearded, bejeweled serpent that befriends and enriches a sailor cast away on an unknown island. The serpent tells the sailor how he himself came to be on the island: "I used to be . . . with my brethren, my children among them; we totaled seventy-three serpents, children together with brethren. . . . Then a star fell and these [serpents] went forth in the flame it produced. It chanced that I was not with them when they were burned."

This story connects the serpent with fire in the sky, and it may even record in poetic terms the observed breakup of a comet. The brethren, or full-sized serpents, would represent the larger fragments, while the children, or smaller serpents, would be the lesser bits and pieces. Each perished in the flame of its own descent, like the fireball that rose from the Tunguska blast.

Another aspect of this story is explained by the effects of a passing comet on the atmosphere. The serpent in "The Shipwrecked Sailor" is radiantly colored with lapis lazuli and other precious gems. As we discussed in chapter 5, this story appears to spring from the same ancient mythological root as the stories of Quetzalcoatl, the brilliantly feathered serpent of Mesoamerica and a god associated with many of the pyramids of that region. Interesting enough on its own, but why all the color in the Egyptian snake and the Mesoamerican god?

The answer may lie in the display a comet would make when it passed through the upper atmospheric layer called the magnetosphere. As the name implies, the magnetosphere is dominated by Earth's magnetic field, so that it catches and holds charged particles. A passing comet would trail an astronomical abundance of charged particles, turning the sky into a purple or green dome streaked with streams of color that burst forth like the most brilliant aurora borealis raised to the power of 10. The mythic image of Quetzalcoatl sailing toward the sunrise on a raft of serpents combines all these images—the water, the dragon-serpents, the brilliant flame-shaped colors of his cloak, all moving toward the east, the source of the zodiacal light before dawn. This mixture of cosmic fear and awe may contain the origin of the pyramid.

Fighting the Bull of the Stars

Yet another mythological stepping-stone on the path of fear and awe leads us even closer to the beginning of the great monuments. Many words ago, in chapter 1, we noted the curious fact that the bones of a bull were found in a sarcophagus in the Khafre Pyramid. No doubt the religious significance of the bull springs in part from the ancient religion of Nabta Playa, where cattle were sacrificed and interred, perhaps to revere them as the source of life for a herding people. Still, there is more to this than an ancient inheritance from pastoralists.

The bull's presence at Giza is hardly unique; the ancient world was awash in depictions of sacred bulls. The likenesses of a bull and a cow were interred with the king and queen and their court in ritual burials during Dynasty 1 at Ur (circa 2500–2350 B.C.). Immense, vibrantly masculine bulls dominate the exquisite frescoes of the Minoans, particularly at the palace of Knossos on Crete, which dates from the first half of the second millennium B.C. Bulls are central to the naturalistic religious imagery of Çatal Hüyük, a city that flourished in the seventh millennium B.C. in the Anatolian region of modern Turkey. And, even further back, at approximately 15,000 B.C., the Hall of the Bulls was painted by Paleolithic artists in a cave at Lascaux, France. The Hall of the Bulls shows, too, that there is more to these bulls than big bovines with impressive horns.

Discovered in 1940, Lascaux's paintings of animals have generally been considered imitative magic. That is, hunters drew a picture of the animal they wished to kill, then went out and killed it. Curiously, though, the Lascaux people ate mostly reindeer. If the pictures are magical hunting rites, why did they draw so many animals, such as wooly ponies, bulls, and bison, that they rarely hunted for food?

The best explanation has been given by Frank Edge, a teacher of mathematics and cosmology at Mitchell Community College in Statesville, North Carolina, who sees the Hall of the Bulls as a map of the summer sky. The key to Edge's understanding is his recognition of seven dots painted over the shoulder of one of the bulls as the star cluster called the Pleiades. The Pleiades are part of the constellation of Taurus the bull, and their appearance within the depiction of a bull shows that even this far back the constellation we know as Taurus was seen as a bull. The bull in the stars is something we have inherited from the prehistory of our culture.

The Pleiades were of interest not only to the people of Lascaux. The Teotihuacános laid great religious significance on this star cluster and aligned the Pyramid of the Sun with it. The later Aztec pyramid of Tenayuca shows a similar alignment. The Hebrew writer of the book of Job called attention to the Pleiades. Yahweh is so powerful, the biblical poet proclaims, that he set the stars in the sky: "The Bear, Orion too, are of his making, / the Pleiades and the Mansions of the South." When Yahweh challenges Job for his inability to understand the divine design, he taunts, "Can you fasten the harness of the Pleiades, or untie Orion's bands?" The Greeks, too, had a myth about the Pleiades: They were seven maidens fathered by Atlas. The hunter Orion desired them all, and he pursued them in vain, until Zeus protected the maidens by turning them into stars. The pursuit continues, though, as the constellation of Orion rises behind the Pleiades and follows them across the sky. Orion also connects the Pleiades to the Egyptian pyramids of Giza because, as we saw in chapter 3, the ground plan of Giza serves as a map of Orion, the dwelling place of Osiris, in the Milky Way. And Orion was of importance in Mesoamerica as well. Building J at the ancient Zapotec center of Monte Albán was aligned with the point in the western sky where Alnilam, the center star of Orion's belt, sets. Three dots representing the three stars of Orion's belt served as the symbol for Cocijo and Tláloc, two Mexican rain gods.

Fascination with the Pleiades continues to this day. Andean farmers set the date to plant corn after watching the star cluster for a week in late winter. The Heaven's Gate cult members who committed mass suicide in San Diego in 1997 thought they would go to their heavenly reward in the Pleiades. Jehovah's Witnesses formerly believed the Pleiades to be the site in the sky where Jehovah dwelt and whence Jesus repaired after his resurrection from the dead.

A clue to this longstanding multicultural interest in the Pleiades comes from the book of Job. Consider this description of Yahweh's power:

> *And who can fathom how he spreads the clouds, or why such*
> *crashes thunder from his tent?*
> *He spreads out the mist, wrapping it about him, and covers*
> *the tops of the mountains.*
> *He gathers up the lightning in his hands, choosing the mark*
> *it is to reach. . . .*
> *Listen, oh listen, to the blast of his voice and the sound that*
> *blares from his mouth.*
> *He hurls his lightning below the span of heaven, it strikes to*
> *the very ends of the earth.*

This could be yet another biblical description of a shower of meteors flaring through the sky and detonating in the air or on the ground. Recall that the Pleiades are part of the constellation of Taurus the bull and that a twice-yearly meteor shower called the Taurid shower comes out of the portion of the sky where Taurus lies, and suddenly the bull in the Khafre Pyramid becomes more understandable. The bull god was sacrificed and mummified, much as a pharaoh would have been, as a way of stilling the anger he sent crashing down from the sky.

The association of bull killing with the angry sky is made unmistakably explicit in one of the rituals surrounding the goddess Cybele, who was worshipped in the form of a meteorite. The bull sacrifice ceremony known as the *taurobolium* was particularly popular in the second century A.D. In it the person dedicating the bull sacrifice lay in a deep pit roofed with heavy planks with holes drilled in them. A bull was led onto the planks and there sacrificed with a spear through the chest or a knife in the neck, so that all its blood poured out and down on the person below. At first this seems like a gruesome heathen baptism. But when we remember Roger of Wendover's description of blood falling from the skies as meteor showers lit up the skies, and when we remember that those flaming objects came from the constellation of the bull, then the *taurobolium* becomes a sacred reenactment of the bloody rain brought on by the goddess worshipped in the form of a meteorite. The bloody rain of the goddess, which was the poetic explanation given to the falling of meteoritic and cometary material, not only become memorialized in ancient—and now often misunderstood—rituals but also drove peoples from their homelands to seek refuge in new territories. Thus very real events that had turned into ritual in practices like the *taurobolium* may have directly influenced the building of the greatest and most enduring of architectural forms: the pyramid.

Of Comets and Pyramids

The fact of Earth's periodic cataclysmic encounters with the remains of fragmenting comets is directly connected to the pyramids in two ways. The first pyramids we know of were built to reach up into the skies to fathom the mystery of this awesome power, at once destructive in its effects and beautiful in its cosmic perfection. In the same way that a plunging meteor connected the sky to the earth, the pyramid again linked the earth to the sky. In ascending the pyramid—whether actually climbing up it, as in Mesopotamia, Mesoamerica, or Cambodia, or metaphorically by means of the mythical rising of the pharaoh's spirit from an Egyptian pyramid—one moved toward this realm of power so awesome that it had to be divine. Certainly the religions of the sky-gods, including Christianity and Judaism as well as the ancient Egyptian and Mesopotamian theologies, are rooted in the experiences of circa 3150, 2345, 1628, and 1159 B.C.

Second, those periodic blasts of catastrophe shattered the customary ways of the earth's peoples. Cities burned, farmlands became deserts, nations and tribes were forced to move. The fleeing of the Shang elites into the Pacific was not a unique event. It happened, I suspect, time and time again, as people from a pyramid-building culture were forced by the angry skies to pull up stakes and take themselves—and their knowledge of pyramid building—to some new and unknown land.

Nine
Seeking the Source

AS WE HAVE SEEN, COMETARY CATASTROPHES HAVE THE ability to change the course of a civilization's history, destroy its traditions, even plunge it into a dark age. That much we know from ancient history. If such events happened within the reach of historical knowledge—which begins more or less with the first recorded civilizations, in about 3500 B.C.—they must have happened before that time as well. Could it be that a cometary catastrophe destroyed civilizations that we do not now know about? Are the pyramids themselves reminders of something and someplace forgotten deep in the distant past? Are the earliest pyramids in Peru, China, Mesopotamia, and Egypt the beginning point for all the pyramids that followed? Do they form the hub of pyramid building's wheel in both the Old and New Worlds? Or are they themselves the spokes of a hub that lies even further back, in an earlier time lost to history?

These questions are hardly new. The notion of a time before our own is a common element in the mythic inheritance of the Western world. In the Old Testament book of Genesis, the Garden of Eden represents the lost world, a place of abundance and immortality taken away by divine fiat as punishment for Eve's original sin. The ancient Egyptians told of the First Times *(Zep Tepi)*, an ancient epoch when order and harmony prevailed and then, sadly, broke down. As elaborated by the poet Hesiod (circa eighth century B.C.) in his *Theogony*, the Greeks saw the world before their own time as a succession of ages in which perfection was replaced step by step by deepening chaos and disorder.

Easily the most famous, and the most written about, lost world also has its origin in Greek culture: Atlantis. Described in the fourth century B.C. by Plato, the account of Atlantis in the *Timaeus* and *Critias* dialogues contains fewer words than a typical short story, yet it has spawned an immense industry of books, television programs, videos, and speakers' tours—each speaker or writer claiming to have found the "real" Atlantis. To date, dozens of locations in Europe and North Africa have been proposed as the site of the lost civilization, as well as more distant places such as Greenland, Iceland, Scandinavia, eastern North America, Bermuda, the Azores, the Canaries, the Cape Verde Islands, the Mid-Atlantic Ridge, the Yucatán Peninsula, the Caribbean Sea, Cuba, South America, Ghana, Zimbabwe, Mesopotamia, and an impossibly ice-free Antarctica.

The Atlantis question isn't simply one of facts and figures, though. It also involves human aspirations and a longing for something better than the world we know. Followers of the psychic Edgar Cayce hold that the records of Atlantis were buried near the Sphinx and that if only we can recover them, their ancient wisdom will change our lives forever and for the better. Some popular, and fanciful, writing about the Atlanteans ascribes to them the power of levitation, the ability to move immense stones with sound waves, and the use of flying machines some 12 millennia before the Wright brothers.

The same kind of New Age cachet attaches to the legends of Lemuria, sometimes equated with Mu, yet another lost continent. Promoted by people like the twentieth-century authors James Churchward and Javier Cabrera, Lemuria, or Mu, is said to have been an Atlantis-sized continent thousands of miles across, with a population of many millions of people, that sank into the South Pacific over 10,000 years ago. Today all that remains of Lemuria are its mountain peaks, which poke up out of the sea to form islands like Hawaii, Fiji, and Tahiti. According to the legend, Lemuria was a tropical paradise whose inhabitants lived free of conflict and disease in homes with transparent roofs; apparently they were unafraid of baring all to their neighbors. Adept at extrasensory perception and mental telepathy, the Lemurians were vegetarian, agricultural, and completely organic, living in harmony with nature. The legend holds that when Lemuria sank into the South Pacific, not all its great wisdom was lost. Maps of the continent were preserved in pre-Inca Peru, where they were discovered by Javier Cabrera, one of the writers who has promoted the legend. The Lemurian elders and their wisdom remain available for consultation through psychic channeling. And the survivors of Lemuria fanned out over the face of Earth to become the Tibetans, the Mayas, the Native Americans, and the Eskimos, peoples who keep alive oral traditions of great antiquity.

In fact, Lemuria is a modern legend arising from nineteenth-century science that was first corrupted, then twisted and turned beyond all recognition. As for Atlantis, I remain convinced that Plato's story is, at least in part, a fictionalized account of a great Mediterranean war at a time of intense climatic change between the tenth and eighth millennia B.C., an idea put forward and well argued by Mary Settegast in her *Plato Prehistorian.*

Still, even at the mythic level, Lemuria and Atlantis, like the Garden of Eden, the First Times, and Hesiod's poem, point us toward that basic underlying question: Have we lost sight and sense of some ancient source of civilization? Finding an answer to this question could tell us even more about the pyramids and the people who built them.

Looking East

Say "ancient civilization," and almost everyone thinks of pharaonic Egypt or Mesopotamia. The Middle East is seen to be the seat of civilization in the same way that Africa is seen to be the evolutionary cradle of humankind. It was in Africa that early hominids first stood up and fashioned tools. From there, so the story goes, they migrated into Southwest Asia and Europe, slowly evolving toward the new species that you and I come from. Only later did they reach the Far East. Since the hominids in Africa, Europe, and the Middle East had a longer time to evolve, they have been thought to be culturally ahead of their cousins in the Orient. The so-called Movius Line, named after Hallam Movius (1907–1987), the scholar who first described it, divides the early technology of western Eurasia and Africa from that of China and Southeast Asia. While the hominids in Africa and western Eurasia were making relatively sophisticated hand axes and cleavers, their contemporary counterparts in the East were apparently using much simpler tools. Therefore, it appeared to scholars like Movius that the Asian hominids were cut off from the Westerners culturally and genetically and lagged behind them in terms of skill and perhaps intelligence.

Recent research is undercutting this idea and erasing the Movius Line. A team of Chinese and American archaeologists has uncovered a store of sophisticated stone tools such as hand axes in the Bose Basin of southern China that date to 803,000 (±3,000) years ago. The tools show that hominids in the East were just as adept as their contemporaries in the West. They also knew how to take advantage of an opportunity. The tools came from a layer of workable stones uncovered by a meteor that exploded in the air or in a shallow, now-vanished crater and burned off the local forest cover. The researchers were able to date the blast by chemically analyzing its evidence, small glass beads called tektites created from molten rock thrown up by the impact.

The pattern traced by the Movius Line is also thought to have set a geographical limit on the possible site of the first civilization. As a result, most prehistorians have restricted their search for civilization's source to North Africa and southwestern Asia. From there, civilization moved into the Indian subcontinent and then to China, which passed its new cultural skills on to Southeast Asia. Here again, recent research calls for a fresh look.

Discovering how to combine copper and tin to make the alloy bronze was one of the key technological developments that formed the basis of Old World civilization. This hard metal made for better tools and superior weapons, increasing the ability to both build and conquer. Supposedly bronze making was first discovered in the Middle East in the fourth millennium B.C., then the same technology appeared later and independently in the East. Recent archaeological work at Ban Chiang in southern Thailand and Phung Nguyen in northern Vietnam has yielded controversial dates for bronze from the third and fourth millennia B.C. This means that Southeast Asians may have begun smelting bronze well ahead of the Chinese and at about the same time as the first civilized peoples of the Middle East—a curious coincidence for so epoch-making a development.

A similar pattern has been uncovered for agriculture. As far back as 15,000 to 10,000 B.C., people in what is now Indonesia were cultivating wild yams and taro, simultaneous to or even preceding the development of farming in the Middle East. Evidence uncovered by the archaeologist Surin Pookajorn shows that rice was being grown in Thailand at some point in the period between 7260 and 5620 B.C., before the earliest date for its cultivation in China, and it appears that Ban Chiang was a fully developed agricultural community as early as the sixth to seventh millennium B.C.

These intriguing clues indicate that Southeast Asia had the potential to develop civilization before or at the same time as the West. What went wrong?

Three Waves of Water

The earliest ancient civilizations of the Middle East flowered between 3200 and 2500 B.C. As we saw in chapter 8, this profound cultural shift happened close on the heels of a period when the skies were showering Earth with fiery debris from comet fragments. Another important geophysical phenomenon characterized this time. The seas had been rising since the end of the last ice age, and, toward the end of the fourth millennium B.C., the world's oceans hit and held their highest level in the past 20,000 years. Depending on where sea level is measured, the oceans averaged more than 10 to 16 feet deeper in the period between 5000 and 3000 B.C. than their current mean. This was but the last of what had been three marked increases in sea level, or floods, over a period of approximately 15 millennia.

As we saw in following the movements of people from Asia to the Americas in chapter 4, an area of land called Beringia between Siberia and Alaska was exposed about 20,000 years ago, when the sea lay approximately 350 to 400 feet lower than it does now. The climate was warming slowly, and the continental glaciers and polar ice caps were melting bit by icy bit. As a result, sea level rose gradually, a few tenths of an inch per year. Then, starting in about 13,000 B.C., the climate turned cold, warmed, then snapped into the cold zone again, a period known as the Older Dryas. At the end of this second cold snap, in approximately 12,000 B.C., the climate warmed suddenly. Ice packs and glaciers melted at a rapid pace, much faster than before. Under this temperature assault, the European ice sheet collapsed, and a literal flood of freshwater poured into the oceans from North America after the sudden emptying of a large glacial lake called Lake Livingston. In fewer than 300 years the sea rose to about 250 feet below its current level.

The rapid rise of the sea stopped with another cold snap, known as the Younger Dryas, circa 11,000 B.C. This period was even colder than the earlier ice age; temperatures in Greenland are estimated to have been over 35 degrees Fahrenheit below what they are today—and Greenland is a very cold place even now. Then, in approximately 10,500 to 9500 B.C., the climate warmed again, even more suddenly than at the end of the Older Dryas. Again glacier and pack ice melted, again glacial lakes collapsed, and again the sea rose speedily. By one estimate the oceans came up approximately 30 feet in only 160 years. Thereafter the warming steadied, as did the rise in sea level. By circa 6500 B.C., sea level had risen to within some 60 feet of the current depth.

Then the pattern of cold snap followed by sudden warming was repeated yet again. During the cold snap, sea level fell 15 to 20 feet. As the climate again warmed, a flood of fresh water poured into the world's oceans from the collapse of the Laurentide ice sheet over eastern Canada. Two huge lakes, called Agassiz and Ojibway, and a complex of smaller bodies of water lay behind the ice, about 1,500 feet above sea level. When the ice gave way under the warming circa 6000 B.C., the water rushed out and poured into what is now Hudson Bay, then through the Davis Strait into the North Atlantic. The amount of water released has been estimated at between 46,500 and 90,000 cubic miles, enough to raise sea level by four inches almost instantaneously. The ice plate still sitting on Canada's landmass was carried out to sea, where it melted and further added to the rise in the sea. Other areas of shoreward ice would also have broken up, entered the sea as immense icebergs, and slowly melted. The oceans rose by up to an inch and a half a year, until sea level had increased by over 75 feet, making this flood the worst of the three post–ice age inundations. The increase slowed and plateaued in about 4000 to 3000 B.C. After that time, as the climate cooled again and glaciation began anew, sea level fell toward its present level.

Each of these three sudden rises in sea level was more than a case of an overfilling bathtub. As ice melted in the sudden warming, the land beneath the vanished glaciers rebounded at the loss of their weight, setting off tremors, earthquakes, uplift, and subsidence—something of a seismic chamber of horrors. The sudden collapse of ice sheets into the oceans could have set off superwaves, towering walls of water that spread for thousands of miles and sweep suddenly onto low-lying coastlines. And on those same coastlines the sea would have edged up year by year, consuming the land and pushing its inhabitants toward higher ground.

The flooding, both by superwave and slow rise, would have had its most devastating effect in an area of land that on contemporary maps is colored blue for water. In 18,000 B.C., when sea level was much lower, a continent-sized expanse of land in Southeast Asia lay where the southern reach of the South China Sea, the Gulf of Thailand, and the Java Sea are now. When the sea rose, a land area equal in extent to the Indian subcontinent sank slowly beneath the waves, leaving only the relative highlands of the Malay Archipelago, Indochina, Borneo, and the many islands of Indonesia protruding above them. Geologists call this expanse of drowned land the Sunda Shelf or Sundaland. A broad band of land along the Pacific coast of East and Southeast Asia also was inundated. Modern ports like Hong Kong, originally hundreds of miles inland, met the sea for the first time.

Today, the seas that cover Sundaland are relatively shallow, averaging only a few hundred feet deep. Sailing over them, one has trouble imagining that people once lived on the flooded bottom of this sea, raising children and crops, building villages and cities, following a lost culture. As the sea came up, where did these people go? We know they must have taken their tools, ideas, and cultural and religious attributes with them. Could it be that the migrants' baggage also included pyramids and the cultural and religious ideas they represent?

Eden in the East

Some years ago Arysio Nunes dos Santos, a professor of nuclear engineering at the Escola de Engenharia da Universidade Federal de Minas Gerais in Brazil, suggested that Indonesia was the site not only of Atlantis but also of the Garden of Eden, paradise, the isle of Avalon, and virtually every other utopian locale ever thought to exist on the face of the earth. Recently, another writer, William Lauritzen, made the same claim, arguing that Sundaland offers the best fit with Plato's Atlantis. I dismissed the idea as so much prattle until I encountered a fascinating

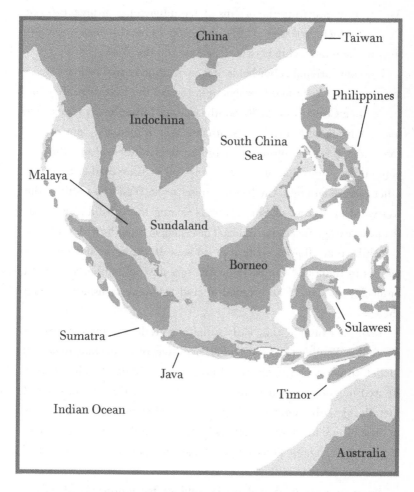

A map of Sundaland, which occupied a large area in what is now the South China Sea, Gulf of Thailand, and Java Sea. The current land masses are shown in dark grey. The light grey areas chart the maximum extent of the land exposed by the lowest sea levels at the end of the last ice age (circa 18,000 B.C.). This land was inundated as the climate warmed and the sea rose.

book entitled *Eden in the East* by Stephen Oppenheimer, a physician who specializes in tropical pediatrics and who formerly served as a professor of pediatrics at the Chinese University of Hong Kong. Oppenheimer has spent much of his professional life working in Southeast Asia and investigating the origins of its indigenous cultures. *Eden in the East*, which appeared in 1998, summarizes his exhaustive scholarship on the relationship between the East and the West.

The conventional belief holds that civilization moved from its Western origin in Egypt and Mesopotamia toward the East, first affecting India, then China, and finally Southeast Asia. Superficially this makes sense. Anyone who travels in Southeast Asia immediately notices the continuing powerful influence of Indian and Chinese culture. But Oppenheimer argues that, if one pulls the veil of time further back, another picture emerges. Civilization arose in the West as a result of the westward migration of Sundalanders fleeing the third and worst of the post–ice age floods, he argues. These people brought with them the key skills that allowed civilization to arise in Sumeria and Egypt as well as in India and China. What one sees now in Southeast Asia is a latter-day version of an original altered by many translations along the way.

Take, for example, the nearly simultaneous development of bronze making in Thailand and the Middle East. According to Oppenheimer's model, this was no coincidence. Rather, the Sundalanders had earlier figured out how to make bronze, and they took their knowledge of metallurgy with them when they fled. Once they settled into their new homes—some in Thailand, others in Mesopotamia—they set to making the metal again. Thus Thailand and Mesopotamia are the spokes; Sundaland is the hub.

A suggestive body of evidence that shows the significance of the period of sea-level rise in the history of the Middle East and lends credence to Oppenheimer's ideas comes from the work of Sir Charles Leonard Woolley, the English archaeologist who uncovered the tombs of the Dynasty 1 of Ur, discussed in chapter 3. As Woolley dug down and reached a layer dated to approximately 3500 B.C., he found copper. Then, as Woolley dug further back in time, all traces of human habitation disappeared for 2,000 years under several yards of silt—the remains, we now know, of the sea's rise toward its peak level in the fourth millennium B.C. Only when he reached the layer representing 5500 B.C., a time when the sea was at about the same level as it is today, did Woolley again find signs of human habitation—but no metal. Thus for a period of two millennia no one could inhabit that land, and during this same period the inhabitants of the area learned how to use copper and acquired the other skills that led to Ur's Dynastic Period. The question is, Did the people of Ur develop metal making and the other attributes of civilization on their own, or were these skills imported from somewhere else during the time of flood? Oppenheimer would argue that refugees from Southeast Asia sailed into the Middle East on the rising waters and, like the Shang Chinese in Mesoamerica over two millennia later, imparted much of what they knew to the locals.

The difficulty of evaluating Oppenheimer's argument directly is the absence of obvious archaeological evidence in Southeast Asia. Except for the highland areas that escaped the three-flood rise in sea level during the past 20 millennia, the settlements of the Sundalanders, particularly those in what once were fertile valleys, deltas, and lowlands, are buried under fathoms of saltwater. But if we can't see where the Sundalanders began, we can follow the route they traveled. Even people who have lost their homes take with them their languages, their genetic makeup, and their stories. Following each of these threads takes us back to the drowned continent of Sundaland.

There is good reason to see Southeast Asia as the original source of many of the world's languages. Austronesian, one of the major groups of Asian languages, was the most widely spoken group of languages on Earth until the spread of European languages during the modern period of colonization. Austronesian (the name means "southern islands") includes the indigenous tongues spoken from Madagascar through the Malay Peninsula and Archipelago and into Polynesia as far as Hawaii and Easter Island, with the exception of the Australian, Papuan, and Negrito languages. The spread of Austronesian languages across such a great expanse of earth, much of which is covered by water, shows the nautical abilities of Austronesian speakers. In addition, the other major group of Southeast Asian languages, which are called the Austroasiatic tongues and which are spoken primarily in northeast India and mainland Indochina, probably began along the coast and migrated into the interior along river valleys, presumably as the sea rose and forced the people toward higher ground.

Based on the linguistic evidence, Oppenheimer posits two waves of migration away from Sundaland as the sea rose, some eastward toward New Guinea and later into Polynesia, and some westward. This westward migration is important in the context of understanding the pyramids. Somewhere around 6000 B.C., as the sea flooded what is now the Strait of Malacca and created a new maritime passage from east to west, rice-growing Austroasiatic speakers made their way to India, taking their languages and their agriculture with them. Others of them may have headed to Mesopotamia as well. The linguist Paul Manansala has argued that Sanskrit and Sumerian are linked to Austroasiatic and Austronesian languages. Other linguists have yet to review Manansala's ideas, but if he is right, the connection argues for the westward migration of the Sundalanders into the area we consider the source of civilization before that civilization arose.

In the same way that languages radiate out from a center in Sundaland, so do human genes. A series of inherited traits that show their oldest form in Southeast Asia, specifically the rainforests of the Malay Peninsula and the Sabah region of Borneo, are also found as far away as Indochina, China, Korea, Taiwan, India, Sri Lanka, Iran, the Persian Gulf, the Arabian Peninsula, Turkey, and Central Europe—again like so many distant spokes on an ancient hub. The most fascinating and telling of these traits is thalassemia, an inherited abnormality of the blood's hemoglobin that causes anemia but also confers increased resistance to malaria. Two forms of the condition, alpha and beta, overlap in a band that begins in western Polynesia; stretches across Indonesia, the Philippines, Indochina and India, Iran, Arabia, and Mesopotamia; then loops around the Mediterranean and reaches deep into North Africa. This pattern argues for an ancient migration out of Southeast Asia both eastward and westward, most likely in the period following the third flood of circa 6000–5500 B.C.

Noah Before Noah and Other Stories

In the context of the pyramids, the most intriguing evidence for the migration of a high-cultured people out of Sundaland comes from the mythological traditions they carried with them. Pyramids, as we have seen, are rooted in the mythic stratum of our minds and cultures. Understanding where those mythological stories came from and what they signify gives us a better handle on comprehending the meaning of pyramids from Uruk to Uxmal.

The first line of evidence comes from stories of the flood, such as the widely known account of Noah in the Old Testament book of Genesis. Noah is but one tale in a worldwide collection of at least 500 flood myths, which are the most widespread of all ancient myths and therefore can be considered among the oldest. Stories of a great deluge are found on every inhabited continent and among a great many different language and culture groups. There is one important exception to this ubiquity: Africa outside Egypt. In his classic *Folklore in the Old Testament*, Sir James Frazer noted that "it may be doubted whether throughout that vast continent a single genuinely native [as opposed to missionary-inspired] tradition of a great flood has been recorded." There is a good geological explanation for this. Africa as a whole has a steep, narrow continental shelf. Any rise in sea level would be less noticeable and have less effect than in many regions of the other continents. And the rapid rise of the terrain near the coast in much of the African continent would mitigate the effect of superwaves sweeping across the oceans from the collapse of ice sheets. In Africa the floods made much less of an impression than they did on the other continents.

The story of Noah derives from a tradition of flood stories that appear among Semitic-speaking peoples of the Middle East and among the Greeks. For example, the Mesopotamian *Epic of Gilgamesh* includes the legend of Utnapishtim, who, like Noah, escaped with his wife in a vessel filled with animals. The Greeks told a similar tale about Deucalion. Warned about the flood in advance, like Noah, King Deucalion built a watertight box and took his queen, Pyrrha, aboard just as Zeus unleashed the waters. When the flood subsided, Deucalion landed on a mountain and sacrificed to Zeus, in the same way that Noah came ashore on Ararat and made an offering to Yahweh. The considerable overlap of the Greek and Semitic traditions indicates that they came from a common source.

India is the best candidate for the location of the original flood story. The Indian flood hero is named Manu, and his story dates back to a time before Indo-European speakers entered India. Most likely it was carried into Mesopotamia and the Greek-speaking eastern Mediterranean along trade routes. The tale of Manu predates the Greek and Semitic flood stories and shows a number of significant links with them, indicating that it is the likely origin.

Like Noah and Deucalion, Manu was warned of the flood in advance and told to build an ark, and after the waters receded he landed on a mountain. There is in this tale a hint of incest. Manu escaped the flood alone. Since he had no wife or consort, humanity would seem doomed to die with him. Manu sacrificed to the waters, and they served up a woman who greeted him as a daughter and offered herself as a divine go-between to help restore humans and animals to populate the earth. This stratagem succeeded, and men, women, and beasts moved over the drying landscape to make new homes for themselves. The incest between Manu and his "daughter" is left unstated, but the tale implies an unusual sexual union underlying the regeneration of the earth's surface.

This theme is echoed in Noah's story. After the flood, Noah planted grapes, made wine, and drank too much. He passed out in some awkward position that left him unclothed and exposed. His son Ham happened upon this display and told his brothers, Shem and Japheth, about it, apparently enjoying a sexually inappropriate joke at his father's expense. When Noah awoke, he cursed Ham for looking at him in an undressed state. This hint of sexuality between parent and child in the biblical account is another clue to India as the origin of the flood story.

Preliminary archaeological research suggests that this flood was real, not a literary invention. In the Gulf of Cambay off the state of Gujarat on India's west coast, possible evidence of extensive human habitation along what once was a river has been discovered 130 feet underwater. Preliminary radiocarbon dating of a single piece of carved wood retrieved from the Gujarat site dates the area to around 7500 B.C. This is about 3,500 years before the rise of the Harappan civilization cities in the Indus Valley, which has generally been thought to be South Asia's first civilization. However, a single sample constitutes far too little data to be certain that the site dates back that far into the past. But if the evidence holds up, it indicates that India's coastal dwellers were forced out of their cities and villages by a rising sea.

Analysis of the Manu legend indicates that its literary form comes from a mix of flood myths found in northern and eastern India and parts of Burma and Vietnam. Still, this is not its point of origin. That lies farther southeast, in Sundaland.

The Austronesian-speaking peoples of Southeast Asia and Polynesia have more flood stories than any other language or culture group. This is significant, because evolutionary biologists, linguists, and anthropologists seeking the origin of a family of species, a language group, or a cultural phenomenon look for the place where that construct is most diverse and numerous. As a simple example, let us say you want to determine the origin of the Germanic languages. In Europe you find that people speak not only German but also such related tongues as Danish, Frisian, Norwegian, Swedish, Icelandic, and Dutch. In addition, the

German spoken in Central Europe has any number of distinct dialects, such as Yiddish, Swiss German, and Swabian. You would also discover that German is spoken in a number of other isolated areas around the world, such as the Volga River region of Russia, northern Chile, and the upper Midwest of the United States. Given the absence of regional dialects in these other areas and also of related but distinct languages, you would conclude that the Germanic language group originated in Central Europe, where it is most numerous and diverse, and was carried into Eastern Europe and the Americas by German-speaking immigrants. And you would be right.

In the same way, the multitude and diversity of flood stories from the Austronesian traditions suggest that this region of the world was the origin of the flood myths found among the Semites, the Greeks, and the Indians. In addition, various specific elements of the Greek and Semitic stories also originated among the Austronesians. An example is the flood tale told about the Iban people of Sarawak. The hero Trow floated about in a makeshift ark with his wife and a number of domestic animals. When the flood subsided and the ark came to rest on dry land, he realized that one woman could not repopulate the world. He made substitute wives of wood and stone and impregnated them. This fascinating fiction is reminiscent of the myth of Deucalion. To repopulate the world, he threw stones over his head, which Zeus turned into men. When Deucalion's queen, Pyrrha, did the same, the stones became women. Incest like that hinted at in the Noah and Manu legends figures into other Southeast Asian and Polynesian stories. Various Austronesian traditions feature a bird that flew out from the saved hero and his family to see if the flood was subsiding, just as Noah did, first with the raven and then with the dove.

A flood plays a role in Genesis not only in the story of Noah but also in the opening verses that tell one version of the biblical creation of the world. This beginning does not start from nothing; it opens with water: "Now the earth was a formless void, there was darkness over the deep, and God's spirit hovered over the water." Next God creates light—

in advance of creating the sun—then divides the waters into two, those under the vault of heaven and those over it. And on the third day God says, "'Let the waters under heaven come together in a single mass, and let dry land appear.' And so it was. God called the dry land 'earth' and the mass of waters 'seas.'" This account sounds less like an actual creation of the world than a re-creation of its form after a devastating sea flood.

In later books of the Old Testament the watery chaos of the first days is linked to a terrible serpent that lives in the sea. Often called Leviathan, as in the books of Isaiah and the Psalms, this marine dragon is a terrible and dangerous creature, one that can be overcome only with divine power. The creature appears again and again in the Middle Eastern and Western traditions. The ancient Egyptian myths of creation include a sea monster that features in the chaos of the first days and acts as a guardian of the underworld. In the Babylonian creation myth, the hero Marduk slays the water monster Tiamat before he creates humankind. A similar story appears in the saga of Perseus, who, on his way to kill Medusa, rescues the virgin Andromeda chained to a seaside rock as a sacrifice to a sea-dwelling dragon. The beast had been sent by Poseidon, the god of the sea, to wreak havoc on the land; only the offering of a young virgin of high rank could stop its onslaught. Hercules kills the Hydra, a giant water snake that is the offspring of the odious half-reptile Typhon. Finally there is the marvelous Anglo-Saxon poem about Beowulf, who slays the monster Grendel by tearing off its arm, then searches out and destroys Grendel's unnamed mother, a horrific mother of all monsters who inhabits a cave at the bottom of a loathsome black lake.

In India the water dragon appears in the story of Krishna, the hero incarnation of the great god Vishnu. Called Kaliya, this monster lived in a deep river pool, destroyed animals and crops with its poison, and finally ceased its terrible ways when mollified by Krishna's music. In the creation story of the Brahmin caste, the world begins, much like the opening verses of Genesis, as an immense watery chaos on which floats a giant water snake with Vishnu asleep on its coils and dreaming. As we saw in chapter 8, China commonly associates dragons with the overflight of comets and the strange behavior of water, like floods and waves. In one creation cycle, floods are caused by a river god in the form of a dragon who demands that two young virgins be sacrificed to him each year, just as Andromeda was offered to the monster sent by Poseidon. In that story Li Bing plays the part of the hero, rescuing the maidens and subduing the dragon without actually killing it.

Water monsters, many of them playing a role in the myths of the First Days, appear all over Southeast Asia, Oceania, and among Sino-Tibetan peoples other than the Chinese. The Dyak crocodile guard guards the underworld as well as a tree of life with a hawk perched in its top branches. The people of Fiji tell of a creator serpent that lived in the sea. In one part of Micronesia, the creator god enlists the aid of a giant conger eel, a snakelike fish dwelling in the sea, to divide land from sky, an action that sounds much like Yahweh's division of the waters from the heavens. The Kuki tribes of Tibet say that the world began as a great sheet of water (the deep of Genesis once again) inhabited by a giant worm. In northern Australia, the indigenous people tell of a goddess who turned into a giant rainbow serpent (shades of Quetzalcoatl) and formed the rivers, mountains, and lakes during a fight with her son.

Notably, many Native American myths begin, like Genesis, with a watery chaos, but they largely lack dragons. Water dragons are also absent from African mythologies. This implies that the tales of water dragons stretching from Australia and Fiji to Anglo-Saxon England are part of a single connected tradition.

The dating of the water dragon stories fits the same kind of westward movement out of Sundaland indicated by the genetic and linguistic evidence. At one extreme sits Australia's rainbow serpent, which some scholars attribute to a tradition beginning sometime between 7000 and 5000 B.C. At the other end is the Anglo-Saxon tale of Beowulf, which tells of events in the early or middle sixth century A.D. It makes sense, too, that Southeast Asia and its many islands would be the original home of the tradition of a marine dragon often associated with creation—or, perhaps more accurately, re-creation following a flood. The Greek writers who recorded the stories of Hercules and Perseus and the biblical scribes who told of Leviathan had almost certainly never seen a saltwater crocodile. The animals do not exist in the Mediterranean; the closest relative is the Nile crocodile, a river dweller. But Southeast Asia in ancient times harbored a large population of saltwater crocodiles, animals that are strikingly larger than their riverine cousins and not the least bit shy about turning humans into a hot meal. One can well imagine the horror of a constantly rising and flooding sea bringing such fearsome animals closer and closer by the day. They would indeed be the guardians of chaos, the monsters who with their sharp teeth and terrible tails were a barrier to all that had been lost. Nothing less than gods could stop them.

Sibling Rivalry and Culture Clash

The well-known Genesis story of Cain killing Abel connects to the mythological background that underlies the building of the Giza pyramids. In the biblical version of the story, Abel the shepherd and Cain the farmer made offerings to Yahweh—Abel of lambs, Cain of fruit and grain. Unfortunately for Abel, Yahweh liked his sacrifice better than Cain's. Driven into rage by jealousy over the extra favor his brother had won with Yahweh, Cain killed Abel. He denied the murder to Yahweh, but the biblical god, seeing through his lie, cursed him and drove him away.

A much older Egyptian story focuses on the rivalry between brother gods, Osiris and Seth. Seth too was jealous and killed his brother. To hide the deed, Seth cut the body up and scattered the parts over the land of Egypt. Isis, the wife of Osiris, methodically gathered them back together. This reassembly of the corpse gave Osiris a renewed but short-lived potency. His penis rose, Isis copulated with him, and her womb filled with Horus, the hawk-headed god. Later, Horus took revenge on Seth, tearing off his testicles and defeating him in a fierce fight.

Both stories, of Cain and Abel and of Osiris and Seth, detail an ancient conflict between cultures. In the biblical story, that strife flares between herders and farmers; in the Egyptian version, the struggle probably refers to the different cultures of Upper and Lower Egypt— the former more African, the latter more Asian and European—which were united by the first pharaoh, Menes, who subjugated the Two Lands just as Horus defeated Seth. In life, the pharaoh was the incarnation of Horus; at his death, he became Osiris, destined to return to the paradise in the sky represented by the constellation Orion, as we saw in chapter 3. The pyramids of Giza arranged like the three stars of Orion's belt memorialized this divine metamorphosis.

The tale of Osiris, Seth, and Horus, which figures so prominently into the mythology underpinning the pyramids of Giza, is not original to Egypt. Related stories come from Sumeria. In a series of poems, various gods and goddesses representing clashing cultures fight it out. Fertility figures into these stories too, as it does in the Egyptian version with the miracle pregnancy of Isis. Other versions can be found in India and among the Saami, or Laps, of arctic Europe, a people who have strong genetic links to South and Central Asia.

Once again, the greatest number and diversity of warring-brother stories come from the region that stretches from eastern Indonesia across Polynesia and Micronesia, the heartland of the Austronesian-speaking peoples. For example, the ornate tale of Kulabob and Manup, from the Moluccas and Micronesia, details the culture conflict and flat-out warfare that accompanied the migration of the Austronesian people from Sundaland and into the Pacific. Other variants are found in the Sepik Basin and in Polynesia. The version of the story that comes from Tonga sounds so much like the biblical tale that the first European to record it went to great trouble to ensure that the Tongans had not been exposed to it by missionaries, who had in fact not yet affected the island's culture. The Tongans told of two brothers, one lazy and the other industrious. The lazy one killed his ever-working sibling, then tried to deny the evil deed to their father, who figured out what had happened, cursed his surviving son, and sent him into exile. As with the stories of watery chaos and marine dragons, the number and diversity of the warring-brother stories point to Southeast Asia, particularly Sundaland, as their source.

The legacy of key myths, like the spread of language and the trail of genetic characteristics, lends credence to Oppenheimer's thesis. He makes a strong case that the people of Sundaland took to their boats to escape the rising waters of the post–ice age floods. Some went east, eventually making their way into the Pacific. Others headed northwest, following the great rivers of Asia into the Himalayas and China. Still others landed in the Indian subcontinent and Mesopotamia, most likely in early Sumerian times.

The arrival of the Sundalanders in India may well have been the catalyst that explains a number of puzzling aspects of ancient Indian culture. In a study of the Vedic hymns, the scholar David Frawley noted that these ancient Sanskrit documents are full of oceanic symbolism. The Indo-Europeans who conquered India and brought Sanskrit with them are thought to have arrived from the north, riding horses into the subcontinent. It does seem odd that horse warriors would know so much about the sea. It is also curious that they would know as much astronomy as they did, a point further explored by Georg Feuerstein, Subhash Kak, and David Frawley. Astronomy, it is pointed out by these authors, is more curiosity than necessity to land-based horse warriors, but it is a matter of life and death to seafarers, who need the stars to guide them. In addition, Frawley, Feuerstein, and Kak push the date of the Vedic hymns back much further than the conventional dating of 2000–1500 B.C. On the basis of internal astronomical evidence, Frawley dates them to 4000 B.C. Feuerstein goes back even further, citing elements of Vedic culture as early as 7000 B.C. Both dates roughly coincide with floodings of Sundaland. In addition, Feuerstein's date fits, perhaps not coincidentally, with the time frame I propose for the building of the Great Sphinx of Giza (see the appendix, "Redating the Great Sphinx of Giza").

Also, the movement from Sundaland in the east to the supposed centers of civilization in the west agrees with the mythology of those western centers of high culture. Genesis puts the location of the Garden of Eden, the beginning point of the human race, somewhere in the east. The Sumerians attributed their civilization to the Seven Sages—strange, fishlike men who emerged from the sea after a journey from the east to teach them the arts of civilization. The Egyptian *Book of the Dead*, which contains a good deal of material from predynastic times, mentions the east numerous times, usually in fear, a place of death from which the soul must be protected. This same book refers to the "domain of Manu across the water," an intriguing possible connection to the Manu of Hindu legend who, like Noah, creates the human race anew after a great catastrophe.

Mesoamerican Echoes

The end points of the migration routes from Sundaland include most of the areas of the Old World where pyramids are found: Egypt, Mesopotamia, India, Cambodia, Indonesian Java, and China. By no means did the migrating Sundalanders build these monuments. Obviously, the migration from the sunken continent of Southeast Asia was long past when the first stupa stones were laid at Sanchi in India. Rather, something of the culture and mythology contributed by these homeless people added to the cultural mix that led to the pyramids.

The connection between the legacy of the Sundalanders and the pyramid-building cultures becomes even more emphatic if we expand our view to the New World, particularly Mesoamerica. The link between Sundaland and Mesoamerica is almost certainly indirect; the legacy of the sunken continent came to the Americas via China and the Mediterranean. Still, these transplanted ideas and stories reached into the cultural core of the people of the New World who became pyramid builders. Many of the distinguishing mythologies of Mesoamerica can be traced back to an origin in Southeast Asia.

Consider the crocodile, which is possibly the Leviathan of Genesis and the dragon of watery chaos among the Austronesians. The Aztec god Cipact is unique as the only alligator deity in Mesoamerica. In certain of the Southeast Asian stories of the creation of the human race, a deity fashions the first man by mixing his or her own blood with clay. A remnant of this story occurs in Genesis. The name of Adam, who is made from dust in one of the biblical creation accounts, means "red earth" or "blood-colored earth." Likewise, as we saw in chapter 5, the Aztecs made images of their god by mixing their own blood with cornmeal.

As we also saw in chapter 5, the Aztecs traced their origin to the goddess Cioacoatl, who also passed sin, suffering, and death into the world. Commonly associated with a snake, Cioacoatl sounds much like Eve in Genesis, who was made by Yahweh from a rib taken out of Adam's side as he slept. Long before Christianity came to the islands, some of the Polynesians told how the first woman Ivi—whose name means "bone" and is pronounced phonetically the same as "Eve"—was made by the divine creator from a bone extracted from the first man's body during sleep.

The serpent figures in an additional motif found in Mesoamerica, the Middle East, and Southeast Asia: the tree of life. A body of myths from Southeast Asia connects a tree of life or immortality with a guardian serpent and a bird that perches in its branches. Readers who know the Old Testament will see an immediate connection to the story of Eve in the Garden of Eden, who is persuaded by a snake to taste the fruit of the forbidden tree. Similar stories are found in Southeast Asia, again in the number and diversity that indicate place of origin. And they appear in Mesoamerica as well. The serpent and the bird are sometimes mixed, as in the figure of Quetzalcoatl, the Feathered Serpent, with the cactus playing the role of the tree. Or they are separate, as in the symbol of the eagle holding a snake in its talons that is the centerpiece of the modern Mexican flag.

In the Genesis story of Eden, the snake offers Eve immortality. This offer coming from a snake was fully credible; because snakes shed their skins, they embodied immortality. In the *Epic of Gilgamesh* the hero Gilgamesh goes looking for the secret of deathless life. After many trials and tribulations, he finds it in a plant growing on the bottom of a river. Gilgamesh plucks this sacred herb, planning to take it back to his city and bestow it as a boon on his people. Then a snake slithers into the scene, swallows the plant, and immediately casts off its skin. Now it owns the secret of immortality, and Gilgamesh must return home empty-handed and as liable to die as any human.

The cast skin as the mark of immortality is one of the many mythological motifs that originated in Southeast Asia, and it explains a particularly bizarre and grisly aspect of Aztec ritual. Certain sacrificial victims were killed by being beheaded, then skinned. A priest wore the raw human hide over his own skin, completing the many steps of a rite that often lasted for days. Attired in this gory way, the priest had taken onto himself the immortality gained by the sacrificial victim. He displayed, too, a cultural connection that stretched back over thousands of years to the drowned continent of Southeast Asia.

And then there are the Pleiades, the group of seven stars from the Taurus constellation with which the Pyramid of the Sun in Teotihuacán and the Aztec pyramid of Tenayuca are aligned. The Pleiades were used extensively as navigational aids by many ancient cultures, including the Greeks and the Austronesians. The Australian Aboriginals tell a story of the origin of the Pleiades as seven sisters pursued by a terrible hunter who lusted after them, a tale that directly echoes the Greek myth about Orion's vain chasing after the maiden daughters of Atlas. Curiously, the Hindu god Varuna, the Greek Ouranos, and the Egyptian Osiris are all associated with Orion. And, given the connection of Osiris to the pharaohs, once again we are drawn back into the mythological foundation that underpins the pyramids of Giza.

Warm and Cold, Wet Comets and Dry

Oppenheimer's argument that the inundation of Sundaland by the second and third of the three post–ice age sea floods prompted a westward cultural migration that sparked the rise of civilization in the fourth millennium B.C. is provocative. Yet an important element is missing. Oppenheimer details the evidence to show that post–ice age floods did occur, yet he is uncertain just why the climate alternately cooled and warmed, melting the polar and continental glaciers. This point lies outside the primary purview of his book, but it is one that deserves looking into here.

The climate history of the past 20 millennia shows two distinct patterns. Following the glacial maximum of 18,000 B.C., the climate generally warmed. Overall this trend has continued to the present day. Yet in the midst of this slow and gradual warming, the climate suddenly cooled, then warmed with equal or greater suddenness at a faster-than-normal rate. This happened three times, with extensive, fast flooding, in approximately 11,500 B.C., 9500 B.C., and 6000 B.C. To understand what may have been happening, we must look for two mechanisms: one to account for the slow post–ice age warming, the other for the sudden alternation of cold and accelerated warming.

The slow cycle is the easier one to explain, thanks to the pioneering work of the Serbian mathematician Milutin Milankovitch in the 1920s and 1930s. Milankovitch maintained that ice ages come and go due to the complex interaction of a number of separate orbital cycles which in turn are modified and influenced by minor fluctuations beyond the present scope of discussion—all of them happening simultaneously. The first of the orbital cycles is called eccentricity. That is, Earth's orbit around the sun follows the path not of a circle, but an ellipse, which means that the orbit is slightly oval. What's more, the ellipse slowly gets longer, then shortens again, varying about 2 percent approximately every 100,000 years. When Earth is farther away from the sun in its larger orbit, it receives less energy and cools, whereas it receives more energy and warms when it is closer.

Eccentricity is modified by a second cycle. The slightly elliptical orbit of Earth not only lengthens and shortens but also slowly rotates around the sun with respect to the stars, making a full rotation approximately every 111,000 years.

The third cycle Milankovitch identified involves Earth's tilt. The axis on which Earth rotates isn't perpendicular to the plane of the orbit. Rather it is tilted, currently by approximately 23.5 degrees. This tilt, known technically as obliquity, varies between 21.6 and 24.5 degrees over a 41,000- to 44,000-year cycle. In the low latitudes closer to the equator, tilt affects climate little. But at high latitudes, particularly near the poles, the influence of tilt is profound. When Earth reaches maximum obliquity of 24.5 degrees, the winter dark extends farther into lower latitudes and the cold is deeper. When the obliquity moves toward the minimum of 21.6 degrees, the winter dark is confined to higher latitudes and the winter is warmer.

Obliquity interacts with the fourth of Milankovitch's cycles: precession. Earth isn't perfectly spherical; it flattens at the poles and bulges at the equator; a radius drawn from Earth's center to the equator is 13.5 miles longer than one drawn to either pole. This extra mass in the middle makes Earth technically an oblate spheroid. In addition, Earth's axis of rotation tips in relation to the plane (also known as the ecliptic) of its orbit around the sun. Both the sun and the moon, and to a much lesser extent the other planets, tug gravitationally on the greater mass of the tipped Earth's equatorial bulge and, because of this slightly imbalanced pull on the planet, slowly move the axis of rotation. As a result, Earth spins not like a wheel on an axle, round and round in the same plane, but with the wobble of a top moving across a table. This slow wobbling, known as precession, affects the seasonal balance of ra-

diation because it changes the timing of the points in the annual orbital cycle at which Earth is farthest and closest to the sun. A single,
complete precessional "wobble" takes about 26,000 years, but because
it interacts with the rotation of Earth's orbit, it affects the timing shift
on a cycle of about 21,000 to 22,000 years. Between them, tilt and precession can alter the amount of solar radiation in high latitudes by
some 15 percent.

Thorough study of ice cores combined with analyses of deep-sea sediments indicates that temperatures on Earth were warm about 103,000,
82,000, 60,000, 35,000, and 10,000 years ago. These data fairly closely
fit Milankovitch's precessional cycle of approximately 21,000 to 22,000
years and the tilt cycle of 41,000 to 44,000 years, combined with the
changing eccentricity of the planet's orbit, and they provide a good explanation for the long, slow warming trend of the post–ice age period.
They do nothing, though, to explain the sudden chills followed by sudden heat waves that preceded the three great sea floods.

The most likely explanation lies not in a gradualist pattern like the
Milankovitch cycles but in the seemingly more random patterns of
Clube and Napier's coherent catastrophism. Behind the three sea floods
lies the periodic breakup of a comet and the plunge of its fragments
onto the surface of the planet.

As the sudden demise of the dinosaurs at the end of the Cretaceous
Period shows, a large comet (or asteroid or meteorite; at least some asteroids and meteorites appear to be the cores of comets) hitting on land
or shallow water can create a dust veil sufficient to cool the planet suddenly and kill off many forms of terrestrial and aquatic life. A similar
cooling event, although on a much smaller scale, apparently occurred
about 2.15 million years ago when the small asteroid Eltanin, estimated at 0.6 to 2 miles across, crashed into the then relatively shallow
waters of the Bellingshausen Sea off the coast of Antarctica. The
heavy atmospheric dust veil caused by a continental impact not only
shields the sun's light but also creates a greenhouse effect, blocking the
release of Earth's heat into space. Over time, the planet's surface tem-

perature tends to equalize, even if it declines overall. Since most of the surface heat is found in the oceans, the lower-latitude oceans would cool while the higher-latitude oceans warm. This heat-exchange process would cause numerous violent storms, which would also arise from rapid atmospheric cooling over the continents in the face of much slower temperature changes over the oceans. Constant heavy rains would fill depressions in the continental interiors, such as the immense lakes accumulating behind the Laurentide Ice Sheet in eastern Canada. At higher latitudes, storms would deposit immense snowfields that would slowly compress to add to existing glaciers or to form new ones. By the time the dust veil fell back to Earth within about three years, a new pattern would have been established—growing glaciers in the higher latitudes, a colder overall ocean temperature with lower sea level, and reduced evaporation. This chill would be likely to last, too, owing to the reflection of sunlight off the increased areas of ice and snow and continued atmospheric dusting from volcanic activity or perhaps even more impacts.

But a comet or other piece of space debris coming down in deep ocean would have a strikingly different effect. Because of the fragment's speed, it might penetrate to the bottom, even in the deepest trenches, and slam into the ocean floor. The immense volume of water displaced by the impact would rise in a towering column, then fall back, forming a system of tsunamis that decline over distance, then gather force again when they encounter the sea bottom in the shallow water of the continental shelves. Depending on the size of the fragment, waves up to several hundred feet high would strike the continents, sweeping coastal communities before them and flooding vast areas of low-lying land.

When the tsunamis subsided and the oceans drained back to their new levels, the climate would not return to normal. Even a moderate impact could possibly break the thin oceanic floor, releasing the hot magma of the mantle, possibly in a violent explosion, perhaps in a slow, sustained venting. Either way, a large amount of seawater would evaporate and escape into the atmosphere as large rain clouds, which would be carried around the globe. With an oceanic impact there is no atmospheric dusting to chill the planet. Rather, the release of heat from the mantle and the added evaporation of the ocean turn the climate wet and warm.

Understanding this difference between land and ocean impacts allows for an interesting speculation. The sudden cold snaps in the past 20 millennia probably resulted from large comet fragments hitting land or shallow water along the continental shelves. Eventually the climate headed back into its slow warming, based on the Milankovitch cycles, which was accelerated now and again by oceanic splashdowns of large comet fragments. Smaller fragments, which have a less dramatic impact, would have helped keep the temperature heading up, glaciers melting, and sea level rising. Since the surface of the earth has significantly more water than land, a steady bombardment by smaller fragments is more likely to lead to warming than chilling or to mitigate the short-term cooling effects of simultaneous land impacts.

Alexander and Edith Tollmann, geologists at the University of Vienna, have argued that a series of large oceanic impacts, coupled with smaller land collisions, in the middle of the eighth millennium B.C. is the cause of Noah's flood. Working partly from folkloric traditions, they even go so far as to date the impact precisely at 3 A.M. (in Austria's time zone) in 7553 B.C. on what would have been September 23 in that precalendrical epoch.

Greenland ice-core data show that something major did happen right around the time the Tollmanns propose. A very strong acid layer, which would indicate extreme volcanic or cometary activity, has been dated to 7630 B.C. ($\pm$ 170 years). In addition, the radiocarbon content of ancient tree rings from 7553 B.C. indicates some kind of major event. Working from evidence in folklore, the Tollmanns argue that a comet with seven large fragments struck the world's oceans more or less simultaneously in the Tasman Sea southeast of Australia, in the South China Sea, in the west-central Indian Ocean, in the North Atlantic, in the central Atlantic south of the Azores, in the Pacific off Central America, and farther south in the Pacific just west of Tierra del Fuego. The impacts set up giant tsunamis, triggered volcanic eruptions and earthquakes, pulsed waves of inferno-like heat outward, threw clouds of dust and water vapor into the upper atmosphere, and filled the air with nitric acid, some of which precipitated in snow and rain over the Greenland ice sheet and lent its signature to the layer in the ice core.

The deep-ocean craters left by this rain of fire and space ice are practically impossible to find, but the Tollmanns claim to have identified a smaller land-based crater that dates to the right period. It is called the Köfels crater and is located in the Ötz Valley of the Austrian Tyrol—curiously, and probably totally coincidentally, the same general area as the 1991 discovery of the Iceman discussed in chapter 8. The Tollmanns have dated the site to 7440 B.C. (± 150 years), a number that lines up approximately with the Greenland ice-core and the tree-ring radiocarbon data.

The Tollmanns' claimed precision about the exact hour and day of the comet strikedown is unsupportable. If comet P/Shoemaker-Levy 9 is a model, the impacts occurred over a series of days, perhaps even months or years. Still, their idea is intriguing food for thought. The impact documented by the Tollmanns may correlate with the breakup of a large comet in this time period discussed by Clube and Napier, the remains of which are known as the asteroid Olijato. Though the 7553 B.C. event may not have been the direct cause of the final flooding of Sundaland, it could have set the stage for the warming that led some 1,500 years later to the catastrophic collapse of the Laurentide Ice Sheet and the sudden release of thousands of cubic miles of water into the world's oceans.

Healing the Wounds of Ancient Days

It is likely that rising waters forced the Sundalanders to flee, and we probably know what caused the sea level to come up. But we still do not know the shape and form of the culture these people carried with them to their new homes. Were they a typical Stone Age people distinguished solely by their nautical expertise? Or did they possess such highly civilized ways, arts, and skills that the preserved memory of their accomplishments appeared centuries later in Plato's descriptions of Atlantis?

Answering these questions requires archaeological information that is as yet lacking. The sea has covered Sundaland and buried the remains of any civilization that might have lived there.

Given the absence of archaeological information, what can we say about the Sundalanders? It is reasonable to suggest that these people had a well-developed, even high culture. They may have been smelting copper and perhaps making bronze even before their homeland was flooded. The Sundalanders could well be the people who brought metalworking to Sumeria and helped that land to make the crucial transition from the Stone Age to the Bronze Age. And the proposed early date for rice growing in ancient Thailand indicates too that they were accomplished agriculturists. Cities can grow only when the grain to feed the populace is sufficient, and all civilizations require an adept farming class. The Sundalanders could have contributed this necessary agronomic expertise and provided a crucial building block to the rise of civilization in Mesopotamia.

Oppenheimer argues that the Sundalanders may also have brought an exquisite system of social hierarchy and stratification to India and Mesopotamia and thence to Egypt. The Austronesians, he notes, are practiced in making social distinctions and adept at using religious, political, and economic methods to preserve class structure. Without a doubt, a hierarchical, king-oriented culture is a key to the pyramid cultures of old. It is indeed possible that the model of social organization incorporated in the pyramid cultures may have been less a homegrown Mesopotamian and Egyptian phenomenon than an import from flooded Sundaland.

At an even deeper level, the greatest contribution of the Sundalanders could be a mythology birthed in chaos and catastrophe. As we saw in chapter 3, pyramids often played a ritual role in healing ancient mythical divisions, such as the rift separating the waters from the sky and the earth from the heavens. It is striking that the mythologies of the pyramid builders build upon so many tales of separation, scattering, and division. Take the tale of Osiris and Seth as a classic example; after Seth murders Osiris, he divides the body into many small pieces and hides them in various parts of Egypt. Buddhist stupas memorialize a similar division of the Buddha's body, since each stupa is said to contain some small part of the great man's remains. When the Babylonian hero Marduk defeats the terrible monster Tiamat, he cuts her body in half and creates the world on her divided carcass. The biblical story of the Tower of Babel is another tale of division; an original unity comes to its end in a chaos of many tongues.

Alan Alford, an independent researcher of ancient mythology and civilizations and the author of the 1998 book *The Phoenix Solution: Secrets of a Lost Civilisation*, has added catastrophe to mythological separation and division to make it the basis of ancient Egyptian religion. Alford calls this idea, which builds on the research of the astronomer Tom Van Flandern, the exploded-planet hypothesis. According to Alford's thinking, the ancients collected and venerated meteorites. The Romans, who worshipped a large black meteorite as the mother goddess Cybele, were just one example of a long tradition in which humans regarded objects that fell from space as sacred. To this day a black meteorite occupies the Kaaba of the Great Mosque of Mecca, the holiest site in Islam. According to Muslim tradition, the archangel Gabriel made a gift of the meteorite to the patriarch Abraham. In ancient Egypt, iron was very rare, found only in meteorites. Since meteorites came from the skies, the Egyptians thought the gods must have bones of iron. Since meteorites were composed of rocks and other earthly substances, they reasoned that there must be another "earth" in the heavens, which exploded and hurled its pieces upon the Two Lands.

Alford's idea is more interesting as a complex religious metaphor embodying a distant history than as a literal observation of astronomy.

The people who left Sundaland knew more than a little about separation. They were forced to leave their way of life behind, to take to their canoes and sail to someplace new and unknown over the horizon. Like the planet the Egyptians thought had scattered its rocky insides over the surface of the earth, they exploded outward. And they connected their forced exodus to the fiery events of the sky. It is unlikely that they knew of the different effects of land and sea cometary impacts upon climate, but then again they didn't need to. When the heavens were disturbed by fiery lights, when stars spread across the sky in the shape of writhing snakes, the huge waves came, the ground rumbled in earthquakes, and the waters rose.

From such experiences grew the mythological ideas that led to the pyramids. These massive monuments re-created an ancient order, a time long lost, when unity and harmony prevailed. They healed the separation of terrible, catastrophic days now only dimly remembered. Pyramids provided platforms reaching into the heavenly anterooms of sky-gods whose anger and violent caprice the pyramid builders had every good reason to fear. At any moment, those gods could again fill the heavens with fiery lights and prompt the waters to rise. The pyramid builders addressed their capricious deities in the language of sacrifice. They sent prayers of blood skyward to beg for a return to that peaceful time lost long ago and far away.

Ten
Civilization's Beginning, Isolation's End

IT IS TIME TO STEP BACK FROM THE DETAILS AND TRACE THE plot line of the story that lies behind the pyramids.

The earliest civilization likely arose in Sundaland, which disappeared under a rising sea sometime between 6000 and 4000 B.C. and was abandoned by its inhabitants. There is good reason to believe that the rise in sea level that concealed Sundaland beneath the waves was connected with cometary activity in the skies. Since pyramids are symbolically connected with comets, and since comets had such an immense effect on the fate of Sundaland, the Sundalanders may have originated the ancient pyramid tradition. As they fled their sinking home, moving principally northwest and east, they would have carried their culture, and the pyramid tradition, with them. Those who went northwest contributed to the cultural melange that gave rise first to the pyramids of Sumeria, Egypt, and Mesopotamia and later to those in India, Southeast Asia, and China. It is possible that the Sundalanders heading eastward voyaged as far as the coast of Peru, where the pyramids of Aspero arose by the end of the fourth millennium B.C. This American pyramid tradition appears to have gone extinct until it was reinvigorated by contact beginning in the late twelfth century B.C. with Old World Pacific Rim mariners, particularly the Chinese. That prompted a wave of New World pyramid building among the Olmecs in Mexico, which spread across Mesoamerica and eventually made its way back to Peru and Bolivia.

Still, there are important gaps in this story, whole chapters that remain missing. We would know more if we were lucky enough to uncover records telling of the arrival of Old World emigrants in the New World and describing their influence among the locals. The closest to such evidence that we have is the South American oral traditions that tell of the arrival of white bearded gods. Beyond that there may be little to find, since the European invasion in the late fifteenth and sixteenth centuries destroyed almost the entire legacy of Native American codices and records. In addition, except for the arrival of masses of Shang Chinese at La Venta in the twelfth century B.C., Old World mariners probably appeared in dribs and drabs—a boat here, a boat there—less a wholesale change than a subtle influence in the extended development of a complex culture.

The absence of records is hardly unique in our reconstruction of history. For example, despite the abundance of histories and literature from the Mediterranean and the careful exploration of its archaeological sites, our knowledge of the ancient civilizations of the region remains incomplete. Consider the ancient Hebrews before the early and middle first millennium B.C. If it weren't for the Bible, we would know remarkably little about them. The Old Testament names approximately 40 kings of Israel and Judah (the Hebrew kingdom was divided for two centuries), yet we can find references to only about a dozen of them in records other than the Hebrew scriptures, and almost all of these are from the time after Solomon. Somehow, personalities as outstanding as Saul, David, and Solomon and events as momentous as the arrival of the Hebrews in Egypt, their enslavement, and the Exodus never made it into Egyptian records. That is a surprising omission, given that by ancient standards the Egyptians were a highly literate society whose scribes were meticulous and complete in their documentation. Perhaps these events, so important in Hebrew mythology, caused little stir among the Egyptians. Or perhaps the records that the Egyptians made have perished, possibly never to be found. Likewise, and hardly surprising, we lack written records documenting Old World mariners' landing in the New World.

In the absence of historical documents from the ancient past, we do have the pyramids themselves. These monuments speak to us in the unusual vocabulary of stone and light. To hear what they are saying, we must drop our preconceptions. With open eyes and minds, we have to lean close, look deep, and attend carefully.

The first part of the pyramids' message concerns the deep and essential oneness shared by all humans. The psychic unity that independent inventionists have relied on since Frazer's classic formulation fails to explain the spread of the pyramids, yet its core concept is valid: All humans in all places share common concerns. Equally to the point, we share a common history, in which civilization began in a single place and then spread across the face of the earth. Sundaland was the likely beginning point. As the waters of the post–ice age seas rose, these displaced people had to move. The Sundalanders who went west to India and Mesopotamia mixed with local peoples and added to the cultural melange from which the civilizations of the fourth millennium B.C. arose. With that rise came the great pyramid-building civilizations of the Old World. The Old World pyramid builders later did for the New World what the Sundalanders had done for them. They contributed skills and ideas to advanced indigenous cultures that helped shape the sophisticated civilizations of Mesoamerica and the Andes.

It is likely there is an even deeper unity among all the earth's people, one far older than the sinking of Sundaland. Douglas C. Wallace and his colleagues at Emory University have traced a female world genetic tree that follows the lines of mitochondrial DNA to show all humans arising from 18 women somewhere in Africa approximately 144,000 years ago. Over time, the descendants of the eighteen moved throughout Africa and then into Europe, Asia, and finally the Americas, leaving their genetic footprints along the way. Similar work, this time on the male side of the line through the Y-chromosome, by Peter A. Underhill and Peter J. Oefner of Stanford University points to an original 10 men who are the forefathers of all modern humans. Following this line of analysis, Bryan Sykes, an Oxford University researcher, has used mitochondrial DNA evidence to show that all Europeans can be traced to seven maternal groups. Sykes calls them the Seven Daughters of Eve, and he has even given them names: Helena, Jasmine, Katrine, Tara, Ursula, Valda, and Xenia.

Luca Cavalli-Sforza of the University of Padua believes that the male chromosomal lineages are connected to the development of languages. One hundred fifty thousand years ago, the argument goes, the small number of humans then living all spoke the same tongue. As various groups migrated into new lands and lost contact with one another, language inevitably changed and evolved. Even though Cavalli-Sforza's male-lineage language tree is still speculative, serious scholars are using linguistic evidence to look for the original tongue that all humans spoke before that first migration long, long ago.

It was only a little over 200 years ago that Sir William Jones first proposed that languages as apparently different as Sanskrit, Latin, Greek, German, Persian, and Gaelic come from a common parent language. This insight has allowed comparative linguists to assemble families of languages such as the Indo-European group that Jones defined. Language families like Indo-European, Sino-Tibetan, and Austronesian can now be grouped into macrogroups and linked historically, much as related contemporary animal or plant species can be found to have a common ancestor back in time. Some of the scholars working on this problem hold that most of the peoples of Europe, much of western Asia, and portions of Africa were speaking languages they call Nostratic long before the development of agriculture. Pushing this understanding even further back into time points to the existence of an original tongue, variously called Proto-World, Proto-Human, or Proto-Global.

Merritt Ruhlen and his colleague John D. Bengston have developed more than 40 word roots they are certain indicate a connection among all the world's tongues and demonstrate the existence of an original single language. As a simple example, consider the English word "hole," which appears in French as *cul* in the compound word "cul-de-sac" and in German as *Hölle* (hell). Next comes the !Kung (Bush people of the Kalahari Desert) *!koro* (hole), Finnish *kolo* (hole), Korean *kul* (cave), Japanese *kur-* (hollow), Tamil *akkuL* (armpit), Tibetan *kor* (hole, pit), and Caucasian *kur* (pit). The appearance of the same word root in tongues as distant as English and Korean points to a common point of origin.

In language and in culture, what we see as difference is in fact a layer of distinction wrapped around a core of unity. Difference is the icing; unity, the cake.

Humankind's unity is more than an idea or a point of data. It is an understanding that can change how we live. Whenever humans kill other humans because of the supposed differences between them—Jew versus Arab, Indian versus Pakistani, Serb versus Kosovar, Catholic versus Protestant, Hutu versus Tutsi, black versus white—the combatants are failing to attend to and build on the unity that joins them. They are missing the point. The more each of us understands the reality of unity and incorporates it into our lives, the better we can help build a just world in which the core humanity of all the earth's residents is honored and respected.

The pyramids also have an important lesson to teach us about the influence of cometary activity on human history and prehistory. Living in an era when the heavens are quiet, we fail to understand how profound an effect the rain of cosmic fire and ice had on our forebears. Not so long ago, the peoples of the earth knew the skies as a source of great danger, a reality the pyramids commemorate. Every stage of pyramid building can be tied to events in the heavens. The sinking of Sunda-land and the dispersal of its people as a result of sea-level rises owing to comet impacts were critical to the development of the cultures and civilizations of the Middle East. The earliest phase of pyramid build-ing—in Mesopotamia, China, and coastal Peru followed soon by Old Kingdom Egypt—accompanied repeatedly close encounters and actual collisions with the cometary fragment stream of which the asteroid Olijato is the principal extraterrestrial survivor. In the twelfth century B.C., the loss of the Mandate of Heaven during a period of high come-tary activity propelled the Shang refugees toward Mesoamerica. Egyp-tian and African evidence at La Venta argues for a migration out of the Mediterranean and across the Atlantic during the same time of disorder in the skies. Another movement from China during the Q'in Dynasty made a likely contribution to Teotihuacán and, from there, to the many pyramids of the Mayan region. A similar mix of East Asian, Medi-terranean, and African elements influenced the creation of the great monuments of the Andes. In each case the transoceanic movement of pyramid builders occurred because of the disruption of Old World so-cieties by events in the heavens.

Comets did more than simply alter the shape of pyramid-building cultures by migration and dispersal. The pyramids themselves were a creative response to the danger in the skies. Duncan Steel has sug-gested that the first stage of Stonehenge, built circa 3200–3100 B.C. during Olijato's heyday, was both an astronomical observatory that warned of the time of greatest danger and a bomb shelter that pro-tected against the barrage from the skies. Newgrange, with its thick roof of sod covering corbeled stone, would also have offered excellent protection. But these monuments and the pyramids that followed them served as more than elaborate foxholes or fallout shelters. The many astronomical alignments and the rich foundation of mythology they incorporated represent attempts to understand the cosmos and to re-store it to a right and safe order. In the same way that you and I want to comprehend through science what makes the universe tick, the ancients were reaching toward ultimate cause in the vocabulary of their sacred buildings.

This reach for control and understanding underscores the pyramids' third major message: Very ancient cultures were much more sophisticated than we have been led to believe. The technological focus of our own culture leads us to look to technology as the dividing line between primitive and advanced. Unless a people has personal computers, safety razors, and 1.2 automobiles per household, some of us may think of that group as culturally backward and, a priori, intellectually bereft. But there was nothing backward or stupid about the culture that carved the earliest portions of the Great Sphinx of Giza between circa 7000 and 5000 B.C. These people had highly developed artistic ability, the engineering skill to turn a big idea into an equally big monument, and the organizational acumen to focus labor and economic resources on a grand scale.

If we drop our preconceptions about Stone Age backwardness, we find repeated examples of knowledge, sophistication, and insight throughout the precivilized world. Many ancient societies had a detailed and specific knowledge of astronomy, an idea explored in great detail in *Hamlet's Mill* by Giorgio de Santillana and Hertha von Dechend. And consider, as a further example, the city of Çatal Hüyük in what is now Turkey. This bustling city of the seventh millennium B.C. was home to some 7,000 residents and was a cosmopolitan melting pot of Asian, European, and African immigrants based on a mystery religion of personal transformation and metamorphosis that is a predecessor of ancient Greek worship and key elements of Christianity. Çatal Hüyük is but one manifestation of the advanced culture that the late Marija Gimbutas called "Old Europe."

The more we understand how sophisticated Late Stone Age cultures were, the less abrupt and revolutionary the arrival of civilization becomes. The popular and academic image depicts civilization arising with the suddenness of midday bursting from midnight. Many of the stranger ideas about the development of civilization (such as Zechariah

Sitchin's notions of extraterrestrials who crossbred with early hominids to create humans who could build cities and write) rest on just such an assumption raised to the third power. I suspect that the change was much less abrupt, even leisurely. Once the key elements were in place, the dawn of civilization was long, slow, and not unexpected.

There is a final nuance to the pyramids' message. Cultures came together in specific and unique ways that led to civilization, the pyramids, and the world you and I inhabit. There was nothing preordained about this progression. Civilization may be every bit as rare a creation as the fast-disappearing plants and animals of our planet. Were we to destroy this cultural world, through some madness like global nuclear war or severe environmental destruction, civilization could be snuffed out and the conditions that led to its birth might never occur again. "Civilization is the gift of the ages," the pyramids are saying. "Build the future in a way that acknowledges, preserves, and respects the precious—and very ancient—inheritance we stand for."

Appendix:
Redating the
Great Sphinx of Giza

D ETERMINING THE EXACT DATE WHEN THE MAGNIFICENT
Great Sphinx of Giza was constructed is a critical exercise in understanding where and when civilization arose.

The research I did in Egypt on determining the date of the Sphinx's
origin marked a major shift in my intellectual and professional life. Before that, I had accepted the conventional view that civilization arose
around 3500 B.C. and that the Sphinx, supposedly built circa 2500 B.C.,
was one of the monuments that marked early civilization's great flowering during Egypt's Fourth Dynasty (circa 2575–2465 B.C.). Then I realized that the weathering and erosion patterns of the Sphinx and the
surrounding rock meant that the monument had in fact been built in
an earlier, wetter epoch of Egyptian prehistory. As we will discuss further in the pages that follow, the oldest portions of the Great
Sphinx date back to at least circa 5,000 B.C., and perhaps even earlier.

Clearly some sophisticated, well-organized, aesthetically sensitive—yes, civilized—group had carved this monument long before people with such skills were supposed to have taken up residence along the banks of the Nile.

For all its wonder and beauty, the Sphinx is more than the Sphinx. It is the most striking evidence we have of civilization long before civilization is said to have begun. The age of the Sphinx is the key to unlocking the mystery of primordial civilization, and the scientific evidence underlying the dating of this great monument has much to tell us about where we came from.

An Argument from Circumstance

The Great Sphinx of Giza is immense: 66 feet high, 240 feet long, with a human face and headdress 13 feet wide, all carved from solid limestone bedrock. Standing in the shadow of the Great Pyramid of Khufu, which is the sole survivor of the Seven Wonders of the Ancient World, the Great Sphinx serves as a living messenger from an age long past.

Egyptologists have long assumed that the principal monuments of Giza were built during the Fourth Dynasty, and they have ascribed various monuments to the legacies of specific pharaohs. The Great Sphinx, it has been agreed since about 1950, belongs to Khafre. A number of lines of evidence support this attribution.

For one, the Great Sphinx fits into a ground plan that also includes the Sphinx Temple, the Valley Temple, Khafre's Causeway, and the Khafre, or Second, Pyramid. Given the artistic unity of this portion of the site, the assumption is that one builder assembled the entire complex. In addition, an exquisite sculpture of Khafre was discovered in the Valley Temple in 1860. The sculpture adds to the likelihood that Khafre was the pharaoh responsible for the temple and, by association, for the Great Sphinx as well—or so it is assumed.

Further evidence is provided by the Dream Stela, an inscribed pillar of granite that was carved and set between the Sphinx's paws by the New Kingdom Pharaoh Thutmose IV (Tuthmosis IV) in approximately 1400 B.C. A significant legend surrounds the stela.

The body of the Great Sphinx lies below the level of the Giza Plateau in a pit, the so-called Sphinx enclosure, from which limestone was quarried to build other structures. Sand carried into the enclosure by the constant desert winds gradually fills the enclosure if it is not removed regularly. This is exactly what happened during the social and political breakdown that followed the collapse of the Old Kingdom in about 2150 B.C. After a few decades, only the head of the Sphinx, as enigmatic as ever, protruded above the sand.

The story goes that a young prince of Egypt riding in the desert paused for a nap in the shade of the buried Sphinx. While he slept, Khepera, a form of the sun god Ra and the divinity that occupied the Sphinx, came in a dream and told the prince that if he cleared away the sand, he would ascend the throne of Egypt. The prince did as the Sphinx bade him, and although he was not the natural heir to the throne, he did become pharaoh. To honor the vision that brought him to power, Thutmose IV had the Dream Stela carved and placed in front of the Sphinx.

Unearthed in the nineteenth century, the Dream Stela was reported to contain the first syllable of Khafre's name. Unfortunately, this particular part of the inscription has flaked away and can no longer be studied except from reports made at the time of the discovery. Furthermore, even if Khafre's name did appear on the stela, its presence does not prove that he was the Sphinx's original creator. He may simply have been associated with a preexisting Sphinx, just as Thutmose IV was over a thousand years later.

The third line of evidence comes from Mark Lehner and some other Egyptologists who maintain that the face of the Sphinx is a sculpted portrait of Khafre. Using a computer program to reconstruct the damaged face of the Sphinx, Lehner claimed the image "came alive" when he gave it Khafre's features.

This likeness-to-Khafre argument is the weakest of the three lines of evidence. For one thing, it amounts to circular reasoning: When Lehner made the face look the way he thought it should look, then it looked the way he thought it should look. Lehner's notion has been further refuted by Frank Domingo, then a forensic officer with the New York City Police Department, who went to Egypt in October 1991 to do what forensic officers do—develop an image of the Sphinx's damaged face as if he were reconstructing a criminal's likeness from the victim's fractured memory. Domingo concluded that Khafre and the Sphinx are not only different people but also different races. Khafre had a distinctly European face, yet the Sphinx looks African, with a heavier jaw positioned at a different angle and a wider nose.

Though the other two lines of evidence ascribing the Sphinx to Khafre are marginally better, it remains the case that there is no direct, unassailable, physical evidence linking the monument to that particular pharaoh. Still, from the point of view of the conventional wisdom, attributing the Sphinx to the Fourth Dynasty or perhaps a little earlier does make sense. Superficially, the Great Sphinx appears to fit in with the general scheme of Old Kingdom structures on the Giza Plateau. If it were not for the hard scientific evidence supporting an earlier time frame for the Sphinx, we would have no reason to doubt an Old Kingdom or early dynastic attribution for the statue.

Pulling the Rug Out from Under Convention

My research on the Sphinx has pushed its date of origin far into the supposedly uncivilized past, raising the specter that the standard story of civilization has got it wrong. And I am not alone in my opinion. Recent independent research by two other scientists, discussed further in the following pages, corroborates my hypothesis and reinforces the growing belief that the Sphinx is indeed much older than we have thought.

As readers of my earlier book, *Voices of the Rocks,* know, I went to Egypt for the first time at the invitation of John Anthony West. West, an independent (academically uncredentialed) yet highly adept Egyptologist, was of the opinion that the Sphinx dated to a much earlier time than Khafre's reign. West, though, lacked the scientific training to conduct the needed testing. As a geologist, I had the background and skills needed to examine West's notion that the Sphinx showed weathering patterns indicating a far greater age than the reign of Khafre.

My own interest in the issue was more than merely technical. Originally drawn to subjects like art history, physical anthropology, and human evolution, I chose geology as my field of academic emphasis because of the wonderful intellectual ferment it offered. Geology is less about answers than questions. It has given me the opportunity to look deeply at issues that intrigue and fascinate me.

One of those issues has to do with the origin of our species and its civilized way of life. Ever since I discovered a 1,600-year-old Roman coin at a flea market when I was 12, then spent hours in the library doing the diligent scholarly research needed to accurately date this piece of ancient money, I have been fascinated by looking into seemingly lost worlds. My doctoral dissertation at Yale University concerned a long-extinct group of mammals, and I found it intriguing to build a detailed image of these creatures from nothing more than the fossil record. The opportunity to go to Egypt with West offered the same fascination. Setting an accurate date for the Great Sphinx based on physical evidence could prove critical to the entire picture of civilization's earliest days.

Still, when I first arrived in Egypt I felt certain that the conventional view of the monument's date was accurate. It was actually surprising, and certainly sobering, to realize that the standard story didn't fit the data.

West's curiosity sprang from an observation made decades ago by the mathematician and esotericist René Aor Schwaller de Lubicz. An Egyptological gadfly like West, Lubicz noted that the Great Sphinx displayed a weathering pattern different from that of the other Giza monuments. Lacking training as a physical and natural scientist, Schwaller de Lubicz was uncertain of the mechanisms of weathering. But to me as a geologist, the pattern was clear.

The monuments of the Giza Plateau are subject to two kinds of weathering. In Egypt the wind blows steadily during certain parts of the year, driving sand that scours and wears. Wind-driven sand can weather and erode stone unevenly, abrading away the softer layers and leaving the harder ones, sometimes yielding a pronounced steplike profile. Water weathers and erodes rock differently, typically creating a rolling, undulating surface that gives the rock a coved appearance, often with pronounced vertical fissures that are wider at the top than the bottom and that follow natural joints or lines of weakness in the bedrock.

Different monuments at Giza display different patterns of weathering.* For example, structures dated unambiguously to circa 2600–2300 B.C., the early and middle Old Kingdom, and built from the same limestone as the Sphinx, show prominent weathering by wind and relatively little by water. That pattern fits with the current Egyptian climate, in which arid, windy conditions are broken by only rare, scant rainfall.

The Sphinx too showed wind weathering and erosion, particularly on the head, which lies above the level of the plateau. Below that level, on the body of the Sphinx, there is little wind weathering. However, weathering and erosion by rainfall, with its striking coved appearance and deep vertical fissures, is marked and obvious on the walls of the surrounding Sphinx enclosure, particularly the one to the west.

If we assume for the moment that the Sphinx and its enclosure were excavated at the same time as the indubitably Old Kingdom structures, then something very strange was happening at Giza. Some structures weathered one way and others weathered another, both at the same time. That doesn't make sense. But what if different structures were built at different times under different climatic conditions and thus were subject to different patterns of weathering?

Further evidence that this could be the case came from the Valley and Sphinx temples. These two structures, situated in front of the

---

* The term "weathering" is being used here and in the following paragraphs in the colloquial sense of "weathering and erosion" to indicate the general degradation of the rock.

Sphinx, were built with blocks of the same limestone, quarried from the enclosure when the body of the Sphinx was first carved. It is absolutely certain that the limestone blocks composing the Sphinx Temple were quarried from the enclosure. Although some researchers have suggested that the Valley Temple blocks may have come from some other, currently unlocated, quarry, it is probable that the limestone blocks of the Valley Temple also originated from the Sphinx enclosure. The temple limestone blocks were subsequently faced over with an outer layer of granite ashlars marked with Old Kingdom inscriptions dated to the approximate time of Khafre's reign. Interestingly, the ashlars are weathered very differently from the underlying limestone blocks. The granite shows only minimal wind weathering at most, yet the limestone beneath reveals the uneven surface to be expected from long-term exposure to rainfall. Egyptian stonemasons actually fitted some of the ashlars to the wavy surface of the limestone to make a smooth and aesthetically pleasing outer layer. Clearly the limestone had been subject to rainfall weathering much like the Sphinx, and then was repaired with the granite outer layer at a later date, possibly during the reign of Khafre.

The words "Egypt" and "rain" rarely appear in the same sentence, yet Egypt has not always been the desert it is today. Toward the end of the most recent ice age, circa 13,000 B.C., periods of heavy, repeated rain typified the climate of the Mediterranean. What is now desert in Egypt was then green, well-watered grassland dotted by clumps of trees. Alternating drier and wetter periods followed one another; the last rainy period extended until between 3000 and 2350 B.C., when arid conditions more or less the same as the current climate set in and water weathering yielded to wind.

This climatological history, combined with the weathering and erosional features seen on the stone, indicates that the Great Sphinx as well as the Sphinx and Valley temples were originally built at a time when Egypt was wet and rainy. And they must have been built far

enough back in that rainy period to allow the obvious, substantial water weathering to take place.

Data indicating just how far back came from seismological testing
conducted in the Sphinx enclosure by the seismology expert Thomas
Dobecki. The data gave Dobecki and me a look at a cross-section of the
structures under the Sphinx, revealing an interesting pattern of uneven subsurface weathering.* The Sphinx itself faces east. The northern, southern, and eastern floors of the Sphinx enclosure are weathered
to a depth that varies between six and eight feet below the surface. The
western floor, however, is weathered less deeply, to a maximum of just
four feet. The difference isn't due to variations in the rock; the exposed
floor of the enclosure on all sides belongs to the same stratum of limestone. Rather, the western floor has been weathering for a shorter period of time. Obviously, it must have been excavated at a considerably
later date.

The western end of the Sphinx enclosure shows further evidence of
two-stage construction. There are two excavation walls at this end of
the enclosure. The higher wall, which lies farther west, is deeply coved
and fissured by rain and runoff. It must have been dug out when
Egypt's climate was wet and rainy, well before the Old Kingdom. The
second, lower wall, which is closer to the Sphinx's rump, shows much
less precipitation weathering. It was along the base of this lower wall
that the western seismic line, showing a depth of only four feet of
weathering, was taken. The lower wall may have been excavated later
than the higher wall. Certainly the western floor of the enclosure,
where we took our seismic readings, was excavated later than the re-
mainder of the enclosure, at a time when Egypt had already turned
dry, perhaps during the Old Kingdom.

---

* Subsurface weathering essentially consists of mineralogical and fabric changes of the rock that occur once the
surface is exposed to the atmosphere; to the untrained eye, the rock may or may not look as if it is weathered.
Over time, such weathering penetrates progressively farther (deeper) into the rock. This weathering can be detected with seismic wave velocity data.

The evident two-stage construction of the Sphinx enclosure and the Valley and Sphinx temples suggests a likely scenario. All three structures were built well before the reign of Khafre, when heavy rain regularly washed across Egypt. Later Khafre claimed the site for himself by refurbishing the temples and altering the Sphinx. Originally, I suspect, the sculpture's body emerged from the bedrock as if it were an integral part of the plateau. By carving the rump and digging out the western enclosure to a second, lower level, Khafre divided the monument from the rock and gave it its own separate aesthetic existence. There is the possibility that the lower wall was also carved out in pre-Khafre times and that Khafre's workers doing the repair merely widened a preexisting passage behind the rump of the Sphinx, and it was this area of widening that we sampled seismically.

The two-stage construction hypothesis also helps explain another anomaly of the Sphinx: the curious size of its head. When the sculpture is viewed from the side, the head appears disproportionately small. This is by no means a convention of Egyptian art; all the monuments I know of have a correct body-head proportion except, notably, the Great Sphinx of Giza. When I inspected the head up close, I saw relatively recent chisel and tool marks. This evidence, along with the appearance of the stone itself, has led me to believe that the current head, complete with the dynastic headdress of an early pharaoh, was recarved from an earlier, larger head—perhaps, given the leonine form of the rest of the sculpture, that of a lion. This recarving possibly took place at the same time as the excavation of the rump, or it may have happened earlier.

The Sphinx and the temples had to have been built long enough before Khafre that the rains could weather them sufficiently to require repair, circa 2500 B.C. Just how long would that weathering take? In other words, how old is the Sphinx?

The seismology data provide a scale. My analysis of the nature and depth of subsurface weathering on the Giza Plateau indicates that it has taken approximately 4,500 years for the subsurface weathering at the younger, western floor of the Sphinx enclosure to reach a depth of four feet. Since the weathering on the other three sides is between 50 and 100 percent deeper, it is reasonable to assume that this excavation is 50 to 100 percent—or approximately 2,200 to 4,500 years—older than the western end. If we accept Khafre's reign (circa 2500 B.C.) as the date for the later excavations in the western end of the Sphinx enclosure, then this calculation pushes the date for the Great Sphinx's original construction back to the 4700-to-7000 B.C. range, or 6,700 to 9,000 years ago.

This estimate ties in nicely with the climatic history of the Giza Plateau and also correlates with the nature and degree of the surface weathering and erosion features. This date may not be the last word on the subject, however.

Weathering rates may proceed nonlinearly—the deeper the weathering goes, the slower it progresses because of protection from the overlying material. If we assume this is the case, then my estimated date is only a minimum. The possibility of nonlinear weathering suggests that the very earliest portion of the Sphinx dates to before 7000 B.C. Climatic change complicates the picture, however. Given that conditions on the Giza Plateau prior to the middle of the third millennium B.C. were moister than the arid conditions prevailing since then, it could be argued that initial subsurface weathering may possibly, but not necessarily, have proceeded faster than later weathering, an effect that could counterbalance any nonlinear effect. In crude terms, the early moist conditions might give deeper weathering, which could appear to point to an "older" date, but this effect is opposed by the nonlinear nature of the weathering, which could appear to give it a "younger" date. In the end, after many hours of analysis and rumination, I am satisfied that the two opposing factors roughly cancel each other out, and a rough linear interpretation of the data makes sense. For this reason I come back to my estimate of circa 5000 to 7000 B.C. for the oldest portion of the Sphinx.

Counterpoint

Only civilized people—artistically and technologically adept, well organized, with a pool of available workers and craftspeople from which to draw the needed labor—could have carved the Great Sphinx. But according to the conventional history of civilization's origins, no such people existed when the Sphinx was being carved and the Sphinx Temple was being built, circa 5000 to 7000 B.C. Supposedly the world needed to wait at least another 1,500 years before the Sumerian civilization arose. If the Sphinx suggests that a civilized people existed before civilization itself did, then surely something is wrong with the conventional chronology.

A number of scholars have argued that my research is what is wrong. According to them, I have misinterpreted the evidence. The story of civilization, they say, needs no revision.

Mark Lehner, who is affiliated with the University of Chicago and is often cited as the world's most prominent authority on the pyramids, has said that present climatic conditions in Egypt account for the weathering of the Sphinx. The country has been industrializing rapidly, and Cairo is growing by leaps and bounds because of a high birthrate and steady immigration from rural areas. Extreme air pollution makes the small amount of rain that falls during the Egyptian winter very acidic. As we know from pollution studies in other areas, limestone holds up poorly against acid rain. Thus, Lehner argues, I am mistaking the destruction that has taken place in the recent past for past damage and confusing the new with the old.

There are two fundamental problems with Lehner's argument. First, acid raid doesn't produce the rainfall runoff patterns seen on the walls of the Sphinx enclosure. Second, how does one account for the fact that indisputably Old Kingdom structures constructed from the same limestones are holding up much better than the Sphinx under the same chemical assault?

K. Lal Gauri, a University of Louisville geologist, maintains that the weathering of the Great Sphinx came not from rainfall but from the various effects of chemical weathering, particularly something known as "exfoliation," or the flaking away of the limestone surface. According to Gauri, dew forming at night on the rock dissolves soluble salts on its surface, making a liquid solution that is drawn into tiny pores in the stone by capillary action. During the heat of the day the solution evaporates, and salt crystals precipitate in the pores. The forming crystals exert pressure that causes the surface of the limestone to flake away.

This process is, in fact, an important current weathering factor on the Giza Plateau. However, it alone cannot account for all of the weathering features seen in the Sphinx enclosure and, more important, for the specific distribution of weathering features in the Sphinx enclosure, such as the more intense weathering, erosion, and degradation in the western end of the enclosure. Also, the weathering processes Gauri proposes have their maximum effect under extremely arid conditions when the Sphinx is exposed to the elements. But the Sphinx and Sphinx enclosure have been buried under a layer of sand for much of their existence, so on the whole they are protected from these effects. Interestingly, the exfoliation Gauri proposes should be operating on all the limestone of the Giza Plateau, yet somehow no other surface shows the same type of weathering and erosional profile as the Sphinx enclosure. Colin Reader, whose work is discussed further below, has astutely pointed out that Twenty-sixth Dynasty tombs (circa 600 B.C.) cut into the rock along the back, or western, wall of the Sphinx enclosure itself, have been subjected to the processes Gauri describes for over 2,500 years, yet they still exhibit clear chisel marks and lack the type of weathering and erosional profiles seen on the Sphinx and the walls of the Sphinx enclosure.

The conclusions are inescapable. I do not deny that salt crystal growth is indeed damaging the Sphinx and other structures at present, but this process does not explain the ancient degradation patterns seen on the Sphinx's body and in the Sphinx enclosure but appearing virtually nowhere else on the Giza Plateau.

James Harrell, also a geologist, proposes a variation of Gauri's argument. According to him, the culprit is sand piled for centuries against the Sphinx and wetted by rainfall, Nile floods, and capillary action. Flooding, though, would have undercut the base of the Sphinx and the enclosure, yet there are no such features. Nor does wet sand around the base of the Sphinx explain the obvious and pronounced weathering on the upper portions of the enclosure walls and the body of the monument. Indeed, there is no known mechanism whereby wet sand piled against a limestone surface will produce the weathering and erosional profile seen on the body of the Sphinx and on the walls of the enclosure. Sand, even wet sand, may actually have helped to preserve the Sphinx. Furthermore, capillary action, far from being a mechanism capable of keeping numerous feet of piled sand wet over many centuries, is a negligible factor in loose sands in arid areas. Furthermore, according to Harrell's theory, the Twenty-sixth Dynasty tombs cut into the back wall of the Sphinx enclosure should show a similar weathering profile to that seen on the Sphinx and Sphinx enclosure walls. They do not, however. Harrell's wet-sand theory simply does not work.

There is another major problem with the work of Harrell and, for that matter, Gauri. Neither exfoliation nor wet sand can create the coved rock and vertical fissures, or runnels, in the rock that are wider at the top than at the bottom and are a prominent feature of the western end of the Sphinx enclosure. Runnels come from running water. Harrell may even recognize this obvious flaw in his argument. In a comment to a *U.S. News & World Report* writer about the competing claims for the Sphinx's age, Harrell said, "[N]one of us can prove our point."

Harrell has also claimed that the seismic work does not reveal subsurface weathering but simply detects the dip in the rock strata of the underlying formations. This is incorrect. The weathered layer found under the floor of the Sphinx enclosure does not follow the bedding of the strata, which are clearly visible on the sides of the Sphinx enclosure. The differential subsurface weathering pattern that Thomas Dobecki and I recorded cuts across the dip of the strata and parallels the floor of the enclosure, as is to be expected of weathering. If the seismic data were simply recording bedding, then the depth of the "weathered layer" should appear deeper along the south flank of the Sphinx than the north flank, since the bedding dips not only toward the east but also toward the south. Yet this is not the case. The profiles along the north and south sides of the Sphinx show virtually the same depth of weathering. Furthermore, the dramatically shallower depth of the weathered layer immediately behind the rump of the Sphinx is totally incompatible with the notion that the seismic data simply record original bedding in the limestone. It is consistent, however, with my scenario of a Sphinx excavated in two stages.

Harrell also asks how I know that the low-velocity seismic layer detected under the floor of the Sphinx enclosure represents weathered limestone. In fact, the evidence is clear. First, the rock currently exposed on the surface of the floor of the Sphinx enclosure is weathered limestone. It is very strange to argue that the surface is weathered yet the subsurface is unweathered, even though the seismic data indicate no difference between them. Second, Dobecki and I did seismic testing just north of the Great Sphinx on exposed, weathered rock from the same limestone members the Sphinx and the floor of the enclosure are carved from. The data we recorded from the exposed, weathered stone were compatible with the data we found in the layers around and under the Sphinx. There is no good reason to think that our data show anything but subsurface weathering.

Another interesting revelation of our 1991 seismic studies is the finding that the floor of the Sphinx Temple, which sits directly east of the Sphinx but at a lower level, is uniformly weathered to a depth of only four to five feet. If the Sphinx Temple was built when the original body of the Sphinx was excavated, one would expect it to show the same six to eight feet of subsurface weathering below the floor that is seen below the oldest portions of the Sphinx enclosure floor. However, detailed examination of the Sphinx Temple floor and original walls of the Sphinx Temple has yielded convincing evidence, in the form of cut marks around pillars on bedrock pedestals and cut marks on the original walls, that the actual floor of the Sphinx Temple was cut down and lowered by approximately 1.5 to 2.5 feet during ancient renovations, presumably in Old Kingdom times circa 2500 B.C. Add the removed floor material to the current depth of subsurface weathering and it is clear that the original floor of the Sphinx Temple did indeed sustain the subsurface weathering expected from a construction date well before the time of Khafre.

Ian Lawton and Chris Ogilvie-Herald, in their book *Giza: The Truth,* have also criticized my analysis of the seismic data. Unfortunately, they make a number of incorrect assumptions and perpetuate misunderstandings. For instance, Lawton and Ogilvie-Herald claim that I assumed that "the subsurface weathering has been caused by rainfall seeping down through the bedrock floor of the enclosure"; in fact, I never postulated that to be the case at all. They then further argue that since the Sphinx enclosure has been filled with sand for much of its existence, the sand has protected the underlying bedrock floor from subsurface weathering. However, subsurface weathering is essentially a change in the rock that proceeds once its surface is exposed to the air or atmosphere, such as occurred when the core body of the Sphinx was excavated. Rainfall has little or nothing to do with it. In addition, loose porous sand piled up in the Sphinx enclosure does not significantly protect the bedrock from this type of weathering. Lawton and Ogilvie-Herald fail to understand this fact.

Lawton and Ogilvie-Herald further claim that "it is almost certain that the subsurface erosion has been caused far more by hydraulic and capillary action over the many millennia since the bed was laid down than by relatively recent rainfall and exposure." They are simply wrong. Subsurface weathering, not erosion—where the rock is actually carried away—is under consideration here, and postulating unknown and undocumented mechanisms of "hydraulic and capillary action" as a way to explain the data is essentially meaningless. Furthermore, their explanation of hydraulic and capillary action does not address the discrepancies in subsurface weathering within the Sphinx enclosure.

Lawton and Ogilvie-Herald go on to say that "it is clear that the west wall [of the Sphinx enclosure] behind the rump [of the Sphinx]—which according to Schoch's theory must have been carved only c. 2500 B.C.— shows exactly the same vertical and rounded profiles as the [presumably older] south wall." They conclude that this obvious contradiction refutes my analysis. Actually it does nothing of the kind. Lawton and Ogilvie-Herald fail to mention that two "back walls" lie behind the rump of the Sphinx. The higher "back wall," which lies farther to the west, does indeed show rain weathering (their "vertical and rounded profiles") and dates to pre–Old Kingdom times. The seismic studies indicate that the lower "back wall," set directly behind the rump of the Sphinx and lacking rain weathering, may have been excavated much later, possibly in Khafre's reign (circa 2500 B.C.). At that time, as I have said, the rump of the Sphinx was reworked and possibly carved down to the same level as the floor of the Sphinx enclosure on the other three sides.

These same authors argue against the two-stage construction of the so-called Valley and Sphinx temples, pointing out that some granite blocks have actually been worked into the Valley Temple and underlie an uppermost course of limestone blocks. Likewise, Old Kingdom tools have been found around and under detached limestone blocks of the Sphinx Temple. They take this evidence to "prove" that the temples, and therefore the Sphinx itself, must date to Khafre's time. However, it is to be expected that Old Kingdom tools would be found around the temples and that newer granite blocks would be incorporated into the temples during the rebuilding and refurbishing phase of Khafre's time. There was a great deal of building going on on the Giza Plateau during the Fourth Dynasty, and we should expect to find evidence of it.

Another geologist, Farouk El-Baz, who directs Boston University's Center for Remote Sensing, argues that the Sphinx was carved from already-weathered rock. The Great Sphinx is, he maintains, what we geologists call a yardang, a hill of stone harder than the surrounding rock and carved out by weathering over the eons, like the mesas of the American Southwest. This idea, though, flies in the face of the obvious fact that all but the head of the Great Sphinx lies below the level of the Giza Plateau and had to be excavated from the limestone bedrock. The head, it is true, may have been a yardang carved in place by ancient Egyptian stonemasons. The rest of the sculpture had to be excavated first, then carved.

Finally, there is the counterargument of Zahi Hawass, the Egyptian archaeologist who is the director of the Giza Plateau site. Hawass claims that the Sphinx was carved from limestone of such poor quality that it needed repair almost immediately. The Sphinx has indeed been repaired repeatedly. The question is, When did those repairs occur, and what do they signify?

The earliest repairs to the Great Sphinx utilized limestone blocks that conform to the style followed by Old Kingdom masons. Hawass maintains that the repairs were done during the Old Kingdom, most likely soon after Khafre had the Sphinx carved from the limestone bedrock. Lehner disagrees. He holds that New Kingdom masons scavenged Old Kingdom blocks from other Giza sites and used them for the repairs. But stop and think about this idea. Each repair block had to be shaped to fit, so making use of existing material would have saved little labor over using new and would have destroyed many of the diagnostic Old Kingdom characteristics of the blocks. This makes it reasonable to assume that Hawass is right and that the first repairs to the Sphinx were made during the Old Kingdom.

This solution, however, presents Hawass with a serious problem. How could the Sphinx have weathered so fast that it needed repair almost immediately after construction? To begin with, the Sphinx is carved from what we geologists call a competent limestone, one that stands up well enough to weathering to perform effectively as a building material. Also, tombs adjacent to the Sphinx and cut from the same limestone during the Old Kingdom did not require immediate repair, as the Sphinx did. How can it be that the same material weathered so differently at the same site?

The limestone is not the issue. Rather, the Sphinx had already been in place for so long that it was severely weathered by the time of the Old Kingdom and needed refurbishing. When Khafre set to work, the Sphinx was already very old.

As John Anthony West has so eloquently pointed out, another problem plagues the counterarguments: They are inconsistent with one another. The Sphinx's weathering is not attributable to capillary action, modern acid rain, wet sand, ancient yardang processes, *and* particularly poor-quality limestone. Each of the arguments, weak on its own merits, is contradicted by one or more of the other arguments. They are all attempts to salvage the circumstantial case that Khafre built the Sphinx. To allow that the Sphinx is older than Khafre is to admit the inadmissible: The conventional scenario, which holds that civilization originated in Sumeria in 3500 B.C. and migrated from Mesopotamia to ancient Egypt in the late fourth millennium B.C., is wrong.

Corroboration

The scholars who support the circumstantial case for Khafre as the builder of the Sphinx are ignoring or discounting important evidence besides mine. For example, there is the matter of the so-called Inventory Stela, which is also known as the Stela of Cheops' Daughter. The stela's inscription, which dates from the sixth or seventh century B.C. and claims to be a copy of an Old Kingdom text, says that the Sphinx was already in existence in the time of Khufu, who took the throne of Egypt 31 years before Khafre. According to Selim Hassan—curiously, the archaeologist who, on the basis of his field work in the 1930s, first advanced the argument that Khafre built the Sphinx—the inscription goes on to say that Khufu repaired the Sphinx's headdress after it was hit by lightning or a thunderbolt, a narrative that is consistent with the obvious Old Kingdom repair work done to both the Sphinx and the Valley and Sphinx temples.

Contemporary Egyptologists reject the Inventory Stela as an ancient forgery, however. To accept it as authentic would, of course, overturn the conventional wisdom.

Then there is the testimony of the ancients. Selim Hassan surveyed all literary references to the monument from the earliest known writings through Roman times. Every one of them placed the Sphinx in an era earlier than the Giza pyramids. Indeed, the oral traditions of some of the villages near Giza hold that the Sphinx is at least 5,000 years older than Khafre.

The Inventory Stela, Hassan's survey of classical literature, and the village traditions are circumstantial evidence, but they are consistent not only with my research but also with two more recent geological studies of Giza, both of which point to a Great Sphinx much older than Khafre.

Writing in *InScription: Journal of Ancient Egypt*, the geologist David Coxill confirms my observations of the weathering patterns at Giza, weighs the counterarguments, and supports my hypothesis that the Sphinx must date from a time of heavy rainfall well before the Old Kingdom. Coxill hesitates to push that date back to the 7000–5000 B.C. range on the basis of seismological data, but he agrees that the Sphinx "is clearly older than the traditional date."

Colin Reader, a geological engineer educated at London University, comes to a similar conclusion following a meticulous study of the Giza weathering patterns and the hydrology of the plateau. He also adds a significant piece of physical evidence. Agreeing with my analysis of the weathering patterns, Reader notes correctly that the enclosure is most heavily weathered and precipitation-eroded at its far western end, in the area behind (that is, west of) the lower wall, which was presumably carved when Khafre fully excavated the rump of the Sphinx and repaired the statue. The explanation for this particularly severe weathering and erosion is surface runoff from rainstorms. Since the Giza Plateau tilts down from the north and west, runoff headed directly toward and through the Sphinx enclosure on its way to the Nile Valley—or at least it did so until the reign of Khufu (circa 2551–2528 B.C.). This pharaoh removed large quantities of stone from quarry pits immediately up-slope from the Sphinx enclosure. After the pits were abandoned, wind-blown sand filled them and soaked up any runoff heading down toward the Sphinx enclosure. Therefore, the heavy weathering and degradation of the western end of the Sphinx enclosure had to have occurred during a period before the quarries were excavated during Khufu's reign.

Reader also argues that the Sphinx is hardly the only Giza monument that requires redating. According to his analysis, Khafre's Causeway (which runs from the Sphinx area up to the Mortuary Temple on the eastern side of Khafre's Pyramid), a portion of the Mortuary Temple itself, and the Sphinx Temple all predate Khafre, who is thought within conventional Egyptology to have been responsible for them. Interestingly, John Anthony West and I had earlier come to the conclusion that part of the Mortuary Temple is older than Khafre, but I have not spoken of this idea at length in public or published it because I wanted to assemble more evidence first. Reader has arrived at the same conclusion on his own—the kind of independent confirmation that warms a scientist's heart.

Reader, however, is unwilling to push the date of the Sphinx back beyond the latter half of the Early Dynastic Period, or circa 2800–2600 B.C. Before this time, Reader says, the ancient Egyptians did not use stone masonry like that seen in the Sphinx and Valley temples and other structures associated with the Sphinx. On this point I am convinced that Reader is mistaken and that the Sphinx is older than he is willing to accept, despite his own very good evidence.

If the Sphinx was carved in the 2800–2600 B.C. period, then there had to be sufficient heavy rainfall during that time frame to heavily weather the monument and its enclosure. The height of the rainy period had ended by 3000 B.C., however, and Egypt was well on its way to becoming desert by 2800 B.C. Mud-brick tombs called mastabas built on the Saqqara Plateau, only 10 miles up the Nile from Giza and dated indisputably to circa 2800 B.C., show little rain weathering even though they are built from a much softer and more vulnerable material and were subject to the same climatic pattern. It simply is not possible that the Sphinx could have been carved as late as 2800 to 2600 B.C. and been weathered so badly under scant rainfall that it required extensive repair by the time Khufu was building his pyramid circa 2550–2530 B.C.

In addition, stone was used architecturally in the Middle East and Egypt well before 2800 B.C. The ancient city of Jericho, situated on the West Bank of the Jordan about 200 miles east of the Nile Delta and dating from 8300 B.C., was surrounded by a stone wall 6.5 feet thick and at least 20 feet tall as well as by a moat 27 feet across and 9 feet deep cut into solid bedrock. A complicated ruin at Nabta Playa in the Western Desert of southern Egypt boasts a series of large, astronomically aligned stone slabs, or megaliths, that date to between 4500 and 4000 B.C. or earlier. An Egyptian predynastic object known as the Libyan Palette (circa 3100–3000 B.C.), and currently housed in the Cairo Museum, shows fortified cities, possibly with stone walls, along the western edge of the Nile Delta. Given this evidence, it by no means strains credulity to assume that the Egyptians were accomplished enough at stonework to erect monuments at Giza well before 2800 B.C.

Despite the disagreement over the era of construction, Reader, like Coxill, corroborates my fundamental observations about the Sphinx. The monument belongs to a time much older than Khafre's.

Acknowledgments

O**NCE AGAIN I MUST ACKNOWLEDGE THAT MANY PEOPLE** have fostered my thinking and studies. In academia, the institution where one finds oneself can sometimes make all the difference. My undergraduate education at the George Washington University (Washington, D.C.) provided me with a solid intellectual foundation, and my graduate training at Yale University (New Haven, Connecticut; Ph.D. in geology and geophysics, 1983) stimulated and honed my curiosity. I remember many glorious hours reading in the Yale libraries and working in the basement of the Peabody Museum of Natural History. In 1984 I accepted a position as a full-time faculty member at the College of General Studies of Boston University and was awarded tenure in 1990. Since 1989 that Egyptological and academic gadfly John Anthony West has continued to goad me on in my studies of ancient history that don't always fit in with the traditional paradigm. I thank him for his persistence in pushing me to continue, even if he and I do not always agree in our interpretations of the data (or what even constitutes legitimate data). Furthermore, it was through the efforts of West that I first got involved in the controversy over the age of the Sphinx. Sometimes I don't know whether to thank him or curse him for dragging me into such a morass. Here I will thank him. Also, I sincerely thank Graham Hancock and Robert Bauval for their continued encouragement and interest in my work. Additionally, I thank Colin Wilson for sharing information with me and supporting my endeavors.

My research in Egypt has been possible only through the cooperation of many individuals. In particular, I thank Mohamed I. Bakr, Ali Hassan, Zahi Hawass, Elsayed Hegazy, and Abdul-Fattah El-Sabbahy for permission to pursue studies on the Giza Plateau. It was through the generosity of Yasuo Watanabe (Japan Medical Dynamic Marketing MDM, Inc., Tokyo) that I was able to first visit Yonaguni Island and explore the Yonaguni monument in September 1997. I returned to Japan in late July and early August 1998 to further study the Yonaguni monument and related structures as a member of the Team Atlantis multidisciplinary underwater research team and documentary film project. I thank Michael Arbuthnot and Iris DeMauro for organizing this effort and inviting me to participate, and Michael Arbuthnot for sharing with me his unpublished manuscript "Diffusion Revisited." In June 2000 I visited Teotihuacán, Mexico, with E. Stratton Horres, Jr., and Jennifer and Mark Young. I thank the three of them for their incredible hospitality, which made for a wonderful trip.

Thanks to the generous invitation of Professor Emilio Spedicato of the University of Bergamo, Italy, I participated in the June 1999 conference entitled "New Scenarios for the Solar System Evolution and Consequences in History of Earth and Man" convened in Milan and Bergamo. This conference was a real eye-opener for me. Consisting of a gathering of scientists and researchers representing various "alternative," "heretical," and "catastrophist" viewpoints, it was one of the most intense and intellectually stimulating three days I have ever experienced. The serious original thinking reported at the conference, and the free flow of ideas during discussion sessions, during a little sightseeing and over meals, helped inspire me to continue to pursue my ongoing studies, as reported both in this book and my previous book, *Voices of the Rocks*. In particular I thank the following attendees of and participants in the "New Scenarios" conference for their stimulating talks and discussions: Alan Alford, Mike Baillie, Flavio Barbiero, Victor Clube, David Eccott, Charles Ginenthal, John Michael (of the Morien Institute), Emilio Spedicato, Alexander Tollmann, and Tom Van Flandern.

I especially thank Alan Alford, Michael Arbuthnot, David Billington, Jr., Thomas J. Brown, David Eccott, James Erjavec, Charles Ginenthal, James L. Guthrie, Graham Hancock, Stratton Horres, Linda Moulton Howe, William Jacobs, Francesca Jourdan, Masaaki Kimura, Jürgen Krönig, Ralph Lyman, John Michael, Richard W. Noone, Colin Reader, Emilio Spedicato, Neil Steede, John Anthony West, and Colin Wilson for sending me articles and references that I found most useful. Also, I thank Michael Arbuthnot, David Billington, Jr., Michael Brass, Francesca Jourdan, John Michael, Matthew Sapero, and John Anthony West for posting various materials pertaining to my research on their various Web sites. In addition, I deeply appreciate the continuing interest in my research shown by Robert and Zoh Hieronimus and Laura Cortner (21st Century Radio), Erskine Payton (of the *Erskine Overnight* radio show), Douglas Kenyon (*Atlantis Rising* magazine), Laura Lee (*Laura Lee* radio show), Hilly Rose (on the *Art Bell* radio show), Mike Siegel (*Coast to Coast* AM radio program), Emad Hammoude (Radio EOF), and Paul Garson (Cyberradio Productions).

Numerous people have been extremely generous in providing me with photographs and permission to use them freely in this book: Klaus Aarsleff, Janis Beaudette, Doris Dumont and Jay Constant, Colette M. Dowell, Ray Grasse, Angie Grenke, Hartwig Hausdorf, Stratton Horres, William R. Iseminger (Cahokia Mounds State Historic Site), Douglas Kenyon (*Atlantis Rising* magazine), Jürgen Krönig, Gordon Landis, Helen Landis, James Parker, Bianca Portela, and Javier Sierra

(*Más Allá de la Ciencia* magazine). All the photographs were very helpful, even though not all of them could be included in this book. I am most grateful for the tremendous assistance I received in this matter. Thank you.

Innumerable other persons have taken an interest in my research more generally and have helped out in various ways. It would be impossible to list everyone whom I have had contact with concerning my research, but I would like to acknowledge the help, support, and interest of a few more people in particular: L. Abdel-Khalek, Alessandro Abdo, Sean Adair, John Adderley, Takao Aharen, Alicia Alexander, Ahmed Ali Mohammed, Bodhi Annan, Kayoe Aoki, Kihachiro Aratake, Janet Arbuthnot, Mary Bailey, Gaber Barakat, Paul Bierman, Tom Campbell, Sita Chaney, John Cheshire, Molly Cheshire, Dennis Coffman, Rita Corriel, Bill and Carol Cote, Barbara Crane, Anh Crutcher, Shun Daichi, Nelson Dale, Peter Daniell, Caroline Davies, Christopher DeFelice, Kate Dickie, Lloyd Dickie, Thomas L. Dobecki, Frank Domingo, Jonathan Eagle, Robert Eddy, M. M. El Aref, Ashraf El Trabishy, Hanny M. El Zeini, Michael Eldredge, Santha Faiia, Vera Fanuzzi, Adriano Forgione (editorial director of *Hera* magazine), Dennis C. Forbes, Brenda Franey, Tim Friend, Nehad Gamal, Alison and Gilbert Gjersvik, Ian Goh, Linda Goldstein, Diane Graszik, Jim Green, Joan Griffith, Terence Guardino, Eileen P. Gurly, Foxy Gwyne, Mary Habib, Khadija S. Hammond, Mohamed Heimeida, Romany Helmy, John Hipsley, Debbie and Stratton Horres, Sandy and Chuck Houghton, Steve Hubbard, James J. Hurtak, Natalia Ignatieff, Nicholas Ignatieff, Sandra Irby, Akiko Ito, Joseph Jahoda, LaNette Kardokus, Jorjana Kellaway, Dale Kimsey, Sarah Kingston, Megumi Kondo, Hiroshi-Kubota, Devendra Lal, Mary Lomando, Yoshimi Matsumura, Michele Matthews, Sarah McDermott, Peter McDougall, Robert G. McKinney, Edmund S. Meltzer, Chie Mikami, Scott Milburn, John E. Miller, Atsushi Mori, Mohamed Nazmy (Quest Travel, Giza, Egypt), Masha Nordbye (who organized a wonderful trip to Yonaguni in July–August 2000), Ahmed Nour-el-Din, T. C. Onstott, Vince Pace, Marshall Payn, Michala Perreault (who, with Strat-

ton Horres, arranged for me to lecture in Dallas in June 2000), Michael
Pill, Cheryl Poppaw, Andris and Margaret Priede, Eglal Refai, Peyton
E. Richter, Paul William Roberts, D. J. Roller, Helen Sage, the late
Boris Said, Sarite Sanders (who accompanied John Anthony West and
me to Egypt in June–July 2000 and helped in many ways), Matthew
Sapero, Akihiko Sato, Joseph Schor, Barbara Scott, Stephen Seufer, Emil
Shaker, Tamer Shawsky, Jeff Shepherd, Diana Shields, C. Simonds,
Lydia Smithers, David Solomon, Richard Speir, Christopher Swayne,
Shunji Takahashi, Midori Uema, Gigi Van Deckter, Kieth VonderOhe,
Robert M. Watts, Celesta West, Joanne Wright, Noelle Wright, Sandy
Wright, Ken Yamada, and Stan Zippan. I apologize to those whom I
have inadvertently missed.

As always, I must acknowledge the support that my immediate family has provided as I have pursued my studies (which have sometimes
entailed my absence from home for weeks at a time). My wife, Cynthia
Pettit Schoch, and my two sons, Nicholas Robert Schoch and Edward
Robert Schoch, have always been there when I needed them. Additionally, my parents, Milton and Alicia Schoch; my sister, Marguerita C.
Schoch; my late grandmother, Adriana M. Goetz; and my parents-in-
law, Robert and Anne Pettit, have always been supportive of all my endeavors.

This book was written while I served several terms as an elected city
councillor in my home "town" (actually, it is a city) of Attleboro, Massachusetts. I thank my neighbors and constituents, fellow elected and
appointed officials, and the city employees for their general patience,
understanding, and support of all my endeavors.

This book could not have been written without the talent, energy,
intelligence, and enthusiasm of my coauthor, Robert Aquinas McNally.
Once again, I could not have asked for a finer collaborator. I remain
deeply indebted to him for all his help.

Robert and I once again benefited from the excellent work of our
two fine literary agents, Sarah Jane Freymann and Judith Riven. Mitch
Horowitz, senior editor at Jeremy P. Tarcher / Putnam, believed in this

book from the moment he laid eyes on the manuscript. His enthusiasm and keen editorial sense saw it through the final revisions and production process to the volume you hold in your hands. Katherine L. Scott did an excellent job copyediting the manuscript. I am privileged and honored to have my work translated into numerous foreign languages. In this respect, Ignacio (Nacho) Ares and Patricia Romero Perez have been incredibly enthusiastic, helpful, and supportive in seeing this book published in Spain. Lutz Kroth has provided unbounded enthusiasm for a German-language edition, and Klaus Gabbert, Ekkehard Kunze, and Christine Behrens have helped immensely with the German version. As Liliane Roth has worked on translating the manuscript into French, she has provided many comments that have proved most useful. It is wonderful to have friends and colleagues around the globe.

Although I never had the opportunity to meet him, here I would like to acknowledge the inspiration and influence of the work and life of the late Thor Heyerdahl. Dr. Heyerdahl (1914–2002) passed away after this book was written but before it was published. I had hoped to send him a copy. In the text I have left the references to him as they were originally penned rather than refer to him as "the late Thor Heyerdahl."

A final comment: All matters of fact and interpretation found in this book are my responsibility. In no way is the mention of any person in the acknowledgments meant to imply that she or he agrees with my opinions and interpretations. This is a book of ideas and suggestions on a subject that is anathema to many traditional historians and archaeologists. My goal, above all else, is to pique and stimulate the reader's intellectual curiosity. I understand that the topics discussed in this book are highly controversial, but that is what makes them so interesting.

Robert M. Schoch
Attleboro, Massachusetts
August 2002

Sources and Readings

THE LISTINGS BELOW ARE INTENDED TO PROVIDE A record of the sources used in writing this book. The dates given after the Internet/World Wide Web addresses (URLs) are the dates when the authors accessed these websites and webpages using the given URLs. Some of these sites and pages may no longer be active or URLs may have changed. In such cases it may be possible for the interested reader to find the applicable or comparable material through a search engine.

Biblical references in the text are taken from the Reader's Edition of the Jerusalem Bible.

Agatucci, Cora. "China Timelines." www.cocc.edu/cagatucci/classes/hum210/ tml/ChinaTML/chinatmlintro.htm. 7 July 2001.

Ahuja, Anjana. "How Seven Women Founded Europe: All Europeans Descend from Just Seven Women, the Founders of Seven Clans." www.foxnews.com/ science/041900/times_7women.sml. 8 July 2000.

Alford, Alan F. "The Phoenix Solution." www.eridu.co.uk/PhoenixSolution. htm. 12 June 1999.

————. *The Phoenix Solution: Secrets of a Lost Civilisation.* London: Hodder & Stoughton, 1998.

Ancient Egypt Research Associates. "Radiocarbon Project." www.fas.harvard. edu/~aera/Giza_Pages/Aeragram_Pages/Aeragram.htm. 11 December 1999.

Anonymous. "California Bones May Complicate Theory on Settlement of Americas." http://www.sfgate.com/cgi-bin/article.cgi?file=/news/archive/ 1999/04/12/state 0246EDT0143.DTL. 12 April 1999.

Anonymous. "China Meteor May Solve Death of Mythic Emperor." http:// asia.cnn.com/2002/WORLD/asiapcf/east/04/09/china.emperor.reut/. 10 April 2002.

Anonymous. "The Chinese Calendar." http://webexhibits.org/calendars/ calendar-chinese.html. 7 July 2001.

Anonymous. "Explorers to Return to Ocean Floor." www.lasvegassun.com/ sunbin/stories/w-sa/2002/may/19/051907529.html. 21 May 2002.

Anonymous. "The First Seafarers." www.bric.postech.ac.kr/science/ 97now/ 98_3now/980311b.html. 16 October 1999.

Anonymous. "5,000-Year-Old 'Pyramid' Discovered in North China." http:// english.peopledaily.com.cn/200107/09/eng20010709_74490.html. 16 July 2001. Also published in *People's Daily,* 9 July 2001.

Anonymous. "Heaven's Gate Tragedy Is Behind Us But Second Sect's Leader Is Still at Large—with Rising Death Toll." www.webshowplace.com/ HeavensGate/home.htm. 2 November 1999.

Anonymous. "The India-Atlantis Expedition." www.india-atlantis.org. 13 April 2002.

Anonymous. "Jehovah's Witnesses and the Pleiades Star Cluster." www. webshowplace.com/HeavensGate/ReconciliationP14.html. 2 November 1999.

Anonymous. "The Legend of Lemuria and Sunken Sundaland." http://asia-pacificuniverse.com/features/lemuria.htm. 5 May 2002.

Anonymous. "Lemurian Paradise." www.crystalinks.com/lemeura.html. 19 June 1998.

Anonymous. "Looking for Lost Riches in Cuba's Seas: Underwater Surveyors Say They May Have Found Sunken City." www.msnbc.com/news/573489. asp?cp1=1. 18 May 2001.

Anonymous. "Lost City Found Off Indian Coast." http://news.bbc.co.uk/hi/ english/uk/england/newsid_1923000/1923794.stm. 13 April 2002.

Anonymous. "Machu Picchu, Peru." www.sacredsites.com/2nd56/21422.html. 1 April 2000.

Anonymous. "The Man in the Ice." www.treesonthemove.com/Media/Ion-Sci/features/maninice/index.html. 16 January 1998.

Anonymous. "The Mayan Calendar." http://webexhibits.org/calendars/ calendar-mayan.html. 8 July 2001.

Anonymous. "The Mystery of the Cocaine Mummies." Broadcast on *Equinox,* BBC Channel 4, 8 September 1996. http://lime.weeg.uiowa.edu/~anthro/ webcourse/lost/coctrans.htm. 6 November 1998.

Anonymous. "Oldest City in the Americas Discovered." www.discoveringar-chaeology.com/articles/042601-oldestperucity.htm. 28 April 2001.

Anonymous. "Proto-World Language." http://members.aol.com/yahyam/ page24/protoworld.htm. 19 October 1999.

Anonymous. "The Pyramids of Guimar, Canary Islands, Spain." www.ferco. org/ferco_pyramids.html. 4 January 2000.

Anonymous. "Rock Chemistry Traces Ancient Traders." *Science* 274 (20 December 1996). Posted on www.trends.ca/~yuku/tran/ xpacif.htm. 24 December 1998.

Anonymous. "Scientists Describe Asteroid's Ancient Ocean Plunge." http:// abob.libs.uga.edu/bobk/ccc/cc120497.html. 13 June 2002.

Arbuthnot, Michael A. "Diffusion Revisited: A Look at the Principles Behind Meggers, Evans, and Estrada's Valdivia-Jomon Hypothesis." Unpublished manuscript. 15 December 1999.

Ashe, Geoffrey. *Dawn Behind the Dawn: A Search for the Earthly Paradise.* New York: Henry Holt, 1992.

———. *Land to the West: St. Brendan's Voyage to America.* London: Collins, 1962.

Sources and Readings

Ashe, Geoffrey, Thor Heyerdahl, Helge Ingstad, J. V. Luce, Betty J. Meggers, and Birgitta L. Wallace. *The Quest for America*. New York: Praeger, 1971.

Associated Press. "Who Passed on the Genes? Key DNA May Be from Dad After All." www.abcnews.go.com/sections/science/DailyNews/dna_evolution991223.html. 8 July 2000.

Bailey, Jim. *Sailing to Paradise: The Discovery of the Americas by 7000 B.C.* New York: Simon & Schuster, 1994.

Baillie, Mike. *Exodus to Arthur: Catastrophic Encounters with Comets*. London: B. T. Batsford, 1999.

Baines, John, and Jaromír Málek. *Atlas of Ancient Egypt*. New York: Facts on File, 1980.

Barber, Elizabeth Wayland. *The Mummies of Ürümchi*. New York: W. W. Norton, 1999.

Bauval, Robert, and Adrian Gilbert. *The Orion Mystery: A Revolutionary New Interpretation of the Ancient Enigma*. New York: Crown Trade Paperbacks, 1994.

Begley, Sharon. "New World Pyramids: Scientists Have Unearthed the Oldest Known City in the Americas, Showing That Urban Civilization Began Here 1,500 Years Earlier Than They Thought." *Newsweek*, 7 May 2001, 60–61.

Behrne, Daniel Randall. "Cultural Patterning as Revealed by a Study of Pre-Columbian Ax and Adz Hafting in the Old and New Worlds." In *Man Across the Sea: Problems of Pre-Columbian Contacts*, ed. Carroll L. Riley, J. Charles Kelley, Campbell W. Pennington, and Robert L. Rands, 139–177. Austin: University of Texas Press, 1971.

Bellos, Alex. "Archaeologists Dig at Each Other Over Findings in Brazil." *San Francisco Examiner*, 20 February 2000.

Bellwood, Peter. "Ancient Seafarers." www.he.net/~archaeol/9703/etc/special report.html. 16 October 1999.

Billington, David. "The Giza Radiocarbon Studies." www.leonardo.net/davidpb/sphinx3.html. 8 December 1999.

———. "Redating the Sphinx." http://members.aol.com/davidpb4/sphinx1.html. 23 December 1999. (A later version of a paper that originally appeared in *World History Bulletin*. 11, no. 1, 1–4 [spring–summer 1994].)

————. "Redating the Sphinx: The Debate." http://members.aol.com/davidpb4/sphinx2.html. 23 December 1999.

————. "A Response to *Giza: The Truth.*" http://members. aol.com/davidpb4/lawton.html. 3 March 2000.

Birnbaum, Edwin. *Sacred Mountains of the World.* San Francisco: Sierra Club Books, 1992.

Blaha, Stephen. *Cosmos and Consciousness: Quantum Computers, SuperStrings, Mysticism, C++ Programming, Egypt, Quarks, Mind-Body Problem, Aliens, Linguistics, and Turing Machines.* Bloomington, Ind.: 1stBooks Library, 2000.

Boslough, Mark, and David Crawford. "Frequently Asked Questions About the Collision of Comet Shoemaker-Levy 9 with Jupiter: Post-Impact Questions and Answers." www/isc.tamu.edu/~astro/sl9/ cometfaq2.html. 11 April 1998.

Bowdan, Scott. "A Comet's Fiery Dance at Jupiter." *The Galileo Messenger,* May 1995. Also available on www.jpl.nasa.gov/sl9g1129.htm. 11 April 1998.

Bradley, Michael. *The Black Discovery of America: Amazing Evidence of Daring Voyages by Ancient West African Mariners.* Toronto: Personal Library, 1981.

Britt, Robert Roy. "Comets, Meteors, and Myth: New Evidence for Toppled Civilizations and Biblical Tales." http://dailynews.yahoo.com/htx/space/20011113/sc/comets_meteors_myth_new_evidence_for_toppled_civiliztions_and_biblical_tales_1.html; and www.space.com/science-astronomy/planetearth/comet_bronzeage_011113-1.htm1. 21 November 2001.

Budge, E. A. Wallis. *The Book of the Dead.* London, 1900. Reprint, New York: Bell Publishing, 1960.

Campbell, Joseph. *The Masks of God: Oriental Mythology.* New York: Penguin, 1962.

————. *The Mythic Image.* Bollingen Series C. Princeton: Princeton University Press, 1974.

————. *Mythologies of the Primitive Planters: The Northern Americas.* Part 2, vol. 2, of *Historical Atlas of World Mythology.* New York: Harper & Row, 1989.

Sources and Readings

————. *The Sacrifice*. Part 1, vol. 2, of *Historical Atlas of World Mythology*. New York: Harper & Row, 1989.

Carter, George W. "The Chicken in America: Spanish Introduction or Pre-Spanish?" In *Across Before Columbus? Evidence for Transoceanic Contact with the Americas Prior to 1492*, ed. Donald Y. Gilmore and Linda S. McElroy, 150–160. Edgecomb, Me.: NEARA Publications, 1998.

————. "Pre-Columbian Chickens in America." In *Man Across the Sea: Problems of Pre-Columbian Contacts*, ed. Carroll L. Riley, J. Charles Kelley, Campbell W. Pennington, and Robert L. Rands, 178–218. Austin: University of Texas Press, 1971.

Castle, Tim. "Historian Presses Claim China Beat Out Columbus." http://sg.news.yahoo.com/reuters/asia-95228.html. 16 March 2002.

Cawthorne, Andrew. "Explorers Comb Cuban Seas for Treasure, Mysteries." http://dailynews.yahoo.com/h/nm/20010514/lf/cuba_treasure_dc_1.html. 18 May 2001.

————. "Explorers View 'Lost City' Ruins Under Caribbean." http://abcnews.go.com/wire/SciTech/reuters20011206_346.html. 8 December 2001.

Chandler, David L. "Peru Find Called Oldest City in Americas," *Boston Globe*, 27 April 2001. Posted on www.boston.com/dailyglobe2/117/nation/Peru_find_called_oldest_city_in_Americas+.shtml. 28 April 2001.

Chang, Kwang-chih. *The Archaeology of Ancient China*. New Haven: Yale University Press, 1963; rev. ed., 1968.

Chapman, Paul H. *The Man Who Led Columbus to America*. Atlanta: Judson Press, 1973.

————. *The Norse Discovery of America*. Atlanta: One Candle Press, 1981.

Clancy, Flora Simmons. *Pyramids*. Montreal and Washington, D.C.: St. Remy Press and Smithsonian Books, 1994.

Clube, Victor, and Bill Napier. *The Cosmic Winter*. Oxford, England: Basil Blackwell, 1990.

Coe, Michael D. *America's First Civilization: Discovering the Olmecs*. New York: American Heritage, 1968.

————. *The Maya*. 5th ed. London: Thames & Hudson, 1993.

Cook, Gary J., and Thomas J. Brown. *The Secret Land: People Before.* Castle Hill Village, Christchurch, N.Z.: StonePrint Press, 1999.

Coxill, David. "The Riddle of the Sphinx." *InScription: Journal of Ancient Egypt* (spring 1998) 13–19.

Däniken, Erich von. *Chariots of the Gods? Unsolved Mysteries of the Past.* Trans. Michael Heron. New York: Putnam, 1970.

Deem, James M. Article [On the Mummies of Ürümchi]. www. jamesm deem.com/urumchi.htm. 8 July 2000.

Dixon, E. James. "Coastal Navigators: The First Americans May Have Come by Water." www.discoveringarchaeology.com/0799toc/7special2-navigate.shtml. 27 January 2000.

Dobecki, Thomas L., and Robert M. Schoch. "Seismic Investigations in the Vicinity of the Great Sphinx of Giza, Egypt." *Geoarchaeology* 7, no. 6 (1992): 527–644.

Doran, Edward, Jr. "The Sailing Raft as a Great Tradition." In *Man Across the Sea: Problems of Pre-Columbian Contacts,* ed. Carroll L. Riley, J. Charles Kelley, Campbell W. Pennington, and Robert L. Rands, 115–138. Austin: University of Texas Press, 1971.

Doutré, Martin. *Ancient Celtic New Zealand.* Albany, N.Z.: Dé Danann, 1999.

Duerinck, Kevin F. "Genetics and Human Migration Patterns (Genetic Anthropology)." http://redshift.stanford.edu/P12/human_origins/050200 sci-genetics-evolution.html. 8 July 2000.

Eccott, David J. "Comalcalco: A Case for Early Pre-Columbian Contact and Influence?" *Chronology & Catastrophism Review* 1999, no. 1: 21–30.

Eccott, David. "Evidence of Contact between America and the Old World before Columbus." www.unibg.it/convegni/NEW_SCENARIOS/Abstracts/Eccott.htm. 16 April 2000.

Edge, Frank. "Aurochs in the Sky: Dancing with the Summer Moon. A Celestial Interpretation of the Hall of Bulls from the Cave of Lascaux." Unpublished manuscript. December 1995.

———. "A Celestial Interpretation of the Hall of Bulls from the Cave of Lascaux." www.jse.com/absource.html. 19 December 1997.

————. "Les Aurochs de Lascaux Dansant avec la Lune d'Été." *Kadath: Chroniques des Civilisations Disparues,* no. 90 (spring–summer 1998): 20–34.

Egan, Timothy. "Expert Panel Recasts Origin of Fossil Man in Northwest." http://search.nytimes.com/search/daily/bin/fastweb?getdoc+site+iib-site+99+0+wAAA+Kennewick%7Eman. 16 October 1999.

Ekholm, Gordon F. "Transpacific Contacts." In *Prehistoric Man in the New World,* ed. Jesse D. Jennings and Edward Norbeck, 489–510. Chicago: University of Chicago Press, 1964.

Eliade, Mircea. *Patterns in Comparative Religion.* Trans. Rosemary Sheed. New York: New American Library, 1974.

————. *The Sacred and the Profane: The Nature of Religion.* Trans. Willard R. Trask. New York: Harcourt, Brace & World, 1959.

Fagan, Brian M. *Quest for the Past: Great Discoveries in Archaeology.* Reading, Mass.: Addison-Wesley, 1978.

Farley, Gloria. *In Plain Sight: Old World Records in Ancient America.* Columbus, Ga.: ISAC Press, 1994. Selected chapters posted on www2.privatei. com/~bartjean/mainpage.htm. 30 January 1999.

Fell, Barry. *America B.C.: Ancient Settlers in the New World.* 1976. Rev. ed., New York: Pocket Books, 1989.

————. *Bronze Age America.* Boston: Little, Brown, 1982.

————. *Saga America.* New York: Times Books, 1980.

Feuerstein, Georg, Subhash Kak, and David Frawley. *In Search of the Cradle of Civilization: New Light on Ancient India.* Wheaton, Ill.: Quest Books, 1995.

Fingerhut, Eugene R. *Explorers of Pre-Columbian America? The Diffusionist-Inventionist Controversy.* Claremont, Calif.: Regina Books, 1994.

Foster, Mary LeCron. "Old World Languages in the Americas: I." Paper presented to George F. Carter Honorary Session, Pre-Columbian Transoceanic Transfers, annual meeting of the Association of American Geographers, San Diego, California, 20 April 1992.

————. "Old World Languages in the Americas: II." Paper presented to Language Origins Society, Cambridge University, September 1992.

Fountain, Henry. "Now the Ancient Ways Are Less Mysterious." *New York Times,* 20 January 2000.

Fowler, Brenda. *Iceman: Uncovering the Life and Times of a Prehistoric Man Found in an Alpine Glacier.* New York: Random House, 2000.

———. "The Iceman's Last Meal." www.pbs.org/wgbh/nova/icemummies/ iceman.html. 31 July 2001.

Frawley, David. *Gods, Sages, and Kings.* Salt Lake City, Utah: Passage Press, 1991.

Frazer, James G. *The Golden Bough: The Roots of Religion and Folklore.* 1890. Reprint, New York: Avenel Books, 1981.

Gallant, Roy A. "The Sky Has Split Apart! The Cosmic Mystery of the Century." www.galisteo.com/tunguska/docs/splitsky.html. 10 April 1998.

Gauri, K. Lal, J. Sinai, and J. A. Bandyopadhyay. "Geologic Weathering and Its Implications on the Age of the Sphinx." *Geoarchaeology* 10, no. 2 (1995): 119–133.

Gibbons, Ann. "Chinese Stone Tools Reveal High-Tech *Homo erectus.*" *Science* 287 (3 March 2000): 1566.

Gilmore, Don. "The First Americans—Hot on the Trail." *NEARA Journal* 31, no. 1 (summer 1997): 1–3. Posted on www.neara.org/gillmore.htm. 5 February 1999.

Gilmore, Donald Y., and Linda S. McElroy, eds. *Across Before Columbus?: Evidence for Transoceanic Contact with the Americas Prior to 1492.* Edgecomb, Me.: New England Antiquities Research Association Publications, 1998.

Gimbutas, Marija. *The Civilization of the Goddess: The World of Old Europe.* San Francisco: HarperSanFrancisco, 1991.

———. *The Language of the Goddess.* San Francisco: Harper & Row, 1989.

Giza Plateau Mapping Project. 1995–96 Annual Report. www-oi.uchicago.edu/ OI/AR/95-96/95-96_Giza.html. 8 December 1999.

Goetz, Delia, and Sylvanus G. Morley, trans. *Popol Vuh: The Sacred Book of the Ancient Quiché Maya.* Norman: University of Oklahoma Press, 1950.

Gordon, Cyrus H. *Before Columbus: Links Between the Old World and Ancient America.* New York: Crown, 1971.

Graves, Robert, and Raphael Patai. *Hebrew Myths: The Book of Genesis.* New York: McGraw Hill, 1963.

Grice, Elizabeth. "Explorer from China Who 'Beat Columbus to America.'" www.telegraph.co.uk/news/main.jhtml?xml=%2Fnews%2F2002%2F03%2F04%2Fnexp04.xml. 16 March 2002.

Gruhn, Ruth. "The South American Twist: Clovis First Doesn't Fit the Rich Prehistory of the Southern Continent." www.discoveringarchaeology.com/0799toc/7special11-twist.shtml. 29 January 2000.

Guthrie, James L. "Great Lakes Copper—Still Missing." *NEARA Journal* 30, nos. 3 & 4 (1996): 57–70.

———. "The Newberry Inscription." *NEARA Journal* 33, no. 1 (summer 1999): 21–30.

Haas, Herbert, James Devine, Robert Wenke, Mark Lehner, Willy Wölfli, and Georg Bonani. "Radiocarbon Chronology and the Historical Calendar in Egypt." In *Chronologies du Proche Orient/Chronologies in the Near East,* ed. Olivier Aurenche, Jacques Evin, and Francis Hours, 585–606. BAR International Series 379(ii), 1987.

Hancock, Graham. "Position Statement by Graham Hancock on the Antiquity and Meaning of the Giza Monuments (22 July 1998)." http://martins.castlelink.co.uk/pyramid/forging/hancockps.html. 14 December 1999.

———. *Underworld: Flooded Kingdoms of the Ice Age.* London: Michael Joseph/Penguin, 2002.

Hancock, Graham, and Robert Bauval. *The Message of the Sphinx: A Quest for the Hidden Legacy of Mankind.* New York: Three Rivers Press, 1996.

Handwerk, Brian. "New Finds Worldwide Support Flood Myths." *National Geographic News,* 28 May 2002. Posted on http://news.nationalgeographic.com/news/2002/05/0528_020528_sunkencities.html. 29 May 2002.

Harrell, J. A. "Comments on the Geological Evidence for the Sphinx's Age." www.users.globalnet.co.uk/~lawtoni/as3.htm. 13 March 2000. See also www.ianlawton.com/gttindex.htm. 24 August 2000.

———. "The Sphinx Controversy: Another Look at the Geological Evidence." *KMT, A Modern Journal of Ancient Egypt* 5, no. 2 (summer 1994): 70–74.

Harris, A. "'Tunguska '96,' Bologna, Italy, July 15–17, 1996: A Meeting Report." http://ccf.arc.nasa.gov/sst/10-11-96.html. 15 December 1997.

Hassan, Selim. *The Sphinx: Its History in the Light of Recent Excavations.* Cairo: Government Press, 1949.

Hathaway, James. "Discoveries at Teotihuacán's Pyramid of the Moon Help Unlock Mysteries of Western Hemisphere's First Major Metropolis." http://clasdean.la.asu.edu/news/teomoon.htm. 15 October 1999.

Hausdorf, Hartwig. *The Chinese Roswell: UFO Encounters in the Far East from Ancient Times to the Present.* Boca Raton, Fla.: New Paradigm Books, 1998.

Hawass, Zahi. *The Secrets of the Sphinx: Restoration Past and Present.* Cairo: American University in Cairo Press, 1998.

Hedrick, B. C. "Quetzalcoatl: European or Indigene?" In *Man Across the Sea: Problems of Pre-Columbian Contacts,* ed. Carroll L. Riley, J. Charles Kelley, Campbell W. Pennington, and Robert L. Rands, 255–265. Austin: University of Texas Press, 1971.

Heinrich, Paul V. "Lemuria, a Scientific Frankenstein." www.mm.org/jz/sphinxcc.html. 19 June 1998.

Heyerdahl, Thor. "The Bearded Gods Speak." In *The Quest for America,* by Geoffrey Ashe, Thor Heyerdahl, Helge Ingstad, J. V. Luce, Betty J. Meggers, and Birgitta L. Wallace, 199–238. New York: Praeger, 1971.

———. *Kon-Tiki: Across the Pacific by Raft.* Trans. F. H. Lyon. Chicago: Rand McNally, 1950.

———. *The Ra Expeditions.* Trans. Patricia Crampton. Garden City, N.Y.: Doubleday, 1971.

Heyerdahl, Thor, Daniel H. Sandweiss, and Alfredo Narváez. *Pyramids of Túcume: The Quest for Peru's Forgotten City.* London: Thames & Hudson, 1995.

Hirst, K. Kris. "Kennewick Man, or How I Learned to Hate 60 Minutes," part 4: "Don't We Already Know How the Americas Were Populated?" http://archaeology.miningco.com/library/weekly/aa120698.htm. 13 April 1999.

Hoffman, Michael A. *Egypt Before the Pharaohs: The Prehistoric Foundations of Egyptian Civilization.* New York: Dorset Press, 1979.

Housden, Tom. "Lost City 'Could Rewrite History.' The City Is Believed to Predate Harappan Civilization." http://news.bbc.co.uk/hi/english/world/south_asia/newsid_1768000/1768109.stm. 13 April 2002.

Hristov, Romeo, and Santiago Genovés. "Mesoamerican Evidence of Pre-Columbian Transoceanic Contacts." *Ancient Mesoamerica* 10, no. 2 (1999): 207–213.

————. "Por una cabeza." *National Geographic* (Spanish language edition) 3, no. 5 (November 1998): 12.

————. "The Roman Head from Tecaxic-Calixtlahuaca, Mexico: A Review of the Evidence." Paper prepared for the 66th Annual Meeting of the Society for American Archaeology in New Orleans, Louisiana, April 18–22, 2001. Posted on www.unm.edu/~rhristov/Romanhead.html. 21 January 2001.

————. "Viajes transatlánticos antes de Colón." *Arqueología Mexicana* 6, no. 33 (1998): 48–53.

Ingstad, Helge. "Norse Explorers." In *The Quest for America*, by Geoffrey Ashe, Thor Heyerdahl, Helge Ingstad, J. V. Luce, Betty J. Meggers, and Birgitta L. Wallace, 96–112. New York: Praeger, 1971.

Jacobs, James Q. "Reflections on Prehistory." www.geocities.com/Athens/Olympus/4844/prehisty.html#5. 7 January 2000.

Jacobs, William. "Toke Like an Egyptian." *Fortian Times* 117 (December 1998): 34–38.

Jairazbhoy, R. A. (Rafique Ali.) *Ancient Egyptians and Chinese in America.* Totowa, N.J.: Rowman & Littlefield, 1974.

Jeffreys, M. D. W. "Pre-Columbian Maize in Asia." In *Man Across the Sea: Problems of Pre-Columbian Contacts*, ed. Carroll L. Riley, J. Charles Kelley, Campbell W. Pennington, and Robert L. Rands, 376–400. Austin: University of Texas Press, 1971.

Jett, Stephen C. "Diffusion Versus Independent Development: The Bases of Controversy." In *Man Across the Sea: Problems of Pre-Columbian Contacts*, ed. Carroll L. Riley, J. Charles Kelley, Campbell W. Pennington, and Robert L. Rands, 5–53. Austin: University of Texas Press, 1971.

————. "Dyestuffs and Possible Early Contacts Between Southwestern Asia and Nuclear America." In *Across Before Columbus?: Evidence for Trans-*

oceanic Contact with the Americas Prior to 1492, ed. Donald Y. Gilmore and Linda S. McElroy, 141–150. Edgecomb, Me.: NEARA Publications, 1998.

———. "Introduction: Early Watercraft and Navigation in the Pacific." *Pre-Columbiana* 1, nos. 1 and 2 (June and December 1998): 3–8.

———. "Precolumbian Transoceanic Contacts." In *Ancient South Americans,* ed. Jesse D. Jennings, 337–384. San Francisco: W. H. Freeman, 1978 and 1983.

Jochmans, Joseph. "How Old Are the Pyramids?" *Atlantis Rising,* summer 1996. Posted on http://atlantisrising. com/issue8/ar8pyramids.html. 27 November 1999.

Johannessen, Carl L. "Maize Diffused to India Before Columbus Came to America." In *Across Before Columbus?: Evidence for Transoceanic Contact with the Americas Prior to 1492,* ed. Donald Y. Gilmore and Linda S. Mc-Elroy, 110–124. Edgecomb, Me.: NEARA Publications, 1998.

Johannessen, Carl L., and May Chen Fogg. "Melanotic Chicken Use and Chinese Traits in Guatemala." *Revista de Historia de América* 93 (1982): 427–434.

Johannessen, Carl L., with Wang Siming. "American Crop Plants in Asia Before A.D. 1500." *Pre-Columbiana* 1, nos. 1 & 2 (June & December 1998): 9–36.

Jojin, Alexandra M. "Biography of a Pioneer: Dr. Betty J. Meggers." www. utexas.edu/courses/wilson/ant304/biography/arybios97/jojinbio.html. 12 December 1998.

Kaplan, Lawrence. "*Phaseolus:* Diffusion and Centers of Origin." In *Man Across the Sea: Problems of Pre-Columbian Contacts,* ed. Carroll L. Riley, J. Charles Kelley, Campbell W. Pennington, and Robert L. Rands, 416–427. Austin: University of Texas Press, 1971.

Kehoe, Alice Beck. *The Land of Prehistory: A Critical History of Archeology.* New York and London: Routledge, 1998.

Kelley, David B. [On Chinese Pyramids.] http://hawk.hama-med.ac.jp/dbk/chnpyramid.html. 7 July 2001.

Kelley, David H. "The Identification of the Proto-Tifinagh Script at Peterborough, Ontario." *NEARA Journal* 28, nos. 3 & 4 (1994): 86–98.

Kennedy, Robert A. "A Transatlantic Stimulus Hypothesis for Mesoamerica and the Caribbean, circa 3500 to 2000 B.C." In *Man Across the Sea: Problems of Pre-Columbian Contacts,* ed. Carroll L. Riley, J. Charles Kelley, Campbell W. Pennington, and Robert L. Rands, 266–274. Austin: University of Texas Press, 1971.

Kenyon, J. Douglas. "Atlantis in Antarctica?" http://members.aa.net/~mwm/atlantis/issue7ar7antarctica1.html. 13 March 1998.

Keys, David. *Catastrophe: An Investigation into the Origins of the Modern World.* New York: Ballantine Books, 2000.

Kienast, M., C. Pelejero, J. O. Grimalt, and L. Wang. "The Flooding of Sundaland during the Last Deglaciation: Imprints in Hemipelagic Sediments from the Southern South China Sea." *Eos, Transactions, American Geophysical Union* 80, no. 46, Fall Meeting (1999), suppl. F531. www.eos.ubc.ca/geochem/people/mkienast/tfosd2.html. 5 May 2002.

Kimura, Masaaki. "Paleogeography of the Ryukyu Islands." *Tropics* 10, no. 1 (2000): 5–24.

———. *Riddle of Submarine Ruins in Okinawa: Are They Oldest Constructions of Megalithic Civilization in the World?* Tokyo: Daisanbunmei-sha, 2000. In Japanese.

———. *Submarine Ruins off Yonaguni, Japan.* Japan, 2000. In Japanese with English summary.

Kornbacher, Kimberly D. "Prehistoric Coastal Peru as an Example of Evolution in a Temporally Fluctuating Environment: A Preliminary Inquiry." www.yannoehl.com/archy/saa98/waste/kkornbac/kornbach.html. 7 January 2000.

Kroeber, A. L. *Anthropology.* New York: Harcourt, Brace, 1923.

Kukal, Zdeněk. *Atlantis: In the Light of Modern Research.* Trans. V. Zborilek and C. Emiliani. Amsterdam: Elsevier, 1984. Reprinted from *Earth Science Reviews* 21 (1984).

Lauritzen, William. "Atlantis: Continent Lost." www.earth360.com/hisatlantis.html. 10 May 2001.

Lawton, Ian, and Chris Ogilvie-Herald. *Giza: The Truth: The People, Politics and History Behind the World's Most Famous Archaeological Site.* London: Virgin Publishing, 1999.

Lehner, Mark. *The Complete Pyramids.* London: Thames & Hudson, 1997.

———. *The Development of the Giza Necropolis: The Khufu Project. Mitteilungen des Deutschen Archäologischen Instituts* (Cairo) 41 (1985): 109–143.

———. "The Search for Ra Ta." Interview by A. R. Smith. *Venture Inward* (magazine of the Association for Research and Enlightenment and The Edgar Cayce Foundation), January–February 1985, 6–11; March–April 1985: 6–11.

Leonard, Jonathan Norton, and the editors of Time-Life Books. *Ancient America.* New York: Time Incorporated, 1967.

Lewis, John S. *Rain of Iron and Ice: The Very Real Threat of Comet and Asteroid Bombardment.* Reading, Mass.: Addison-Wesley, 1996.

Liu, Claire. "A Link Between Chinese and American Cultures? The Olmec and the Shang." Trans. Robert Taylor, with Claire Liu; photos by Vincent Chang. *SINORAMA Magazine* 22, no. 5 (May 1997). Posted on http://hawk.hama-med.ac.jp/dbk/605006e1.html. 7 July 2001.

Lorenzi, Rossella. "Rock Art Reveals Egypt Prehistory." www.discovery.com/news/briefs/20001229/hi_hu_rockart.html. 3 January 2001.

Luce, J. V. "Ancient Explorers." In *The Quest for America*, by Geoffrey Ashe, Thor Heyerdahl, Helge Ingstad, J. V. Luce, Betty J. Meggers, and Birgitta L. Wallace, 53–95. New York: Praeger, 1971.

Mackenzie, Donald A. *Pre-Columbian America: Myths and Legends.* Senate Books. London: Random House, 1996. (Originally published as *Myths of Pre-Columbian America.* London: Gresham Publishing Company, 1923.)

Mallery, Arlington H. *Lost America: The Story of Iron-Age Civilization Prior to Columbus.* Washington, D.C.: Overlook, 1951.

Mandelkehr, Moe. "The Causal Source for the Climatic Changes at 2300 B.C." *Chronology & Catastrophism Review,* no. 1 (1999): 3–10.

———. "The Causal Source for the Geological Transients at 2300 B.C." *Chronology & Catastrophism Review,* no. 1 (1999): 11–16.

Markham, Sir Clements R. *The Travels of Pedro de Cieza de Leon.* London: Hakluyt Society, 1864.

Sources and Readings

Sources and Readings

Marx, Robert R. "Romans in Rio?" *Oceans* 17, no. 4 (1984): 18–21.

Marx, Robert, with Jenifer G. Marx. *In Quest of the Great White Gods: Contact Between the Old and New World from the Dawn of History.* New York: Crown, 1992.

Matthews, Robert. "Meteor Clue to End of Middle East Civilisations." http:// news.telegraph.co.uk/news/main.jhtml?xml=%2Fnews%2F2001%2F11% 2F04%2Fwmet04.xml. 4 November 2001.

McCaffrey, Kevin. "Ancient Coins May Map New Understandings of Antiquity." www.mtholyoke.edu/offices/comm/profile/mcmenpub.html. 24 December 1998.

McCarter, P. Kyle, Jr. "Let's Be Serious About the Bat Creek Stone." *Biblical Archaeology Review*, July–August 1993, 54–55.

McCulloch, J. Huston. "The Bat Creek Inscription: Did Judean Refugees Escape to Tennessee?" *Biblical Archaeology Review*, July–August 1993, 47–53.

———. "The Bat Creek Stone." www.econ.ohiostate.edu/jhm/arch/batcrk. html. 24 December 1998.

McGlone, William R., Phillip M. Leonard, James L. Guthrie, Rollin W. Gillespie, and James P. Whittall, Jr. *Ancient American Inscriptions: Plow Marks or History?* Sutton, Mass.: Early Sites Research Society, 1993.

McMenamin, Mark A. "Cartography on Carthaginian Gold Staters." *The Numismatist*, November 1996, 1315–1317.

———. "Phoenician Coins and Phoenician Exploration." *Migration & Diffusion* 1, no. 1 (2000): 67–82.

Meggers, Betty J. "Contacts from Asia." In *The Quest for America*, by Geoffrey Ashe, Thor Heyerdahl, Helge Ingstad, J. V. Luce, Betty J. Meggers, and Birgitta L. Wallace, 239–259. New York: Praeger, 1971.

———. "La Dynastie Chinoise des Shang et l'Enigme des Origines Olmècs." *Kadath: Chroniques des Civilisations Disparues* 92 (1999): 23–36.

Mendelssohn, Kurt. *The Riddle of the Pyramids.* New York: Praeger, 1974.

Nakhla, Shawki, et al. "Dating the Pyramids." *Archaeology* 52, no. 5 (September–October 1999): 26–33.

National Aeronautics and Space Administration. "Comet Shoemaker-Levy Background." www.jpl.nasa.gov/sl9/background.html. 11 April 1998.

[National Palace Museum, Taipei, Taiwan]. "Hou-chia-chuang Tomb No. 1001 [Artifacts from a Shang Dynasty Grave Mound]." www.npm.gov. tw/ exhbition/ctom2000/english/etom2000.htm. 7 July 2001.

Needham, Joseph, and Lu Gwei-Djen. *Trans-Pacific Echoes and Resonances; Listening Once Again.* Singapore and Philadelphia: World Scientific, 1985.

Needham, Joseph, with Wang Ling and Lu Gwei-Djen. *Science and Civilisations in China.* Vol 4: *Physics and Physical Technology,* part 3, "Civil Engineering and Nautics." Cambridge: Cambridge University Press, 1971.

Neihardt, John G. *Black Elk Speaks: Being the Life Story of a Holy Man of the Oglala Sioux.* 1932. Reprint, New York: Pocket Books, 1972.

Nemecek, Sasha. "Who Were the First Americans?" *Scientific American* 283, no. 3 (September 2000): 80–87. Also available at www.sciam.com/2000/ 0900issue/0900nemecek.html. 23 August 2000.

Oppenheimer, Stephen. *Eden in the East: The Drowned Continent of Southeast Asia.* London: Phoenix, 1998.

Ó Ríordáin, Sean P. *Antiquities of the Irish Countryside.* 5th ed., rev. Ruaidhrí de Valera. London and New York: Methuen, 1979.

Pelejero, Carles, Markus Kienast, Luejiang Wang, and Joan O. Grimalt. "The Flooding of Sundaland during the Last Deglaciation: Imprints in Hemipelagic Sediments from the Southern China Sea." *Earth and Planetary Science Letters* 177 (1999): 661–667.

Pethokoukis, James M. "So How Old Do I Look? The Great Sphinx Stumps the Experts Again." *U.S. News & World Report,* 24–31 July 2000, 38. Also available at www.usnews.com/usnews/issue/ 000724/mysteries/sphinx. htm. 18 July 2000.

Platner, Samuel Ball. *A Topographic Dictionary of Ancient Rome.* Completed and revised by Thomas Ashby. London: Oxford University Press, 1929.

Plato. *Timaeus* and *Critias.* Trans. Benjamin Jowett. www.activemind.com/ Mysterious/Topics/ Atlantis/timaeus_and_critias.html. 1 January 1998.

Polynesian Voyaging Society. "1976: Hawai'i to Tahiti and Back." http:// leahi.kcc.hawaii.edu/org/pvs/1976.html. 13 December 1998.

———. "Non-Instrument Navigation." http://leahi. kcc.hawaii.edu/org/ pvs/navigate/navigate.html. 12 December 1998.

Popescu, Roxana M. "Scientists Say Bronze Age Hunter Known as the Iceman Was Killed by Arrow 5,300 Years Ago." www.sfgate.com/cgi-bin/article.cgi?file=/news/archive/2001/07/25/international1534EDT0685.DTL. 26 July 2001.

Pratt, David. "The Great Pyramid." http://ourworld.compuserve.com/homepages/dp5/pyramid.htm. 14 December 1999.

Prescott, William H. *The World of the Aztecs.* Geneva: Editions Minerva, 1970.

Procuta, Egle. "Canadians May Have Found Lost City. Theory of Sunken Town Off Cuba to Get Support from Geologist's Findings." www.canoe.ca/CNEWSScience0203/27_city-cp.htm. 29 March 2002.

Reader, C. D. "Further Considerations on the Age of the Sphinx." www.users.globalnet.co.uk/~lawtoni/as4.htm. 14 June 2000. See also www.ianlawton.com/gttindex.htm, 24 August 2000.

———. "A Geomorphological Study of the Giza Necropolis, with Implications for the Development of the Site." *Archaeometry* 43, no. 1 (2001): 149–159.

———. "Khufu Knew the Sphinx: A Reconciliation of the Geological and Archaeological Evidence for the Age of the Sphinx and a Revised Sequence of Development for the Giza Necropolis." Unpublished. July 1998. Revised version available at www.users.globalnet.co.uk/~lawtoni/as1.htm. 24 January 2000. See also http://www.ianlawton.com/gttindex.htm. 24 August 2000.

———. "A Response to Comments on 'A Geomorphological Study of the Giza Necropolis, with Implications for the Development of the Site.'" *Archaeometry* 43, no. 1 (2001): 163–165.

Reader's Digest, eds. *The World's Last Mysteries.* Pleasantville, N.Y.: Reader's Digest Association, 1976.

Riley, Carroll L., J. Charles Kelley, Campbell W. Pennington, and Robert L. Rands, eds. *Man Across the Sea: Problems of Pre-Columbian Contacts.* Austin: University of Texas Press, 1971.

Rudgley, Richard. *The Lost Civilizations of the Stone Age.* New York: Free Press, 1999.

Ruhlen, Merritt. *The Origin of Language: Tracing the Evolution of the Mother Tongue.* Stanford, Calif.: Stanford University Press, 1994.

Saleh, Mohamed, and Hourig Sourouzian. *Official Catalogue: The Egyptian Museum.* J. Liepe, photographer. Mainz: Verlag Philipp von Zabern, 1987.

Santillana, Giorgio de, and Hertha von Dechend. *Hamlet's Mill: An Essay on Myth and the Frame of Time.* Boston: Gambit, 1969.

Santos, Arysio Nunes dos. "A Novel Theory on Atlantis." www.atlan. org/index. html. 14 March 1998.

Schoch, Robert M. "Comments by Robert M. Schoch on the Geological Analysis of Ian Lawton and Chris Ogilvie-Herald found in Chapter 7 (The Age of the Sphinx) of *Giza: The Truth* (1999, Virgin, London)." http://members. aol.com/davidpb4/schoch.html; and http://users.iafrica.com/m/mi/ mikeyb/Schoch_GizaTheTruth.html. 3 March 2000. Also available at http://www.RobertSchoch.homestead.com/files/CommentsOnLawton. htm. 24 August 2000.

———. "Comments on the 'Comments on the Geological Evidence for the Sphinx's Age, by J. A. Harrell.'" www.RobertSchoch.homestead. com/files/ CommentsOnHarrell.htm. 24 August 2000.

———. "Dating the Sphinx." *Condé Nast Traveler* 28, no. 2 (February 1993): 103.

———. "An Enigmatic Ancient Underwater Structure off the Coast of Yonaguni Island, Japan." www.RobertSchoch.homestead.com/files/Yonaguni Article.htm. 24 August 2000.

———. "Erosion Processes on the Great Sphinx and Its Dating." Society for Interdisciplinary Studies, *Internet Digest*, no. 2 (1999): 8–9. Also available at www.unibg.it/convegni/NEW_SCENARIOS/Abstracts/ Schoch.htm; and at http://teamatlantis.com/schoch/sphinx_abstract_text. html. 2 January 2000. Also available at http://RobertSchoch.homestead. com/files/Bergamo Abstract.htm. 24 August 2000. Related material available at www.morieninstitute.org/sphinx.html. 24 August 2000.

———. "The Great Sphinx Controversy." *Fortean Times* 79 (February–March 1995): 34–39.

————. "L'Âge du Sphinx de Gizeh: Vers une Révision Déchirante?" *Kadath: Chroniques des Civilisations Disparues,* no. 81 (winter 1993–1994): 13–53.

————. "A Modern Riddle of the Sphinx." *OMNI* 14, no. 11 (August 1992): 46–48, 68–69.

————. "[More Sphinx Debate]." *KMT, A Modern Journal of Ancient Egypt* 5, no. 3 (fall 1994): 4–5. Also available at http://users. iafrica.com/m/mi/ mikeyb/Schoch_harrell.html. 2 January 2000.

————. "New Studies Confirm Very Old Sphinx: Orthodox Protests Notwithstanding, Evidence for the Schoch/West Thesis Is Growing." *Atlantis Rising,* no. 23 (May 2000): 39, 41, 68, 69. Also available at www. Robert Schoch.homestead.com/files/AtlantisRisingArticle.htm. 24 August 2000.

————. "On the Geological Evidence for an Older Sphinx." *KMT, A Modern Journal of Ancient Egypt* 5, no. 2 (summer 1994): 6–7.

————. "Reconsidering the Sphinx." *OMNI* 15, no. 6 (April 1993): 31.

————. "Redating the Great Sphinx of Giza." *KMT, A Modern Journal of Ancient Egypt* 3, no. 2 (summer 1992): 52–59, 66–70. Also available at http:// users.iafrica.com/m/mi/mikeyb/Schoch_redating.html. 2 January 2000.

————. "Scholars Debate Age of the Great Sphinx." Letter to editor. *Chronicle of Higher Education,* 15 January 1992, B5. Also available at http:// users.iafrica.com/m/mi/mikeyb/Schoch_Yurco.html. 2 January 2000.

————. "Sphinx Links." *Archaeology* 48, no. 1 (January–February 1995): 10–12. Also available at http://users.iafrica.com/m/mi/mikeyb/Schoch_ Hawass_Lehner.html. 2 January 2000.

————. "The Sphinx: Older by Half?" Interview by A. R. Smith. *Venture Inward* (magazine of the Association for Research and Enlightenment and the Edgar Cayce Foundation), January–February 1992, 14–17, 48–49.

Schoch, Robert M., with Robert Aquinas McNally. "An Update to the Redating of the Sphinx, and Other Pertinent Matters." Epilogue to *Voices of the Rocks: Lost Civilizations and the Catastrophes That Destroyed Them,* 243–249. London: Thorsons, 2000.

————. *Voices of the Rocks: A Scientist Looks at Catastrophes and Ancient Civilizations.* New York: Harmony Books, 1999.

Sources and Readings

Schoch, Robert M., and John Anthony West. "Further Evidence Supporting a Pre-2500 B.C. Date for the Great Sphinx of Giza, Egypt." Paper presented at the Geological Society of America Annual Meeting, Reno, Nevada, 15 November 2000. Abstract published in *Geological Society of America Abstracts with Programs* 32, no. 7 (2000): A276.

Schurr, Theodore G. "The Story in the Genes: Genetic Research Finds More, Older Options for First Americans." www.discoveringarchaeology. com/0799toc/7special14-genes.shtml. 29 January 2000.

Schwaller de Lubicz, René Aor. *Sacred Science: The King of Pharaonic Theocracy.* Trans. A. and G. VandenBroeck. New York: Inner Traditions International, 1982.

Settegast, Mary. *Plato Prehistorian: 10,000 to 5000 B.C. in Myth and Archaeology.* Cambridge, Mass.: Rotenberg Press, 1986–1987.

Severin, Tim. *The Brendan Voyage: A Leather Boat Tracks the Discovery of America by the Irish Sailor Saints.* New York: McGraw Hill, 1978.

Shao, Paul. "China and Pacific Basin Art and Architectural Styles." *Pre-Columbiana* 1, nos. 1 & 2 (June and December 1998): 37–51.

Shortland, A. J., and C. J. Doherty. "Comments on 'A Geomorphological Study of the Giza Necropolis, with Implications for the Development of the Site.'" *Archaeometry* 43, no. 1 (2001): 159–161.

Sitchin, Zechariah. *The Stairway to Heaven.* New York: Avon Books, 1983.

———. *The Twelfth Planet.* New York: Avon Books, 1976.

Sorenson, John L. "Bibliographia Pre-Columbiana." *Pre-Columbiana* 1, nos. 1 & 2 (June & December 1998): 143–154.

———. "The Significance of an Apparent Relationship Between the Ancient Near East and Mesoamerica." In *Man Across the Sea: Problems of Pre-Columbian Contacts,* ed. Carroll L. Riley, J. Charles Kelley, Campbell W. Pennington, and Robert L. Rands, 219–241. Austin: University of Texas Press, 1971.

Sorenson, John L., and Martin H. Raish. *Pre-Columbian Contact with the Americas Across the Oceans: An Annotated Bibliography.* 2d ed., revised. Provo, Utah: Research Press, 1996.

Spangenberg, Lisa L. "Did the Celts and Druids Perform Human Sacrifice?" www.digitalmedievalist.com/faqs/sacrific.html. 28 July 2001.

Spedicato, Emilio. "Apollo Objects, Atlantis, and Other Tales: A Catastrophical Scenario for Discontinuities in Human History." www.unibg.it/dmsia/dynamics/apollo.html. 15 December 1997.

————. "Evidence of Tunguska-Type Impacts over the Pacific Basin Around the Year 1178 AD." www.unibg.it/dmsia/dynamics/year.html. 13 March 1998.

Spindler, Konrad, et al. *The Man in the Ice: The Discovery of a 5,000-Year-Old Body Reveals the Secrets of the Stone Age.* Trans. Ewald Osers. New York: Harmony Books, 1994.

Spotts, Peter N. "New Players in Race to the New World." *Christian Science Monitor,* 21 October 1996.

Stanford, Dennis, and Bruce Bradley. "The Solutrean Solution: Did Some Ancient Americans Come from Europe?" www. discoveringarchaeology.com/0799toc/7special12-solutrean.shtml. 29 January 2000.

Steede, Neil. "Comalcalco: An Early Classic Maya Site." In *Across Before Columbus? Evidence for Transoceanic Contact with the Americas Prior to 1492,* ed. Donald Y. Gilmore and Linda S. McElroy, 35–40. Edgecomb, Me.: NEARA Publications, 1998.

Steel, Duncan. *Rogue Asteroids and Doomsday Comets: The Search for the Million Megaton Menace That Threatens Life on Earth.* New York: John Wiley, 1995.

Stengel, Marc K. "The Diffusionists Have Landed." *Atlantic Monthly* 285, no. 1 (January 2000): 35–48.

Stephens, S. G. "Some Problems of Interpreting Transoceanic Dispersal of the New World Cottons." In *Man Across the Sea: Problems of Pre-Columbian Contacts,* ed. Carroll L. Riley, J. Charles Kelley, Campbell W. Pennington, and Robert L. Rands, 401–415. Austin: University of Texas Press, 1971.

Stower, Martin. "Forging the Pharaoh's Name?" http://martins.castlelink.co.uk/pyramid/forging. 14 December 1999.

Sykes, Bryan. *The Seven Daughters of Eve.* New York: W. W. Norton, 2001.

Tankersley, Kenneth B. "The Puzzle of the First Americans." www.discoveringarchaeology.com/0799toc/7special1-puzzle.shtml. 27 January 2000.

Thompson, Gunnar. *American Discovery: The Real Story.* Seattle: Argonauts Misty Isles Press, 1992.

Thwaites, Tim. "Ancient Mariners." *New Scientist,* 14 March 1998. Available at www.newscientist.com/ns/ 980314/npeople.html. 16 October 1999.

Todt, Ron. "Earliest American Site Dated: Western Hemisphere Inhabited at Least 15,000 Years Ago." www.abcnews.go.com/sections/science/Daily News/first_americans000407.html. 9 April 2000.

Tollmann, Alexander. "The Deluge in the People's Traditions and Geological Evidence." www.unibg.it/convegni/NEW_SCENARIOS/Abstracts/ Tollmann.htm. 1 March 2000.

Tollmann, Edith, and Alexander Tollmann. "The Flood Came at 3 O'Clock in the Morning." *Austria Today,* April 1992, 40–47.

Uceda, Santiago, Elías Mujica, and Ricardo Morales. "Las Huacas del Sol y de la Luna." http://webf0164.ntx.net/huacasol.com/index.html. 4 January 2000.

Van Flandern, Tom. *Dark Matter, Missing Planets and New Comets: Paradoxes Resolved, Origins Illuminated.* Berkeley, Calif.: North Atlantic Books, 1993.

Van Sertima, Ivan. *They Came Before Columbus.* New York: Random House, 1976.

Veber, May. "Pyramids in the Americas." In *The World's Last Mysteries,* 180–187. Pleasantville, N.Y.: Reader's Digest Association, 1976.

Vermaseren, Maarten J. *Cybele and Attis: The Myth and the Cult.* Trans. A. M. H. Lemmers. London: Thames & Hudson, 1977.

Verschuur, Gerrit. *Impact! The Threat of Comets and Asteroids.* Oxford: Oxford University Press, 1996.

Viegas, Jennifer. "Geneticist: All Europeans Descended from Seven Matriarchal Clans." www.abcnews.go.com/sections/science/DailyNews/daughters 000420.html. 8 July 2000.

Vlahos, Olivia. *African Beginnings.* New York: Viking Press, 1967.

Waddell, Edward J. "Justinian I, 527–565 A.D. AE Follis. Antioch. Year 16." www.coin.com/cgi-local/findCoins.cgi?grp=12&page=3. 11 February 2000.

Wade, Nicholas. "DNA Backs a Tribe's Tradition of Early Descent from the Jews." http://archives.nytimes.com/archives/search/fast-web?getdoc+ allyears2+db365+330986+0+wAAA+Lemba. 10 May 1999.

Sources and Readings

Wagner, Thomas. "Scientists Say Vast Asteroid Narrowly Missed Hitting Earth." www.boston.com/dailyglobe2/172/nation/Scientists_say_vast_asteroid_ narrowly_missed_hitting_ Earth+.shtml. 21 June 2002.

Waters, Michael R. "Proving Pre-Clovis: Criteria for Confirming Human Antiquity in the New World." www.discoveringarchaeology.com/0799toc/ 7special9-preclovis.shtml. 29 January 2000.

Watkins, Calvert. "Indo-European and the Indo-Europeans." In *The American Heritage Dictionary of the English Language,* ed. William Morris, 1496–1502. New York: American Heritage, 1970.

Wendorf, Fred, and Romuald Schild. "Late Neolithic Megalithic Structures at Nabta Playa (Sahara), Southwestern Egypt." http://rampages.onramp. net/~mobaldia /WendorfSAA98.html. 11 December 1998.

West, John Anthony. *Serpent in the Sky: The High Wisdom of Ancient Egypt.* Wheaton, Ill.: Quest Books/Theosophical Publishing House, 1993.

————. *The Traveler's Key to Ancient Egypt: A Guide to the Sacred Places of Ancient Egypt.* New York: Alfred A. Knopf, 1989.

————. "Update to the German Edition of *The Traveler's Key.*" http:// users.iafrica.com/m/mi/mikeyb/Sphinx_JAW.html. 27 November 1999.

White, Paul. "The Oz-Egyptian Enigma." *Exposure Magazine* 2, no. 6 (1996). Also available at www.ozemail.com.au/~classblu/egypt/egypt.htm. 14 July 2000.

Whitehouse, David. "Space Rock's Close Approach." http://news.bbc.co.uk/ hi/english/sci/tech/newsid_2056000/2056403.stm. 21 June 2002.

Wilford, John Noble. "Chinese Outdid Columbus, Briton Says." www.nytimes. com/2002/03/17/science/social/17SHIP.html?ex=1017503294&ei=1&en =82c1ad7085e23997. 18 March 2002.

Wilkinson, T. A. H. "Comments on C. D. Reader, 'A Geomorphological Study of the Giza Necropolis, with Implications for the Development of the Site.'" *Archaeometry* 43, no. 1 (2001): 161–163.

Wilson, Colin. *From Atlantis to the Sphinx: Recovering the Lost Wisdom of the Ancient World.* New York: International Publishing, 1996.

Winter, Marcus. *Oaxaca: The Archaeological Record.* Mexico City: Editorial Minutiae Mexicana, 1992.

Sources and Readings

Witcombe, Chris. "Silbury Hill." http://witcombe.sbc.edu/earthmysteries/ EMSilbury.html. 7 March 2000.

Woolley, Sir Charles Leonard. *Ur of the Chaldees*. London: Ernest Benn, 1929.

————. *Ur: The First Phases*. London and New York: Penguin, 1946.

Wuthenau, Alexander von. *Unexpected Faces in Ancient America, 1500 B.C.–A.D. 1500*. New York: Crown, 1975.

Xu, H. Mike. "La Venta Offering No. 4: A Revelation of Olmec Writing?" *Pre-Columbiana* 1, nos. 1 & 2 (June and December 1998): 131–134.

————. *The Origin of the Olmec Civilization*. Edmond, Oklahoma: University of Central Oklahoma Press, 1996.

Yamei, Hou, Richard Potts, Yuan Baoyin, Guo Zhengtang, Alan Deino, Wang Wei, Jennifer Clark, Xie Guangmao, and Huang Weiwen. "Mid-Pleistocene Acheulean-like Stone Technology of the Bose Basin, South China." *Science* 287 (3 March 2000): 1622–1626.

Young, Emma. "Drowned Indian City Could Be World's Oldest." www.newscientist.com/news/news.jsp?id=ns99991808. 27 January 2002.

Zapp, Ivar, and George Erikson. *Atlantis in America: Navigators of the Ancient World*. Kempton, Ill.: Adventures Unlimited Press, 1998.

Zabarenko, Deborah. "Largest Asteroid in Years Misses Earth." http://story.news.yahoo.com/news?tmpl=story&cid=585&ncid=753&e=1&u=/nm/20020621/sc_nm/s pace_asteroid_dc. 21 June 2002.

Index

Açoka, emperor of India, 34–35, 64

Acosta, José, de, 85

Aeneid, Virgil, 121

Africa, and flood myths, 249–50

Aleut people, 86

Alford, Alan, 268

Alvarez, Luis and Walter, 203–4

American Indians. *See* Native Americans

Americas, 3, 39–49, 82–99, 186–87, 211, 271

    See also Mesoamerica; New World

Ammizaduga, king of Babylon, 218–19

Andromedid meteor shower, 207

Angkor Wat, 3, 36, 59, 62–65, 68, 71, 72, 148, 172

Anglo-Saxon Chronicle, 214

Ankh hieroglyph, 228

Antioch, 213–14, 215

Anubis Caves, 126, 135

Aratake, Kihachiro, 51

Archaeometry, 124n

Aristotle, 176

Arroyo Hondo pueblo, 199

Ashanti people, 134

Asia, 85–87, 90, 137–39, 164

    See also China; Southeast Asia

Aspelta, king of Nubia, 32

Aspero pyramids, Peru, 23–24, 47, 99, 226, 271

Asteroids, 204

Astronomy, 73–74, 159, 276

Atlantis, 238, 239, 244–46

Australia, 171–74

Austronesian language, 247–48, 251–52

Aveni, Anthony, 74

Awadalla, Philip, 94n

Axis mundi, 62

Aymara Indians, 181

Aztec civilization, 44, 45–46, 60, 69, 103–4, 211, 259, 260

Babel, Tower of, 26, 78–80, 104, 268

Bahia culture, Ecuador, 147–48

Baillie, Mike, 200, 202, 204–5, 209, 218, 220

Baines, John, 17

Balabanova, Svetlana, 131

Baptism, 109

Bark cloth, 144

Bat Creek Stone, 125, 135, 231

Batres, Leopoldi, 42

Battered-profile pyramids, 23, 61, 229

Bauval, Robert, 75

Index

Beans, green (*Phaseolus vulgaris*), 127

Bengston, John D., 274

Beothuk people, 97

Beowulf, 253, 254

Berber culture, 133

Beringian land-bridge, 85–86, 136, 242

Betanzos, Juan José, de, 120

Bible, and Hebrew history, 271–72
  See also Genesis (Bible)

Biblical practices, New World and, 109

Biela's comet, 206–7

Birs Nimrud, Babylonian ziggurat, 26, 58

Blaha, Stephen, 228

Blowguns, 142–44

Boats, 71–72, 111, 115–16, 178
  See also Reed boats

Bock, Hieronymus, 139

Book of Caverns, Egyptian, 106

"Book of the Community" (*Popol Vuh*),
  101–3, 113

Book of the Dead, Egyptian, 105, 106, 258

Borobudur stupa, 3, 35–36, 64, 172

Bottle gourds (*Lagenaria* spp.), 127–28

Bradley, Bruce, 93–94

Brazil, ancient female skull, 90–91

Brendan, Saint, 96

Bricks, kiln-fired, 150–52, 173

Bronze, 192, 241, 246

Bronze Age, decline of, 217–18, 221–22

Brugh na Bóinne, 226, 227, 228

Buddhism, 34, 55, 65, 66

Buduma boat builders, 179–81

Bulls, and pyramids, 10, 232–36

Burial customs, ancient, 27–28, 32, 34, 37–38,
  46, 66–69, 71, 109–11, 149, 154

Cabral, Pedro Alvares, 140

Cabrera, Javier, 239

Cactus Hill, Virginia, archaeological site, 88

Cahokia, Illinois, ceremonial center, 3, 46

Calendars, 155, 160, 163, 228

Cambodia, temples, 36–37, 148

Campbell, Joseph, 67–68, 73, 99

Canada, paleontological research, 88

Cannibalism, 45

Canoe, seafaring, 188–89

Caral, Peru, 24

Carbon-14 dating, 14–16, 85n

Carthage, Phoenician colony, 134, 176, 191–92

Çatal Hüyük 232, 276

*Catastrophe: An Investigation into the Origins
  of the Modern World*, Keys, 214

Catastrophes, natural, 4, 208–9

Cavalli-Sforza, Luca, 273

Caves, pyramids and, 70–72

Caviglia, Giovanni Battista, 13

Cayce, Edgar, 238

Celts, migrations of, 2

Center of universe, pyramids as, 61–62

Ceremonial complexes, 19–20, 45–48, 63, 149,
  159

Champollion, Jean-François, 126

Chatters, James, 92

Chavín de Huántar, Peru, 47, 72, 135, 165

Chavín people, 159

Cheops boat, 132–33, 178–79

Chia, Stephen, 172

Chichén Itzá, 43–44, 69, 72, 112–13

Chickens, 140–42

Chicxulub impact crater, 204–5

Chih-huang-ti (Shihuangdi), emperor of
  Q'in, 38, 186, 197, 203

China, 37–39, 68, 138, 187, 197–98, 211, 222,
  226, 227, 254, 275
  influences in New World, 154–55, 157–60,
  164

Ch'in Dynasty. *See* Q'in Dynasty, China

Cholula, Mexico, 45–46, 117

Churchward, James, 239

Circumnavigation of globe, 96

Civilizations, ancient, 2–5, 7–10, 20, 100,
  237–49, 270, 272, 276–79

Climate changes, 198–203, 222–23, 226–27,
  242–44, 261–66, 284, 287–98

Clovis artifacts, 86–87, 93, 98

Clube, Victor, 205–9, 226–27, 263, 266

Cocaine, in Egyptian mummies, 131

Codices, Mesoamerican, 100–101, 108

Coe, Michael, 157

Cohenim (Jewish priests), 161

Coherent catàstrophism, 205–9, 263

Columbus, Christopher, 173, 177, 192

Comalcalco, 149–52, 173

Comets, 4, 203–15, 224, 228–36, 263–66, 270,
  274–75

The Complete Pyramids, Lehner, 10

Complexes, cultural, 129–31, 143–44, 146–48

Con-Tiki Viracocha, 118–19, 120, 121

Index

Copper, 156, 192–95
Corn, 137–38
Cortés, Hernán, 45–46, 118
Cosmic events, evidence of, 198–203
Costa Rica, stone spheres, 111
Cotton (*Gossypium*), 128–30
Covarrubias, Miguel, 157
Coxill, David, 296, 298
Creation stories, 57, 102, 252–55, 259
Crocodiles, 255, 259
Culture clash, myths of, 256–58
Culture-givers, mythical, 117–21
Cybele, 216, 235, 268

Dahshur, pyramids at, 29, 30, 61, 71
Dark Ages, European, 173, 177, 212
Dating of monuments, 11–18, 23n, 85n, 171, 278–89
Deacy, Dave, 91
Dead bodies, preservation of, 65–66
Death, rituals of, 109–11
Dechend, Hertha von, *Hamlet's Mill*, 276
Dendrochronology, 199–203
Deucalion, 250, 252
Diffusionism, 77–84, 98–99, 129–35
Dillehay, Tom D., 87, 88–89
Dinosaurs, disappearance of, 203–4, 263
Diodorus Siculus, 134
Divisions, mythical, healing of, 268
Djedefre, pharaoh, 30
Djoser, pharaoh, 28
Dobecki, Thomas L., 12, 285, 291
Dogs, mummified, 110
Domingo, Frank, 281
Douglass, Andrew, 198–99
Draft animals, absence of, 163
Dragons, 224, 229–30, 253–55, 259
Dream Stela, 279–80
Drift voyages, accidental, 185
Drucker, Philip, 158
Dye, purple, 130–31
Dynastic collapses, China, 197–98, 203, 211, 216, 217, 218, 275

Eccott, David J., 150–52
Ecuador, Japanese contact, 145–48
Eden, Garden of, 238, 244–46, 258
Eden in the East, Oppenheimer, 246, 248
Edge, Frank, 233

Egypt, ancient, 8–20, 64, 67, 105, 106, 132–33, 173–74, 219–21, 222, 226, 227
  pyramids, 27–31, 59, 74–75
  See also Giza Plateau, pyramids
Ekholm, Gordon F., 157
Elam, kingdom of, 27
El-Baz, Farouk, 293–94
Eliade, Mircea, 22
El Paraíso, pyramids, 24
Eltanin (asteroid), 263
England, pyramid possibility, 50
Epic of Gilgamesh, 104–5, 250, 260
Eratosthenes, 177
Estrada, Emilio, 145
Etemenenanki (Babylonian ziggurat), 26
Etruscans, 134
Europeans, ancient, in New World, 117–23
Evans, Clifford, 145
Eve, 102, 238, 259–60
Evolutionary research, 94
Exodus of Hebrews from Egypt, 219–21

Famine, worldwide, 212, 215–16
Feathered Serpent Pyramid, 42
Fell, Barry, 125, 150, 195
Feuerstein, Georg, 257
First Times (*Zep Tepi*), Egyptian, 238
Fission-track dating, 171
Fladmark, Knut, 87
Floods, 222, 242–44, 263, 265–66
Flood stories, 8, 103–4, 104–5, 249–55
Folklore in the Old Testament, Frazier, 249
Folsum, New Mexico, artifacts, 86
Foster, Mary LeCron, 117
Founding families, myths of, 103
Frawley, David, 257
Frazier, James G., 77, 97, 249
Freud, Sigmund, and Moses, 121
Fullagar, Richard, 171

Gaius Cestius (Roman praetor), 33
Garden of Eden, 238, 244–46, 258
Gases, release of, 213–14
Gauri, K. Lal, 289, 290
Genesis (Bible), 57, 78–80, 238, 249–60
Genetic studies, 94, 160–62, 248–49, 272–73
Genghis Khan, 211
Geology, 282
Gilbert, Adrian, *The Orion Mystery*, 75

Index

Gilgamesh, 104–5, 250, 260

Gimbutas, Marija, 151, 276

Giordano Bruno (lunar crater), 210

Giza: The Truth, Lawton and Ogilvie-Herald, 292–93

Giza Plateau, 16–19, 29–30, 75–76, 279, 283–88

    Great Sphinx, 11–13, 18, 75, 227, 278–98

    pyramids, 9–10, 14–18, 21–22, 61, 62, 71, 229, 234, 256, 261

God-king concepts, 63–65, 105

Gods, long-nosed, Mayan, 149

Gold, search for, 192

The Golden Bough, Frazier, 77, 97

Gordon, Cyrus, 125

Gosford Glyphs, 173–74

Gourds (*Lagenaria* spp.), 127–28

Great Britain, disasters, 212–14

Great-circle routes, 167–68

Great Lakes copper mines, 192–93

Great Pyramid. *See* Khufu Pyramid

Great Sphinx, 11–13, 18, 75, 227, 278–98

Greeks, ancient, 174, 176, 233–34, 250

Greenland, climate record, 201, 216, 218

Guaca, 70

Guanche people, 51

Gulf of Cambay, Gujarat, India, 251

Guthrie, James L., 192

Hamlet's Mill, Santillana and Dechend, 276

Hancock, Graham, *The Message of the Sphinx*, 75

Harappan civilization, India, 33, 152, 251

Harlan, Tom, 200

Harney Peak, 54, 55

Harrell, James, 290–91

Hartung, J. B., 209–10

Hassan, Selim, 295–96

Hawass, Zahi, 294

Head, Lesley, 171

Heads, stone sculptures, 112, 134, 156–57

Heaven's Gate cult, 234

Hebrew artifacts, in New World, 125, 135

Hebrew people, 79–80, 219–21, 271–72

Hebrew scriptures, New World myths and, 101–4

Heizer, Robert F., 158

Herodotus, 12, 60, 107, 175

Heroes, mythical, 117–23

Hesiod, *Theogony*, 238

Heyerdahl, Thor, 51, 179–81, 190

Hieroglyphics, 116, 125

Hindus, ritual wife sacrifice, 68

Hiram of Tyre, 175

Hirschboeck, Kathy, 201–2

Hokule'a (outrigger canoe), 188–89

Hominids, regional development, 240–41

Homo erectus, 170–72

Horus, 66, 107, 256

Howard-Vyse, Richard, 12, 13–14

Hsü Fu, 186–88, 197, 203

Huaca, 70

Huangdi (Yellow Emperor), 224–25

Huber, P. J., 219

Human sacrifice, 38, 42, 45–46, 48, 56–57, 59, 66–69, 74, 106–7, 211, 260

Humboldt, Alexander von, 85

Huni, pharaoh, 28

Hunting methods, 142–44

Hyksos people, 219

Ice ages, 85–86, 242–43

Ice cores, climate record, 201, 202, 204, 214, 216–18, 223–24, 227, 263, 265, 266

Iceman (Ötzi), 225–26

Imhotep (Egyptian pyramid-builder), 28

Inca civilization, 48–49, 68–69, 211

Incense, ritual uses, 108

Incest, 250–52

Independent inventionism, 77, 82–84, 97–98, 143–44, 162, 166–67, 272

India, 33–36, 53, 138–39, 172–73, 250–51, 258

Indo-Malaysian Archipelago, 169–70

Indus River Valley, 33, 140, 142, 151

Ingstad, Helge, 96

InScription: Journal of Ancient Egypt, Coxill, 296

Intestinal parasites, 142

Inventionism. *See* Independent inventionism

Inventory Stela, 13, 14, 295–96

Iraq, meteoritic crater, 223

Ireland, burial mounds, 50

Iridium, 203–4

Isaiah (Hebrew prophet), 230

Isis, 66

Itzamná, 119

Index

Jade, 154
Jaguar-man, 159
Japan, 39, 51–52, 145–48, 185
Jehovah's Witnesses, 234
Jericho, 298
Jett, Stephen C., 143
Job (Bible), 233, 234–35
John of Ephesus, 213
Jomon pottery, 145–47
Jonah, 175
Jones, William, 273
Julius II, Pope, 84–85
Jupiter, comet collision, 206

Kailas (Tibetan mountain), 34, 55, 56
Kak, Subhash, 257
Kelley, David H., 195–96
Kennewick Man, 91–92
Keys, David, 214
Khaba, pharaoh, 28
Khafre (Chephren), pharaoh, 10, 11, 18, 30,
    279–81, 286–87, 297
Khafre Pyramid, 10, 15–16, 17, 30, 61, 279
    bull bones in, 10, 232, 235
Khufu (Cheops), pharaoh, 10, 12–14, 18,
    29–30, 295, 297
Khufu Pyramid, 9–10, 13–17, 29–30, 61, 66,
    71–72, 75, 115, 228, 279
Kimura, Masaaki, 51, 52
Kings, 63–66, 74
Köfels crater, Austria, 266
Kon-Tiki, 179
Kroeber, A. L., 131–32
Kukulcan, Temple of, 43, 44, 122
Kuleshov, N. N., 137–38
Kuroshio Current, 168, 185, 187
Kush. *See* Nubia

LaMarche, Val, 200, 201–2
Languages, 17, 77–80, 247–48, 273–74
    similarities, 116–17, 141–42
Lanzon Slab, 47, 72
Lapita people, 172
Lascaux, France, cave paintings, 233
Late Stone Age cultures, 276–77
Lauritzen, William, 245
La Venta Pyramid, 40, 59, 63, 71, 112, 134,
    135, 157–60, 164, 187, 197, 271
Lawton, Ian, *Giza: The Truth*, 292–93

Lehner, Mark, 10, 280–81, 288, 294
Lemba people, 161–62
Lemuria (Mu), 239
León, Pedro de Cieza de, 49, 68–69
Leonardo da Vinci, 198
Leviathan, 253, 259
Libations, 109
Libyan Palette, 298
Libyans, ancient, 133
Lishan, China, funerary center, 38–39, 59, 63,
    68, 71, 160, 186, 187
Livy, 216
Lubbock, John, 90
Lucifer, 230
Luzia (ancient Brazilian female), 90–91, 93

McAvoy, Joseph M. and Lynn, 88
Machu Picchu, 49
McMenamin, Mark, 126
Magellan, 138
Magnetosphere, 232
Mahabharata (Hindu epic), 220
Maillard, Pierre, 125–26
Maize, 137–38
Málek, Jaromír, 17
Manasala, Paul, 248
Mandate of Heaven, loss of, 197–98, 203, 211,
    215–16, 217, 218, 275
Manjuro, Nagahama, 185
Manu (Indian flood hero), 250–51
Mastabas, 27–28, 298
Master, Sharad, 223
Mathematical systems, 155
Maya civilization, 45, 101, 148–49, 212, 226
Mayan pyramids, 43–44, 60, 73, 148–49, 152
Medinet Habu, Egypt, 107, 108, 115
Meggers, Betty J., 145–47
Meidum Pyramid, 28–29, 61
Menes (Narmer), king of Egypt, 9, 256
Menkaure (Mycerinus), pharaoh, 10, 18, 30
Menkaure Pyramid, 10, 15–16, 17, 30, 60
Menzies, Gavin, 96
Meru (mythological mountain), 34, 35
Mesoamerica, 39–49, 69, 106, 114–16,
    258–61, 271
Mesopotamia, 25–27, 246, 267
The Message of the Sphinx, Hancock and
    Bauval, 75
Metals, 155–56, 163, 191–96

Index

Meteorites/meteoroids, 216n, 268
Meteor streams, 208–9
Michael, Saint, 230, 231
Micmac people, 96–97, 125
Micronesian people, seafaring skills, 188–89
Milankovitch, Milutin, 261–63
Minoan civilization, 151, 174, 232
Mississippian culture, 46
Mixe-Zoque languages, 117
Moche culture, 48
Mohenjo-daro, 33–34
Monte Albán, 134, 234
Monte Verde, Chile, 87, 88–89
Moon, meteor impact, 209–10
Mori, F., 65
Moses, 121, 230–31
Mountains, symbolic, 54–58
Mount Meru, 34, 35
Movius Line, 240–41
Mu. See Lemuria
Mummification, 65, 110
Mythology, 99, 101–11, 117–23, 249–55,
      267–68
   and pyramids, 54–81

Nabta Playa, 19–20, 22, 133, 298
Na-Dene people, 86
Napier, Bill, 205–9, 226–27, 263, 266
Native Americans, 84–99,
Nebuchadrezzar II, king, 26, 58, 64, 79
Neck rests, ceramic, 147
Needham, Joseph, 153–56, 184
Newberry inscription, 195
Newfoundland, Viking visits, 96–97
Newgrange (burial mound), 3, 50, 228, 275
New World, 24, 95–96, 100–101, 117–23
   reasons for travel to, 185–88, 191–236
   See also Americas; Mesoamerica; North
      America
New Zealand, 51
Nichols, Johanna, 89
Nicotine, in Egyptian mummies, 131
Noah, 8, 57, 103–4, 249–51, 265–66
Norsemen, ancient, 196
North America, 46, 86, 88, 192–93, 222
   See also Americas; New World
Nubia, 31–33, 59, 67–68, 76
Numerology, 102–3
Nunes dos Santos, Arysio, 244–45

Ocean currents, 168, 222
Oefner, Peter J., 273
Ogilvie-Herald, Chris, Giza: The Truth, 292–93
Old Copper culture artifacts, 192–95
Olijato asteroid, 226–27, 266, 275
Olmec civilization, 40, 156–59, 197
Oort Cloud, 205, 207, 229
Oppenheimer, Stephen, Eden in the East, 246,
      248, 257, 261, 267
Optical luminescence dating, 171
Orientation of pyramids, 62–63, 72–73
Orion, 234, 260
The Orion Mystery, Bauval and Gilbert, 75
Osiris, 65–66, 256, 260–61, 268
Ötzi (Iceman), 225–26

Pacal (Mayan king), 44, 69, 70–71, 120, 149,
      154, 155
Pacific Ocean, crossings to New World, 136–65
Palenque, tomb of Pacal, 44, 70–71
Paleo-Indians, 86, 89, 95
Paleomagnetic dating, 171
Panpipes, 147–48
Patrick, Saint, 212–13
Peiser, Benny, 223
Penis amputation, 107–8
Peru, 23–24, 47–49, 68–69
Peterborough stone, 195–96
Phallic cults, 108
Phoenicians, 134, 174–76
Piailug, Mau, 189
Pizarro, Francisco, 118–19, 140
Plagues, Egyptian, 220–21
Plants, cultivated, 127–28, 137–38
Plato, 238
Plato Prehistorian, Settegast, 239
Pleiades constellation, 74, 233–35, 260
Plutarch, 108
Polynesian people, seafaring skills, 188
Pookajorn, Surin, 241
Popol Vuh ("Book of the Community"),
      101–3, 113
Precious metals, search for, 191–96
Pre-Columbian visits to Americas, 123–26,
      134–35
Price, David, 171
Procopius, 212–13
Proto-Tifinagh alphabet, 196
Psalms (Bible), and catastrophes, 218

Index

P/Shoemaker-Levy 9 (comet), 206, 207
Purple dye, 130–31
Pyramid builders, migrations, 209–28
Pyramids, 3, 4, 7, 12–18, 21–27, 50–53, 99,
    226, 232, 235–69, 272–77
    Americas, 39–49, 135, 148
    Asia, 33–39
    comets and, 228–36
    Egyptian, 9–10, 27–33, 222
    myths and, 54–81, 249
    Sundaland and, 270
Pythons, 122

Q'in (Ch'in) Dynasty, China, 37, 38, 64, 216
Quechua language, 117
Quetzalcoatl, 117–18, 120, 122–23, 134,
    231–32, 259
Quiché people, 101–3, 113
Quiros, Pedro de, 188

Ra (Heyerdahl's reed boat), 179–81
Racial characteristics, Mesoamerican, 112–14
Radiocarbon dating, 85n
Rafts, ocean-going, 181–84, 190
Ramesses III, pharaoh, 107, 108
Raza, Asaf, 171
Reader, Colin, 289, 296–97, 298
Reed boats, 115–16, 178–81, 190
Regicide, sacred, 74
Reisner, George, 67
Rituals, similarities of, 106–11
Roger of Wendover, 215, 220, 235
Roman artifacts in Americas, 123–24, 126, 135
Rome, ancient, 33, 167, 177, 216
Ross, Martin, 199
Ruhlen, Merritt, 274
Ruiz, Bartolomeo, 182
Ruwenzoris Mountains, 55–56

Sacsahuamán, 49, 62, 70, 72, 115, 135
Sanchi, Great Stupa, 35
Santillana, Giorgio de, *Hamlet's Mill*, 276
Schwaller de Lubicz, René Aor, 282
Scripture, Mayan, 101–3
Sea level, rise of, 4, 19, 242–49, 263–66, 270,
    275
Sekhemkhet, pharaoh, 28
Senna, Yemen, 161–62
Serpent in the Sky, West, 227–28

Serpent myths, 122, 231–32, 253–55, 259–60
Seth, 65–66, 107, 268
Settegast, Mary, *Plato Prehistorian*, 239
Severin, Tim, 96
Sexuality, ritual, 58
Shang Dynasty, China, 37–38, 197, 203, 217
    trans-Pacific migration, 157–59
"The Shipwrecked Sailor," 123, 231
Sibling rivalry, myths of, 255–58
Silbury Hill, England, 3, 50, 227
Sioux people, and Harney Peak, 54, 55
Sitchin, Zechariah, 14
Skeletal remains, studies of, 91–93, 114
Sky-gods, religions of, 236
Smith, Grafton Elliot, 149
Social structure, Sundlanders and, 267
Solutrean culture, 93–94, 98
Sorenson, John L., 114
Southeast Asia, 148–49, 164, 172–73, 241, 248
Spanish conquest of New World, 100–101
Spherical earth, idea of, 176–77
Sphinx. *See* Great Sphinx
Spindin, Herbert, 149
Stanford, Dennis, 93–94
Star-holed mace, 147
Steel, Duncan, 229, 275
Stele, D. Gentry, 92
Stichin, Zechariah, 276–77
Stine, Anne, 96
Stone heads, 112, 134, 156–57
Stonehenge, 226, 227, 275
Stone spheres, Costa Rica, 111
Stupas, Buddhist, 3, 34–36, 59–60, 62, 65, 268
Submarine pyramids, 51–53
Subsurface weathering, 285, 286–87, 290–92
Sullivan, Paul, 171
Sumerians, 8, 25–27, 57, 58, 66, 74, 258
Sumeru (Mount Kailas), 34, 55
Sun, eclipses of, 214
Sundaland (Sunda Shelf), 4, 170, 244–61,
    267–70, 272
Sun-god figures, origin of, 122–23
Sun worship, 105, 134–35
Surgical procedures, 116
Sykes, Bryan, 273

Taharqa, pharaoh, 32
Takla Makan Desert, 1
Tambora, eruption of, 200–201

Index

Tamped-earth pyramids, 38, 40, 63, 187
Tapanui Craters, New Zealand, 210
Tarshish, Phoenician colony, 175, 176, 192
Tassili culture, 133
Taurid meteor shower, 207, 210, 235
Taurobolium (bull sacrifice), 235
T-cell leukemia, 147
Technology, 276
Templo Mayor (Aztec pyramid), 45
Tenayuca (Aztec pyramid), 3, 45, 74, 233, 260
Tenochtitlán, 3, 45, 69
Teotihuacán, 3, 40–42, 63, 70, 73, 152–53, 212
  Pyramid of the Sun, 41–42, 74, 233, 260
Thailand, 246
Thalassemia, 248–49
Theogony, Hesiod, 238
Thera (Santorini), eruption of, 201–2
Thermoluninescence dating, 171
Thomas, Will, 91
Time, measurements of, 154–55
Tin, 192
Tiwanaku, Bolivia, 47–48, 115, 118, 135, 165
Toca do Boqueirão da Pedra Furada, Brazil, 89
Tollmann, Alexander and Edith, 265–66
Tolstoy, Paul, 144
Toltec people, 44
Tower of Babel, 26, 78–80, 104, 268
Tower temples, Khmer, 36–37
Tozzer, Alfred, 149
Trade, long-distance, Southeast Asia, 172–73
Transoceanic travel, 96, 167–69
Trans-Pacific contacts, pre-Columbian, 137–65
Travel to New World, 185–88, 191–236
Tree rings, climate records, 198–203, 204, 214, 216, 217, 218, 222, 223–24, 227, 265, 266
Trepanning, 116
Tres Zapotes, stone heads, 112, 134, 156–57
Tsunamis, 221, 264
Tunguska, comet explosion, 207, 210
Tykot, Robert, 172

Uaxactún, Pyramid E-VII, 72–73
Underhill, Peter A., 273
Underworld, concepts of, 105–6
Unity, universal, 272–74
Ur, civilization of, 247
Urdaneta Route, 168

Uruk (Erech, Warka), Sumerian city, 25
Ürümchi mummies, 1–2

Valdivia pottery, 145–47, 148
Van Flandern, Tom, 268
Veber, May, 39
Vedic hymns, 257
Vega, Garcilaso de la, 49, 118
Venus (planet), influence of, 73–74
Venus Tablets, 218–19
Vikings, in Newfoundland, 96–97
Viracochas, 118–19, 121–22, 135, 179
Virgil, *Aeneid*, 121
Virginia, archaeological site, 88
Volcanic eruptions, 200–201, 203, 214, 223
Votan, 119–20

Waddell, Edward, 215
Wallace, Douglas C., 272–73
Wallace Line, 170
Water, pyramids and, 71–72
Weapons, 147
Weathering of Giza monuments, 11–12, 283–88
  of Sphinx, 282–98
Weaving methods, 129–30
Wenke, Robert J., 14
West, John Anthony, 227–28, 281–82, 295, 297
Wheel, absence of, 162–63
Wheeled animals, 110–11, 163
White color, and pyramids, 228–29
White Temple of Uruk, 25, 226, 227, 228
Wiercinksi, Andrzej, 114
Wilkinson, Toby, 20
Woolley, Charles Leonard, 26, 67, 73, 246–47
World mountains, 34, 57–60
Writing, 8, 116, 151, 155

Xia Dynasty, China, 37, 197, 203, 218
Ximénez, Francisco, 101
Xu, H. Michael, 157–59

Yahweh, power of, 234–35
Yonaguni monument, 51–52

Zero, concept of, 115, 155
Zheng He (Chinese admiral), 96
Zhou Dynasty, China, 38, 197
Ziggurats, 3, 25–27, 58, 60, 62, 72

About the Authors

ROBERT M. SCHOCH, a full-time faculty member at the College of General Studies at Boston University since 1984, earned his Ph.D. in geology and geophysics at Yale University. Dr. Schoch has been quoted extensively in the media for his work on the Sphinx, and he was featured on the Emmy-winning documentary, *The Mystery of the Sphinx,* hosted by Charlton Heston.

The author of numerous books, ROBERT AQUINAS MCNALLY is a writer and poet whose early education in classical Latin blossomed into a lifelong fascination with ancient civilization and mythology.